Skip·Beat!

Shojo Beat

Skip·Beat!

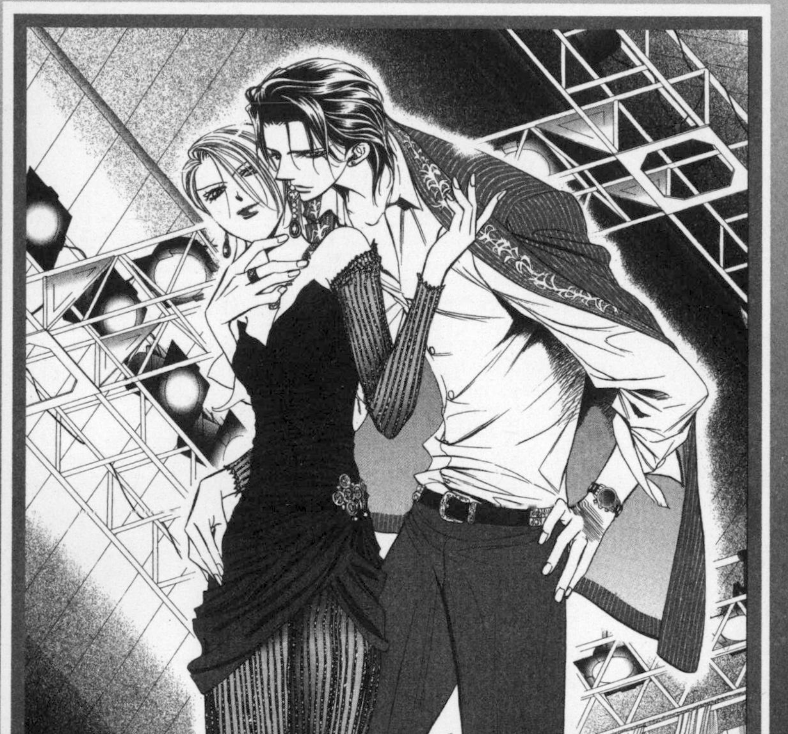

23

Story & Art by Yoshiki Nakamura

Skip·Beat!
Volume 23

CONTENTS

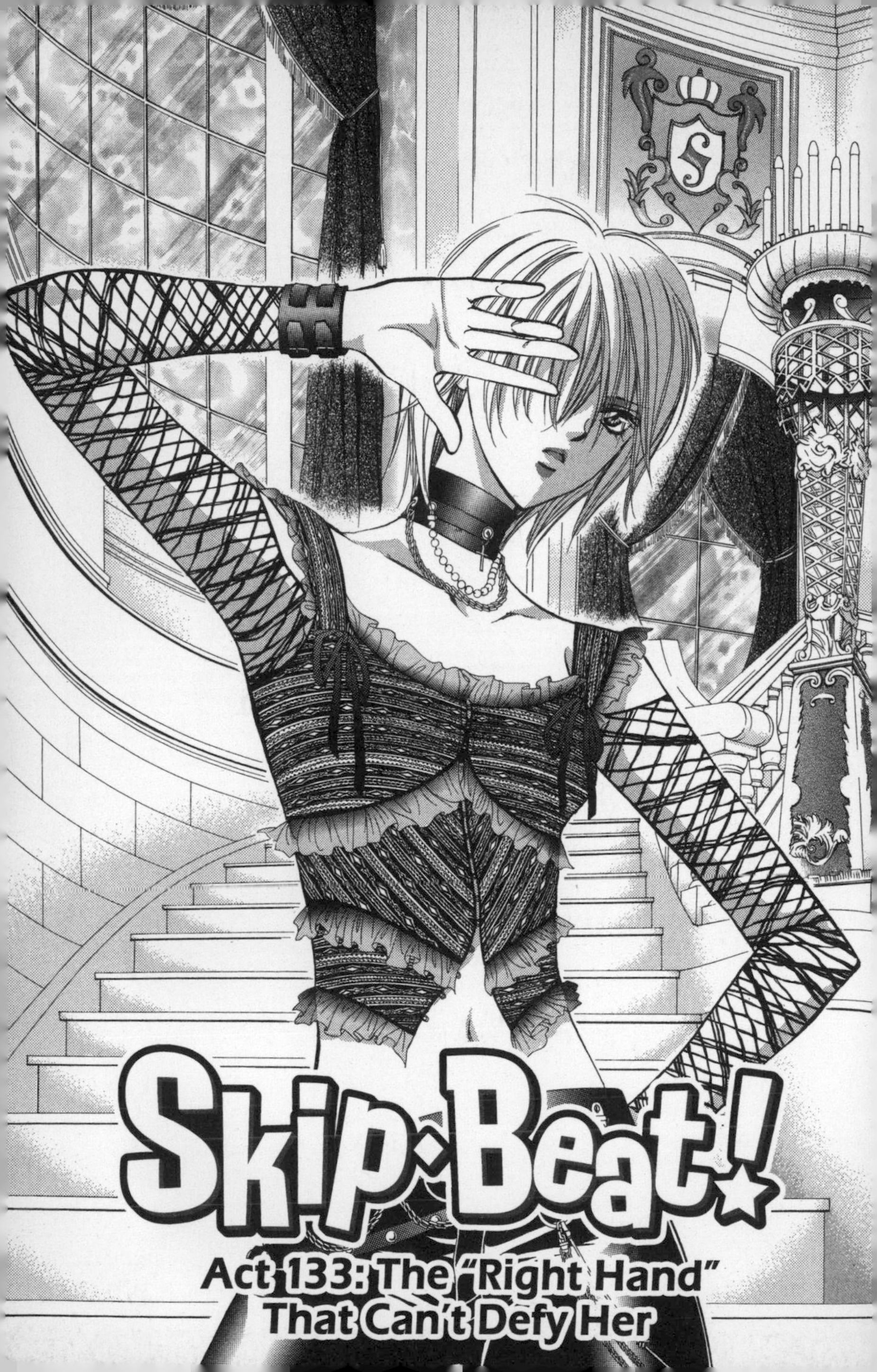
Skip·Beat!
Act 133: The "Right Hand" That Can't Defy Her

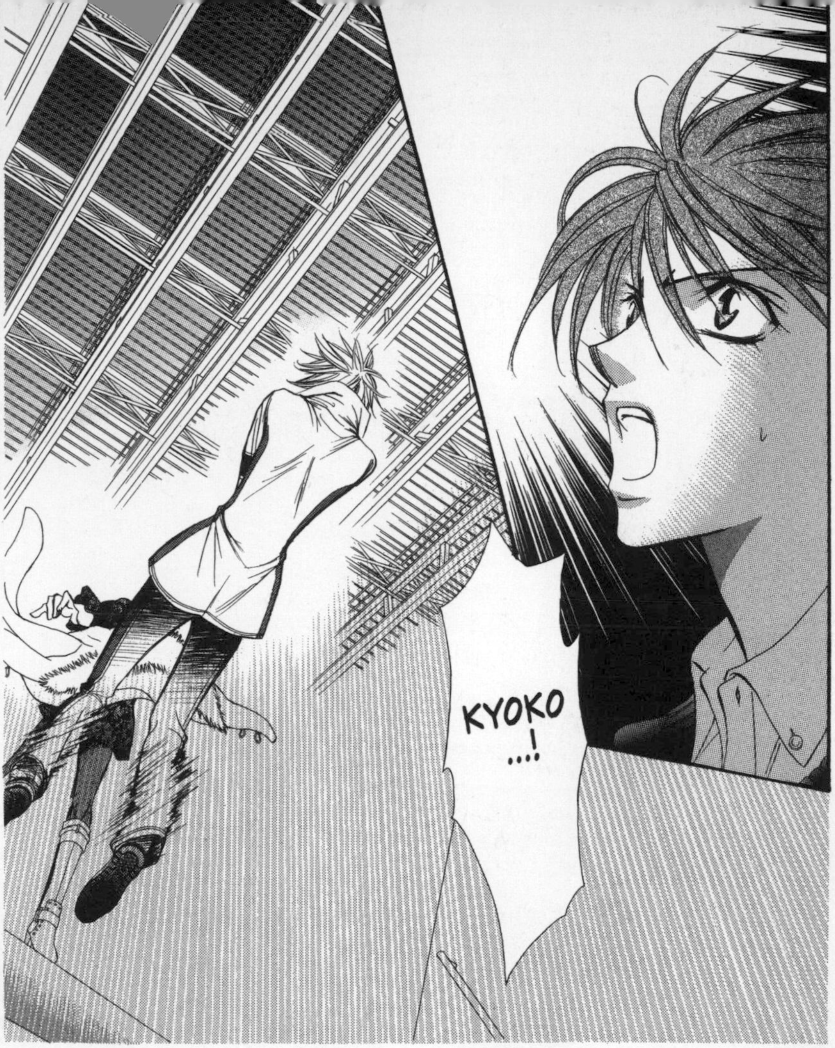
KYOKO ...!

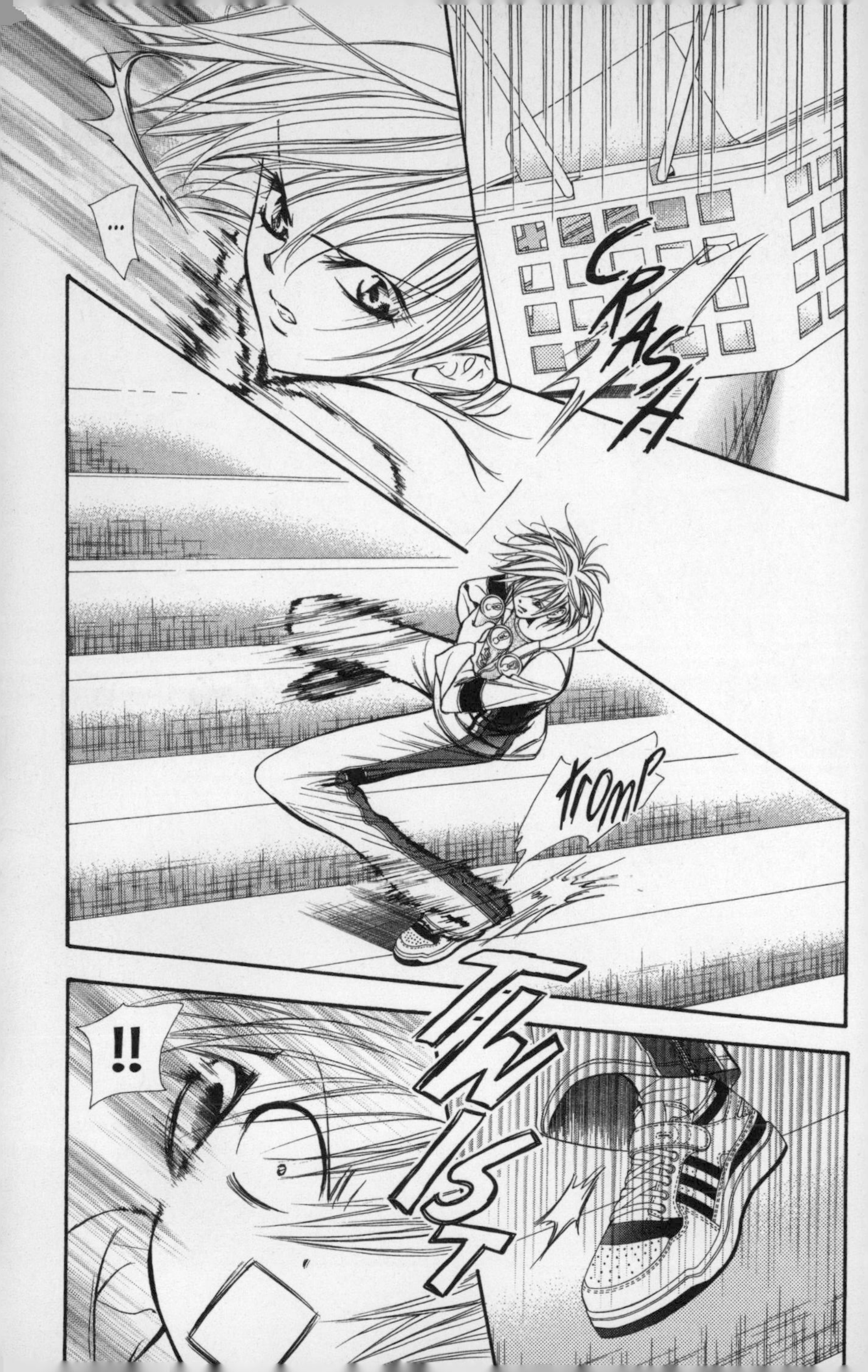
CRASH
...
tromp
TWIST
!!

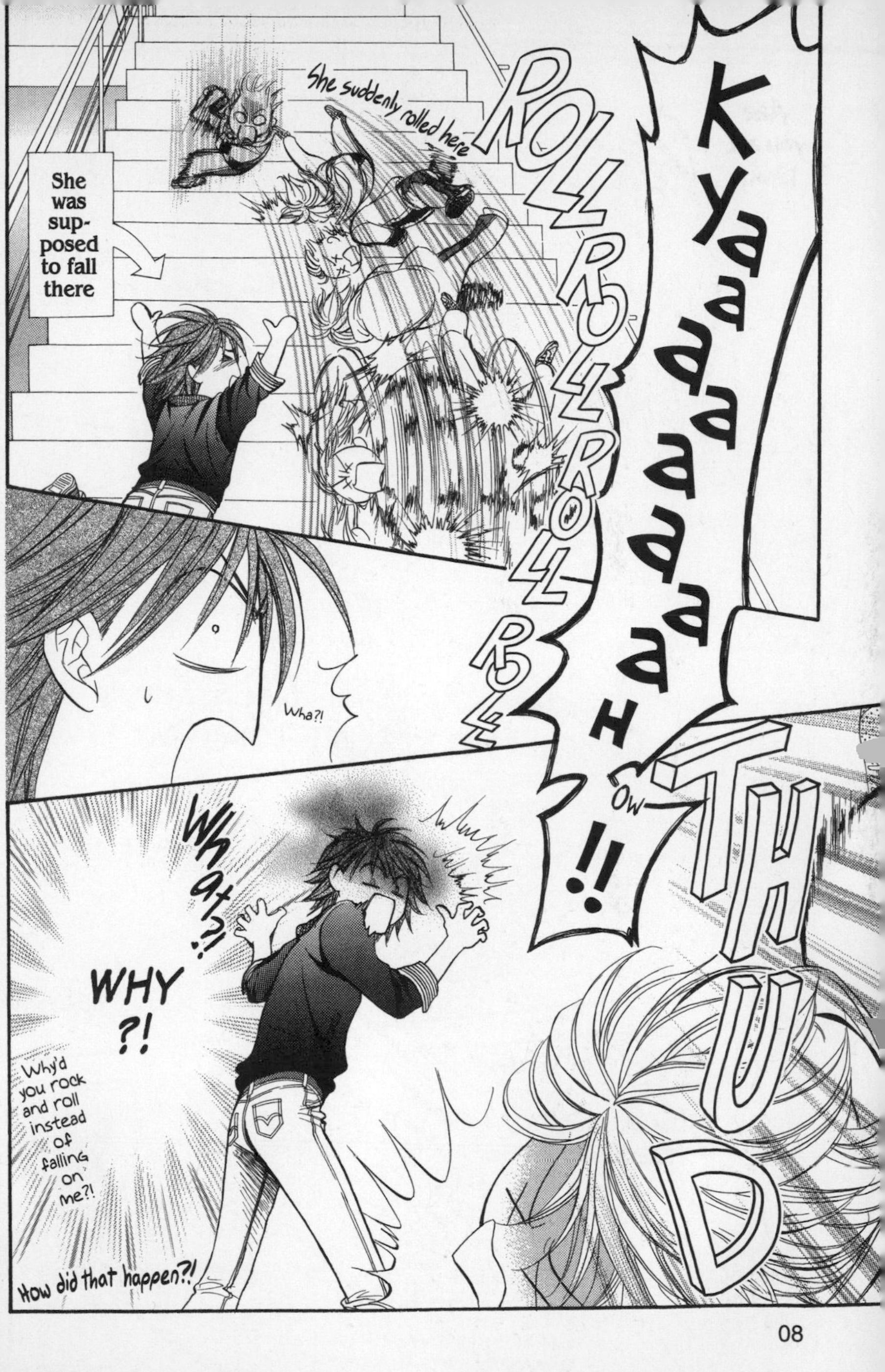

Kyaaaaaaah!!
ROLL ROLL ROLL ROLL
She suddenly rolled here
She was supposed to fall there
Wha?!
THUD
OW
What?!
WHY?!
Why'd you rock and roll instead of falling on me?!
How did that happen?!

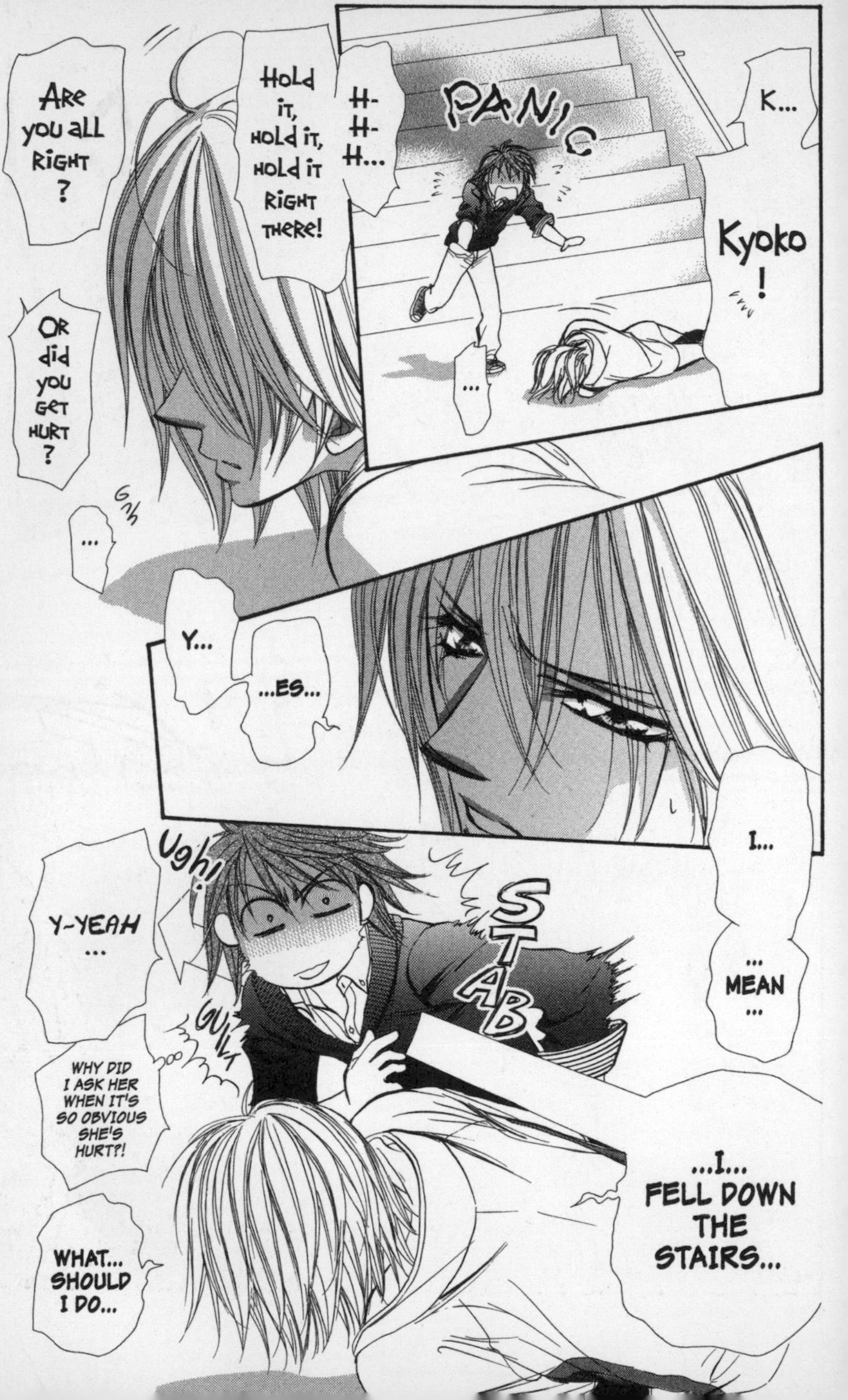
K...
Kyoko!
PANIC
H-H-H...
Hold it, hold it, hold it right there!
...
Are you all right?
Or did you get hurt?
...
Y...
...es...
I... ...mean...
STAB
Ugh!
Y-yeah...
GULP
Why did I ask her when it's so obvious she's hurt?!
...I... fell down the stairs...
What... should I do...

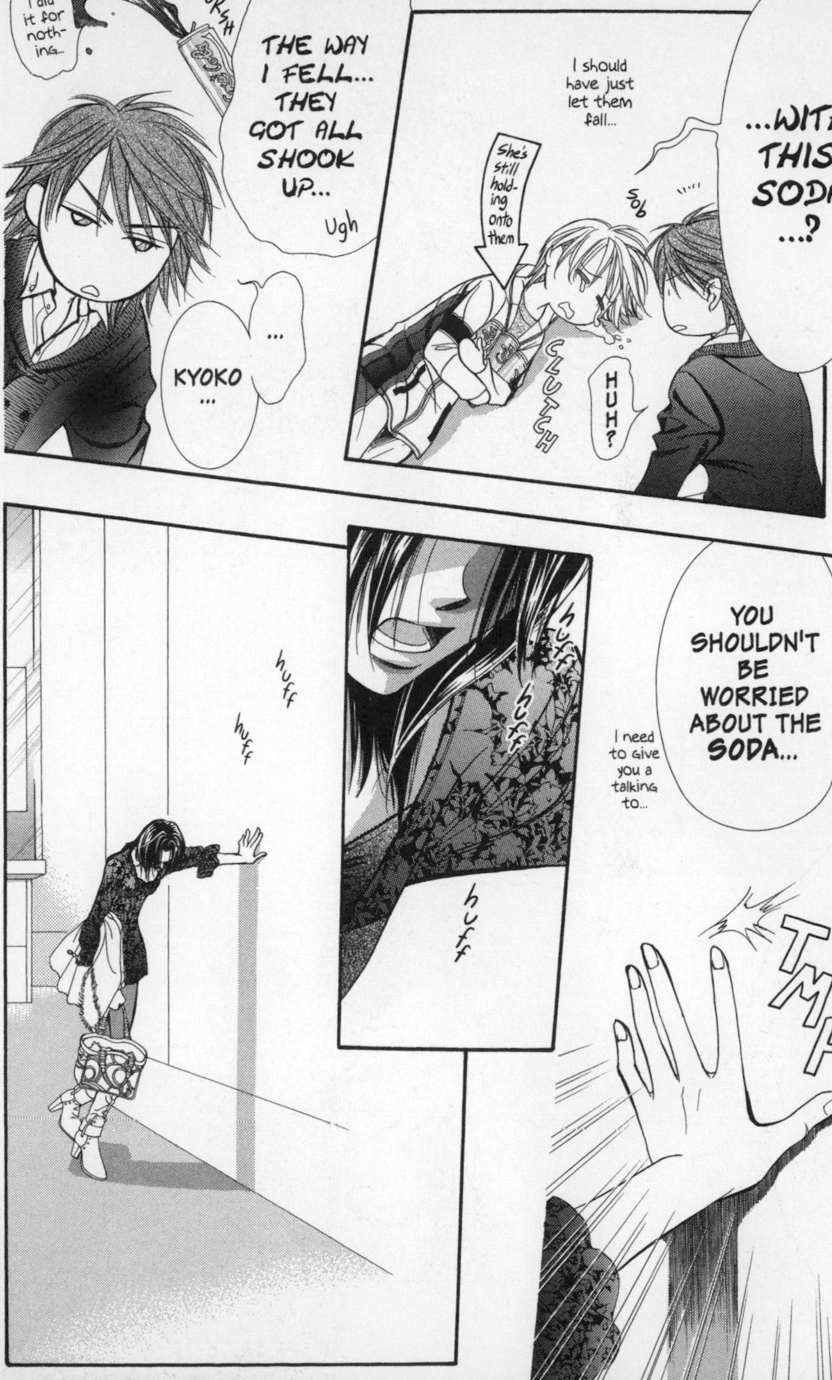
...WITH THIS SODA ...?
I should have just let them fall...
She's still holding onto them
sob
HUH?
CLUTCH
SPLORSH
THE WAY I FELL... THEY GOT ALL SHOOK UP...
Ugh
I did it for nothing...
...
KYOKO ...
YOU SHOULDN'T BE WORRIED ABOUT THE SODA...
I need to give you a talking to...
TMP
huff
huff
huff
huff
huff

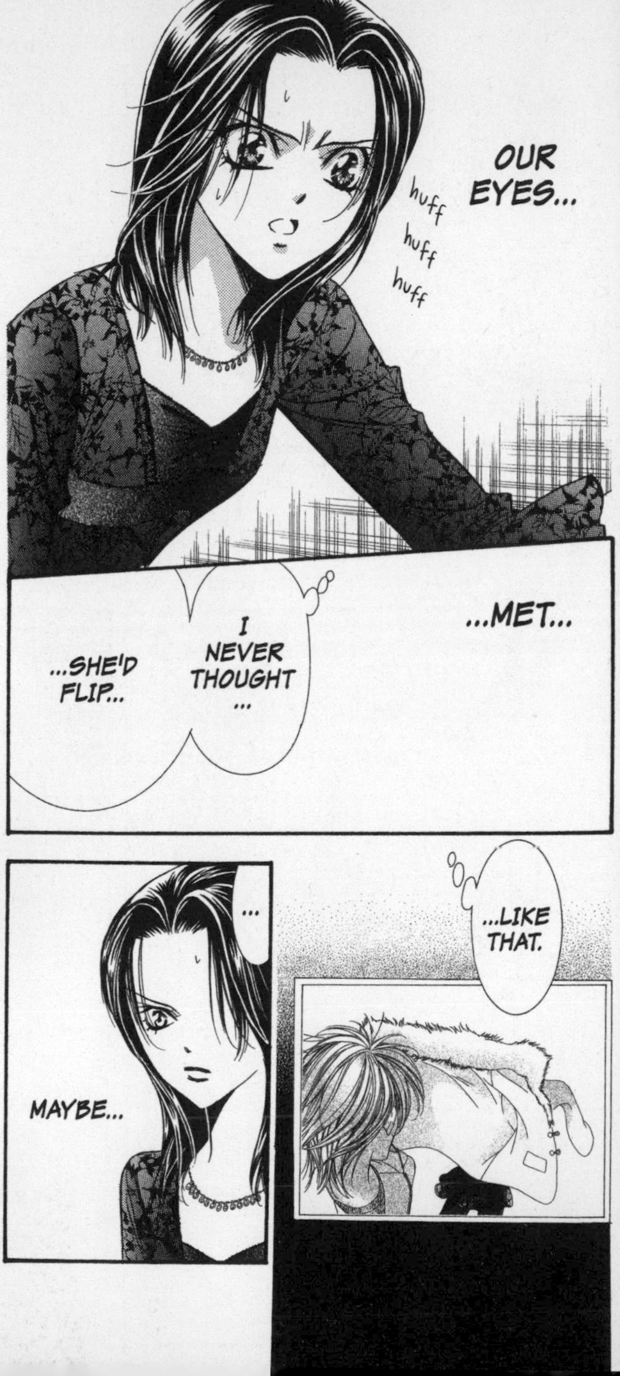
OUR EYES...
huff
huff
huff
...MET...
I NEVER THOUGHT ...
...SHE'D FLIP...
...LIKE THAT.
...
MAYBE...
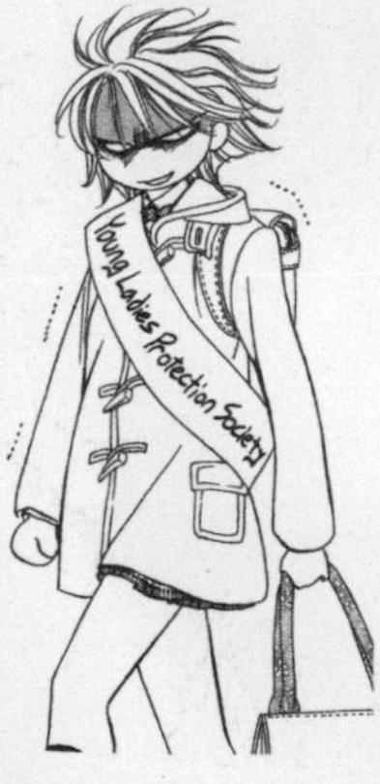
Young Ladies Protection Society

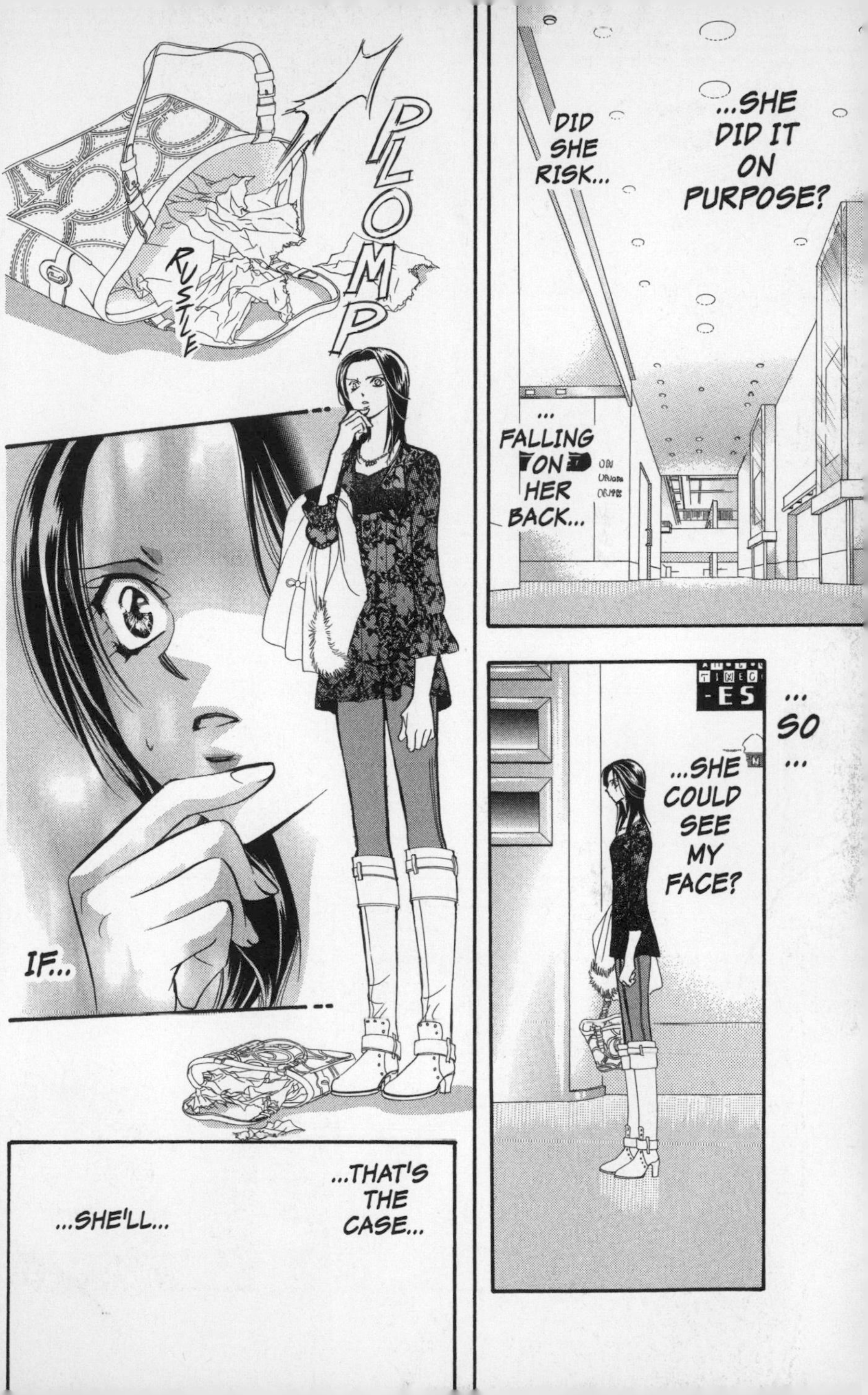
...SHE DID IT ON PURPOSE?
DID SHE RISK...
...FALLING ON HER BACK...
...SO...
...SHE COULD SEE MY FACE?
PLOMP
RUSTLE
IF...
...THAT'S THE CASE...
...SHE'LL...

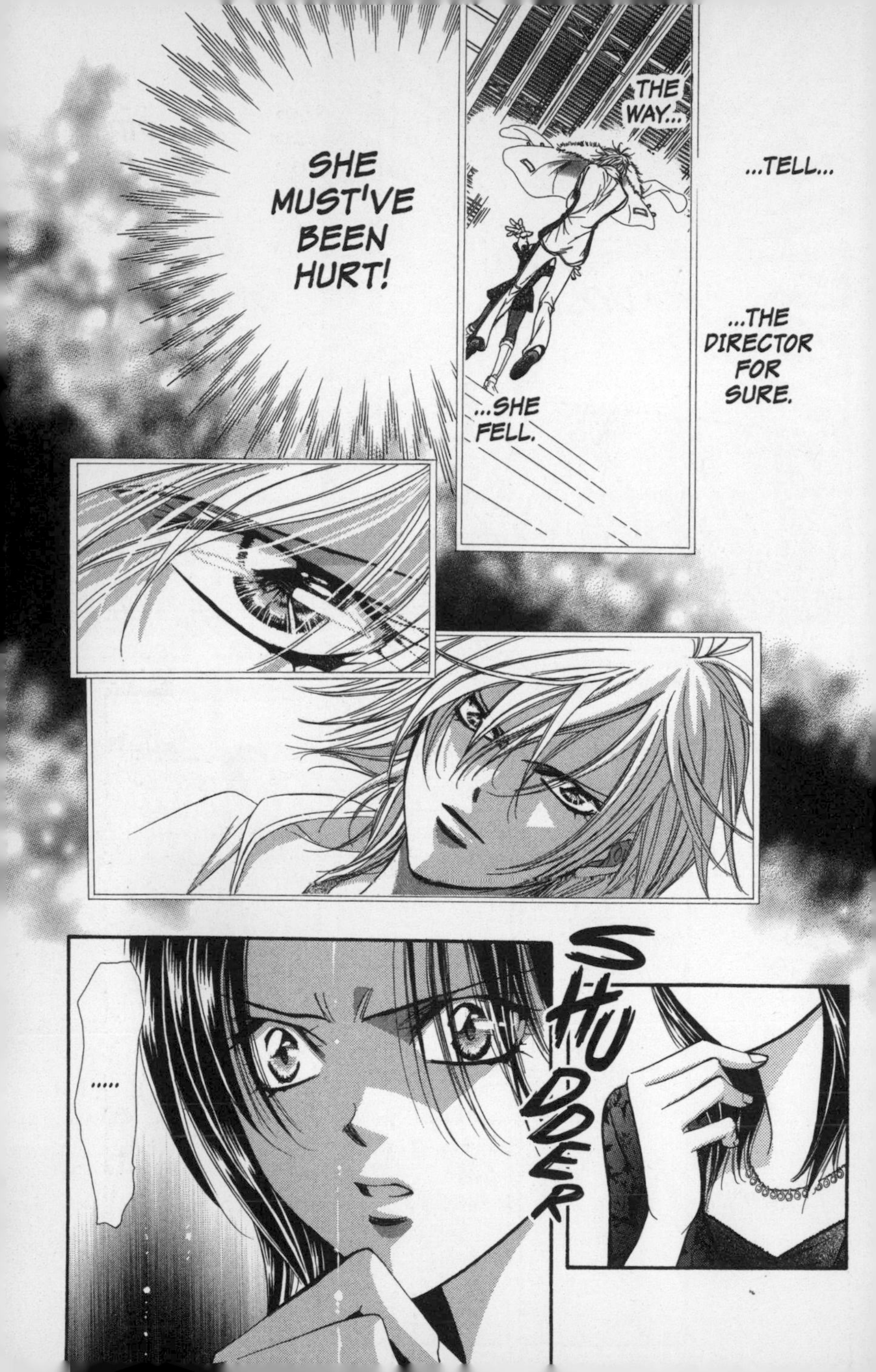
...TELL...
...THE DIRECTOR FOR SURE.
THE WAY...
...SHE FELL.
SHE MUST'VE BEEN HURT!
SHUDDER
.....

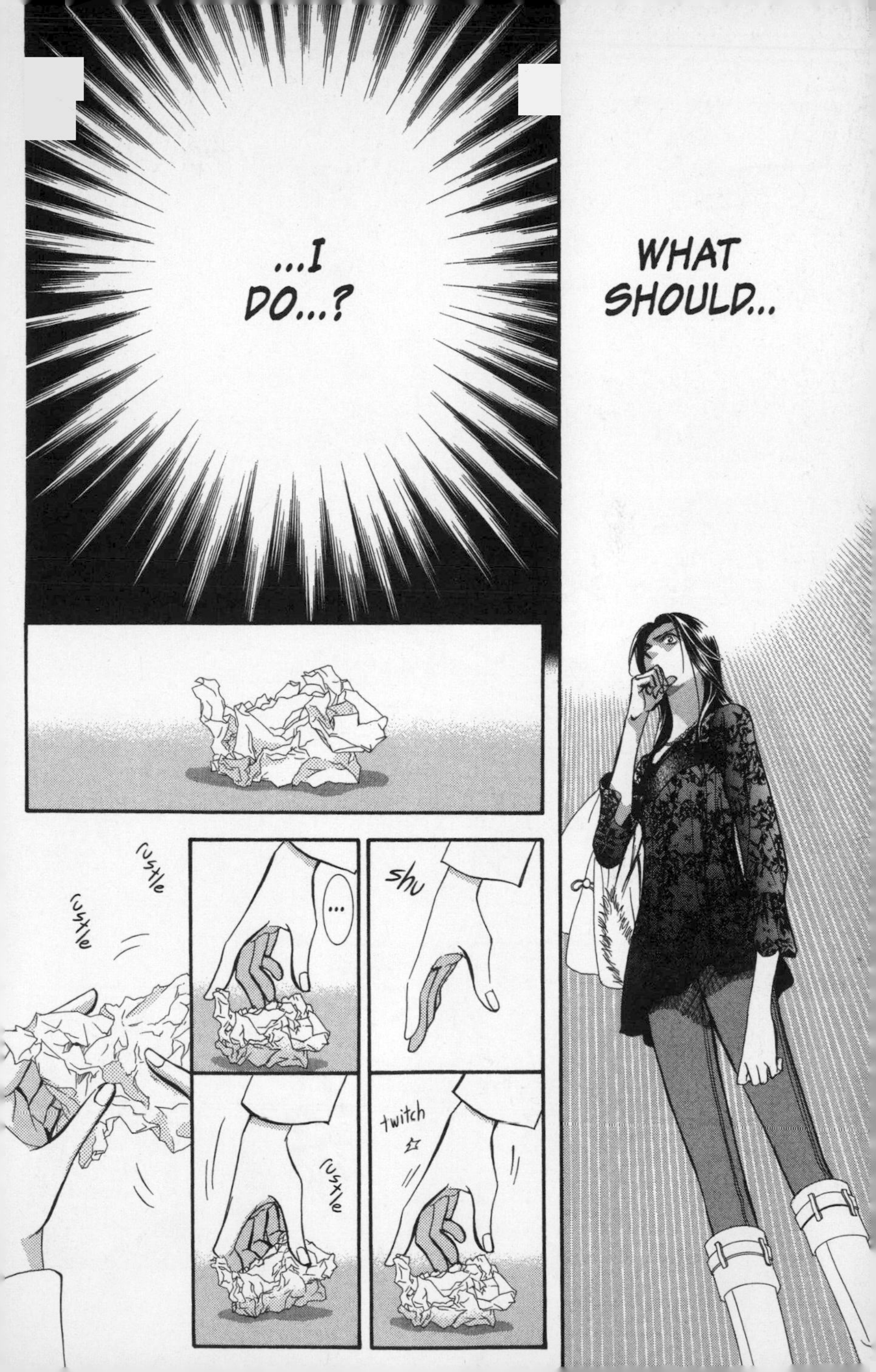
WHAT SHOULD...
...I DO...?
shu
...
twitch
rustle
rustle
rustle

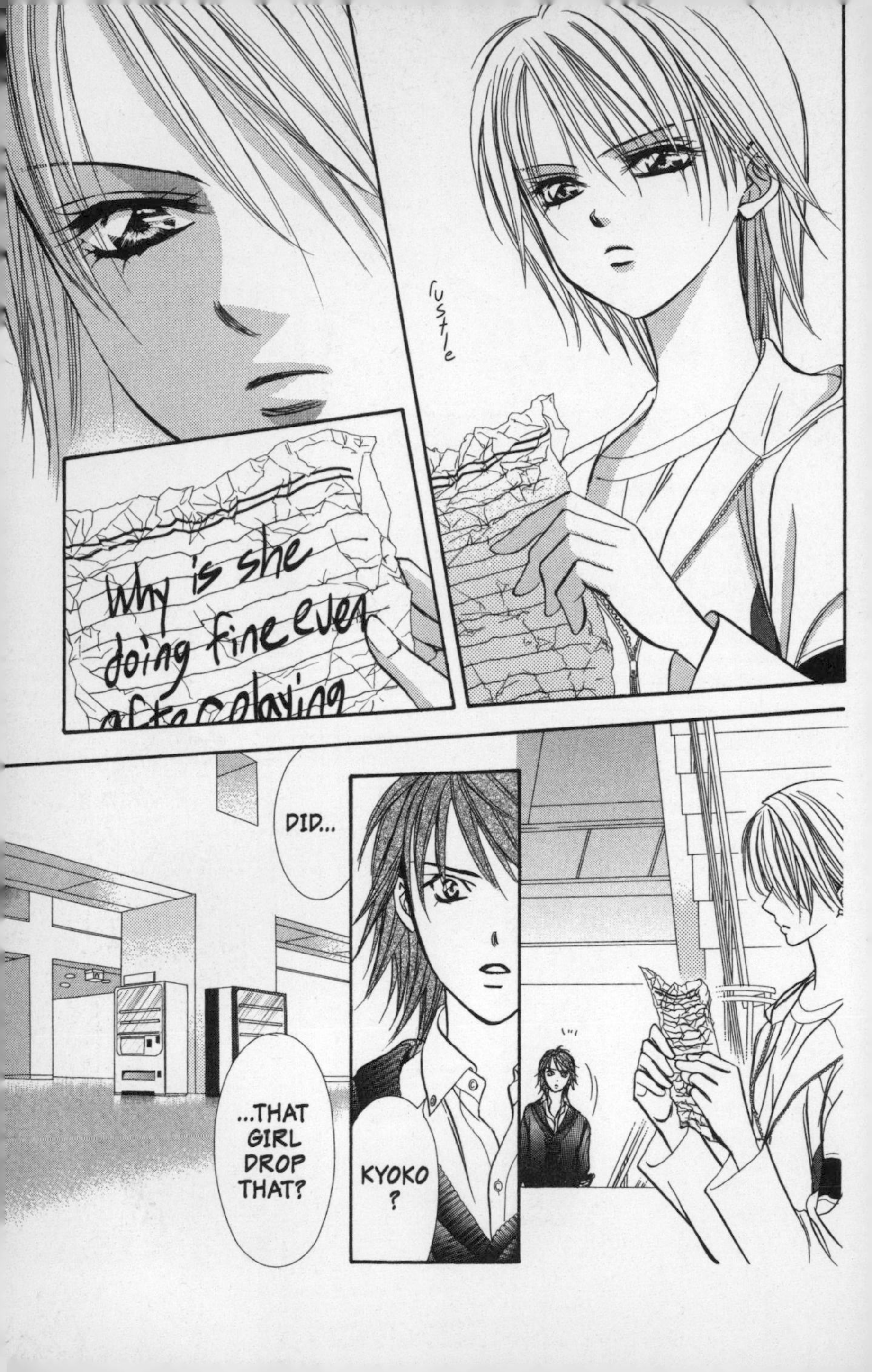
rustle
Why is she
doing fine even
KYOKO ?
DID...
...THAT GIRL DROP THAT?

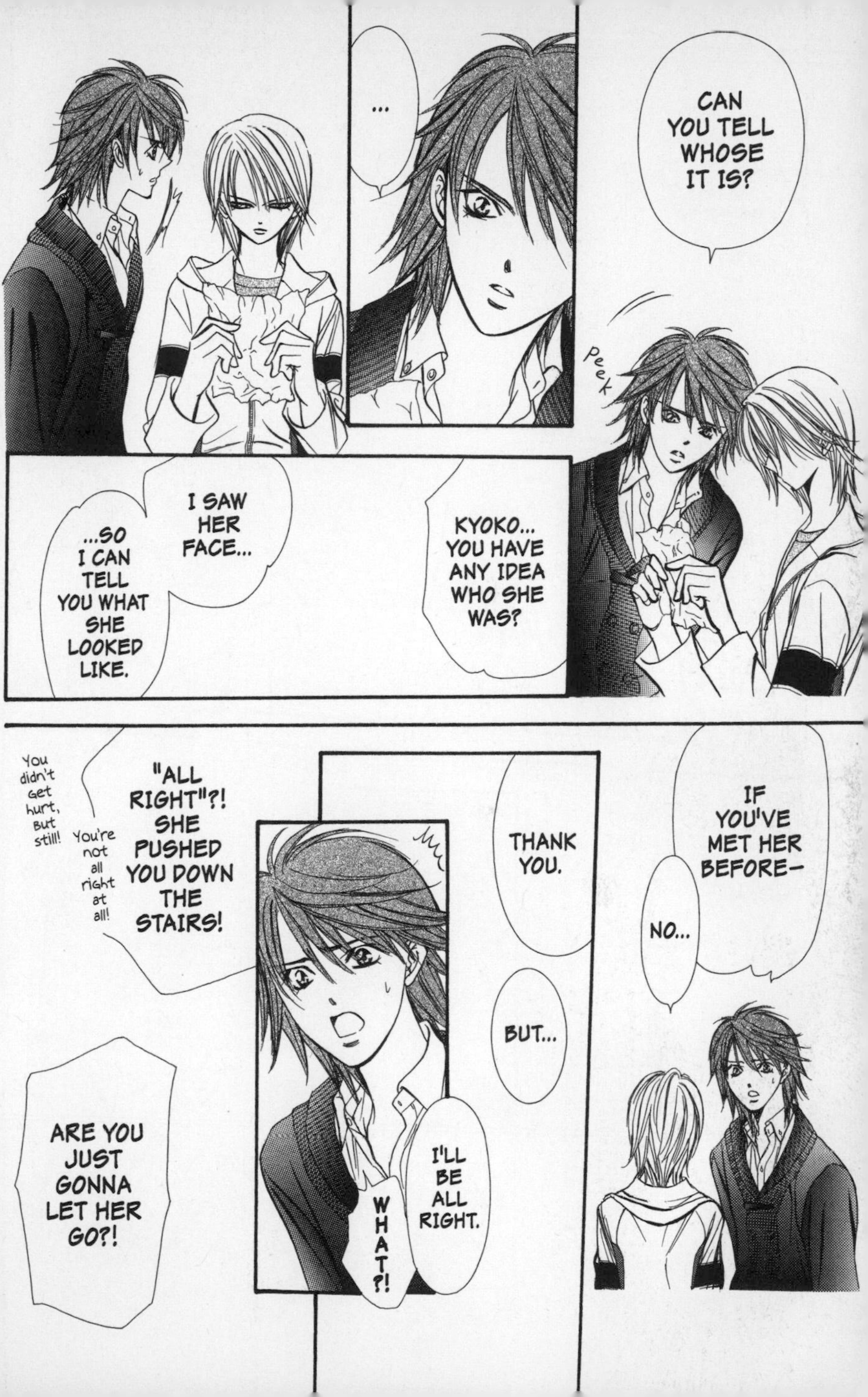
CAN YOU TELL WHOSE IT IS?
Peek
...
KYOKO... YOU HAVE ANY IDEA WHO SHE WAS?
I SAW HER FACE...
...SO I CAN TELL YOU WHAT SHE LOOKED LIKE.
IF YOU'VE MET HER BEFORE—
NO...
THANK YOU.
BUT...
I'LL BE ALL RIGHT.
WHAT?!
"ALL RIGHT"?! SHE PUSHED YOU DOWN THE STAIRS!
You're not all right at all!
You didn't get hurt, but still!
ARE YOU JUST GONNA LET HER GO?!

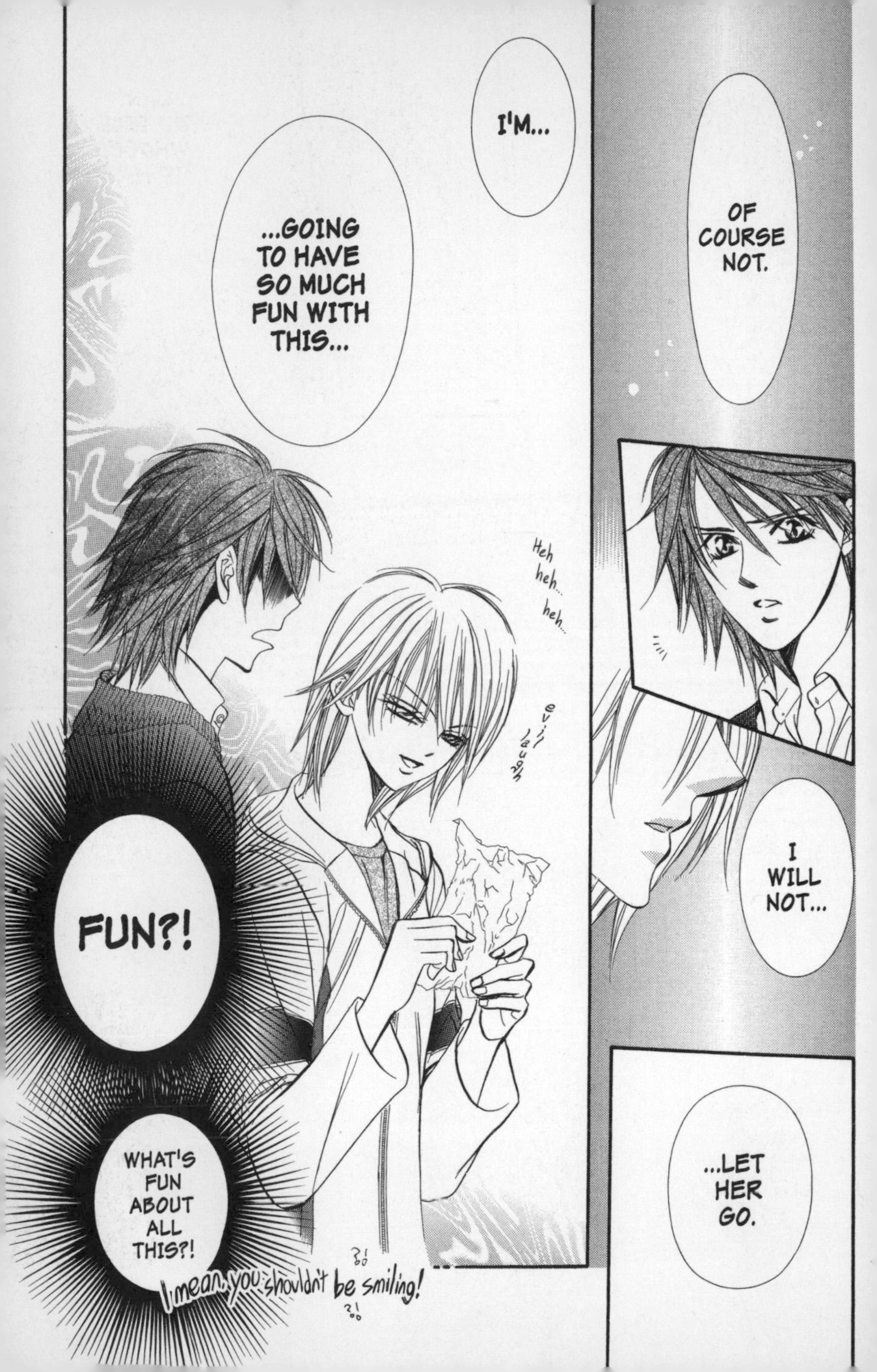
OF COURSE NOT.
I WILL NOT...
...LET HER GO.
I'M...
...GOING TO HAVE SO MUCH FUN WITH THIS...
Heh heh... heh...
evil laugh
FUN?!
WHAT'S FUN ABOUT ALL THIS?!
?!
I mean, you shouldn't be smiling!
?!

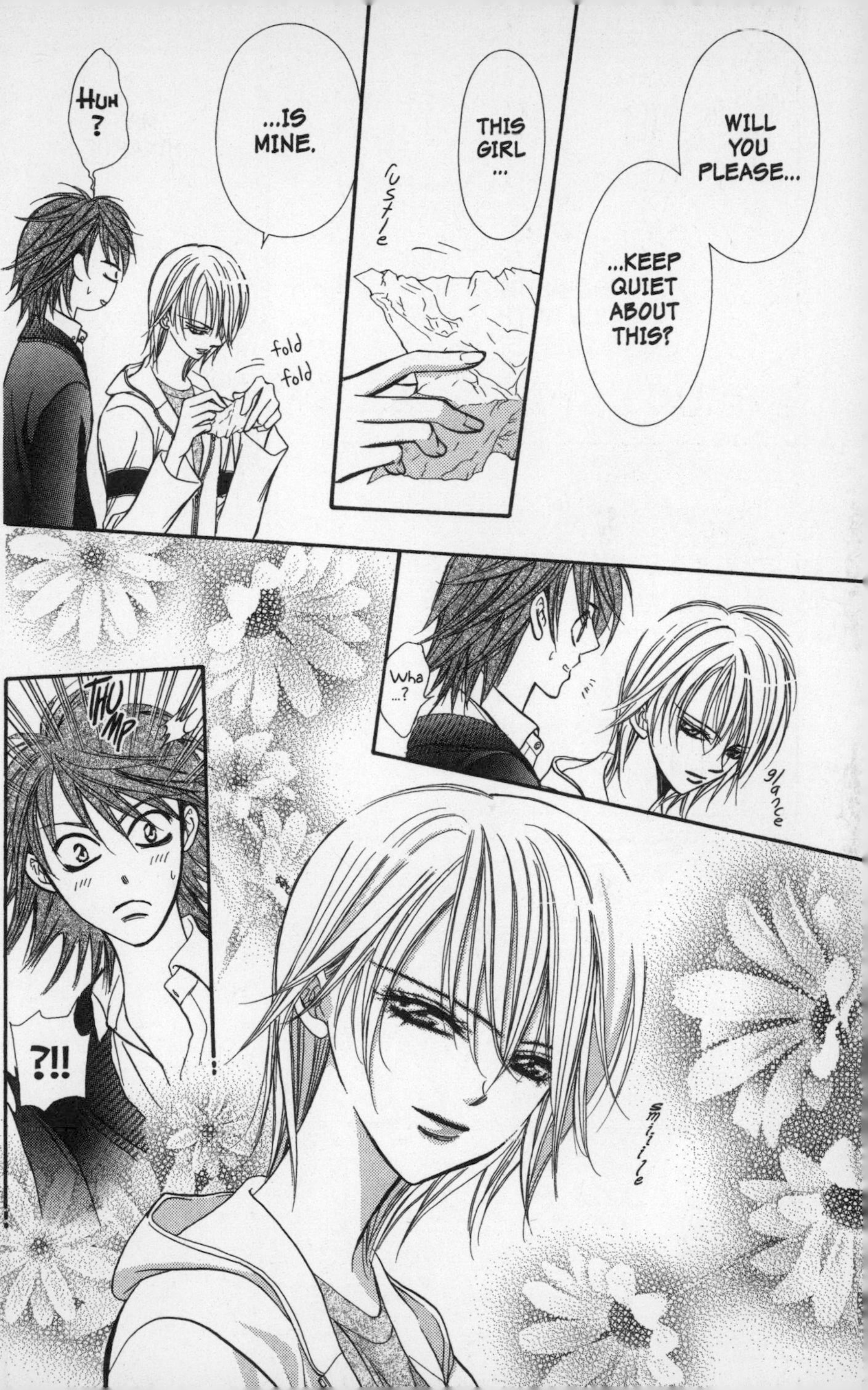
WILL YOU PLEASE...
...KEEP QUIET ABOUT THIS?
THIS GIRL ...
rustle
...IS MINE.
HUH ?
fold
fold
Wha ...?
glance
smiiile
THUMP
?!!

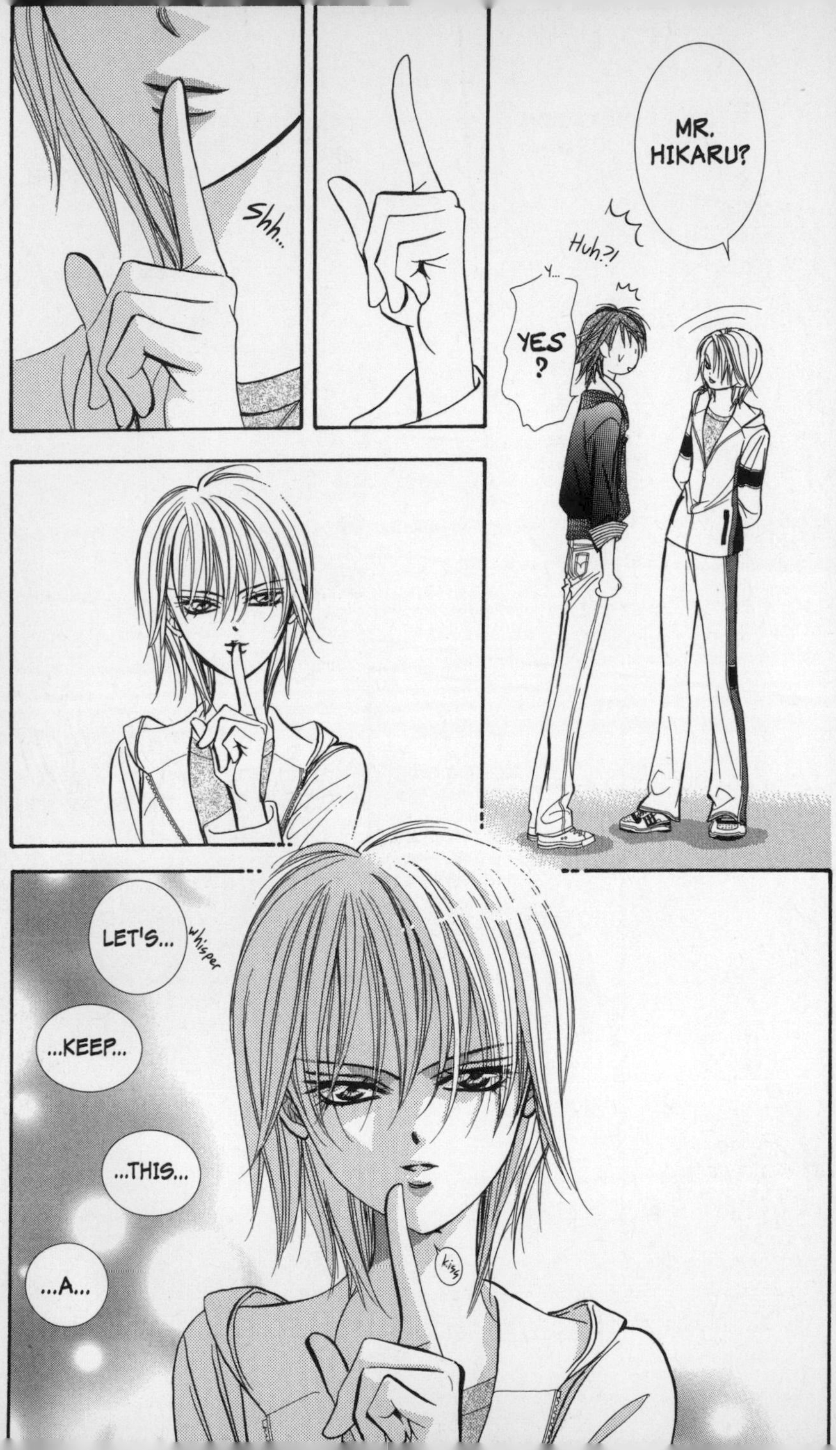
MR. HIKARU?
Huh?!
Y...
YES?
Shh...
LET'S...
whisper
...KEEP...
...THIS...
...A...
kiss

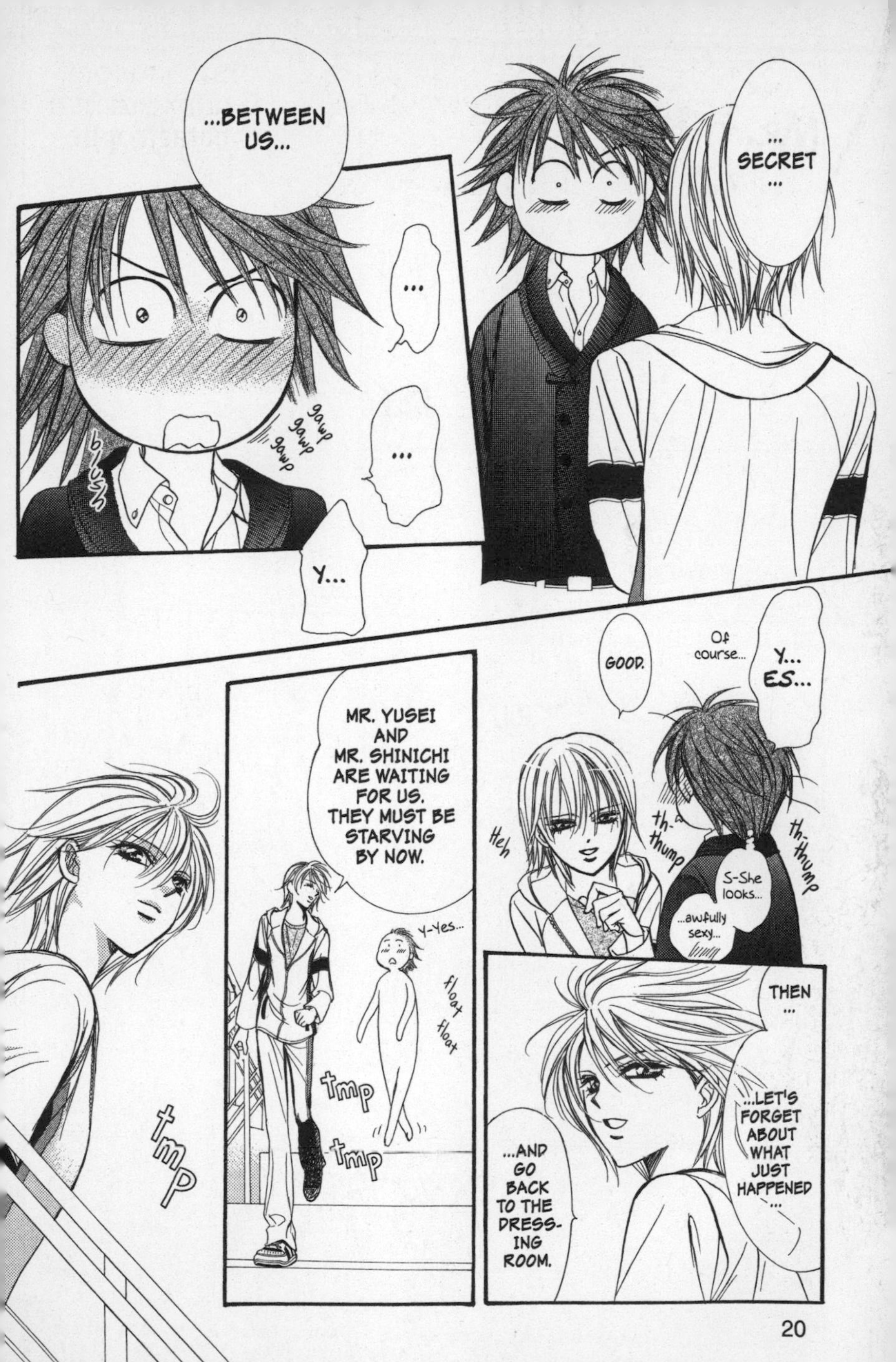
... SECRET ...
...BETWEEN US...
gawp gawp gawp
blush
...
...
Y...
Y... ES...
Of course...
GOOD.
th-thump th-thump
S-She looks...
...awfully sexy...
Heh
THEN ...
...LET'S FORGET ABOUT WHAT JUST HAPPENED ...
...AND GO BACK TO THE DRESS-ING ROOM.
MR. YUSEI AND MR. SHINICHI ARE WAITING FOR US. THEY MUST BE STARVING BY NOW.
Y-Yes...
float float
tmp
tmp
tmp

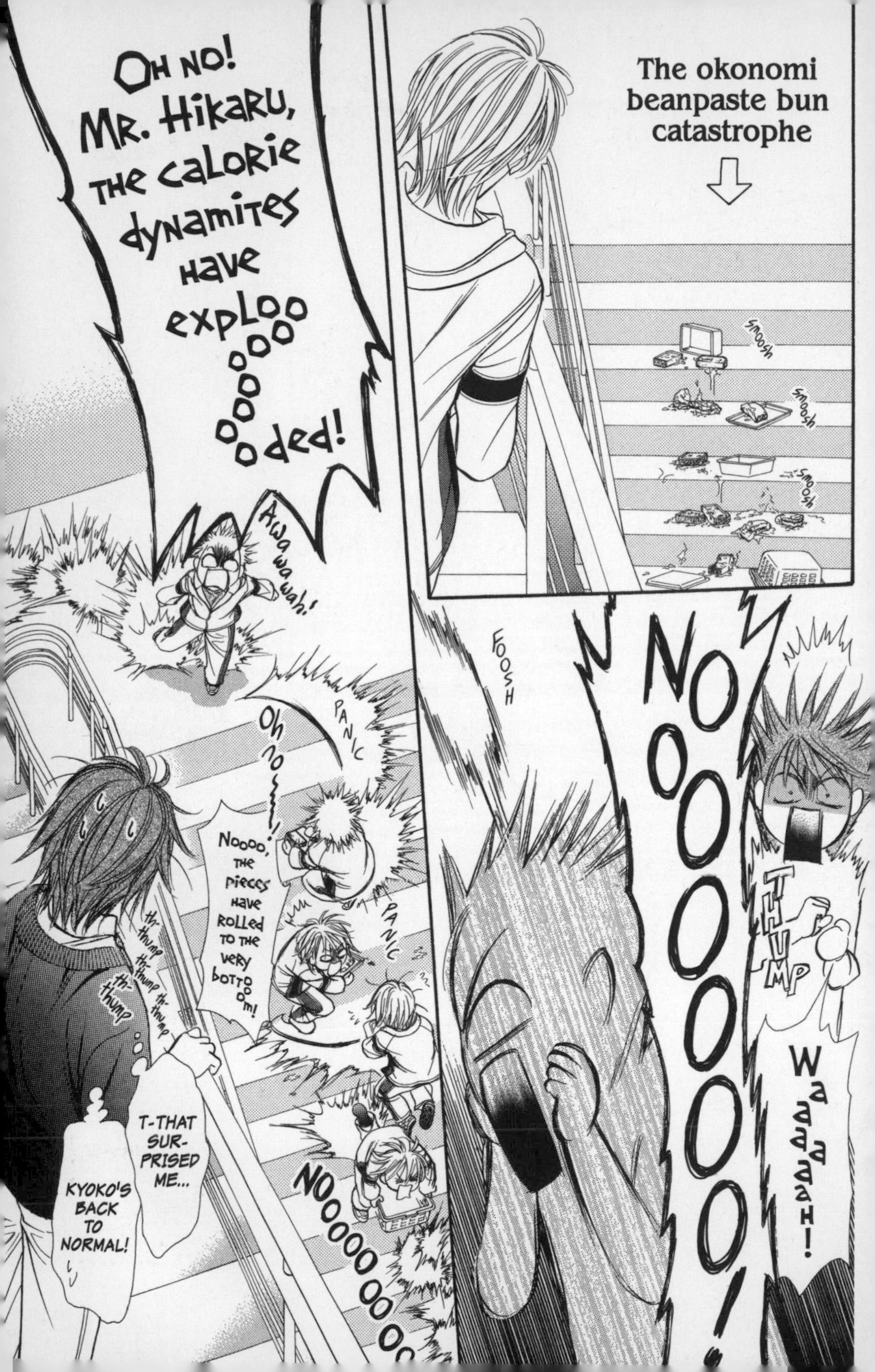
The okonomi beanpaste bun catastrophe
SMOOSH
SMOOSH
SMOOSH
FOOSH
NOOOOOOOOO!
THUMP
Waaaaaah!
Oh no! Mr. Hikaru, the calorie dynamites have explooooooooooded!
Awawawah!
PANIC
Oh no~!
Noooo, the pieces have rolled to the very bottooom!
PANIC
th-thump th-thump th-thump th-thump
T-THAT SUR-PRISED ME...
KYOKO'S BACK TO NORMAL!
NOOOOOOOOO

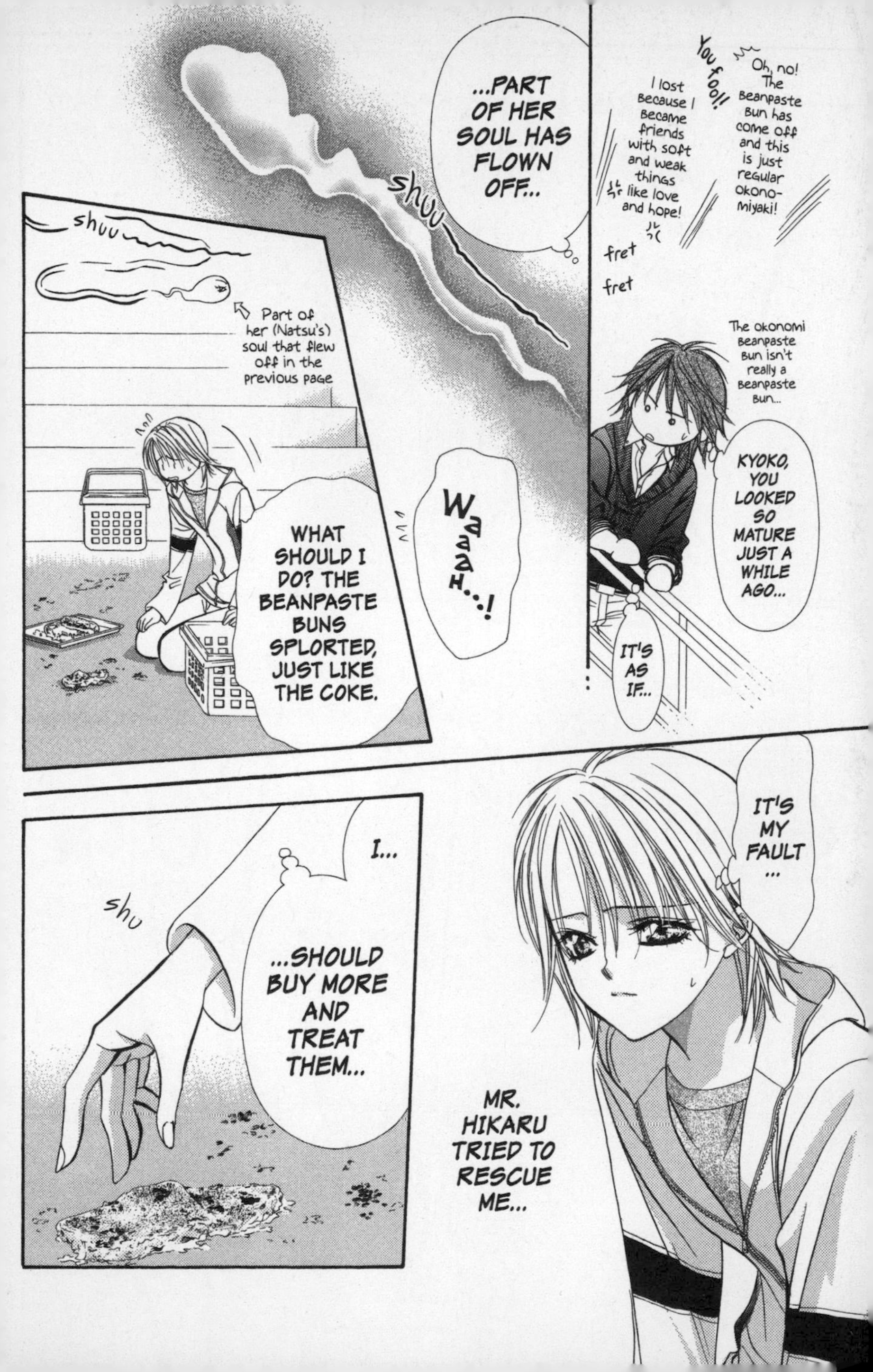
Oh, no! The Beanpaste Bun has come off and this is just regular Okonomiyaki!
You fool!!
I lost because I became friends with soft and weak things like love and hope!
fret
fret
The okonomi Beanpaste Bun isn't really a Beanpaste Bun...
KYOKO, YOU LOOKED SO MATURE JUST A WHILE AGO...
IT'S AS IF...
...PART OF HER SOUL HAS FLOWN OFF...
shuu
shuu
Part of her (Natsu's) soul that flew off in the previous page
Waaah...!
WHAT SHOULD I DO? THE BEANPASTE BUNS SPLORTED, JUST LIKE THE COKE.
IT'S MY FAULT...
MR. HIKARU TRIED TO RESCUE ME...
I...
...SHOULD BUY MORE AND TREAT THEM...
shu

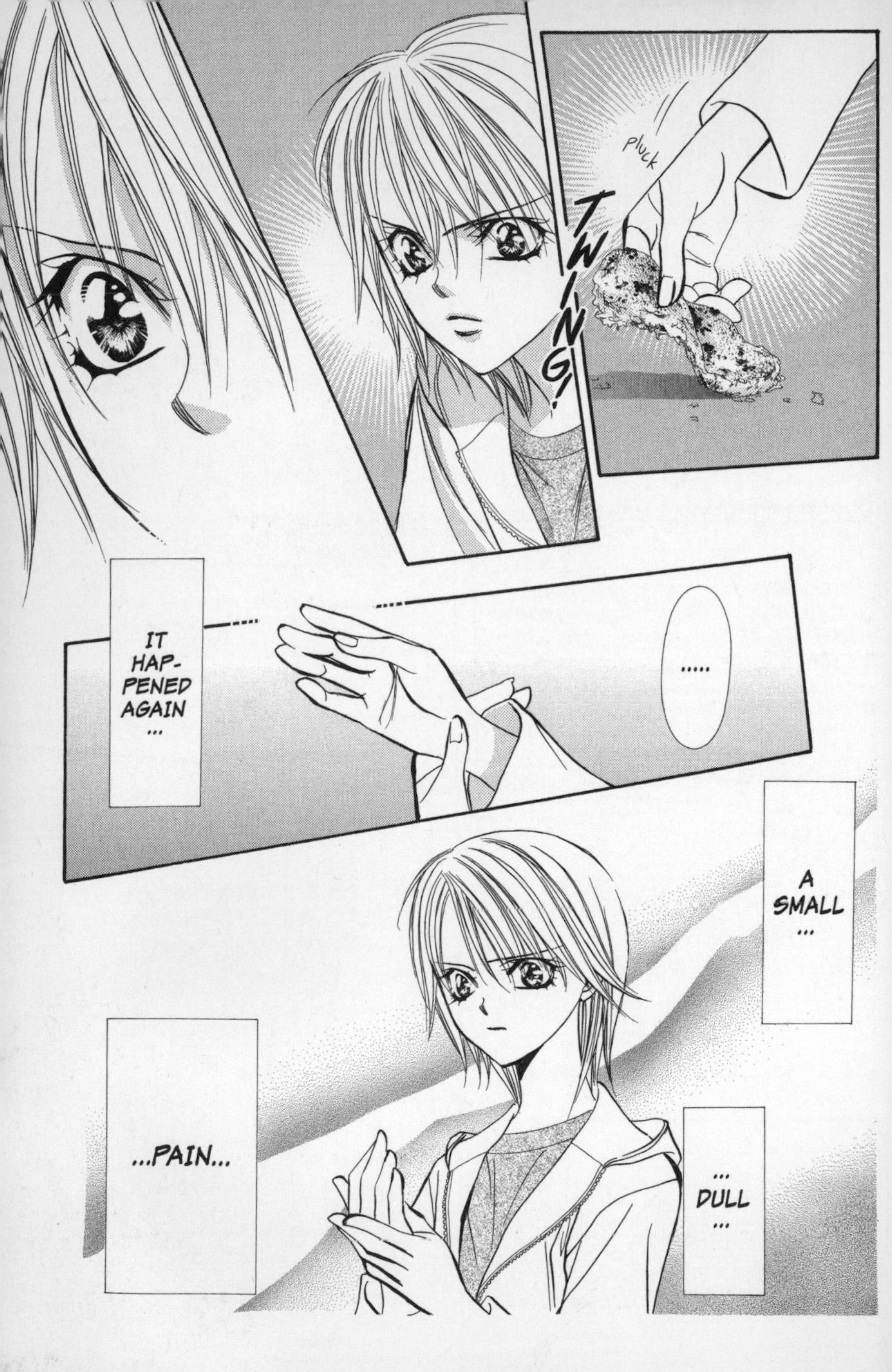
pluck
TWING!
.....
IT HAP-PENED AGAIN ...
A SMALL ...
... DULL ...
...PAIN...

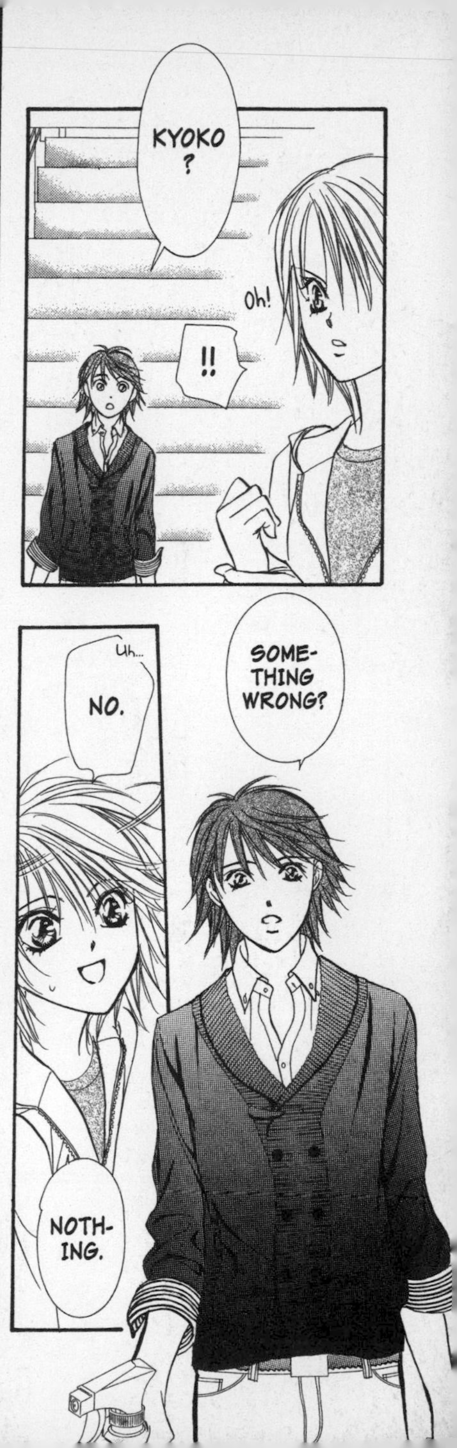
KYOKO ?
Oh!
!!
SOME-THING WRONG?
Uh...
NO.
NOTH-ING.
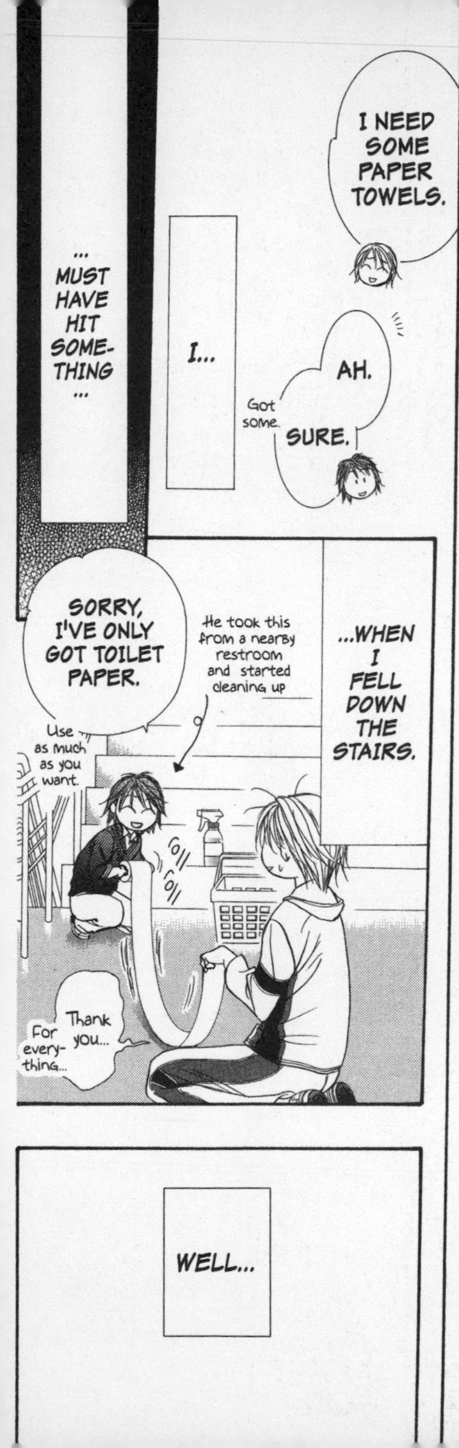
I NEED SOME PAPER TOWELS.
AH.
SURE.
Got some.
I...
... MUST HAVE HIT SOME-THING ...
...WHEN I FELL DOWN THE STAIRS.
SORRY, I'VE ONLY GOT TOILET PAPER.
He took this from a nearby restroom and started cleaning up
Use as much as you want.
roll roll
Thank you...
For every-thing...
WELL...

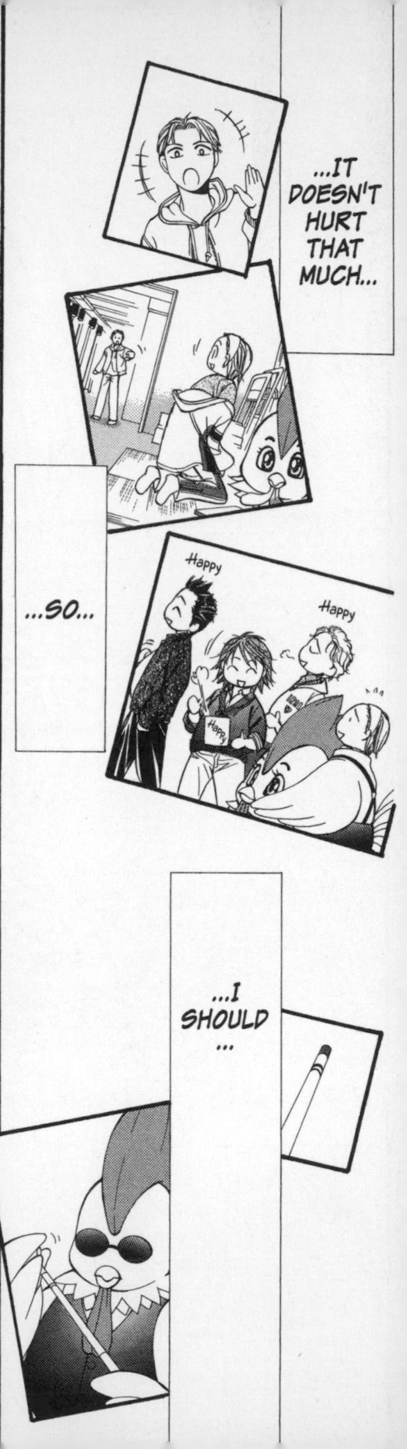
...IT DOESN'T HURT THAT MUCH...
...SO...
Happy
Happy
Happy
...I SHOULD ...
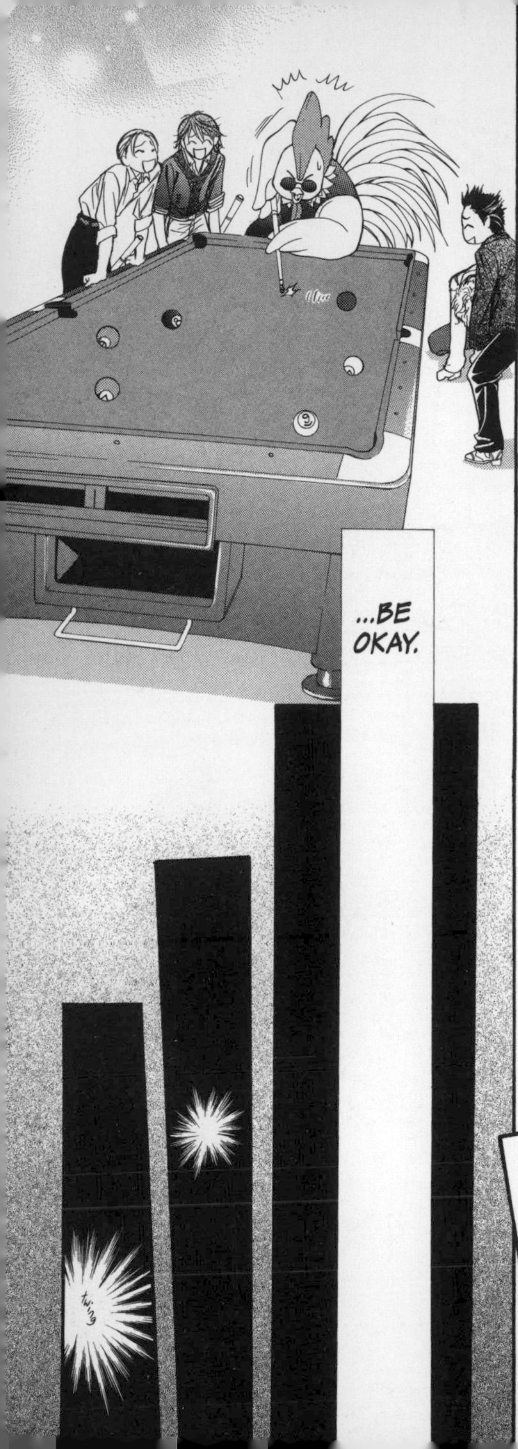
...BE OKAY.
twing

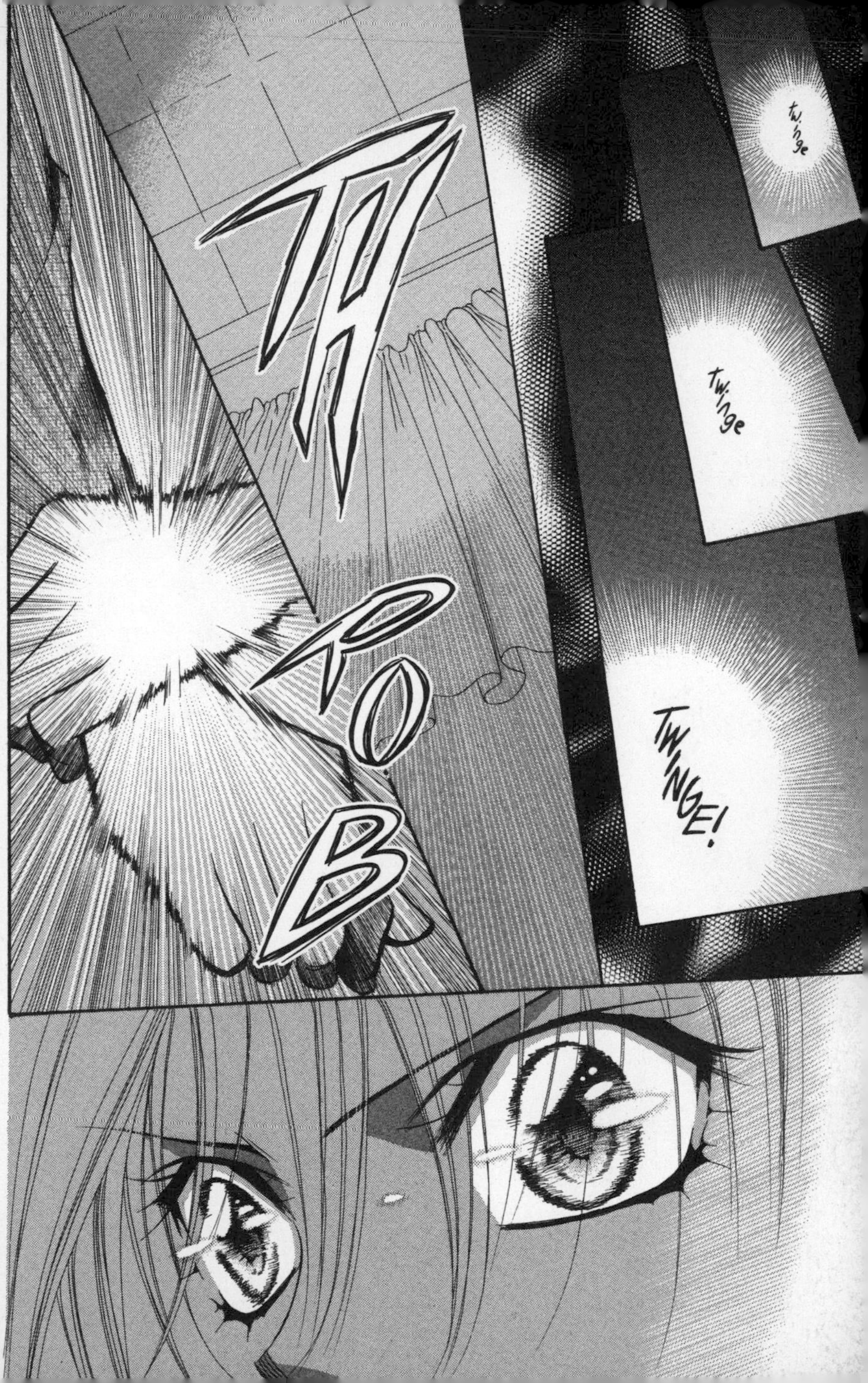
twinge
twinge
TWINGE!
THROB

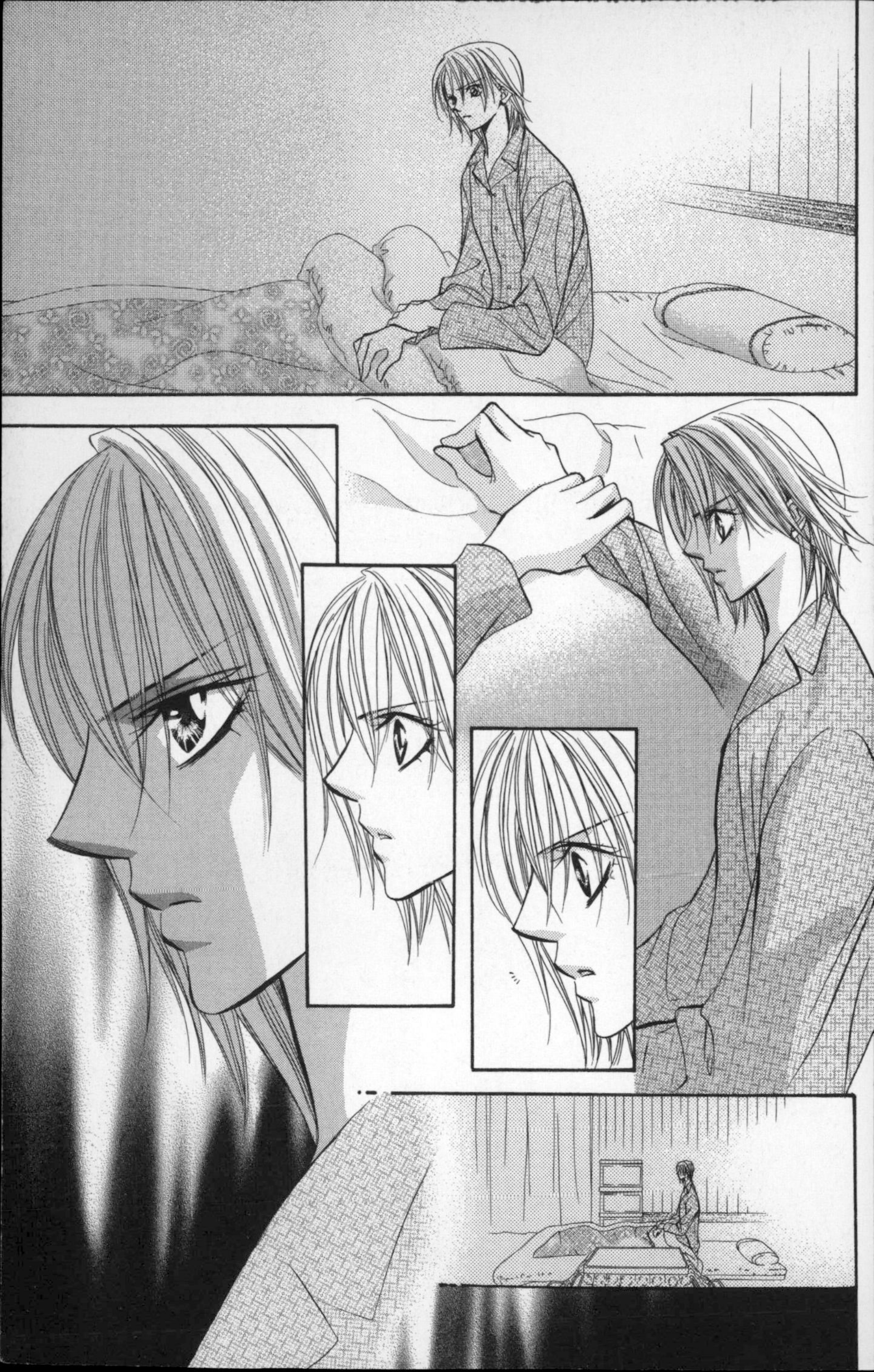

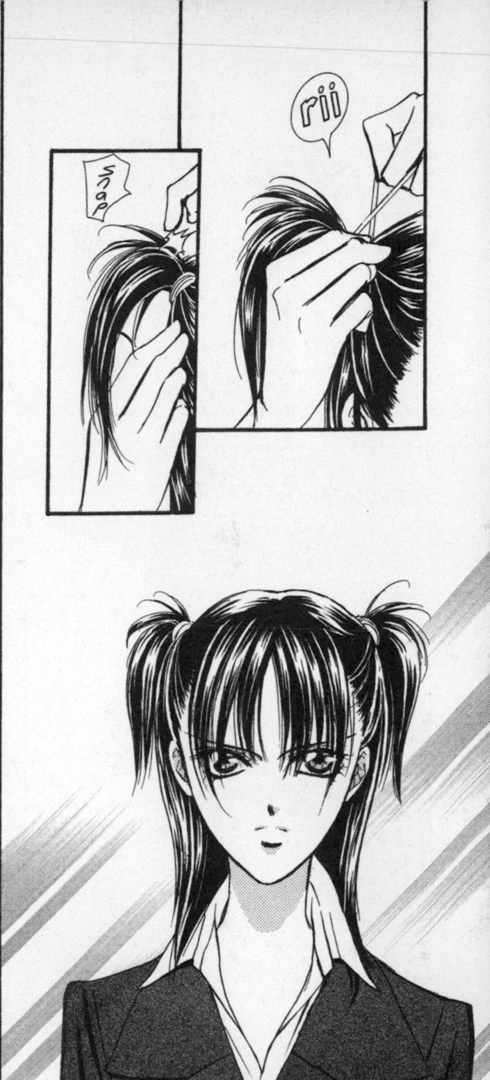
rii
snap

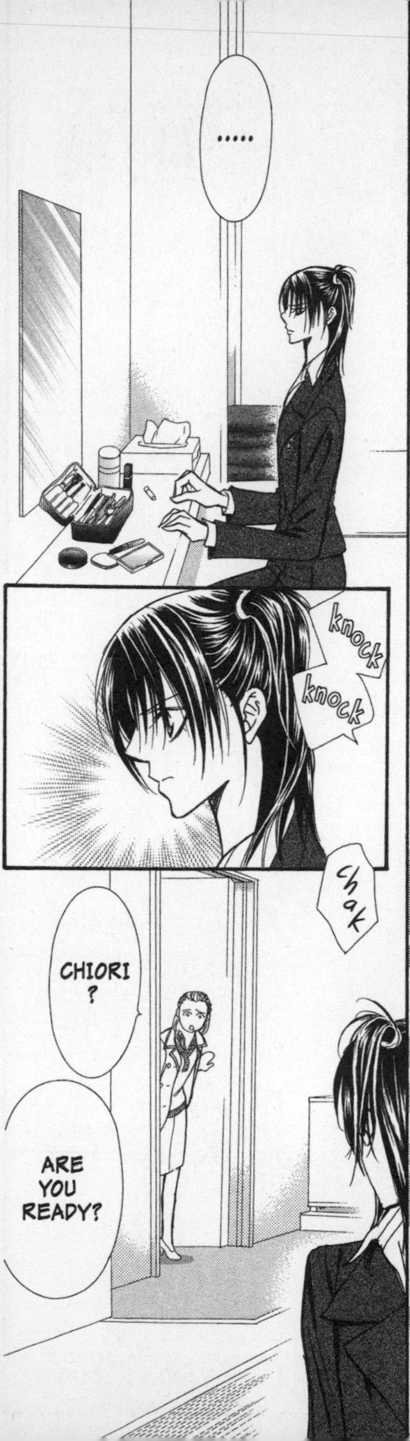
......
knock
knock
chak
CHIORI?
ARE YOU READY?

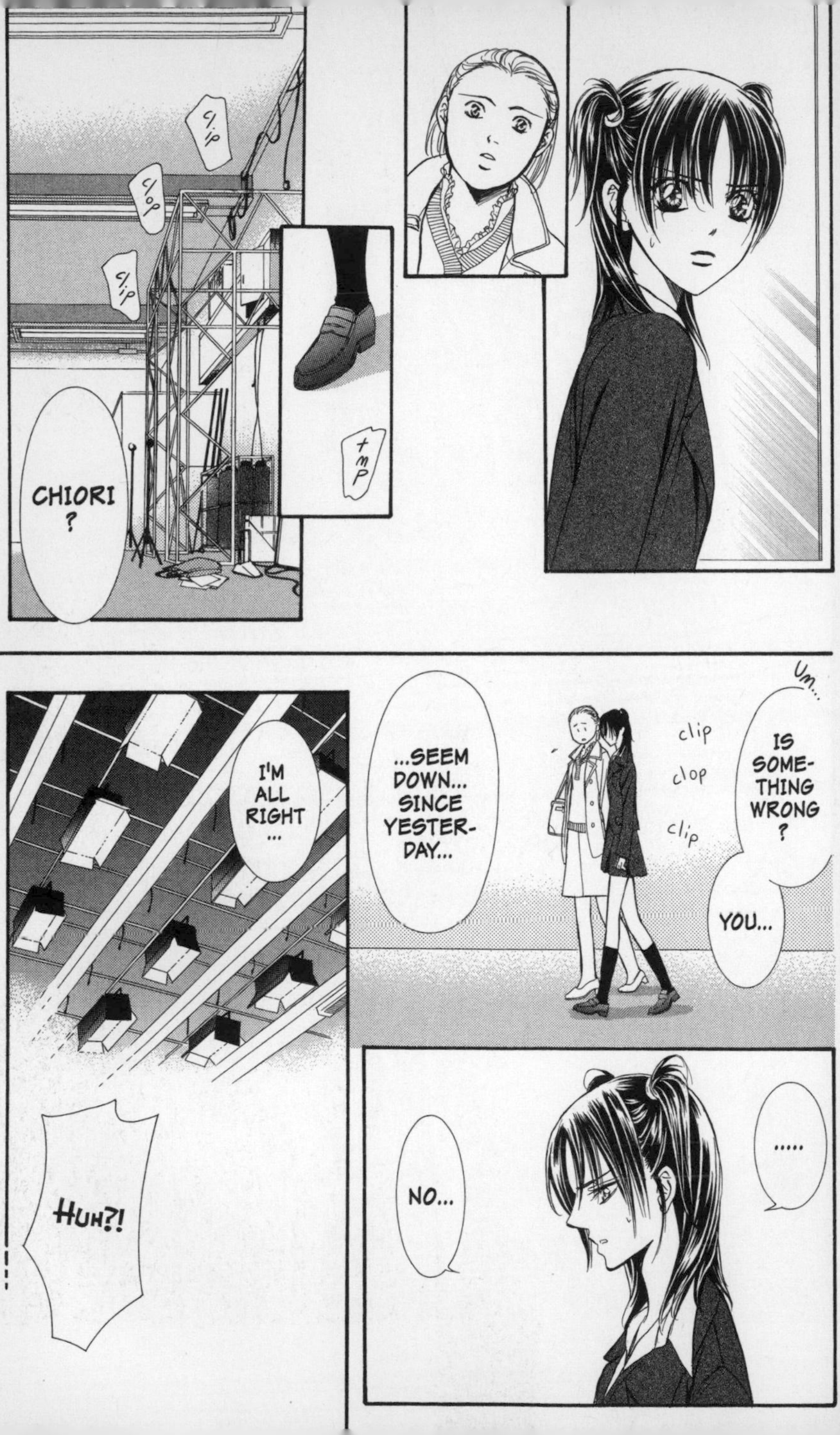
tmp
clip
clop
clip
CHIORI?
Um...
IS SOMETHING WRONG?
YOU...
clip
clop
clip
...SEEM DOWN... SINCE YESTERDAY...
.....
NO...
I'M ALL RIGHT...
HUH?!

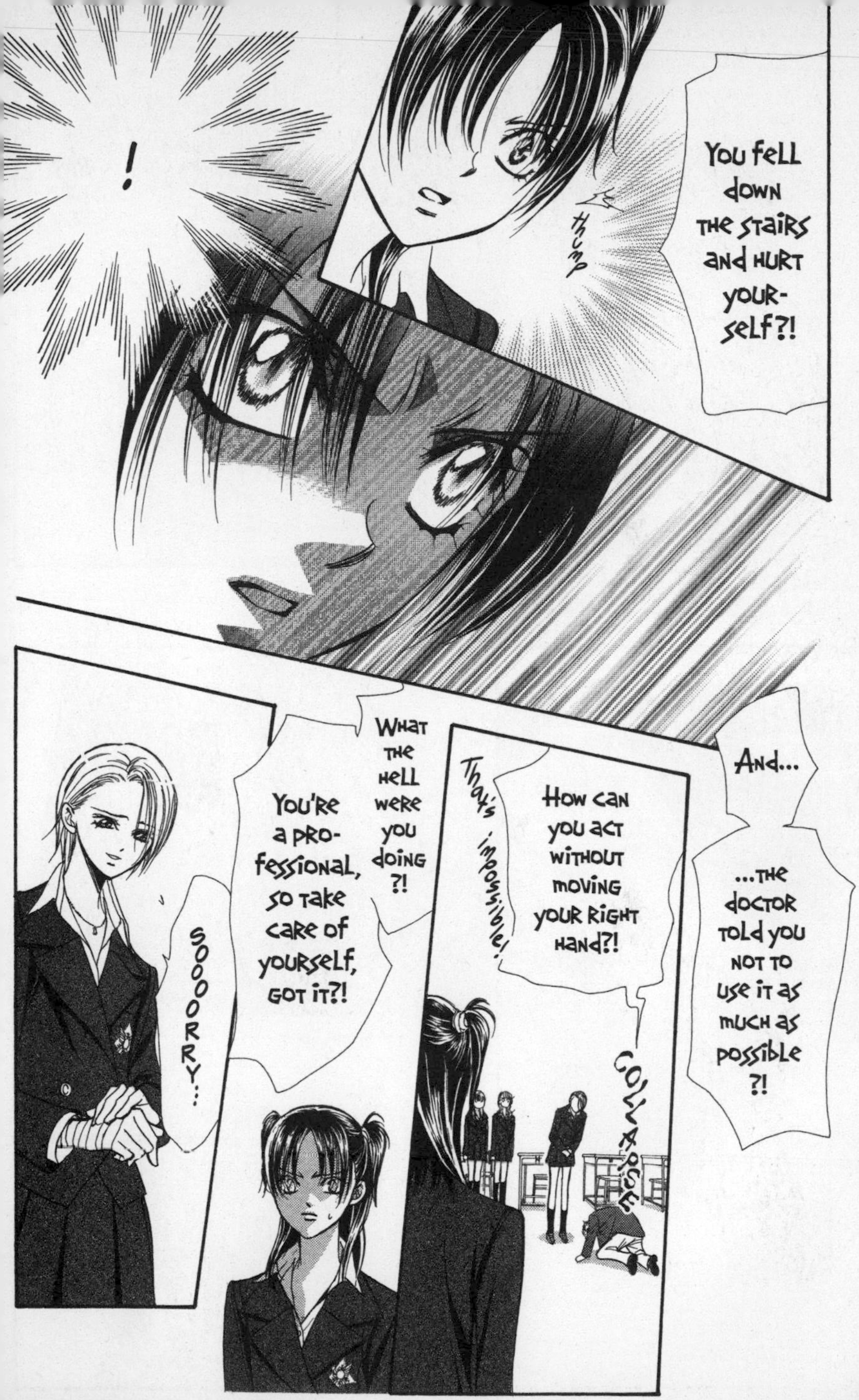
You fell down the stairs and hurt yourself?!
thump
!
And...
...the doctor told you not to use it as much as possible?!
How can you act without moving your right hand?!
That's impossible!
COLLAPSE
What the hell were you doing?!
You're a professional, so take care of yourself, got it?!
SOOOORRY...

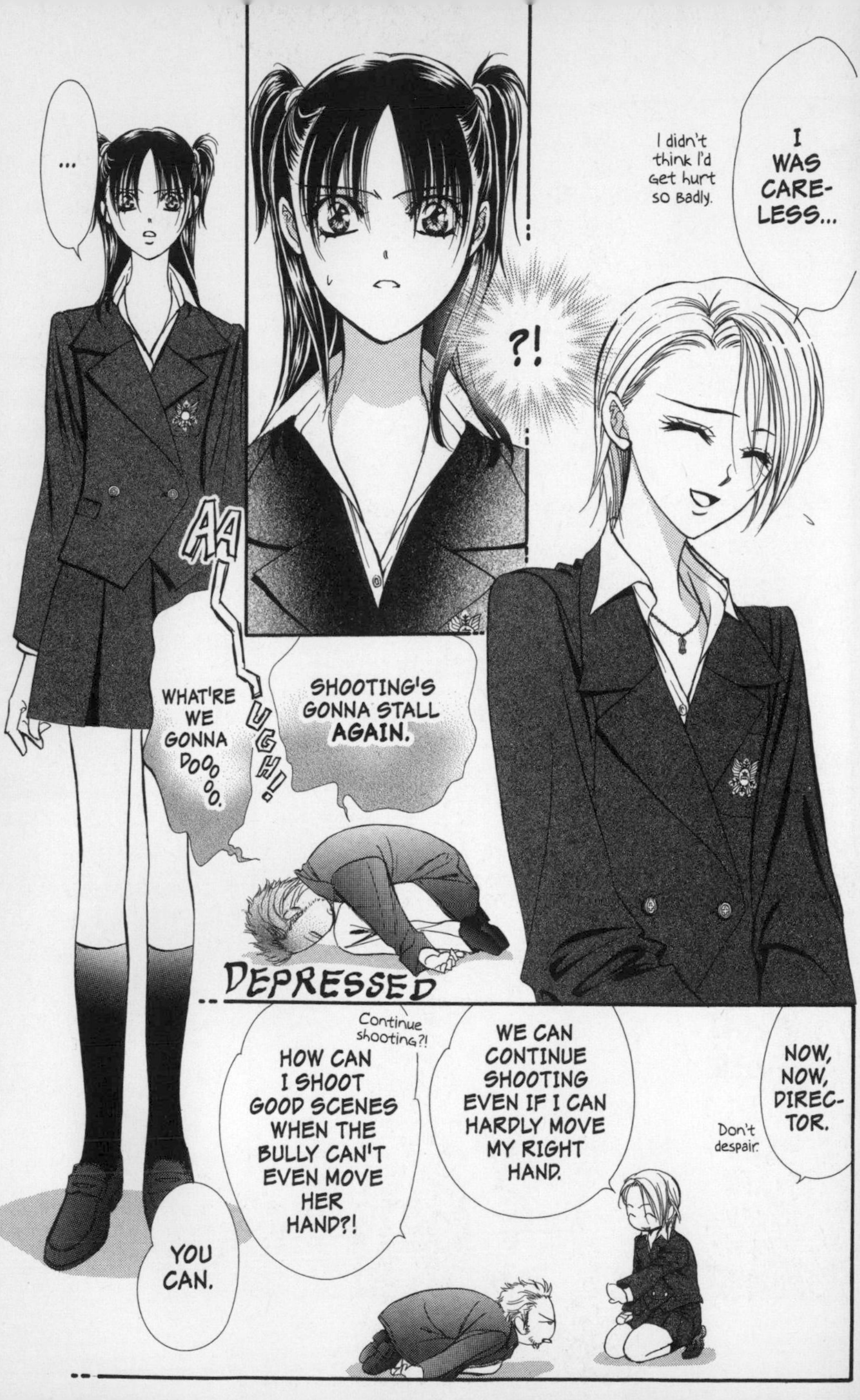

I WAS CARE-LESS...
I didn't think I'd get hurt so badly.
?!
SHOOTING'S GONNA STALL AGAIN.
AAAUGH!
WHAT'RE WE GONNA DOOOOO.
DEPRESSED
NOW, NOW, DIREC-TOR.
Don't despair.
WE CAN CONTINUE SHOOTING EVEN IF I CAN HARDLY MOVE MY RIGHT HAND.
Continue shooting?!
HOW CAN I SHOOT GOOD SCENES WHEN THE BULLY CAN'T EVEN MOVE HER HAND?!
YOU CAN.
...

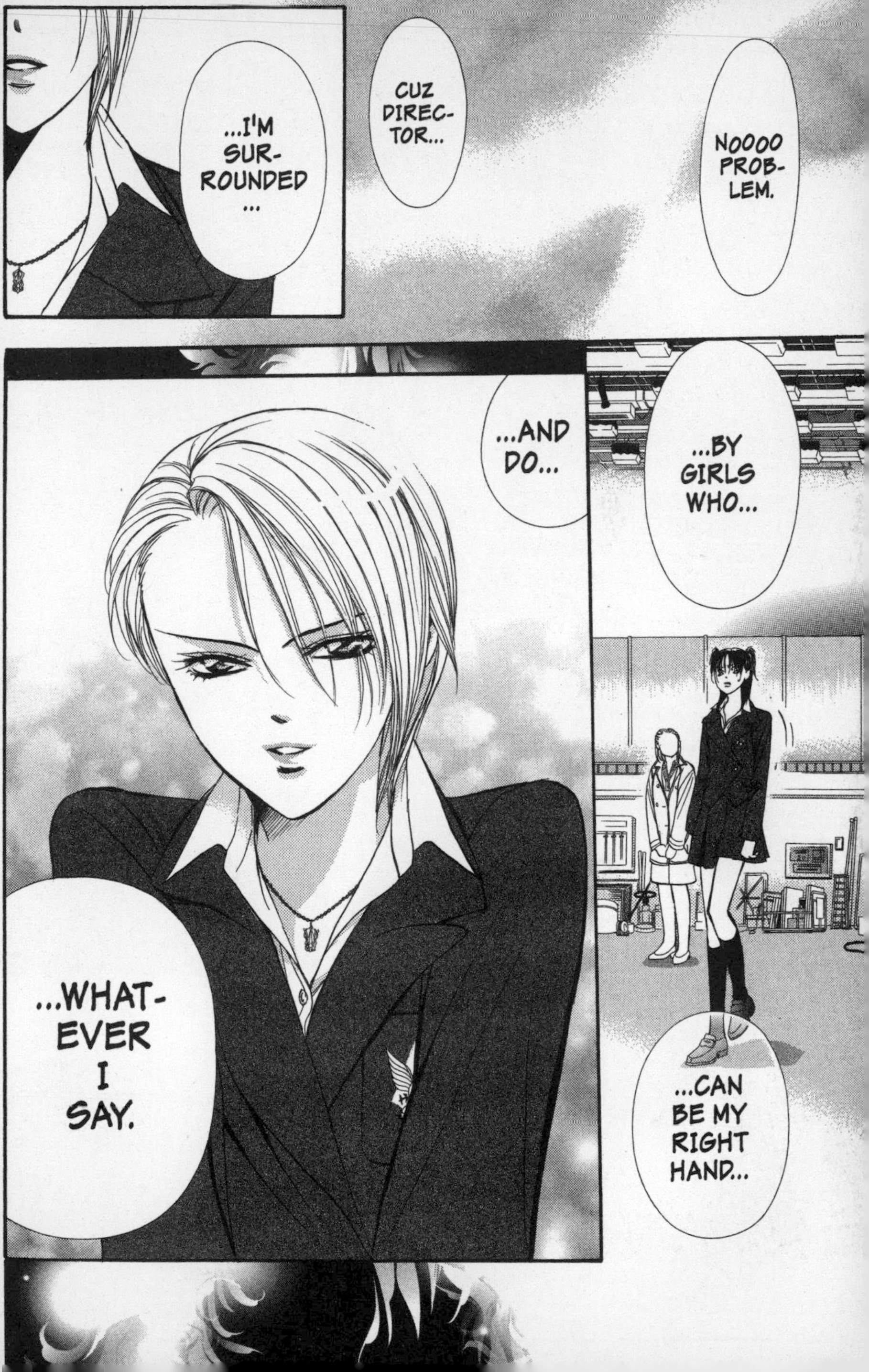
NOOOO PROB-LEM.
CUZ DIREC-TOR...
...I'M SUR-ROUNDED...
...BY GIRLS WHO...
...CAN BE MY RIGHT HAND...
...AND DO...
...WHAT-EVER I SAY.

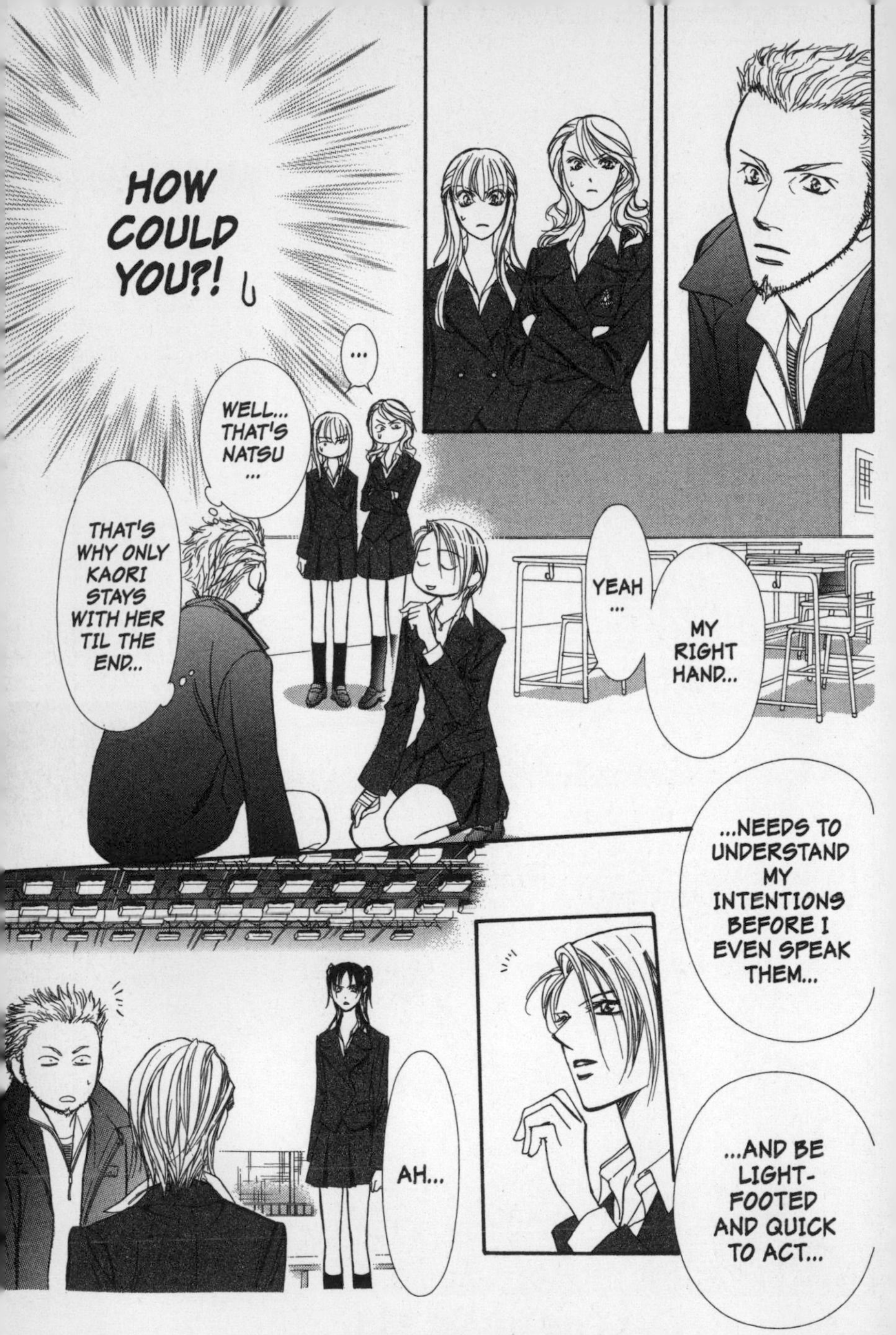
HOW COULD YOU?!
...
WELL... THAT'S NATSU...
THAT'S WHY ONLY KAORI STAYS WITH HER TIL THE END...
YEAH...
MY RIGHT HAND...
...NEEDS TO UNDERSTAND MY INTENTIONS BEFORE I EVEN SPEAK THEM...
...AND BE LIGHT-FOOTED AND QUICK TO ACT...
AH...

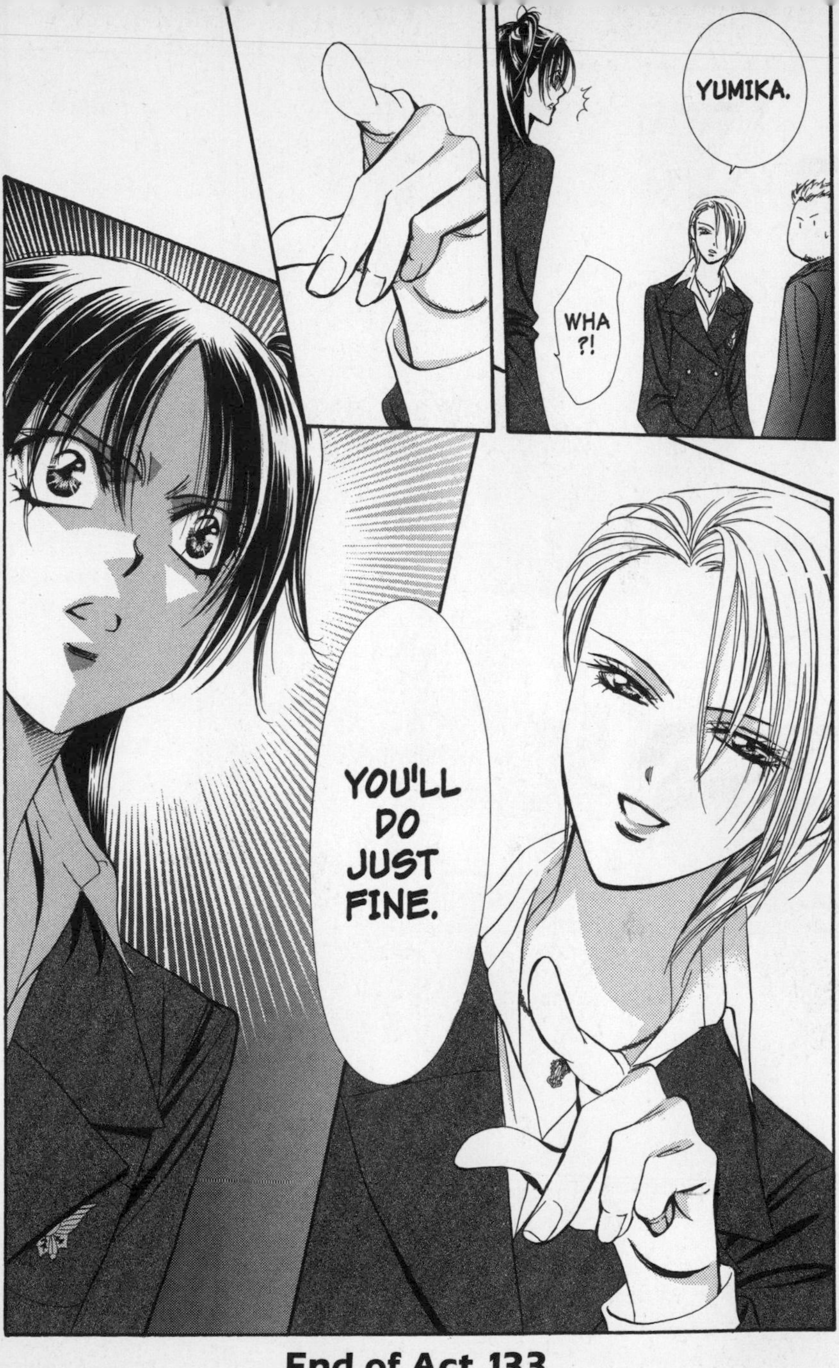
YUMIKA.
WHA ?!
YOU'LL DO JUST FINE.

End of Act 133

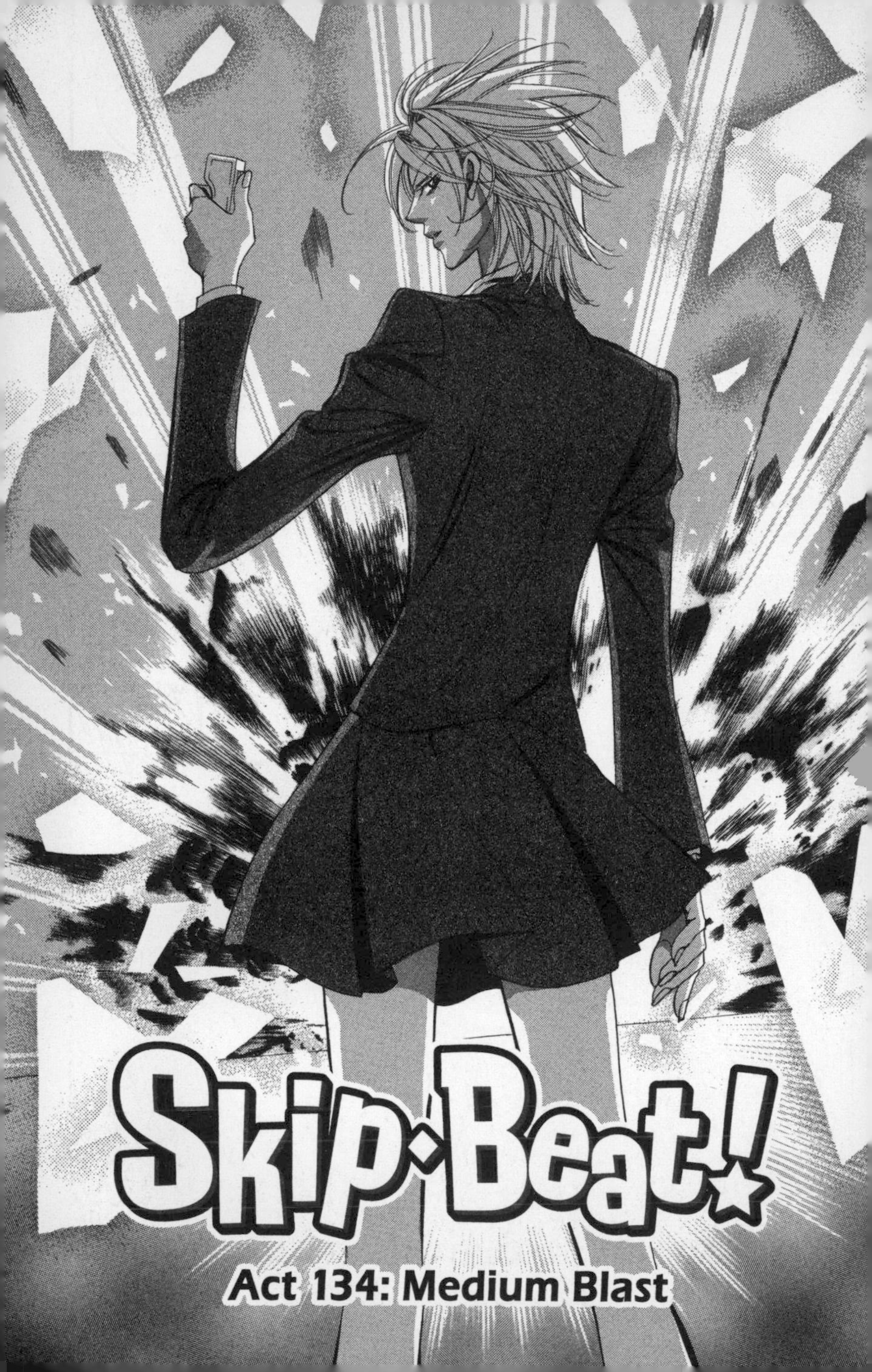
Skip·Beat!
Act 134: Medium Blast

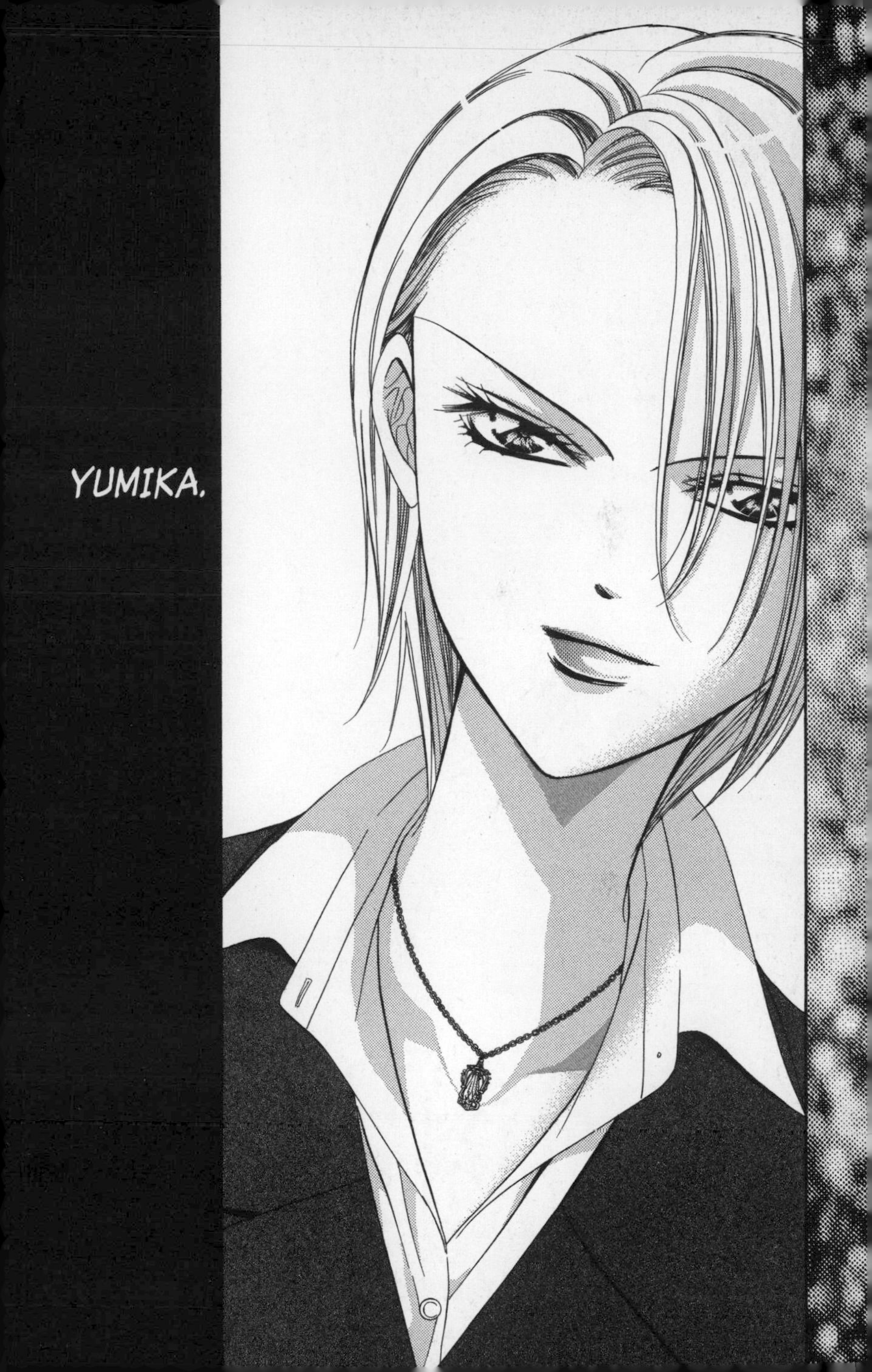
YUMIKA.

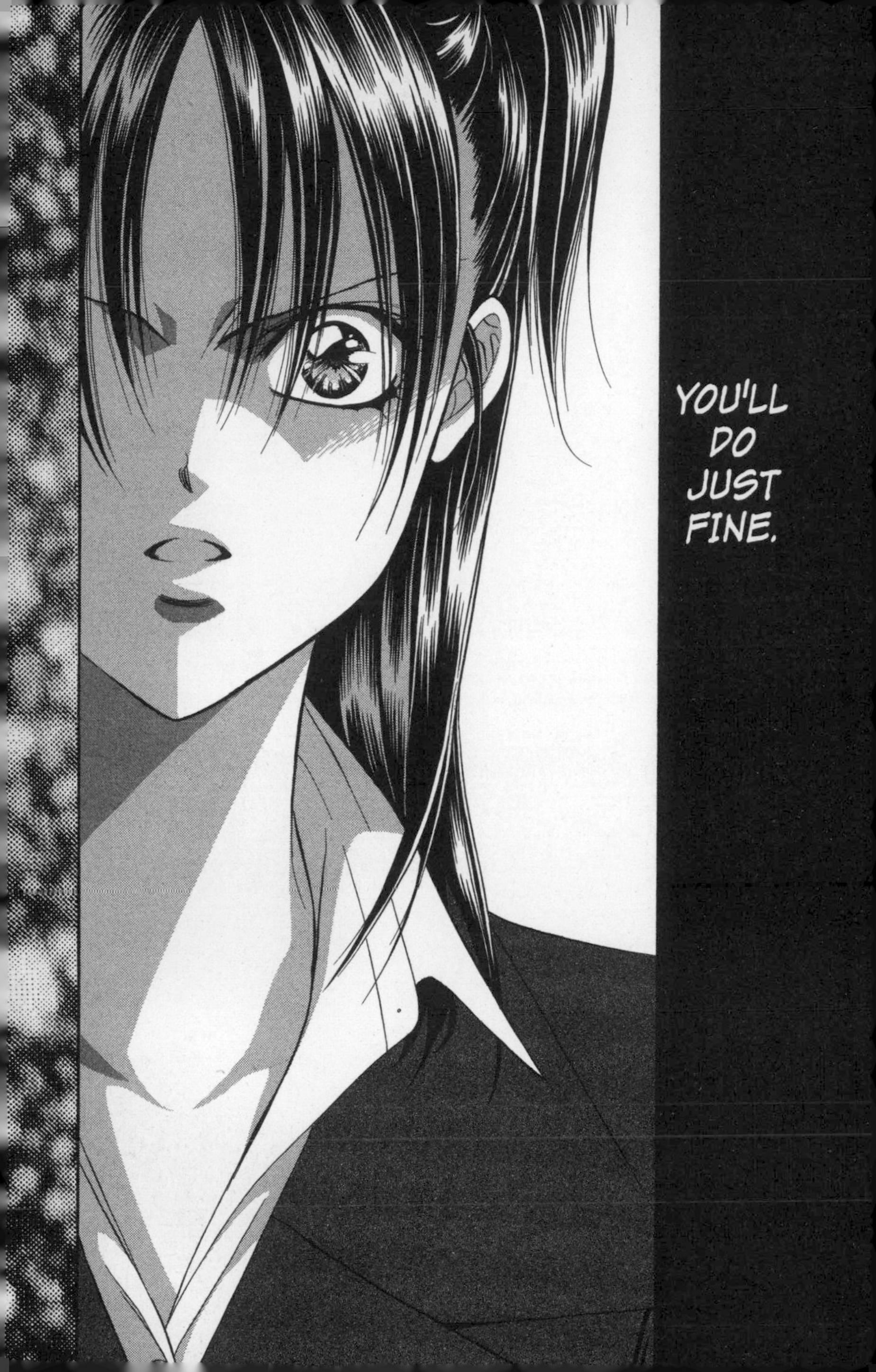
YOU'LL DO JUST FINE.

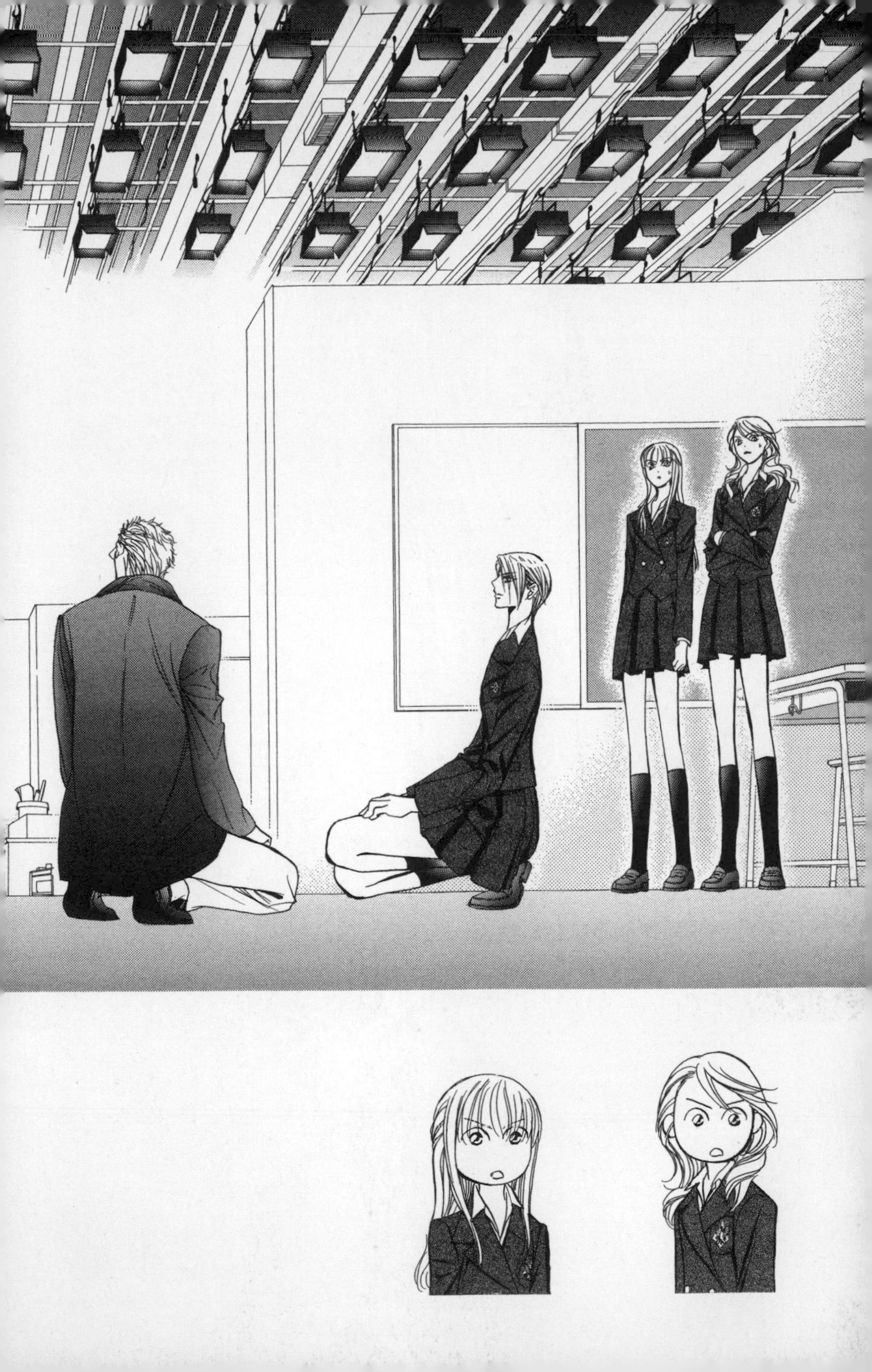

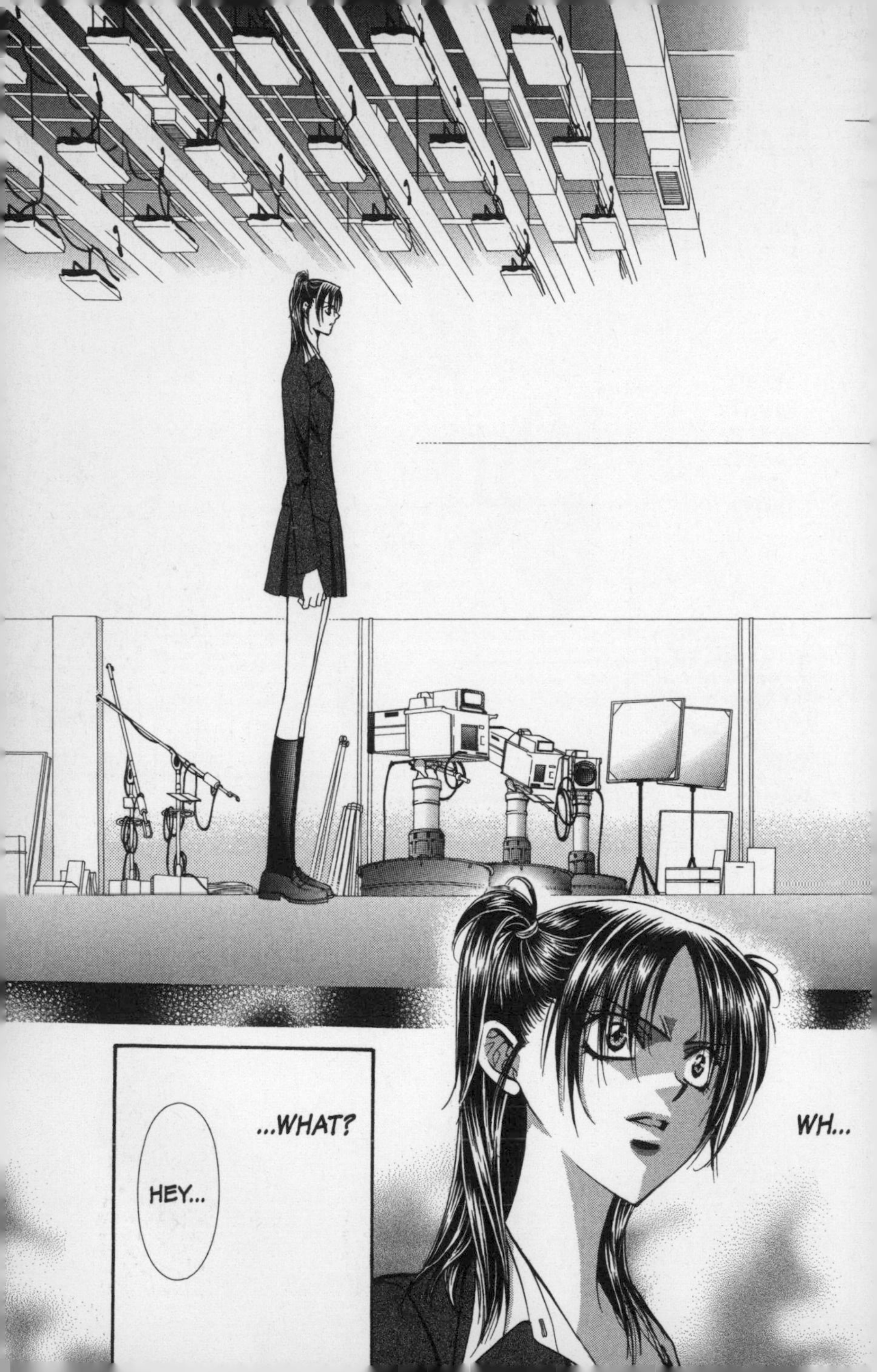
WH...
...WHAT?
HEY...

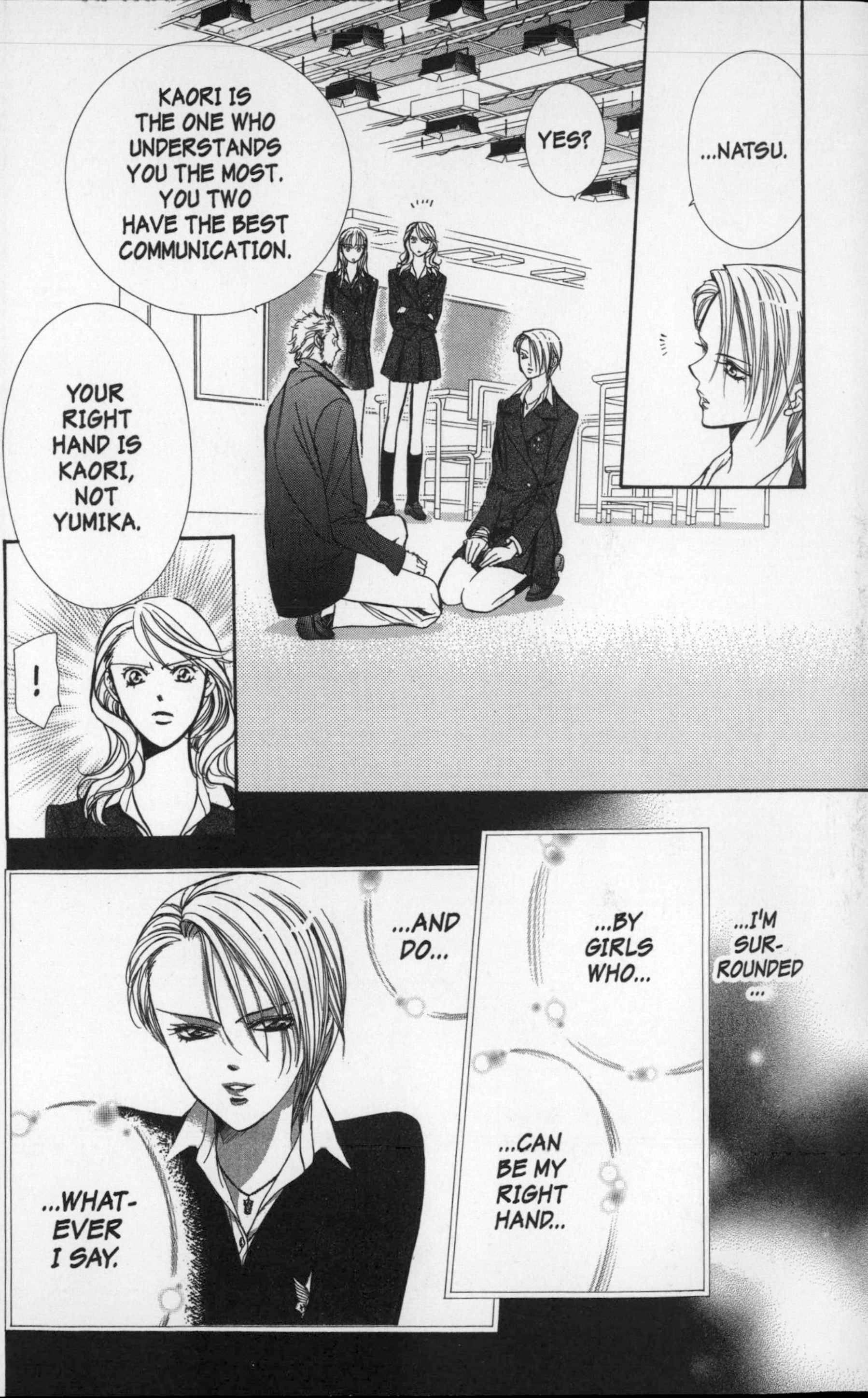
...NATSU.
YES?
KAORI IS THE ONE WHO UNDERSTANDS YOU THE MOST. YOU TWO HAVE THE BEST COMMUNICATION.
YOUR RIGHT HAND IS KAORI, NOT YUMIKA.
!
...I'M SUR- ROUNDED ...
...BY GIRLS WHO...
...CAN BE MY RIGHT HAND...
...AND DO...
...WHAT- EVER I SAY.

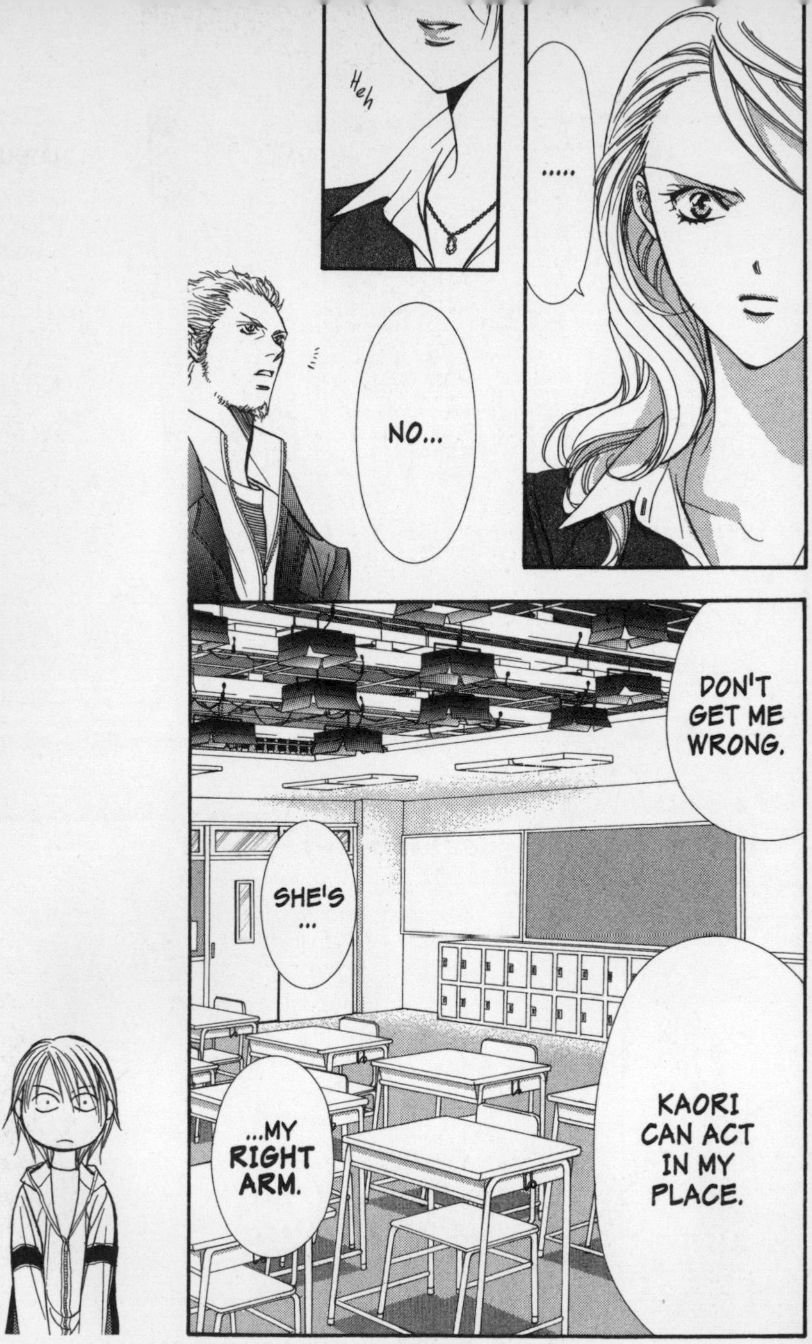
.....
Heh
NO...
DON'T GET ME WRONG.
KAORI CAN ACT IN MY PLACE.
SHE'S ...
...MY RIGHT ARM.

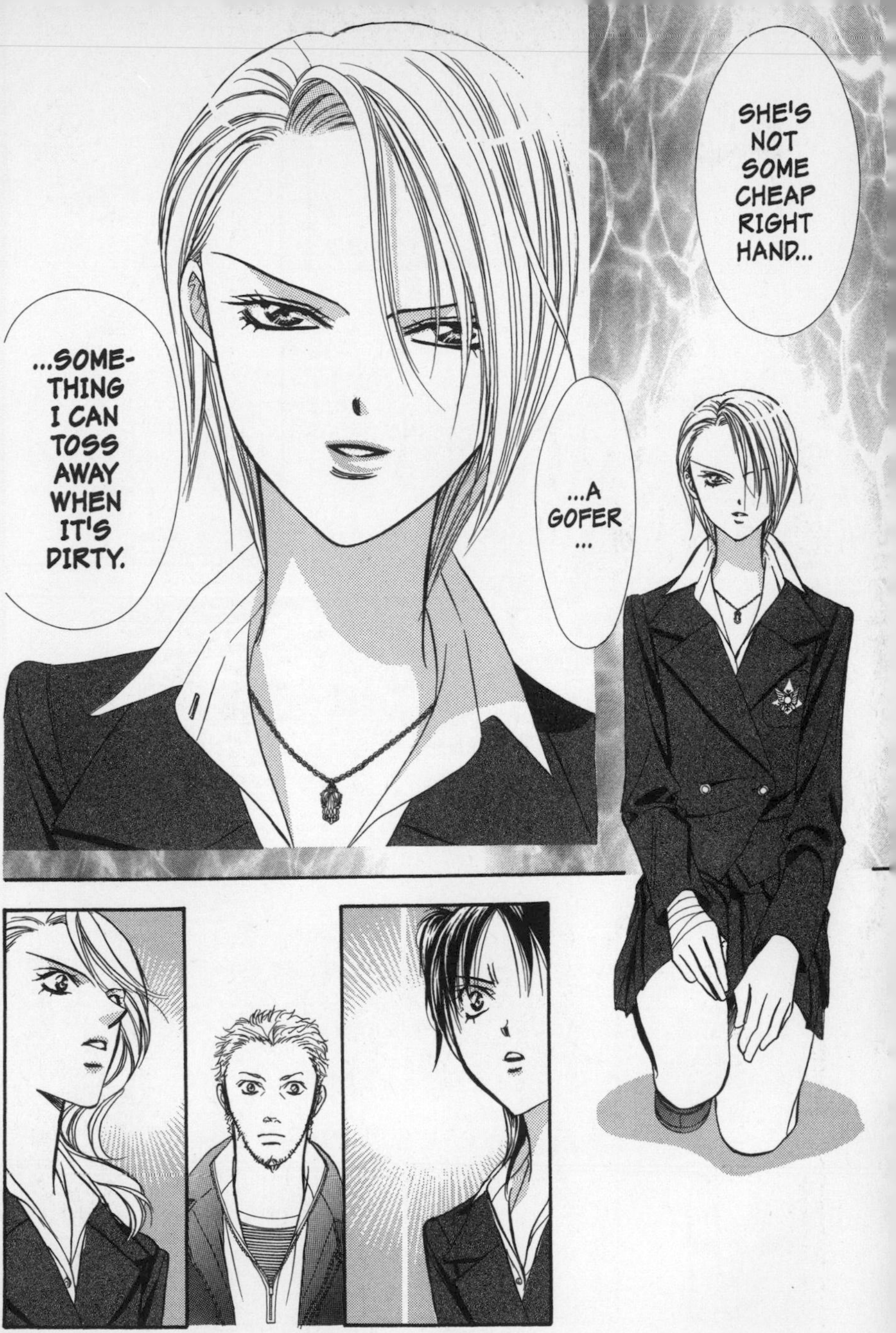
SHE'S NOT SOME CHEAP RIGHT HAND...
...A GOFER...
...SOME-THING I CAN TOSS AWAY WHEN IT'S DIRTY.

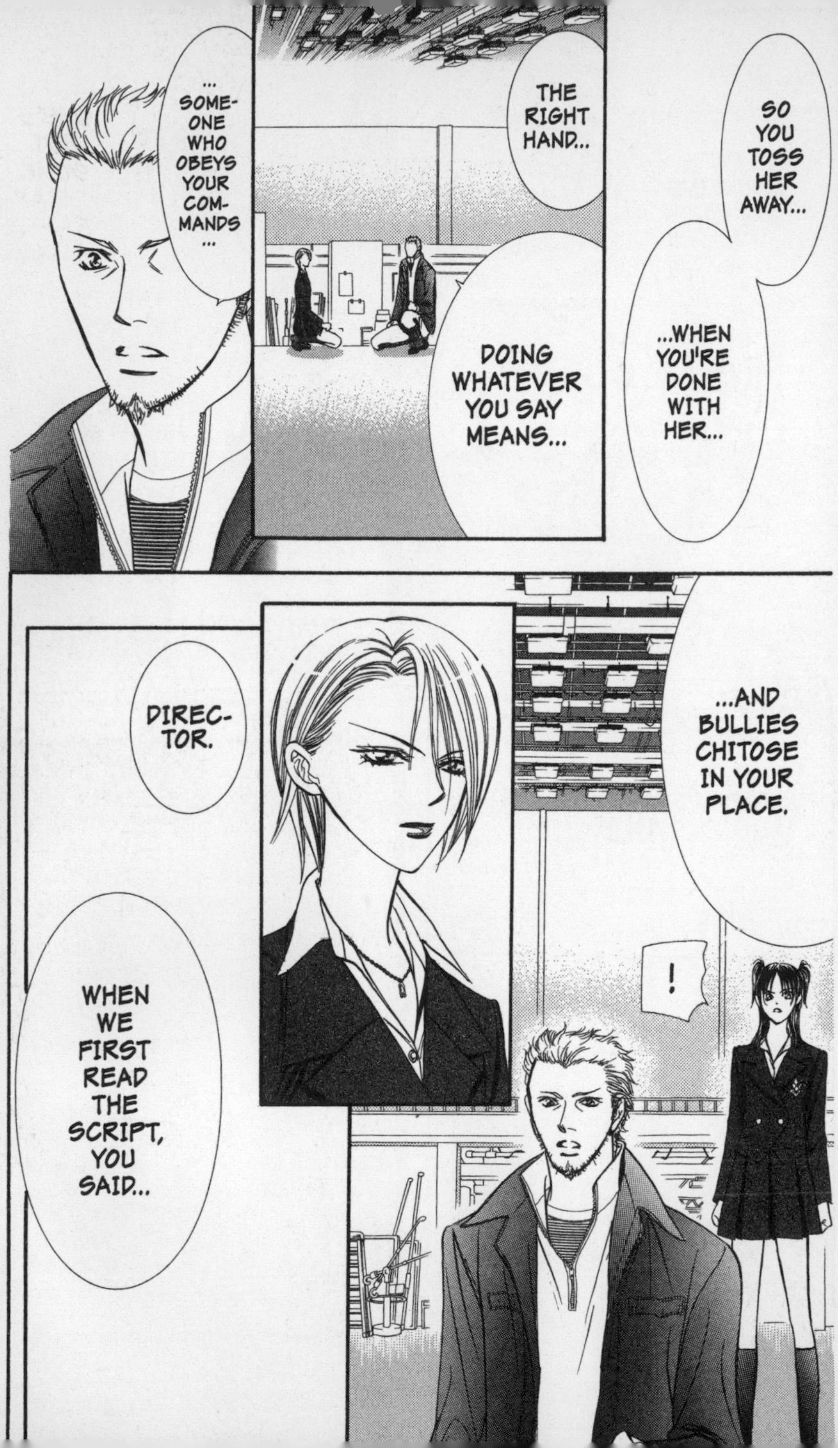

SO YOU TOSS HER AWAY...
...WHEN YOU'RE DONE WITH HER...
THE RIGHT HAND...
DOING WHATEVER YOU SAY MEANS...
... SOMEONE WHO OBEYS YOUR COMMANDS ...
...AND BULLIES CHITOSE IN YOUR PLACE.
!
DIRECTOR.
WHEN WE FIRST READ THE SCRIPT, YOU SAID...

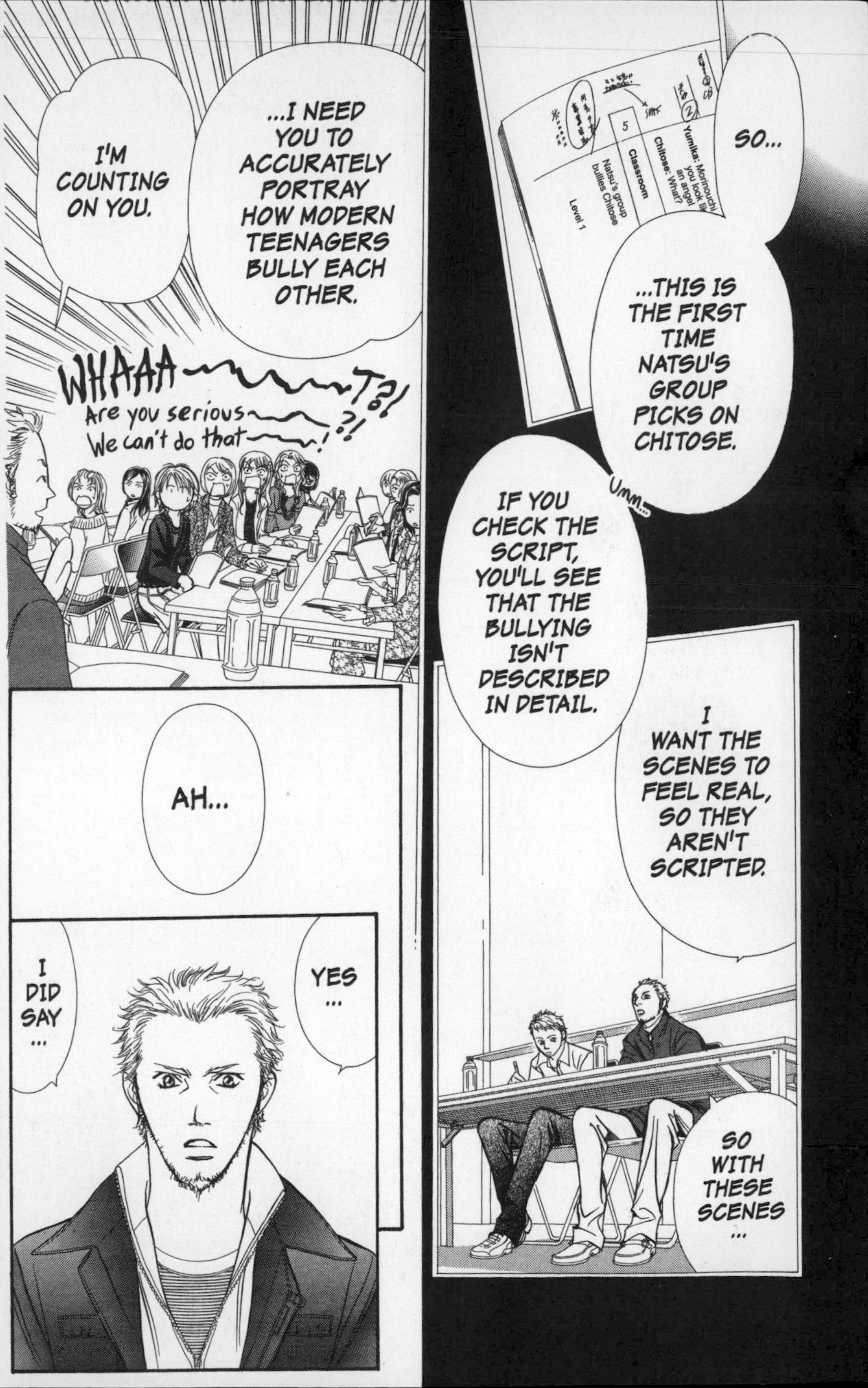
SO...
Yumika: Morinouchi
Chitose: What?
5
Classroom
Natsu's group bullies Chitose
Level 1
...THIS IS THE FIRST TIME NATSU'S GROUP PICKS ON CHITOSE.
Umm...
IF YOU CHECK THE SCRIPT, YOU'LL SEE THAT THE BULLYING ISN'T DESCRIBED IN DETAIL.
I WANT THE SCENES TO FEEL REAL, SO THEY AREN'T SCRIPTED.
SO WITH THESE SCENES ...
...I NEED YOU TO ACCURATELY PORTRAY HOW MODERN TEENAGERS BULLY EACH OTHER.
I'M COUNTING ON YOU.
WHAAAT?!
Are you serious?!
We can't do that!
AH...
YES ...
I DID SAY ...

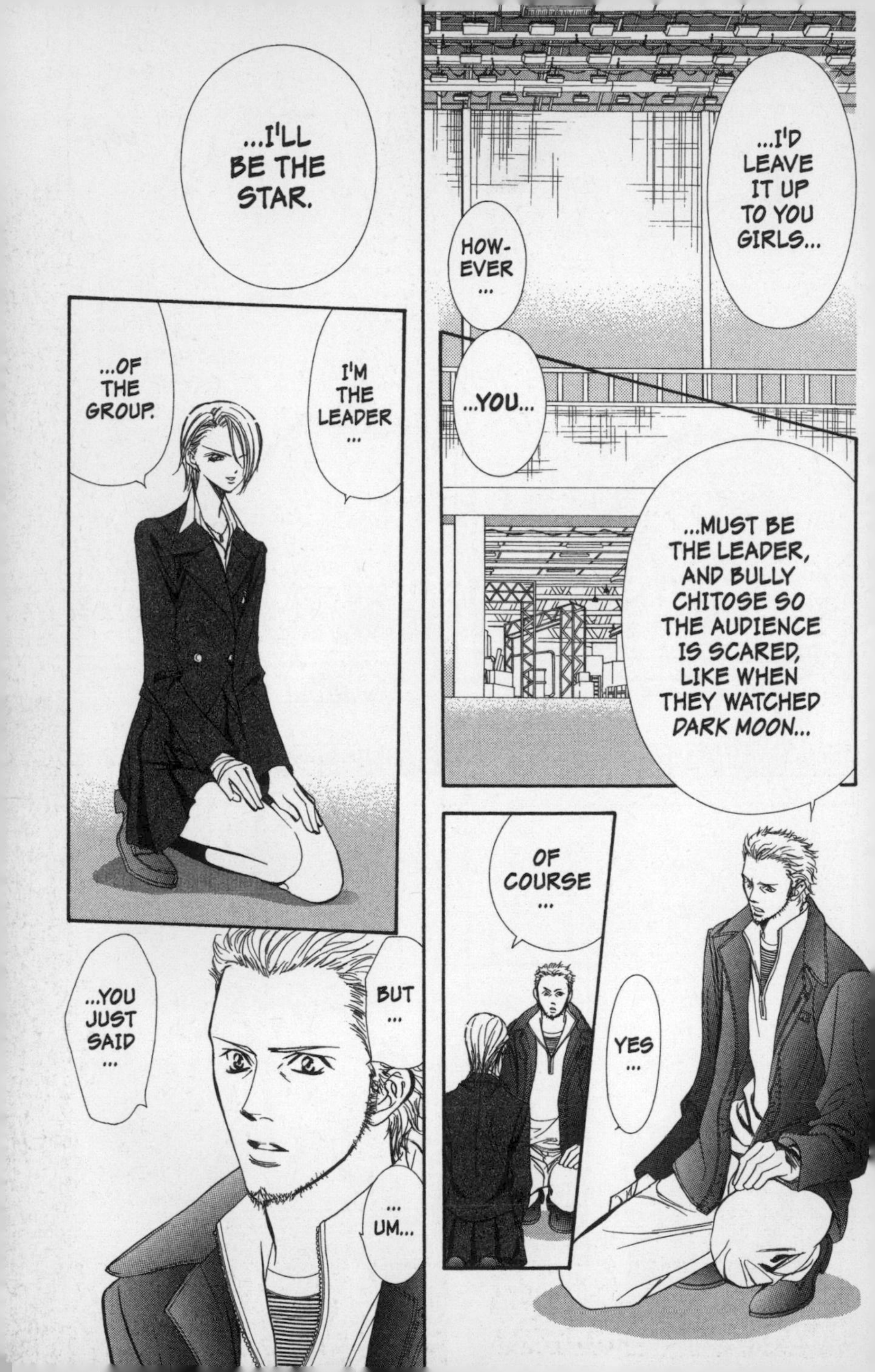
...I'D LEAVE IT UP TO YOU GIRLS...
HOW-EVER...
...YOU...
...MUST BE THE LEADER, AND BULLY CHITOSE SO THE AUDIENCE IS SCARED, LIKE WHEN THEY WATCHED DARK MOON...
OF COURSE...
YES...
...I'LL BE THE STAR.
I'M THE LEADER...
...OF THE GROUP.
BUT...
...YOU JUST SAID...
...UM...

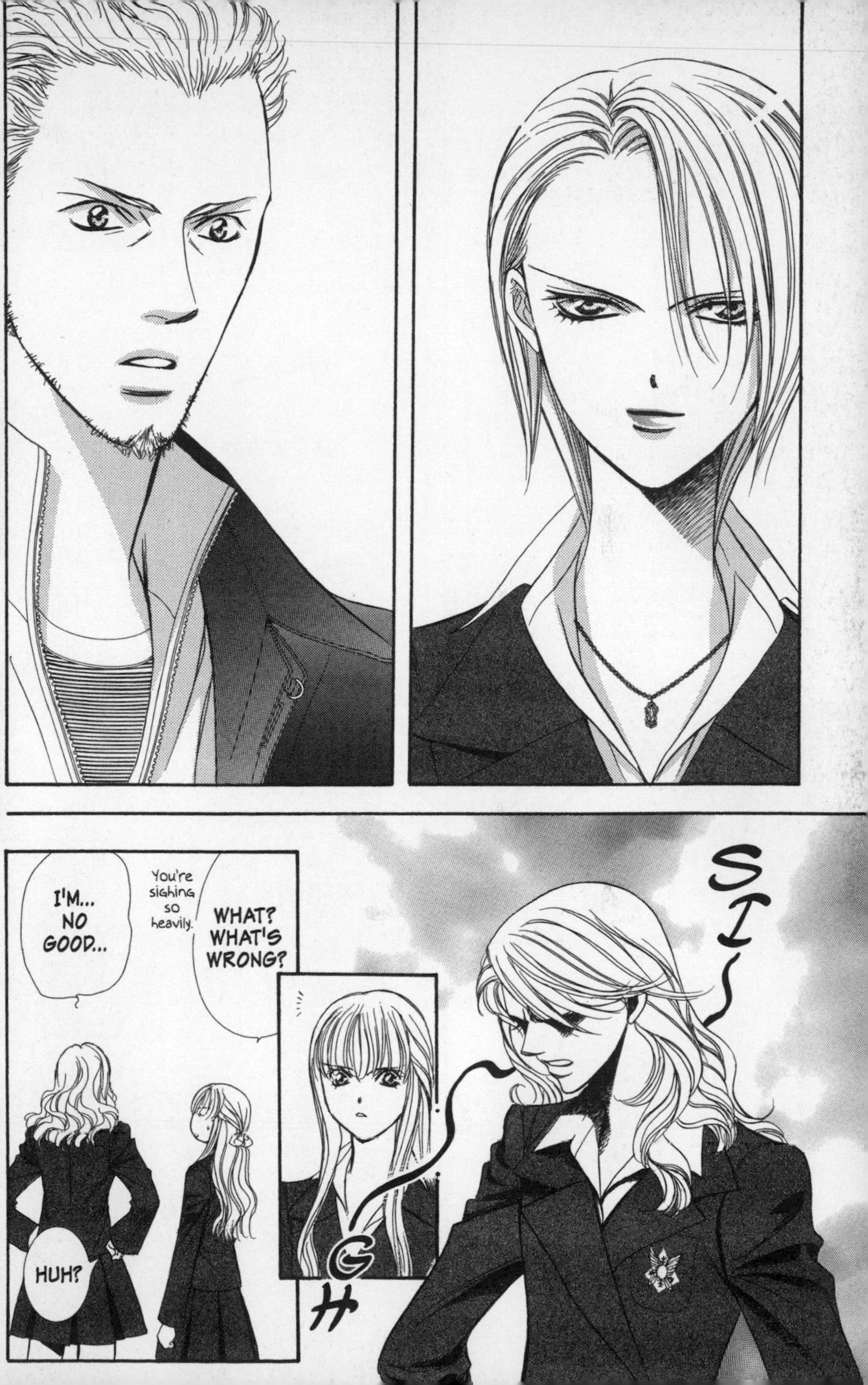
SI
GH
WHAT? WHAT'S WRONG?
You're sighing so heavily.
I'M... NO GOOD...
HUH?

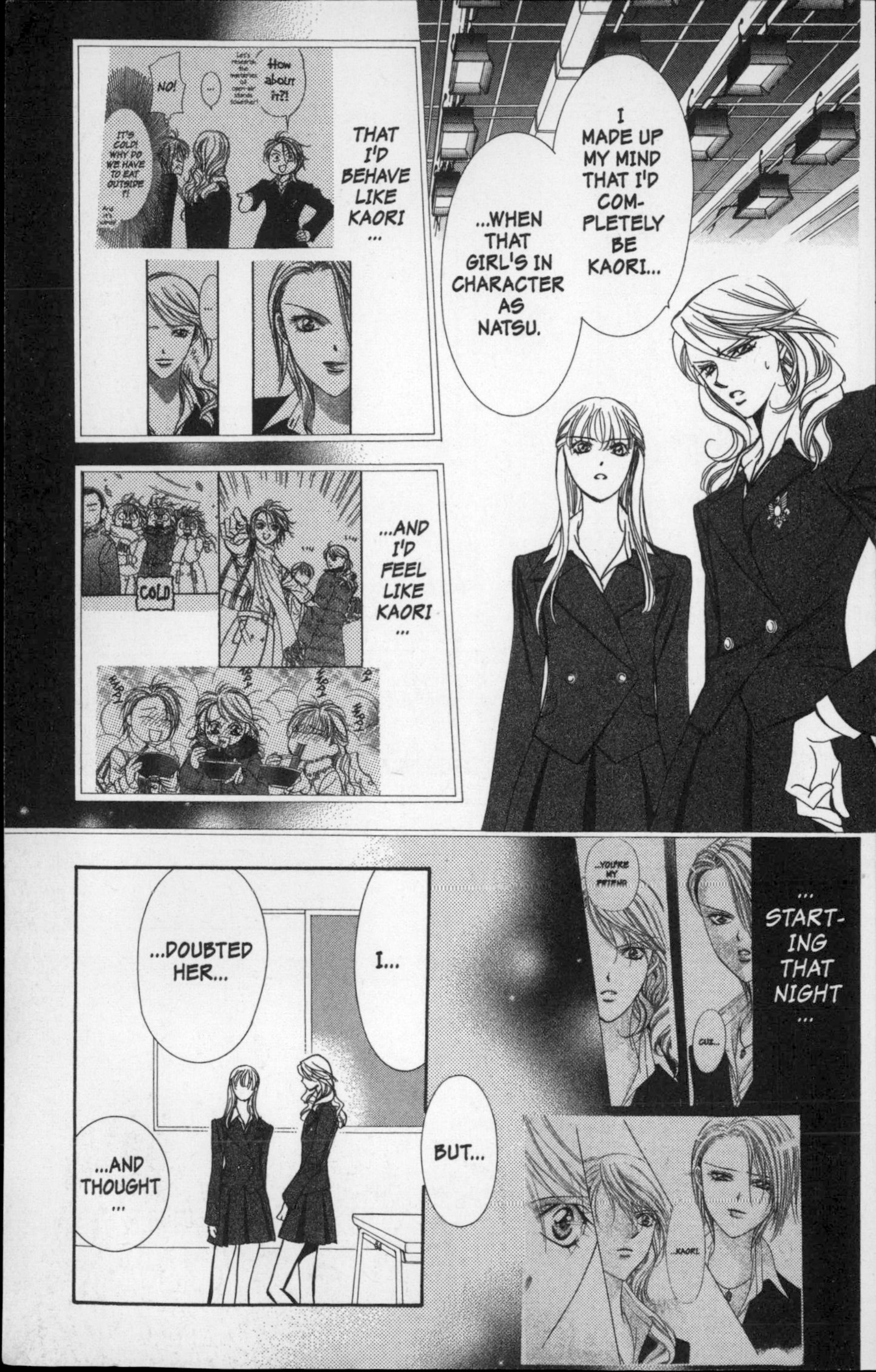

I MADE UP MY MIND THAT I'D COMPLETELY BE KAORI...
...WHEN THAT GIRL'S IN CHARACTER AS NATSU.
THAT I'D BEHAVE LIKE KAORI...
How about it?!
NO!
IT'S COLD! WHY DO WE HAVE TO EAT OUTSIDE ?!
...AND I'D FEEL LIKE KAORI...
COLD
...STARTING THAT NIGHT...
CUZ...
...KAORI.
I...
...DOUBTED HER...
BUT...
...AND THOUGHT...

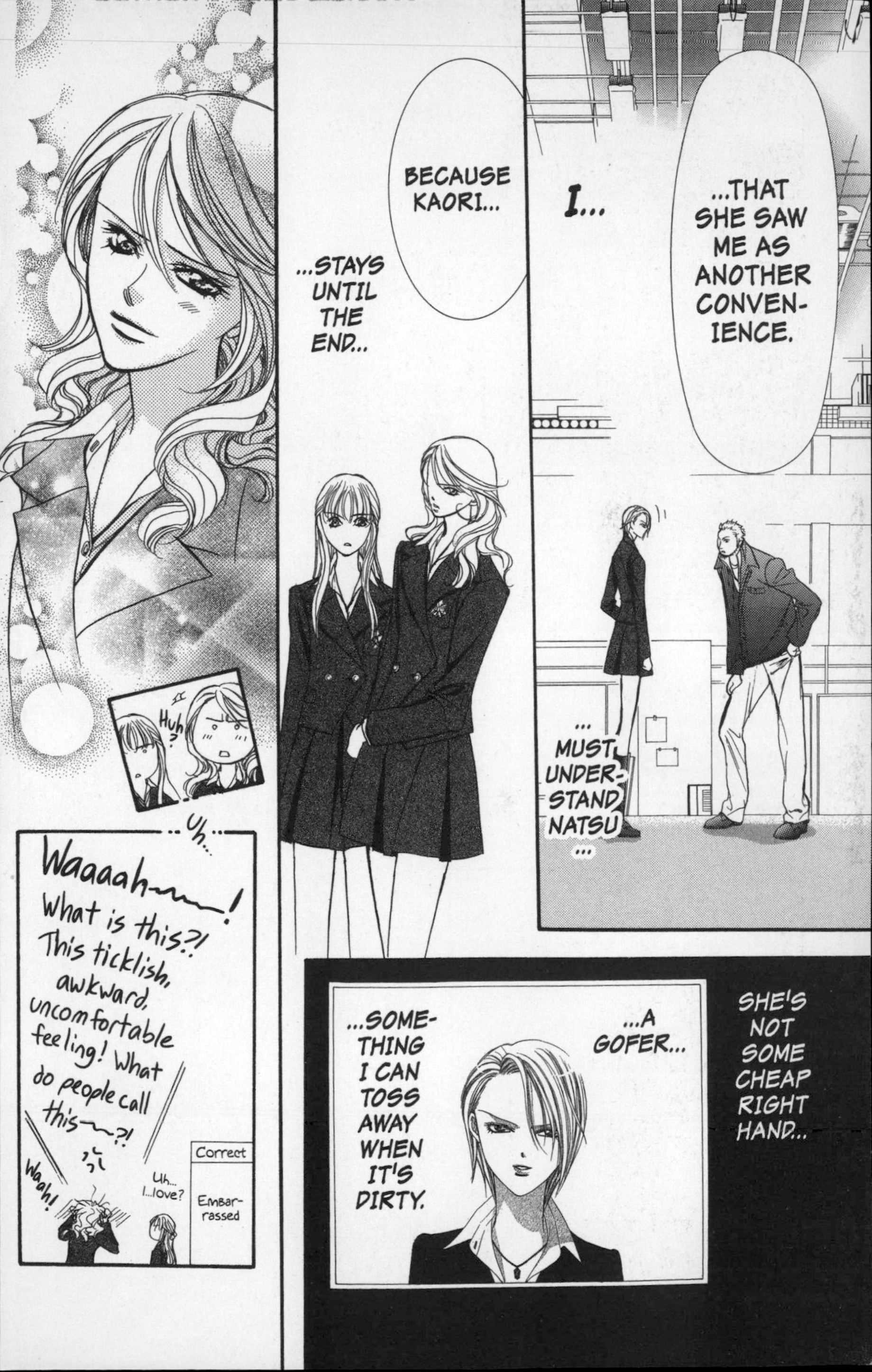
...THAT SHE SAW ME AS ANOTHER CONVEN-IENCE.
I...
...MUST UNDER-STAND NATSU...
BECAUSE KAORI...
...STAYS UNTIL THE END...
Huh?
Uh...
SHE'S NOT SOME CHEAP RIGHT HAND...
...A GOFER...
...SOME-THING I CAN TOSS AWAY WHEN IT'S DIRTY.
Waaaah~~~! What is this?! This ticklish, awkward, uncomfortable feeling! What do people call this~~?!
Waah!
Uh... I...love?
Correct
Embar-rassed

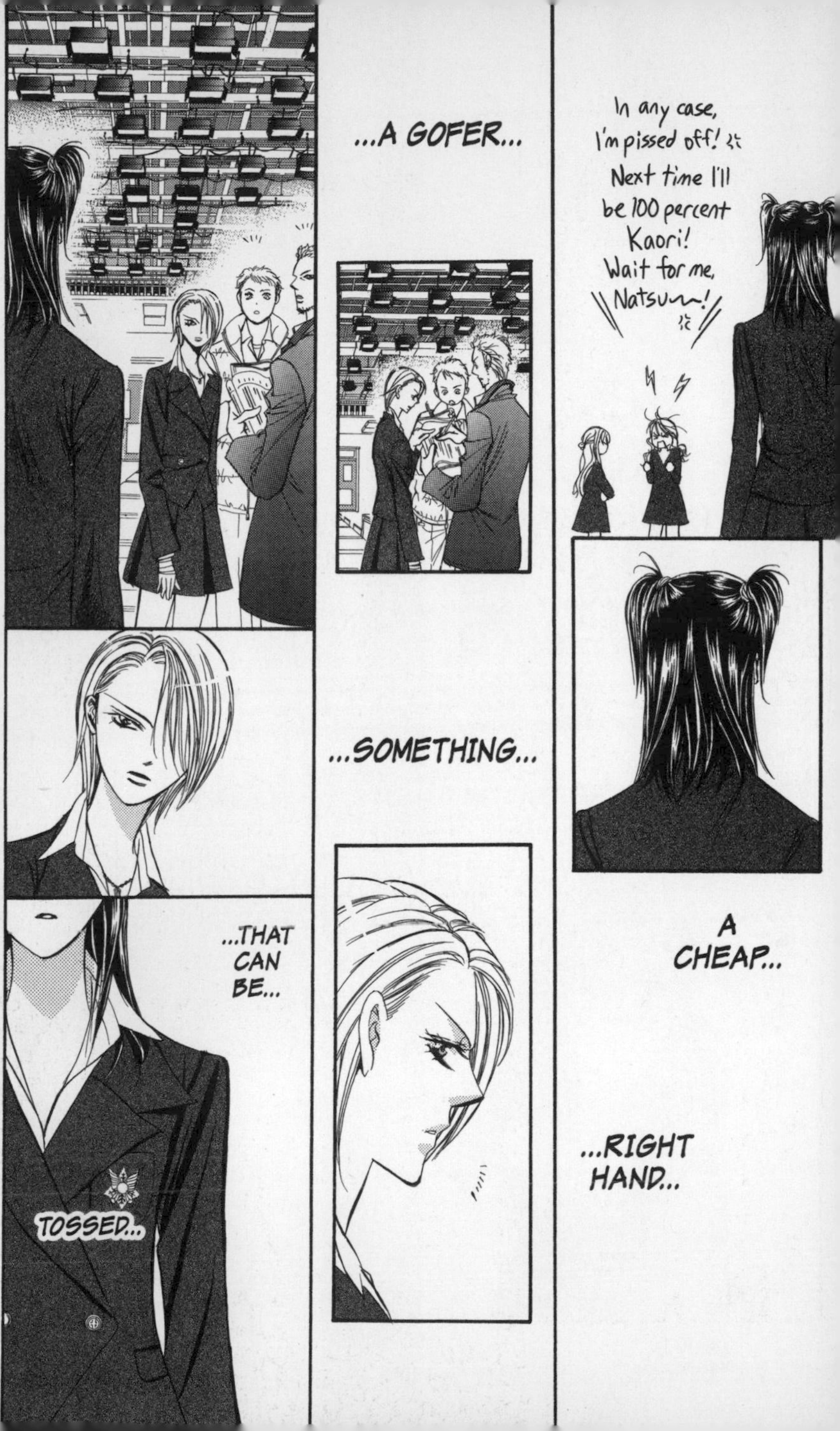
In any case, I'm pissed off! Next time I'll be 100 percent Kaori! Wait for me, Natsu~~!
A CHEAP...
...RIGHT HAND...
...A GOFER...
...SOMETHING...
...THAT CAN BE...
TOSSED...

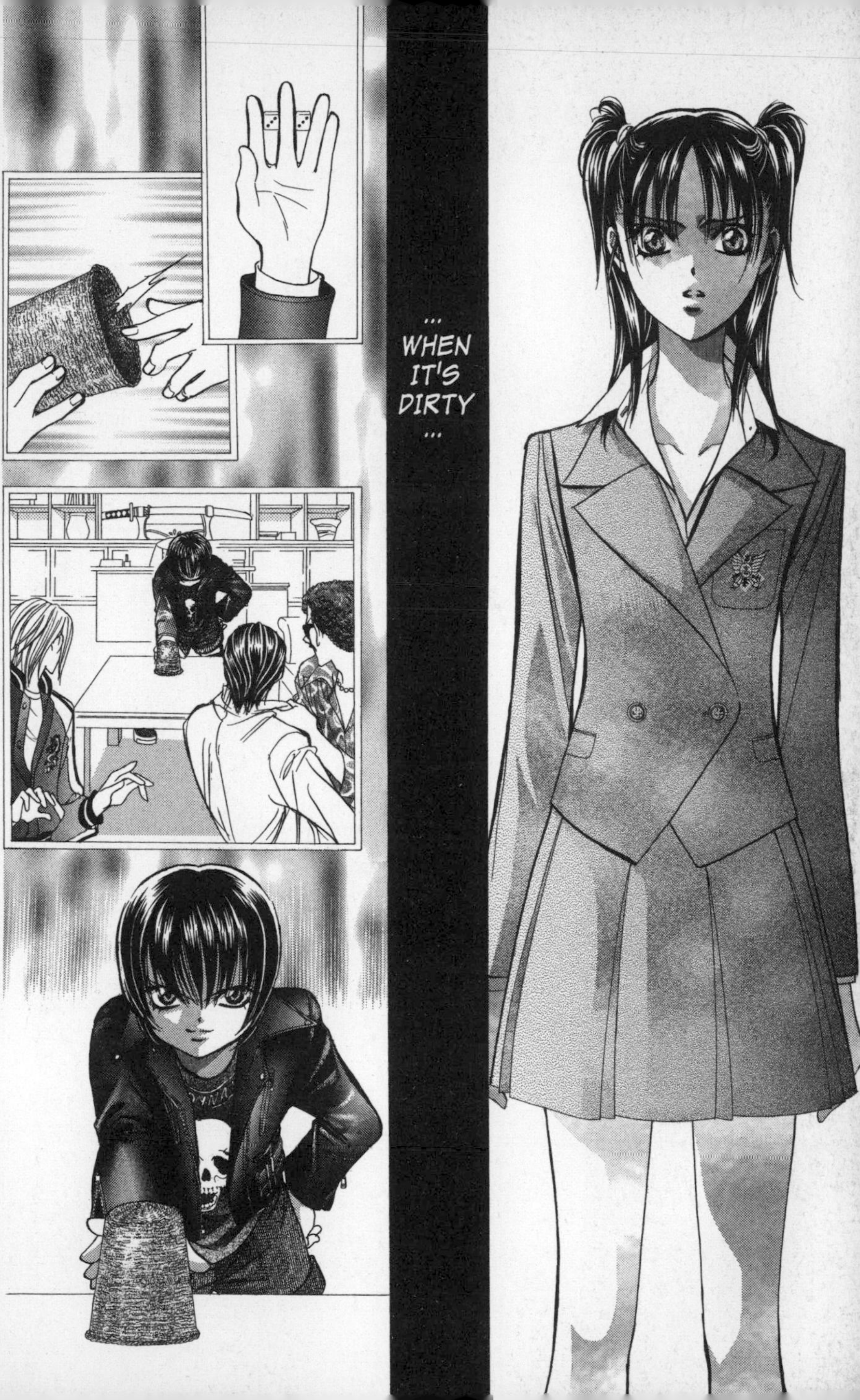
... WHEN IT'S DIRTY ...

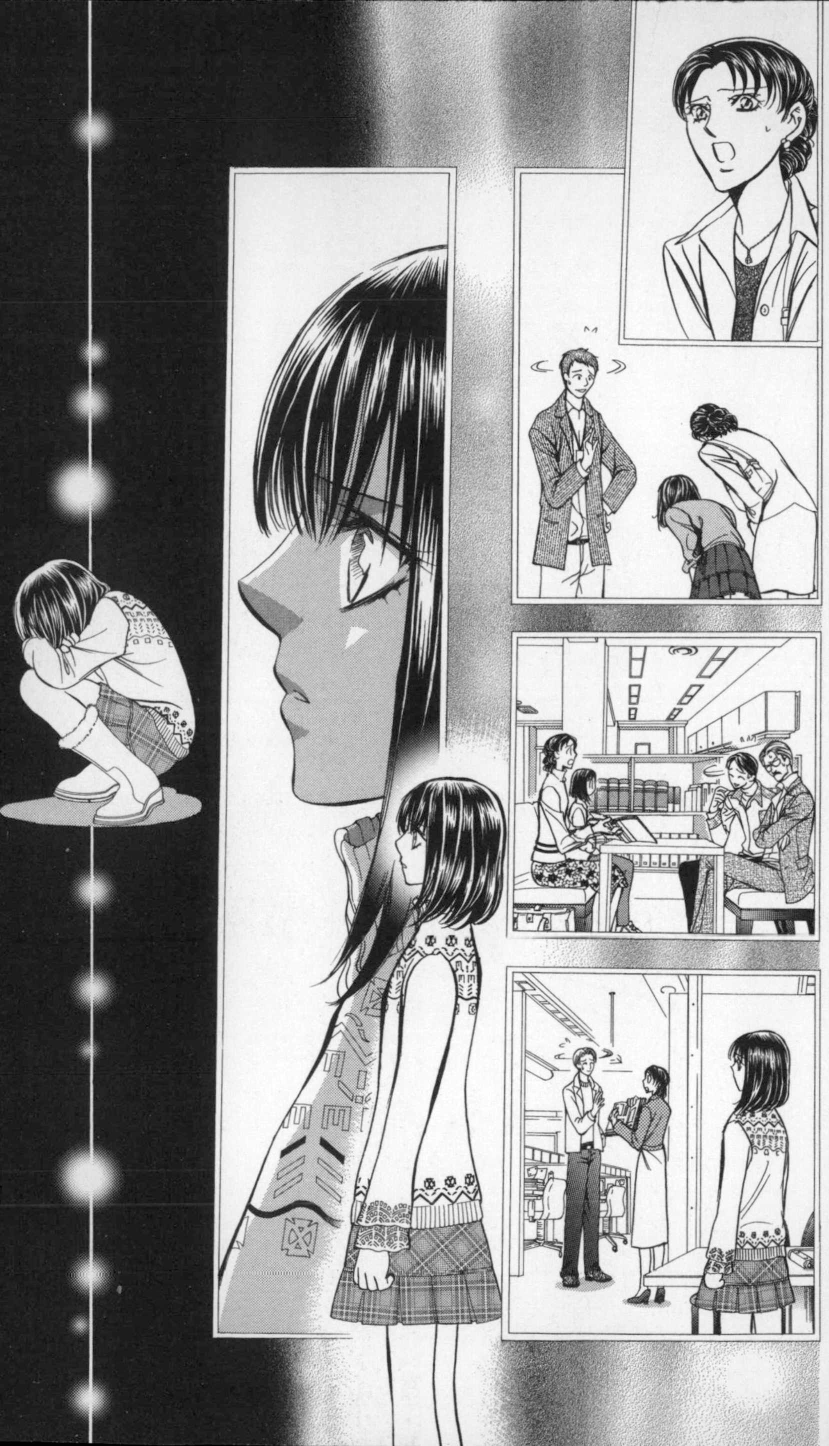

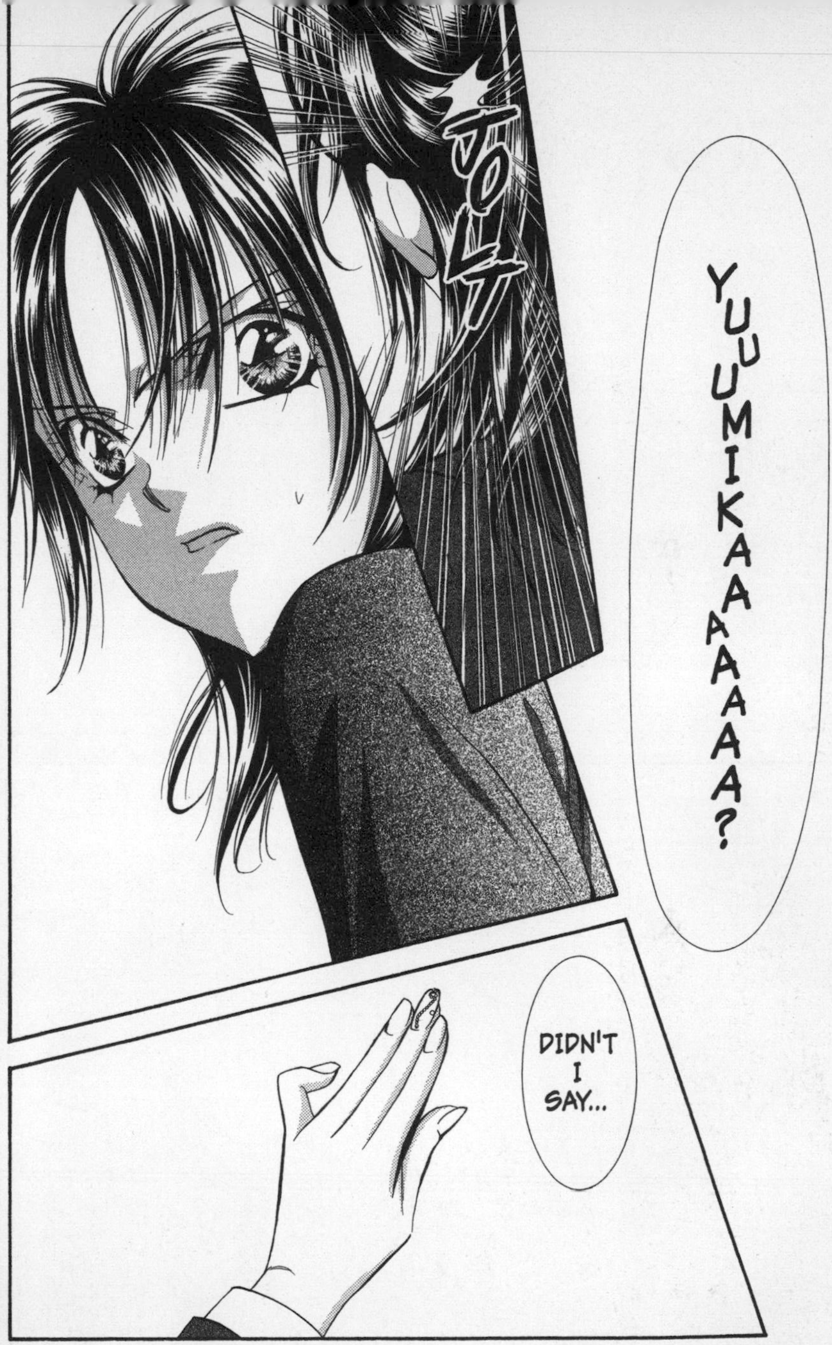
YUUUMIKAAAAAAAA?
DIDN'T I SAY...

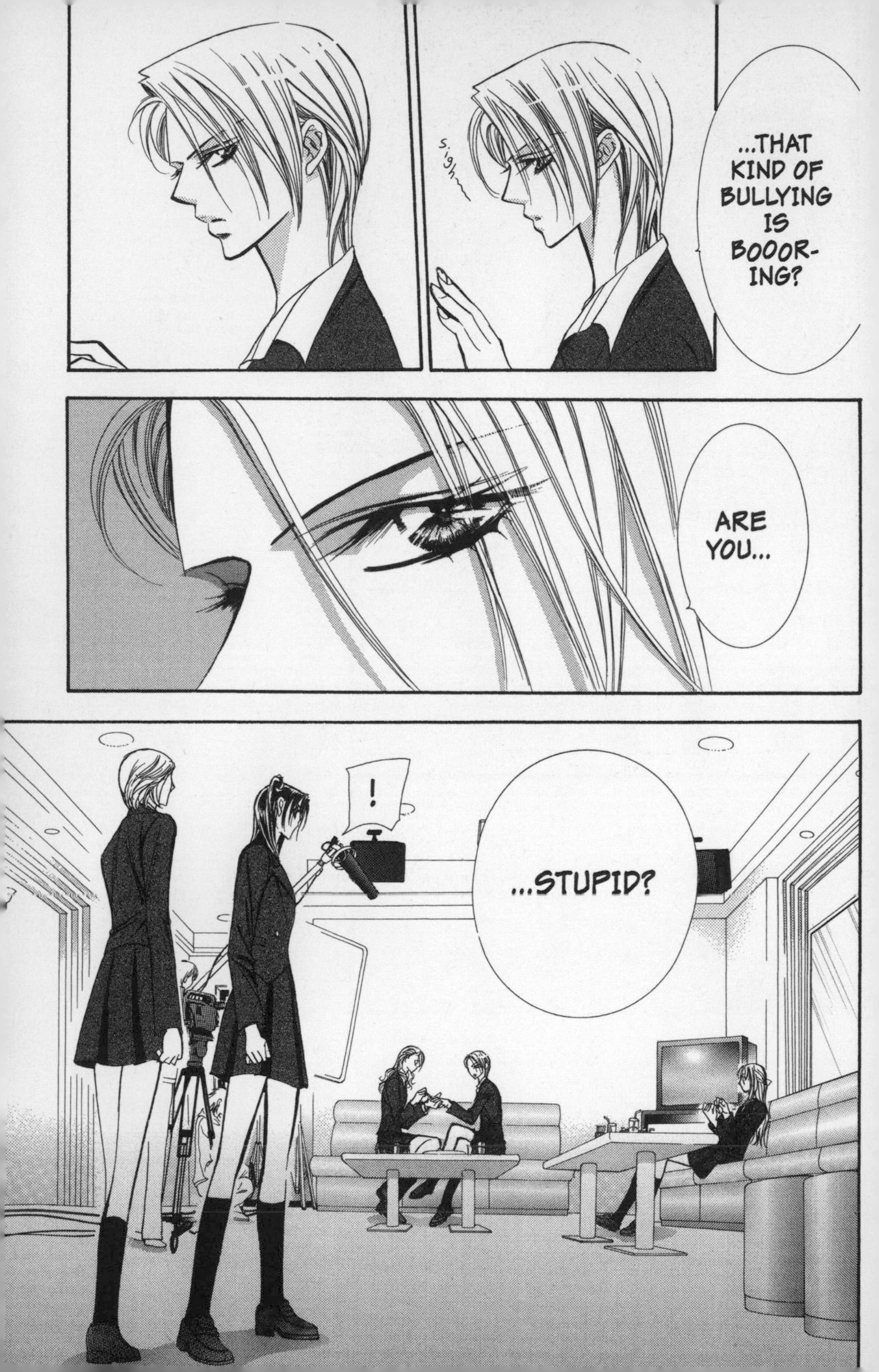
...THAT KIND OF BULLYING IS BOOOR-ING?
sigh
ARE YOU...
...STUPID?
!

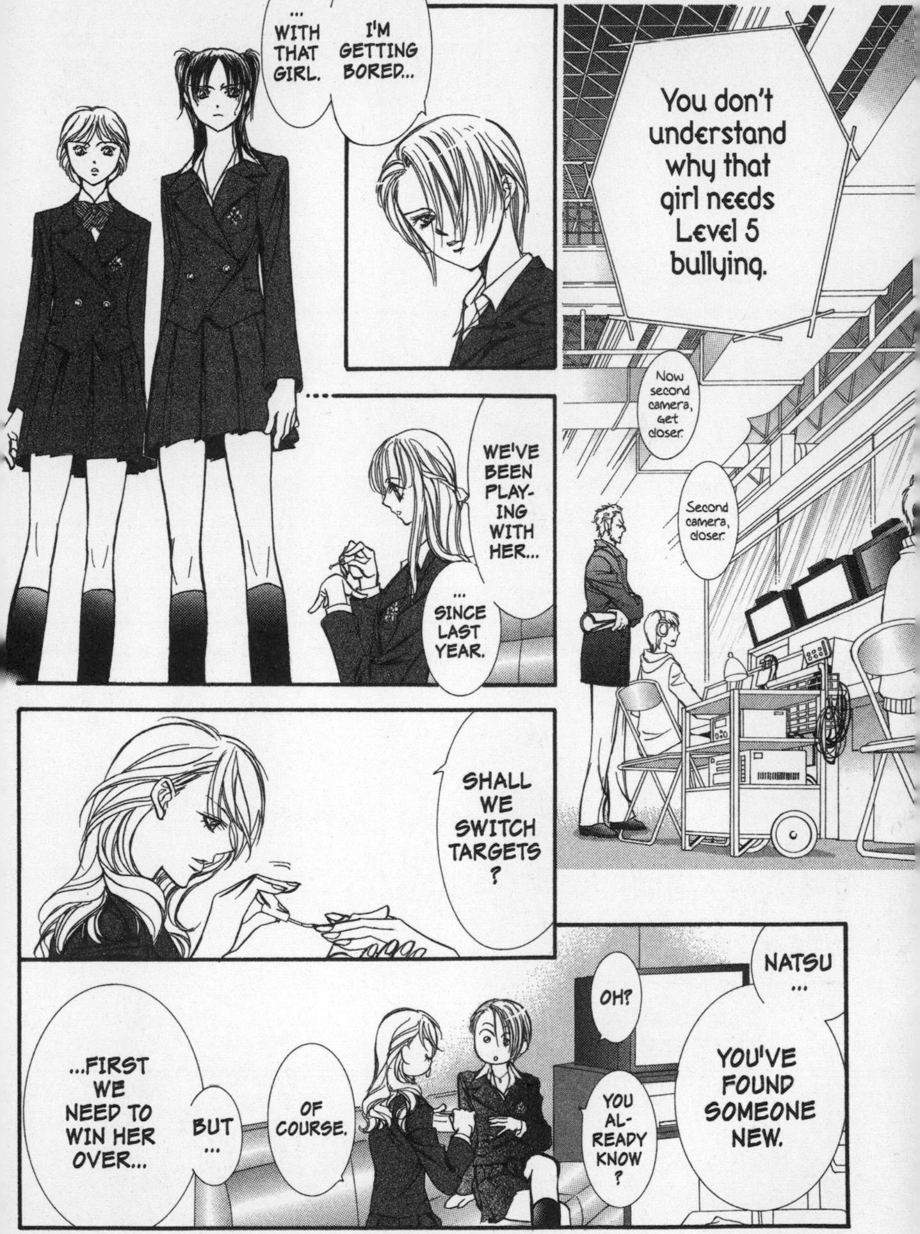
You don't understand why that girl needs Level 5 bullying.
Now second camera, get closer.
Second camera, closer.
I'M GETTING BORED...
...WITH THAT GIRL.
...
WE'VE BEEN PLAYING WITH HER...
...SINCE LAST YEAR.
SHALL WE SWITCH TARGETS?
NATSU...
YOU'VE FOUND SOMEONE NEW.
OH?
YOU ALREADY KNOW?
OF COURSE.
BUT...
...FIRST WE NEED TO WIN HER OVER...

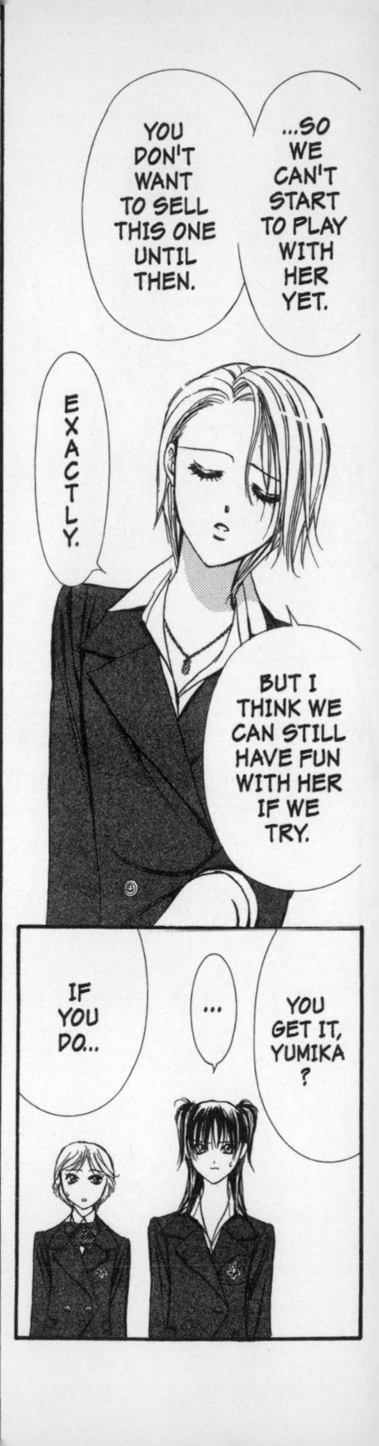
...SO WE CAN'T START TO PLAY WITH HER YET.
YOU DON'T WANT TO SELL THIS ONE UNTIL THEN.
EXACTLY.
BUT I THINK WE CAN STILL HAVE FUN WITH HER IF WE TRY.
YOU GET IT, YUMIKA?
...
IF YOU DO...

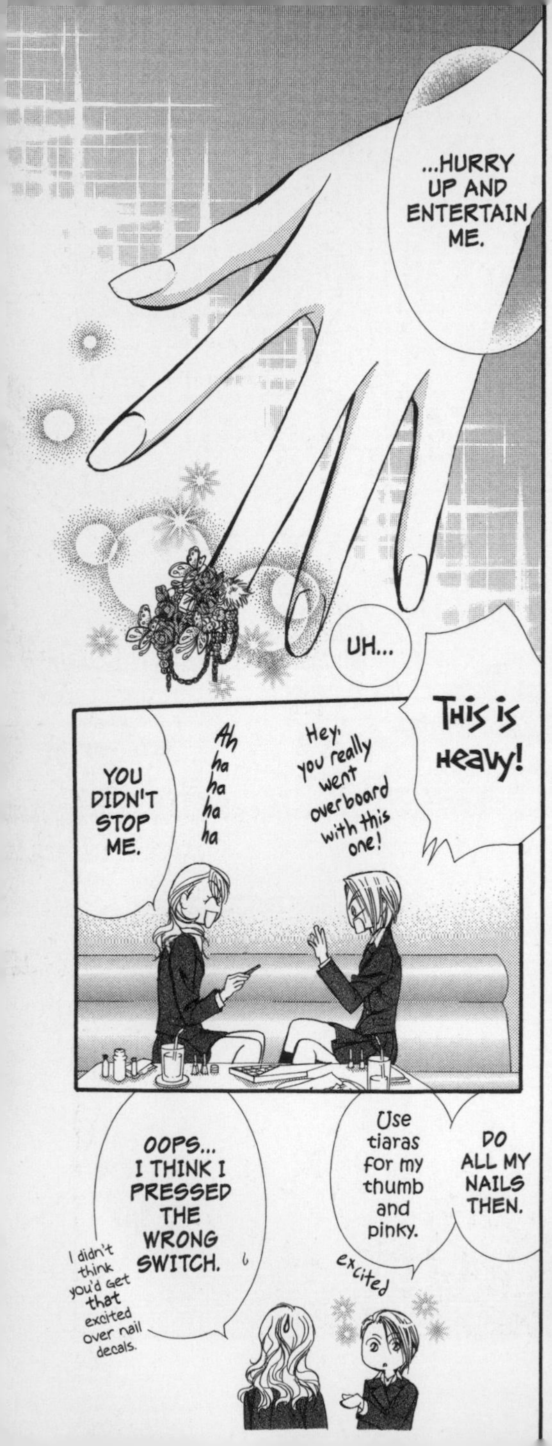
...HURRY UP AND ENTERTAIN ME.
UH...
THIS IS HEAVY!
Hey, you really went overboard with this one!
Ah ha ha ha ha
YOU DIDN'T STOP ME.
DO ALL MY NAILS THEN.
Use tiaras for my thumb and pinky.
excited
OOPS... I THINK I PRESSED THE WRONG SWITCH.
I didn't think you'd get that excited over nail decals.

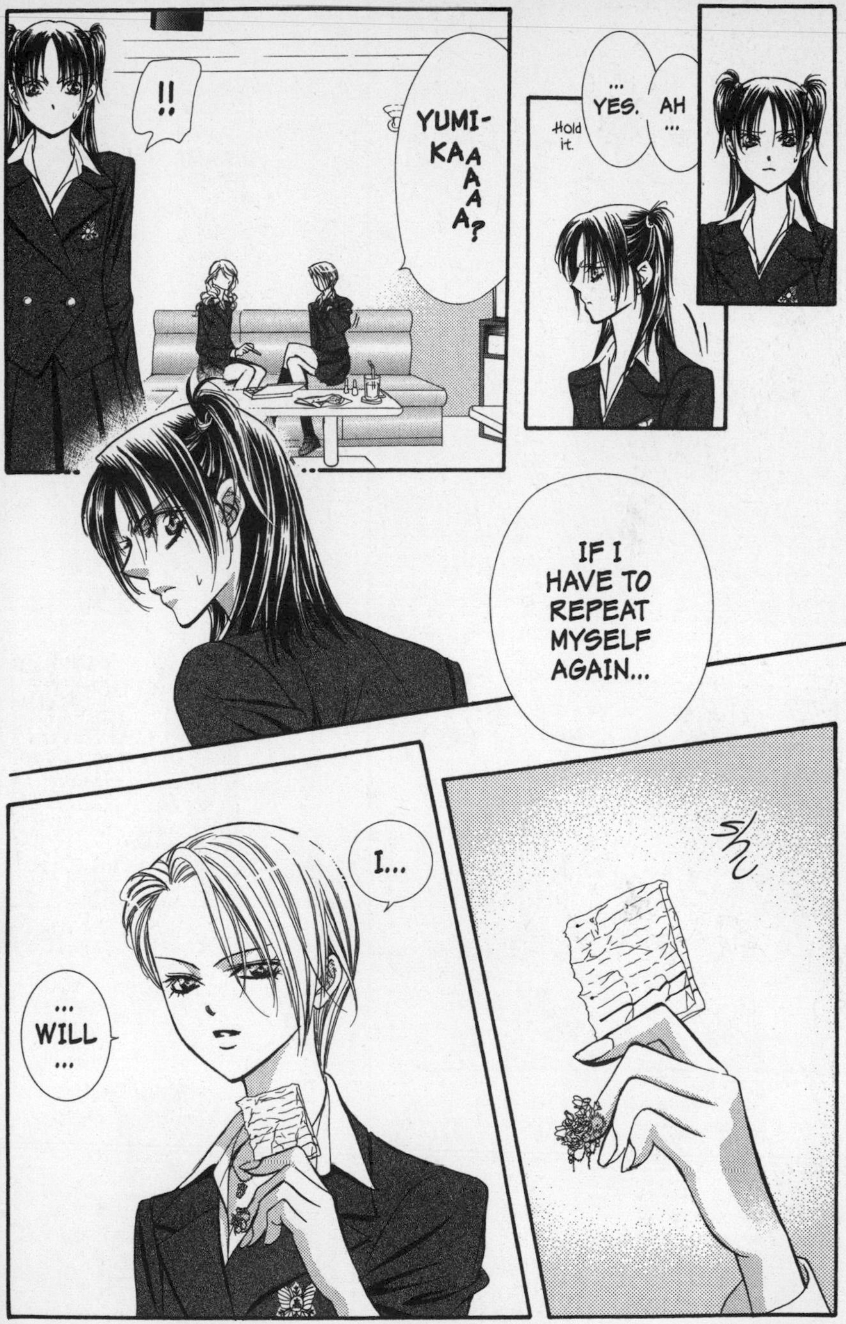
AH...
...YES.
Hold it.
YUMIKAAAAA?
!!
IF I HAVE TO REPEAT MYSELF AGAIN...
shu
I...
...WILL...

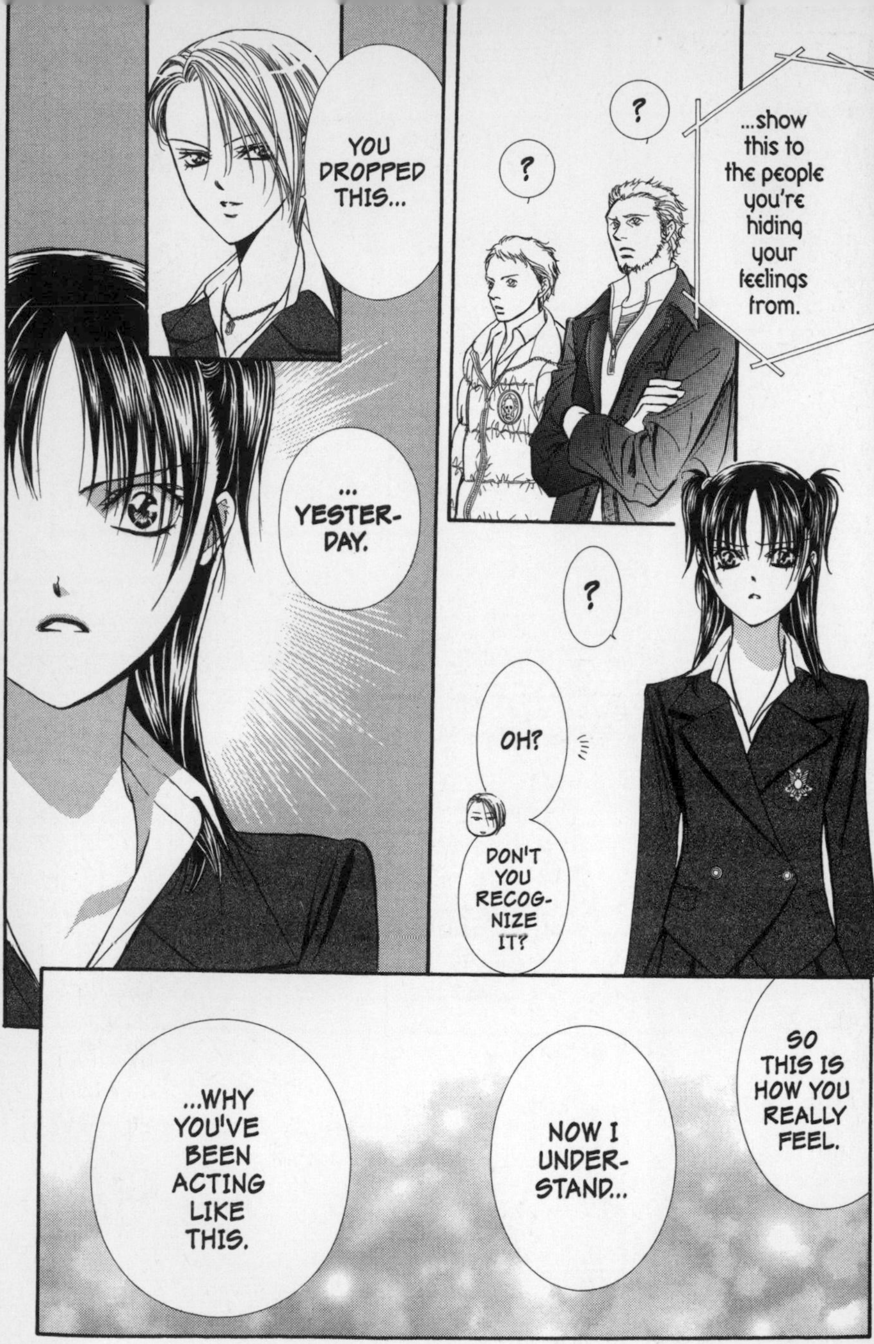
...show this to the people you're hiding your feelings from.
?
?
?
OH?
DON'T YOU RECOGNIZE IT?
YOU DROPPED THIS...
... YESTERDAY.
SO THIS IS HOW YOU REALLY FEEL.
NOW I UNDERSTAND...
...WHY YOU'VE BEEN ACTING LIKE THIS.

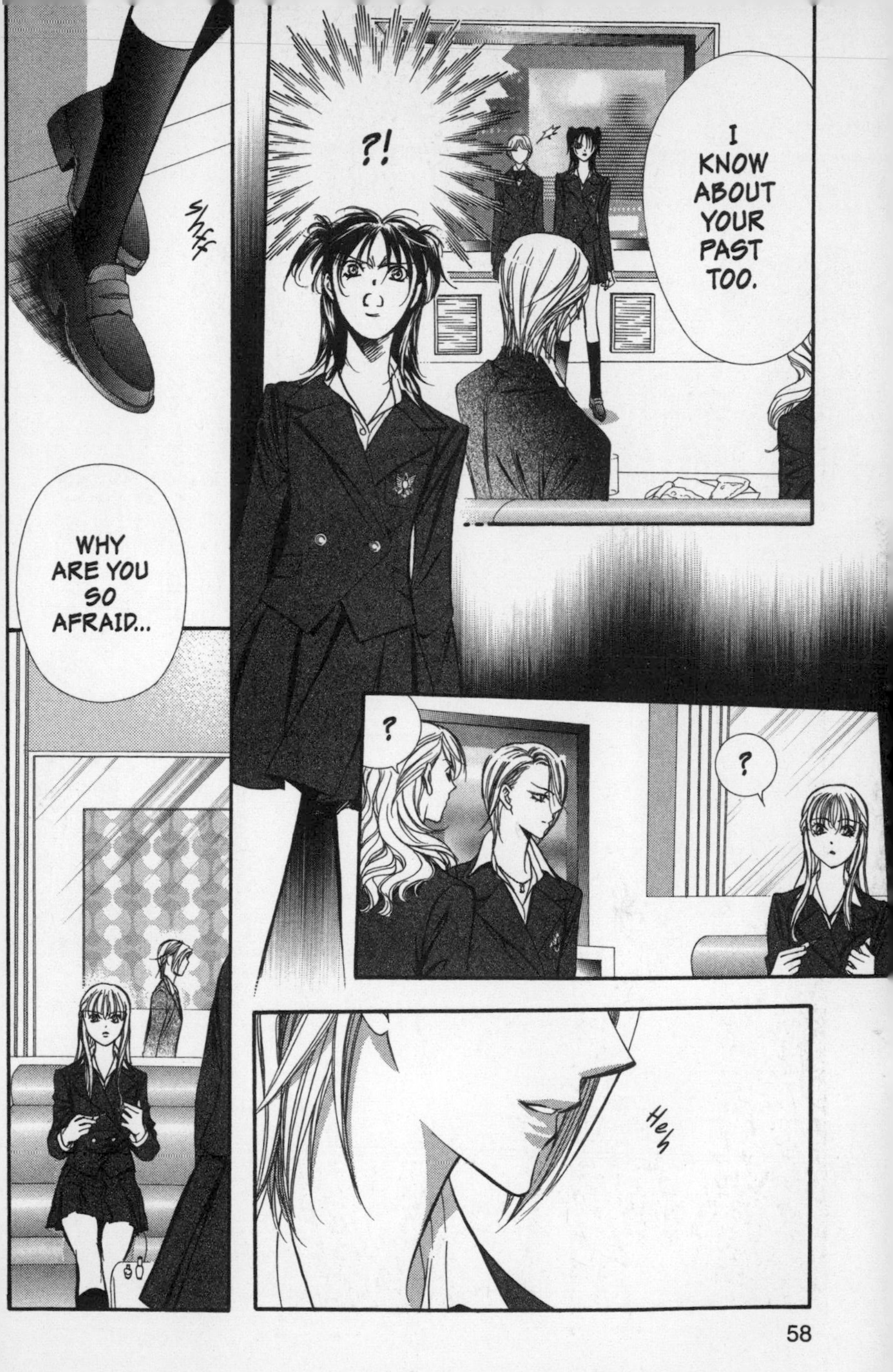
I KNOW ABOUT YOUR PAST TOO.
?!
Shff
WHY ARE YOU SO AFRAID...
?
?
Heh

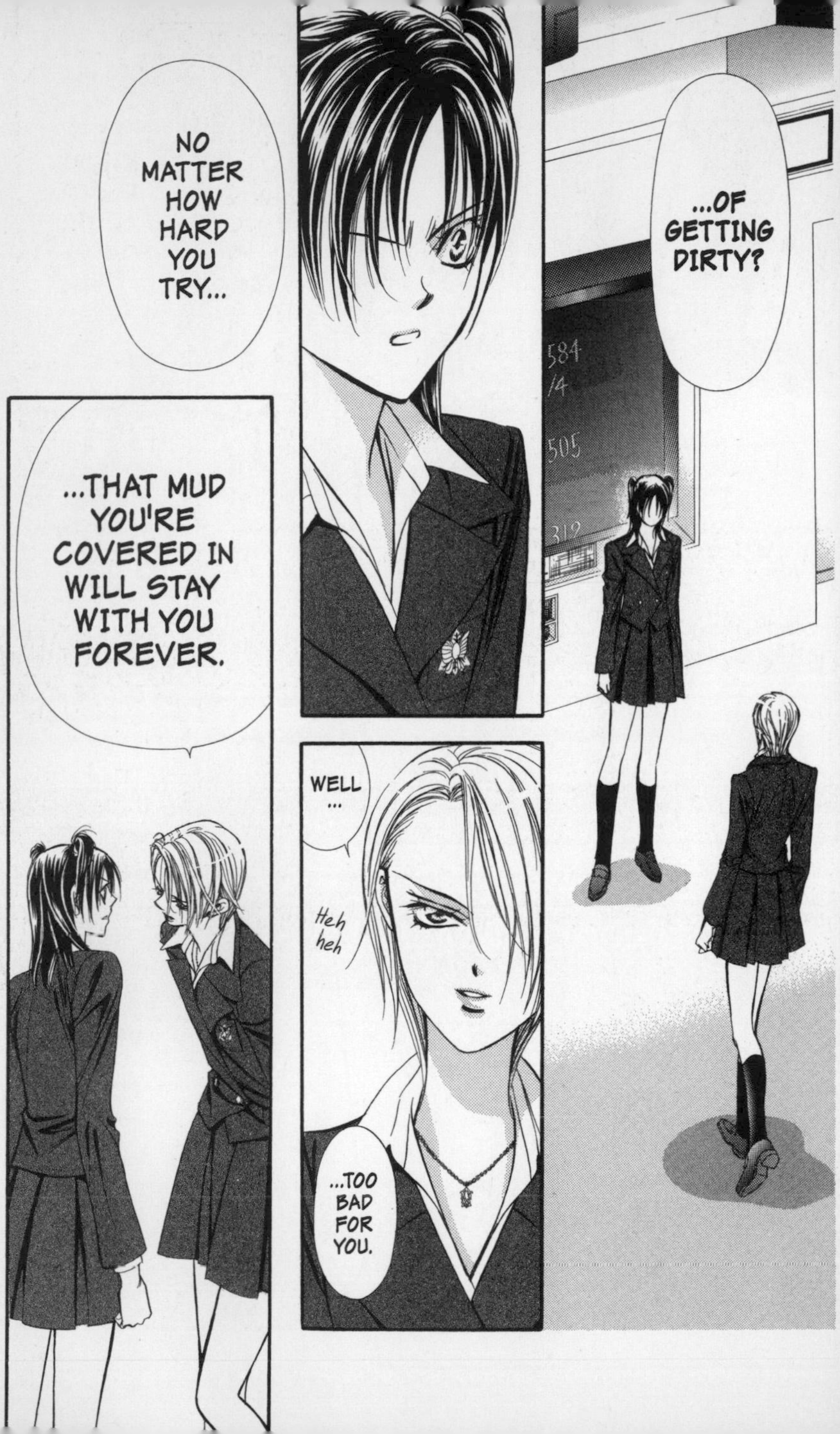
...OF GETTING DIRTY?
NO MATTER HOW HARD YOU TRY...
...THAT MUD YOU'RE COVERED IN WILL STAY WITH YOU FOREVER.
WELL ...
Heh heh
...TOO BAD FOR YOU.

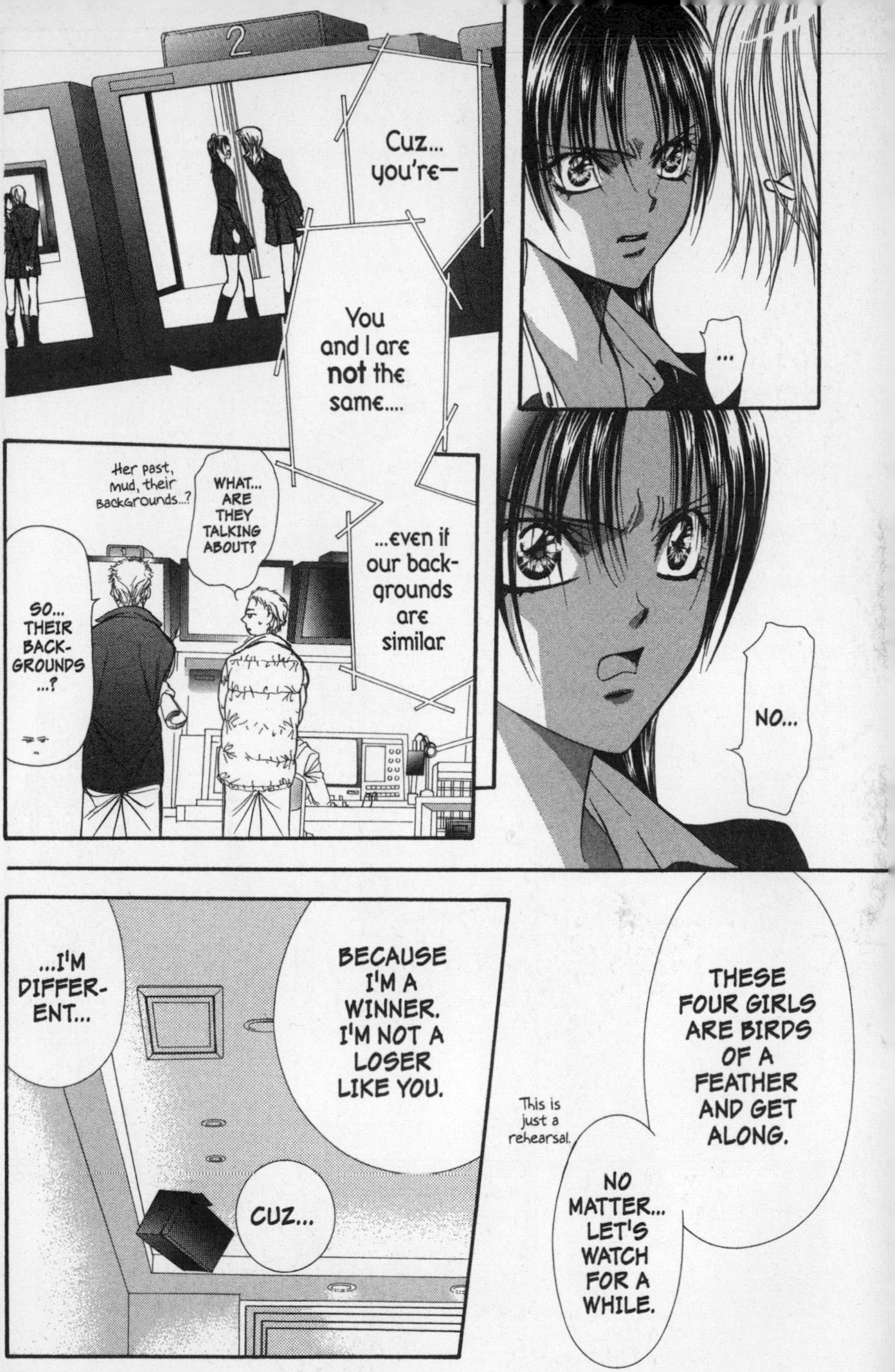
...
Cuz... you're—
You and I are not the same....
...even if our backgrounds are similar.
NO...
WHAT... ARE THEY TALKING ABOUT?
Her past, mud, their backgrounds...?
SO... THEIR BACKGROUNDS ...?
THESE FOUR GIRLS ARE BIRDS OF A FEATHER AND GET ALONG.
This is just a rehearsal.
NO MATTER... LET'S WATCH FOR A WHILE.
BECAUSE I'M A WINNER. I'M NOT A LOSER LIKE YOU.
CUZ...
...I'M DIFFERENT...

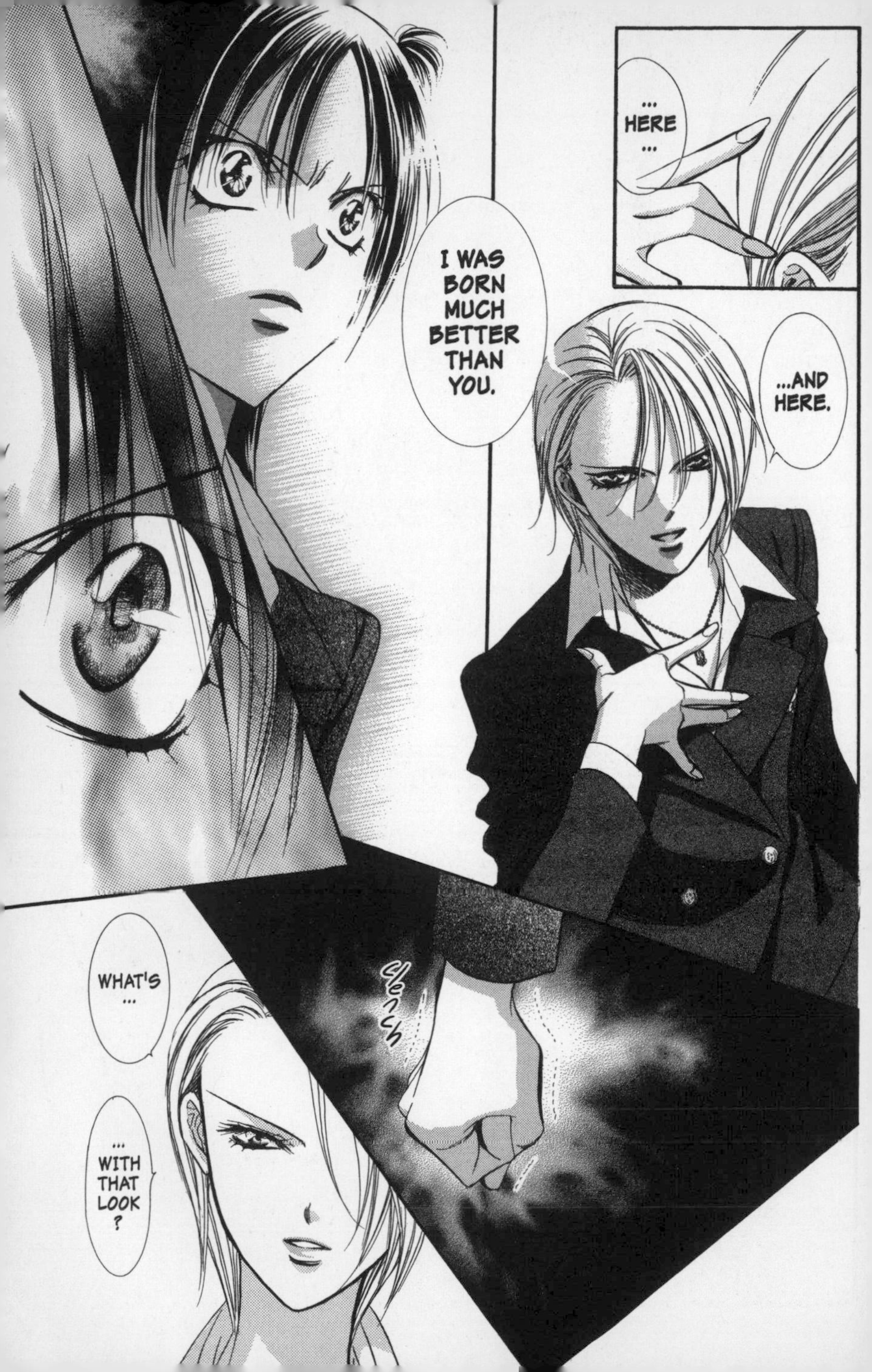
... HERE ...
...AND HERE.
I WAS BORN MUCH BETTER THAN YOU.
clench
WHAT'S ...
... WITH THAT LOOK ?

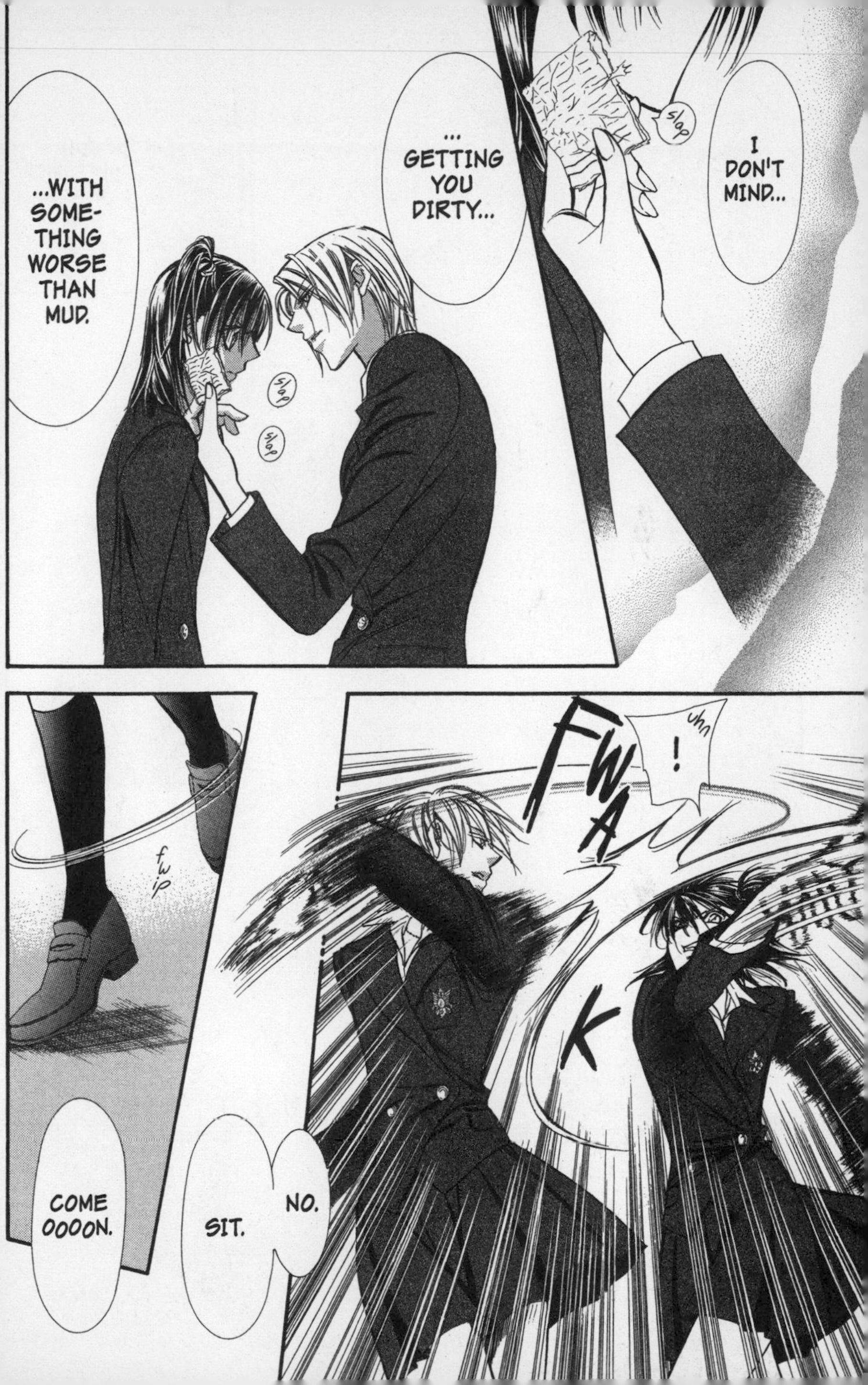
slop
I DON'T MIND...
... GETTING YOU DIRTY...
...WITH SOME-THING WORSE THAN MUD.
slop
slop
FWAK
uhn
!
NO.
SIT.
fwip
COME OOOON.

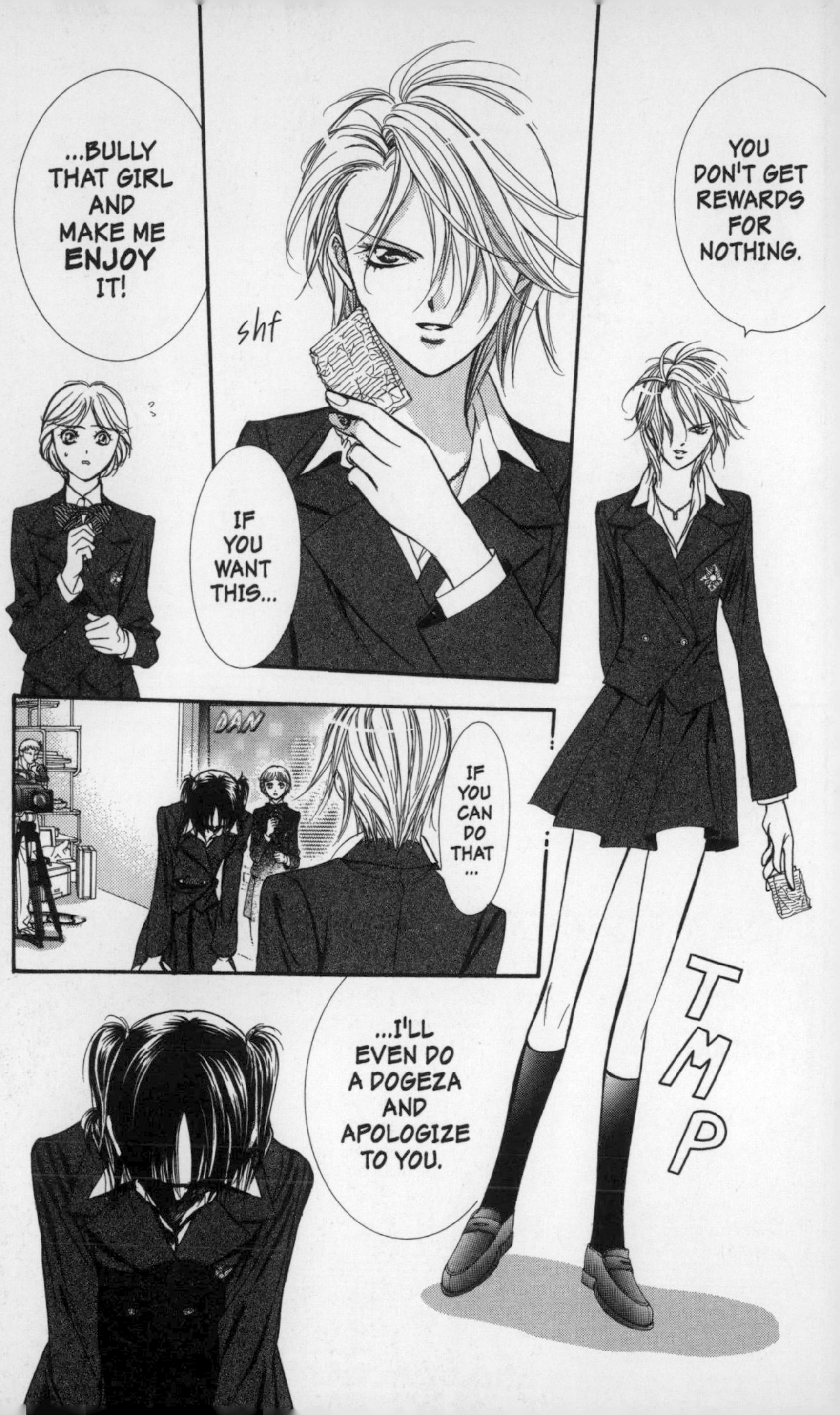
YOU DON'T GET REWARDS FOR NOTHING.
TMP
shf
IF YOU WANT THIS...
...BULLY THAT GIRL AND MAKE ME ENJOY IT!
DAN
IF YOU CAN DO THAT...
...I'LL EVEN DO A DOGEZA AND APOLOGIZE TO YOU.

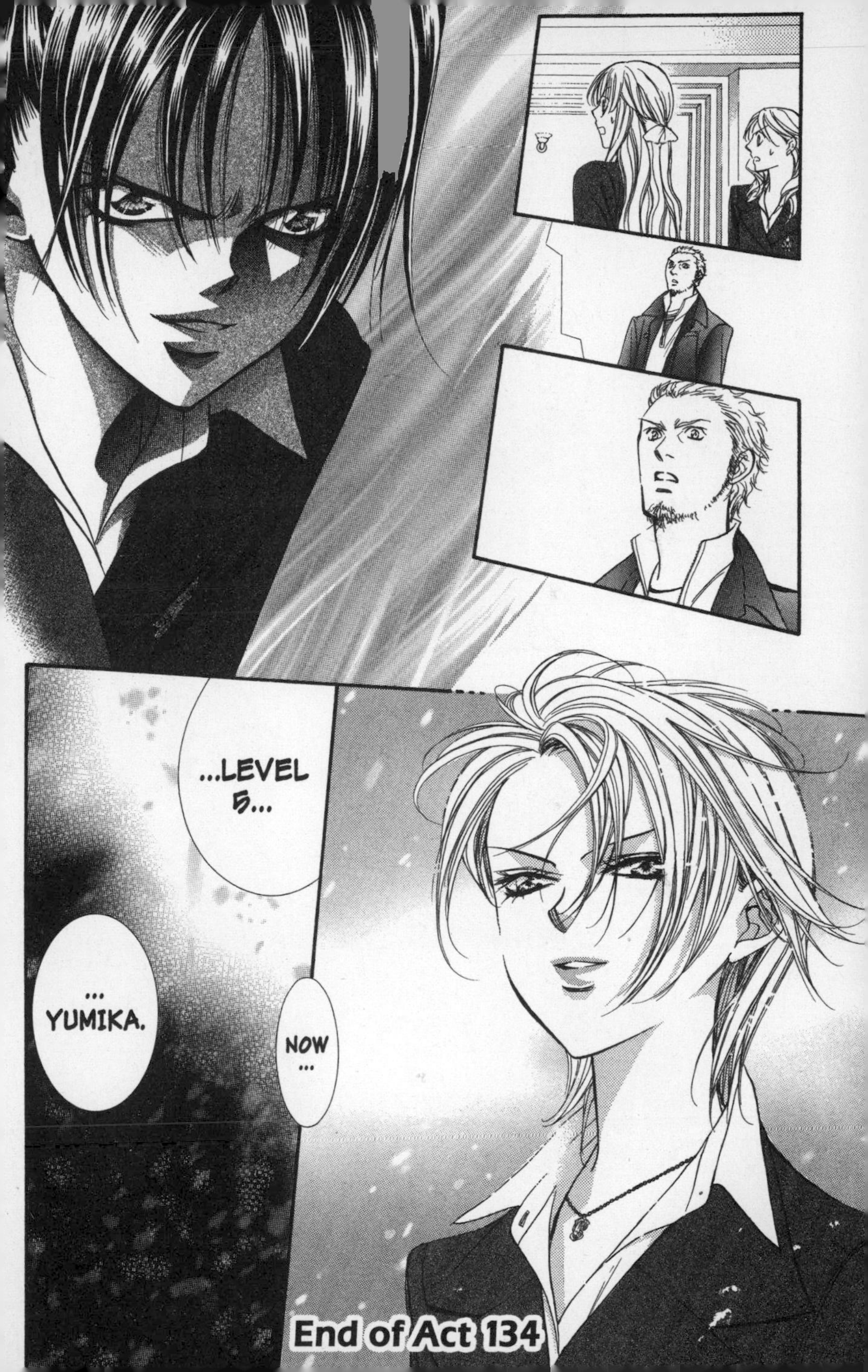
...LEVEL 5...
NOW ...
... YUMIKA.
End of Act 134

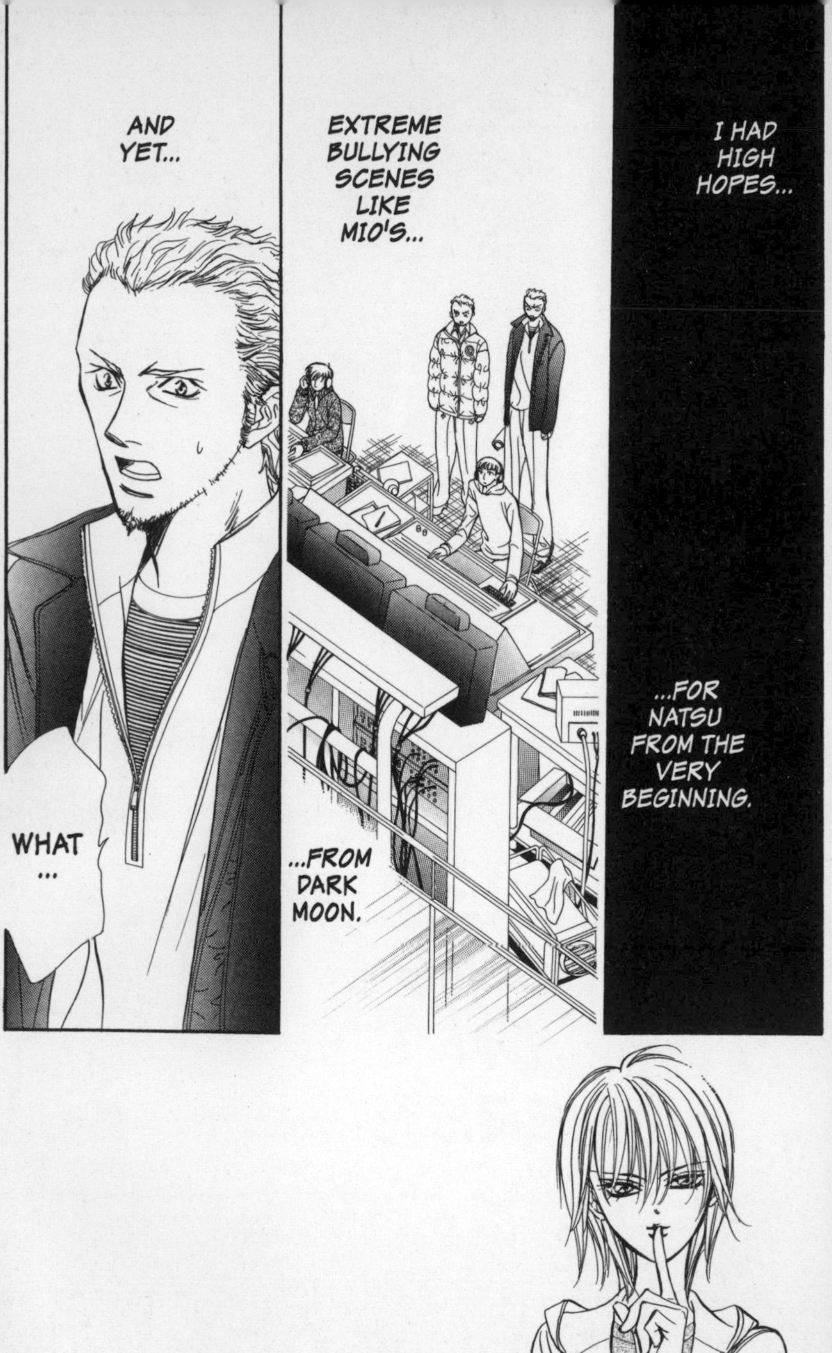
I HAD HIGH HOPES...
...FOR NATSU FROM THE VERY BEGINNING.
EXTREME BULLYING SCENES LIKE MIO'S...
...FROM DARK MOON.
AND YET...
WHAT ...

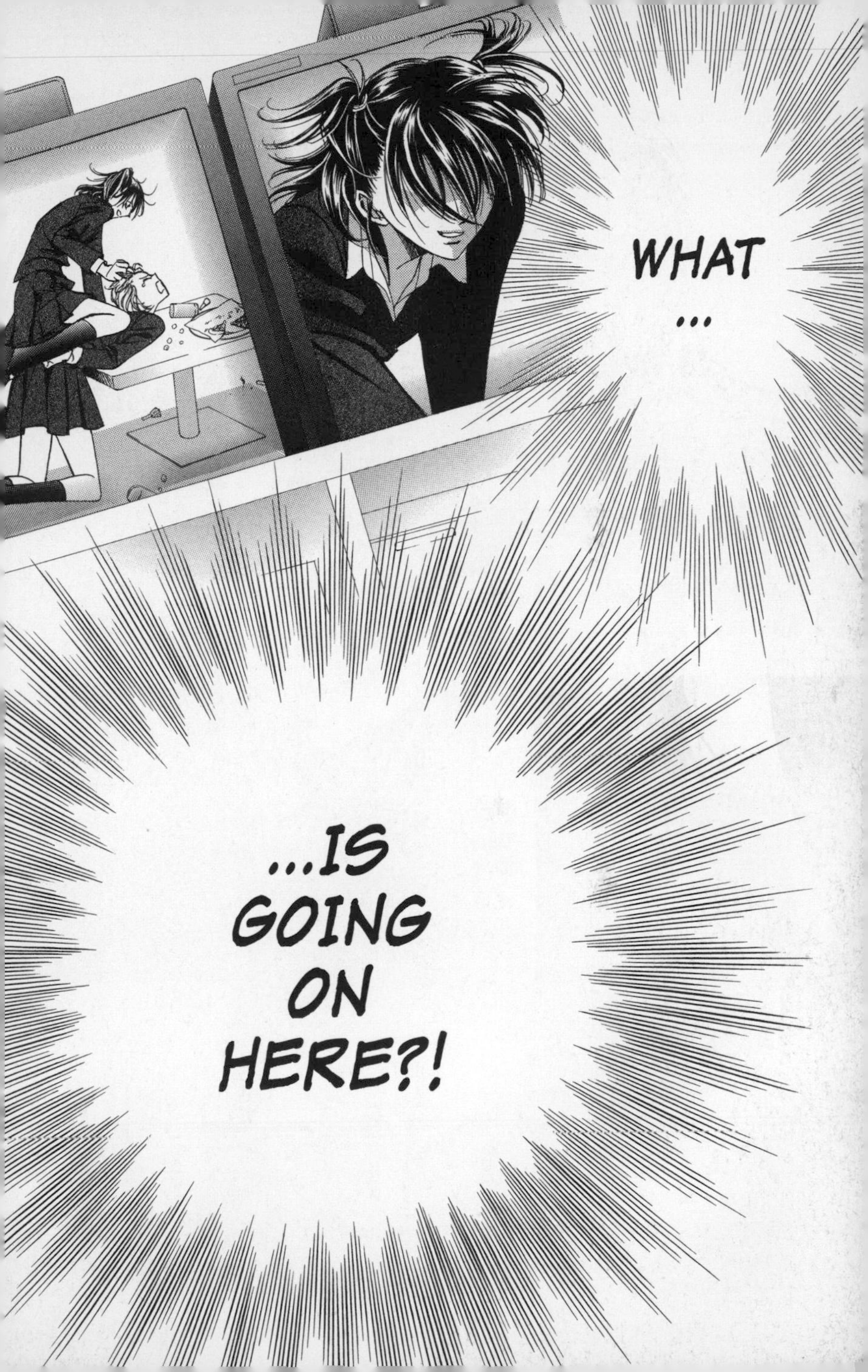
WHAT ...
...IS GOING ON HERE?!

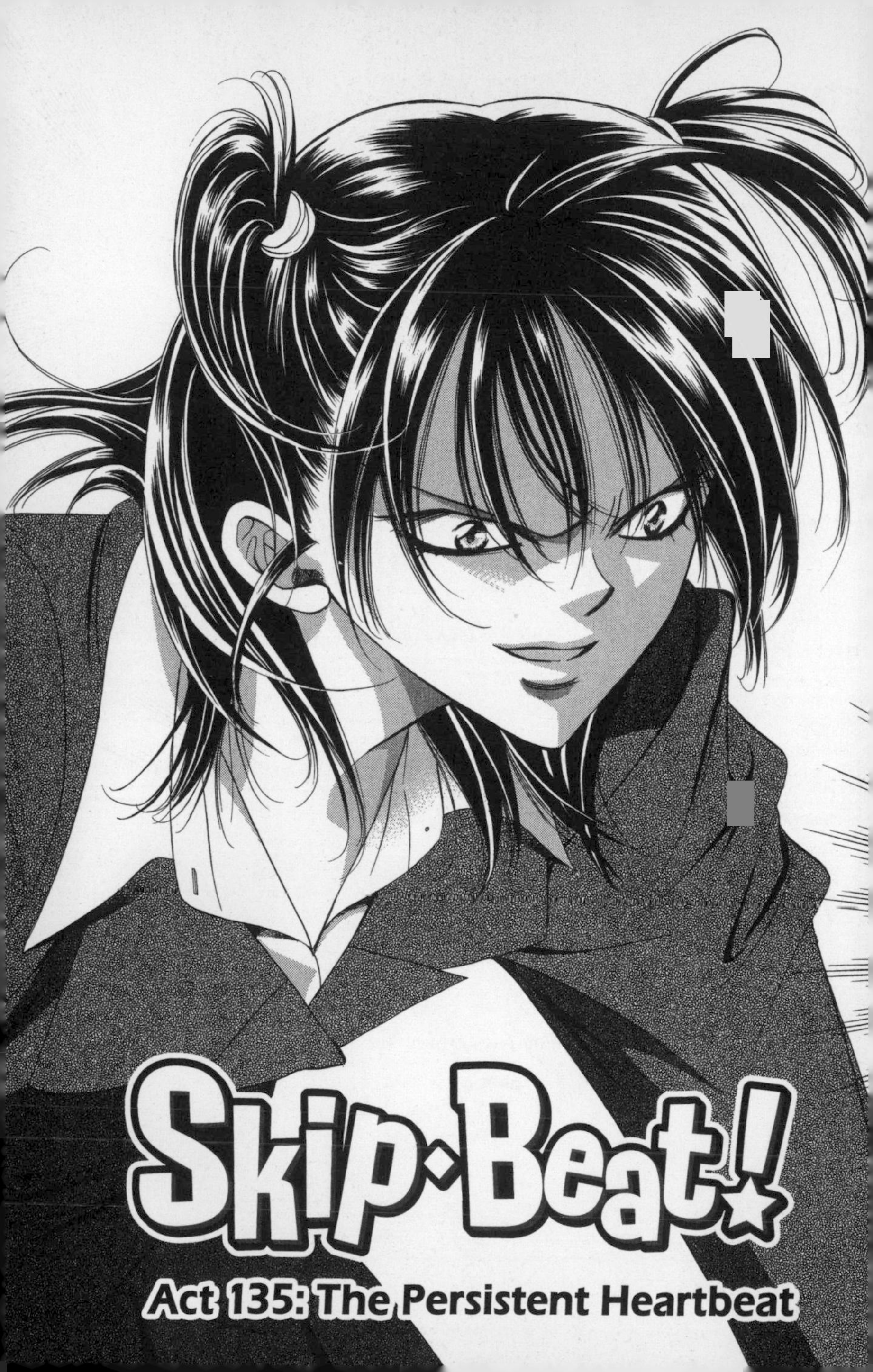
Skip·Beat!
Act 135: The Persistent Heartbeat

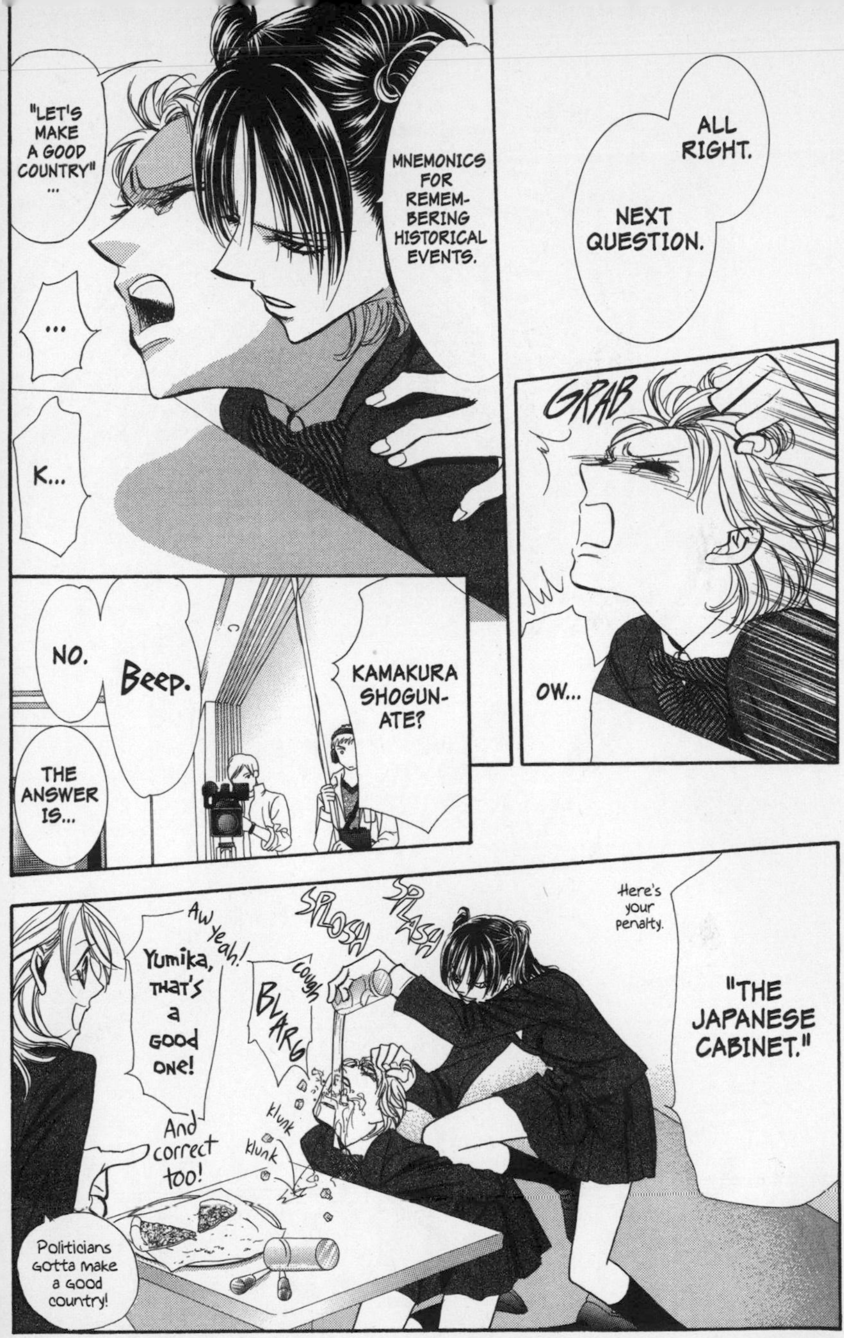
ALL RIGHT.
NEXT QUESTION.
MNEMONICS FOR REMEMBERING HISTORICAL EVENTS.
"LET'S MAKE A GOOD COUNTRY" ...
...
K...
KAMAKURA SHOGUNATE?
Beep.
NO.
THE ANSWER IS...
GRAB
OW...
Here's your penalty.
"THE JAPANESE CABINET."
SPLASH
SPLOSH
cough
BLARG
klunk
klunk
Aw yeah!
Yumika, that's a good one!
And correct too!
Politicians gotta make a good country!

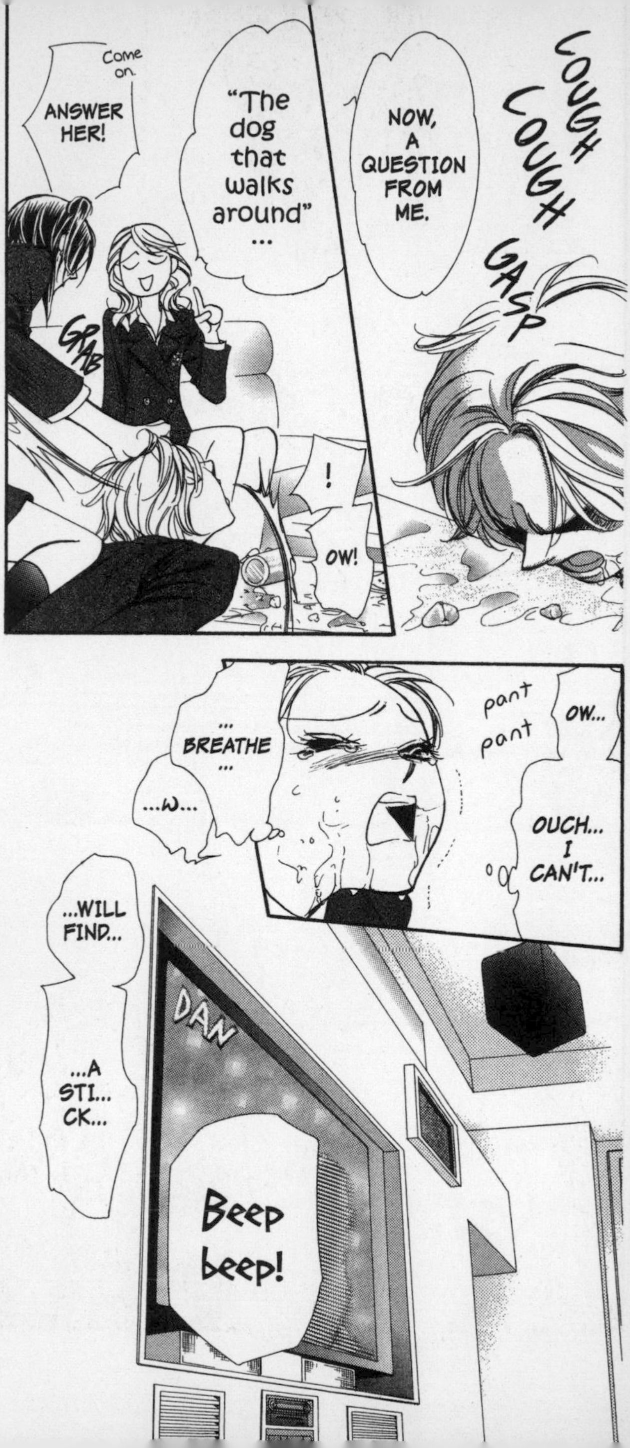
COUGH COUGH
GASP
NOW, A QUESTION FROM ME.
"The dog that walks around"...
Come on.
ANSWER HER!
GRAB
!
OW!
pant pant
OW...
OUCH... I CAN'T...
...BREATHE...
...w...
...WILL FIND...
...A STI... CK...
DAN
Beep beep!

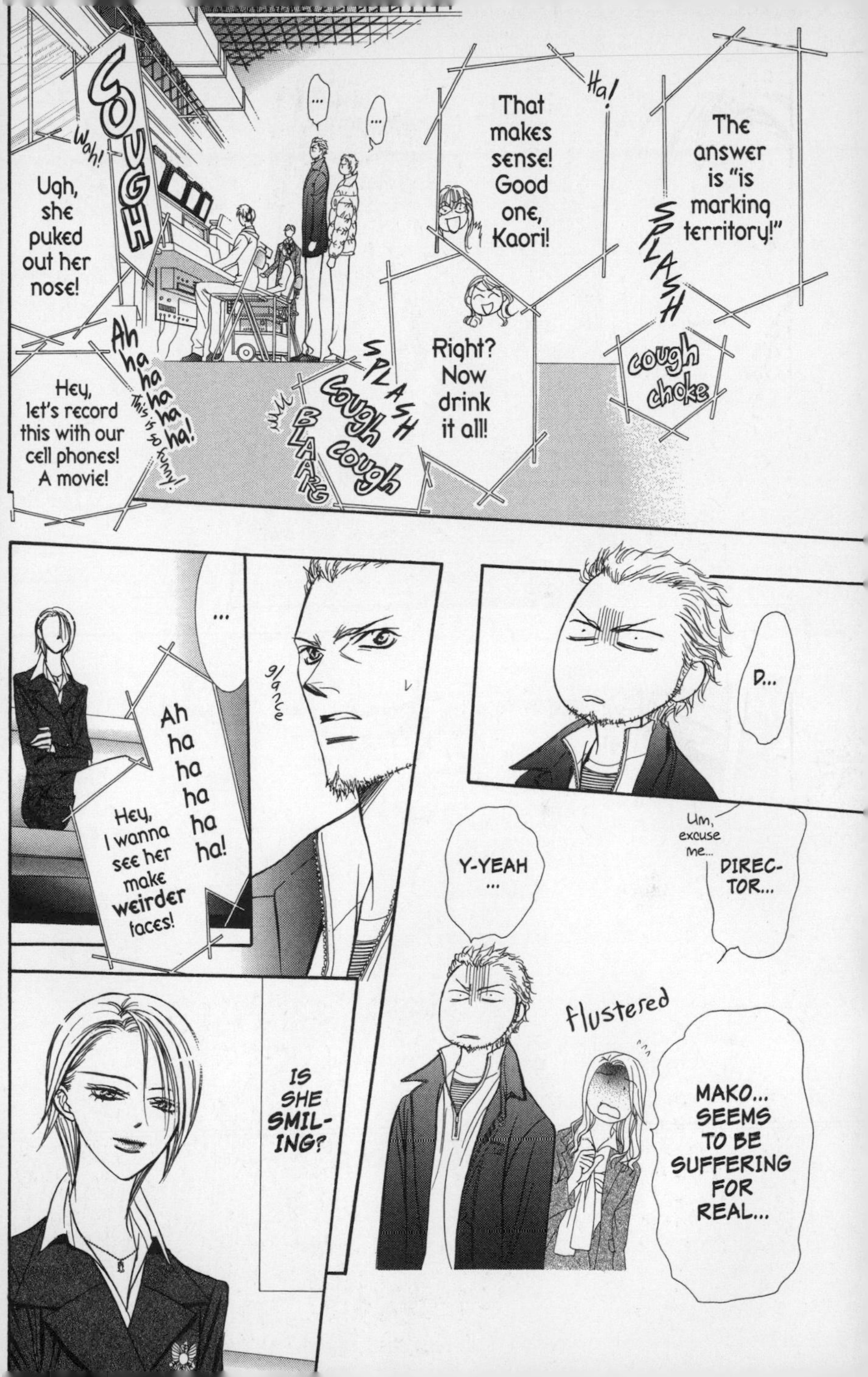
The answer is "is marking territory!"
SPLASH
cough choke
Ha!
That makes sense! Good one, Kaori!
Right? Now drink it all!
...
...
SPLASH
cough cough
BLAARG
Ugh, she puked out her nose!
Wah!
COUGH
Ah ha ha ha ha ha!
This is so funny!
Hey, let's record this with our cell phones! A movie!
D...
...
glance
Ah ha ha ha ha ha ha!
Hey, I wanna see her make weirder faces!
Um, excuse me...
DIRECTOR...
Y-YEAH ...
flustered
MAKO... SEEMS TO BE SUFFERING FOR REAL...
IS SHE SMILING?

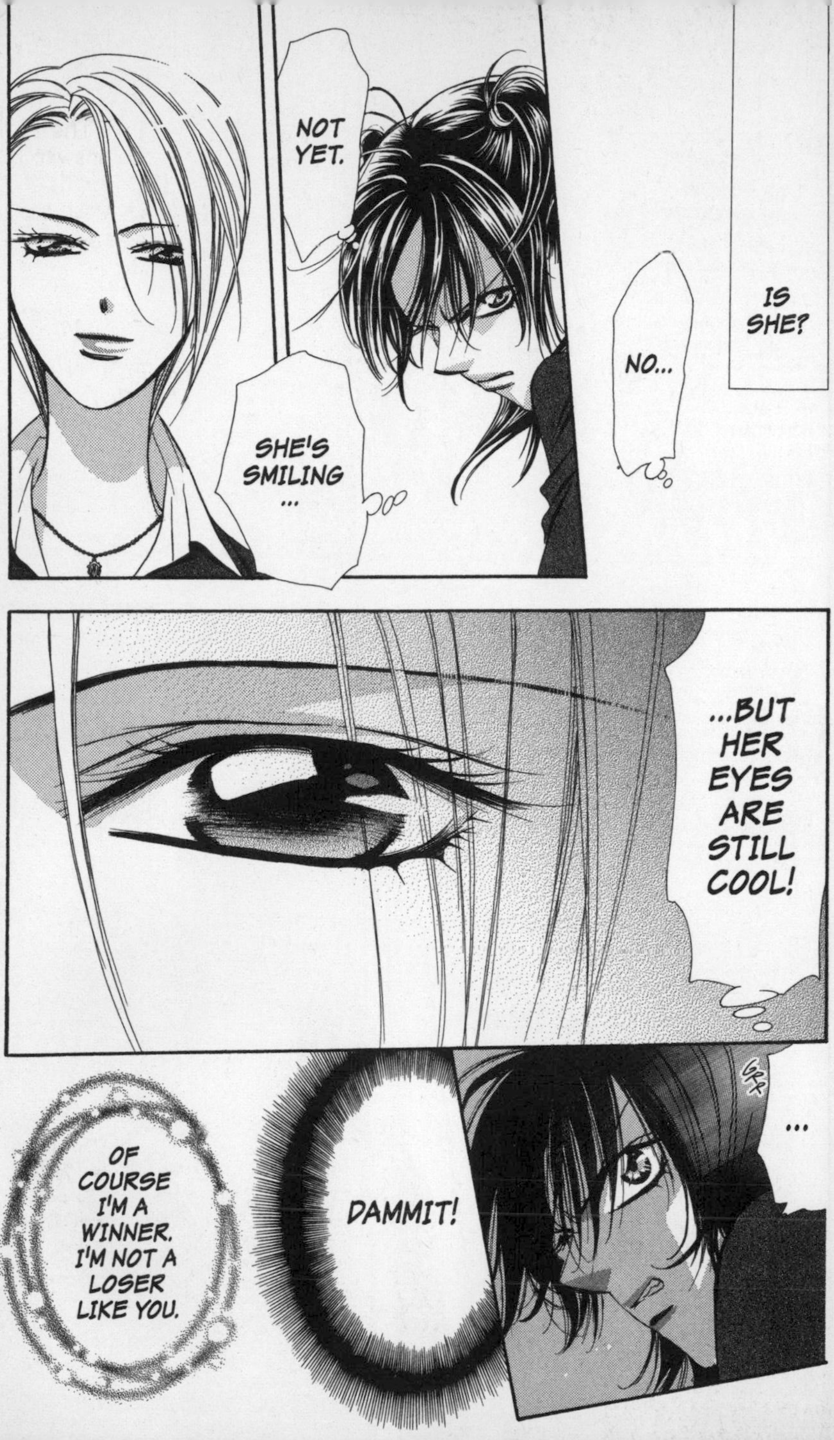
IS SHE?
NO...
NOT YET.
SHE'S SMILING ...
...BUT HER EYES ARE STILL COOL!
GRR
...
DAMMIT!
OF COURSE I'M A WINNER. I'M NOT A LOSER LIKE YOU.

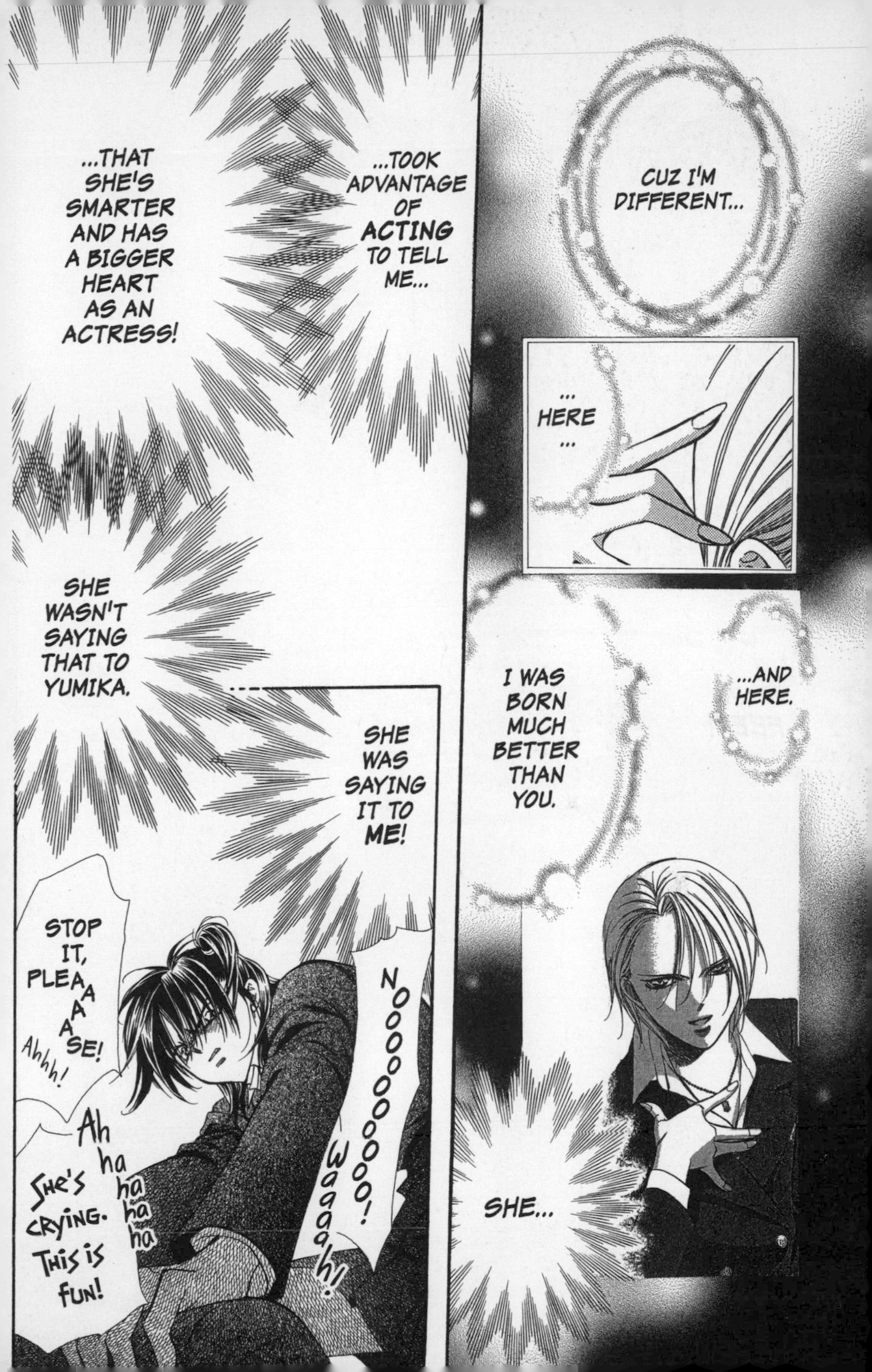
CUZ I'M DIFFERENT...
...HERE...
...AND HERE.
I WAS BORN MUCH BETTER THAN YOU.
SHE...
...TOOK ADVANTAGE OF ACTING TO TELL ME...
...THAT SHE'S SMARTER AND HAS A BIGGER HEART AS AN ACTRESS!
SHE WASN'T SAYING THAT TO YUMIKA.
SHE WAS SAYING IT TO ME!
NOOOOOOOOOOO!
Waaaah!
STOP IT, PLEAAAAASE!
Ahhh!
Ah ha ha ha ha
She's crying. This is fun!

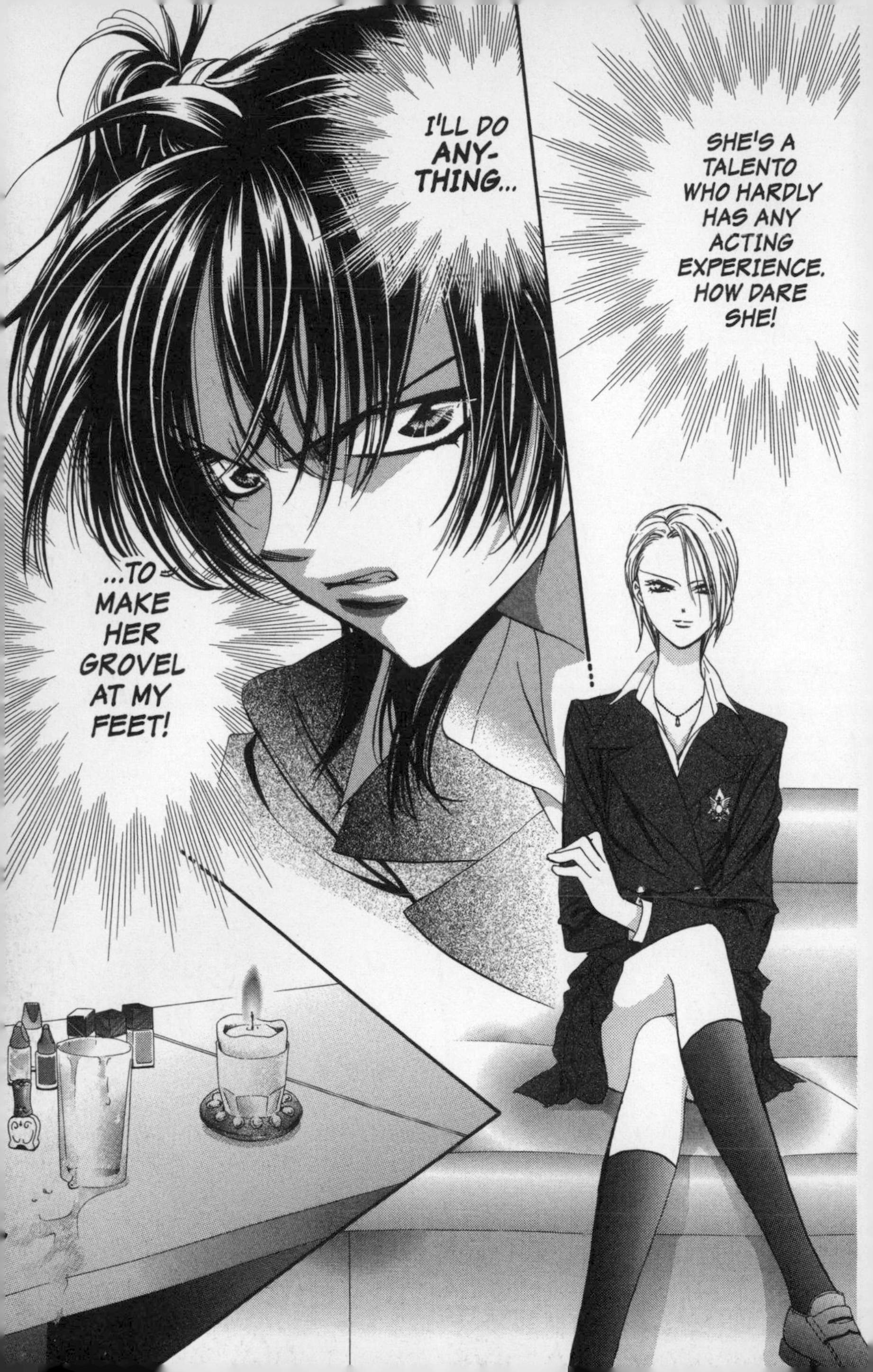
SHE'S A TALENTO WHO HARDLY HAS ANY ACTING EXPERIENCE. HOW DARE SHE!
I'LL DO ANY-THING...
...TO MAKE HER GROVEL AT MY FEET!

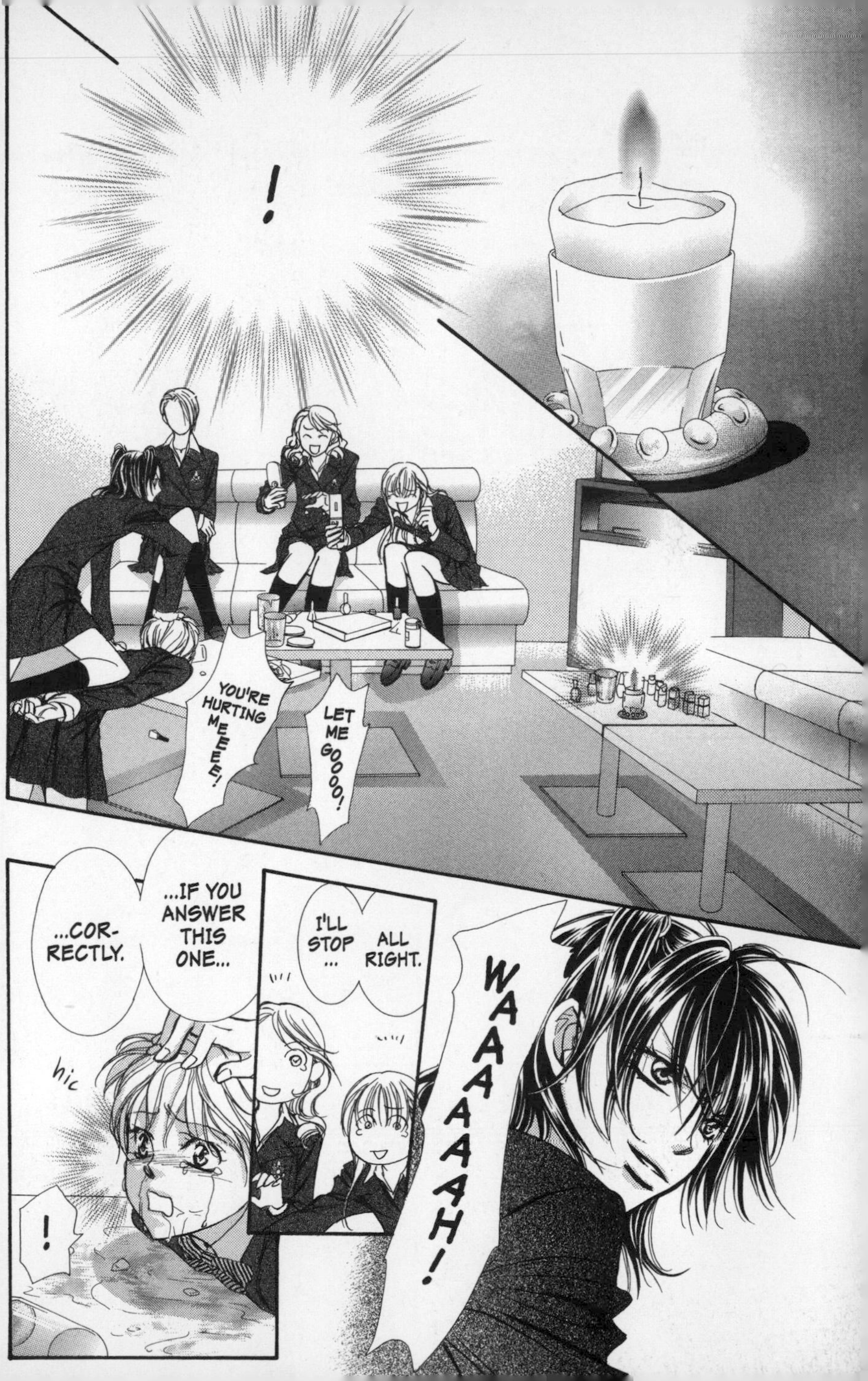
!
LET ME GOOOO!
YOU'RE HURTING MEEEEE!
WAAAAAAH!
ALL RIGHT.
I'LL STOP...
...IF YOU ANSWER THIS ONE...
...COR-RECTLY.
hic
!

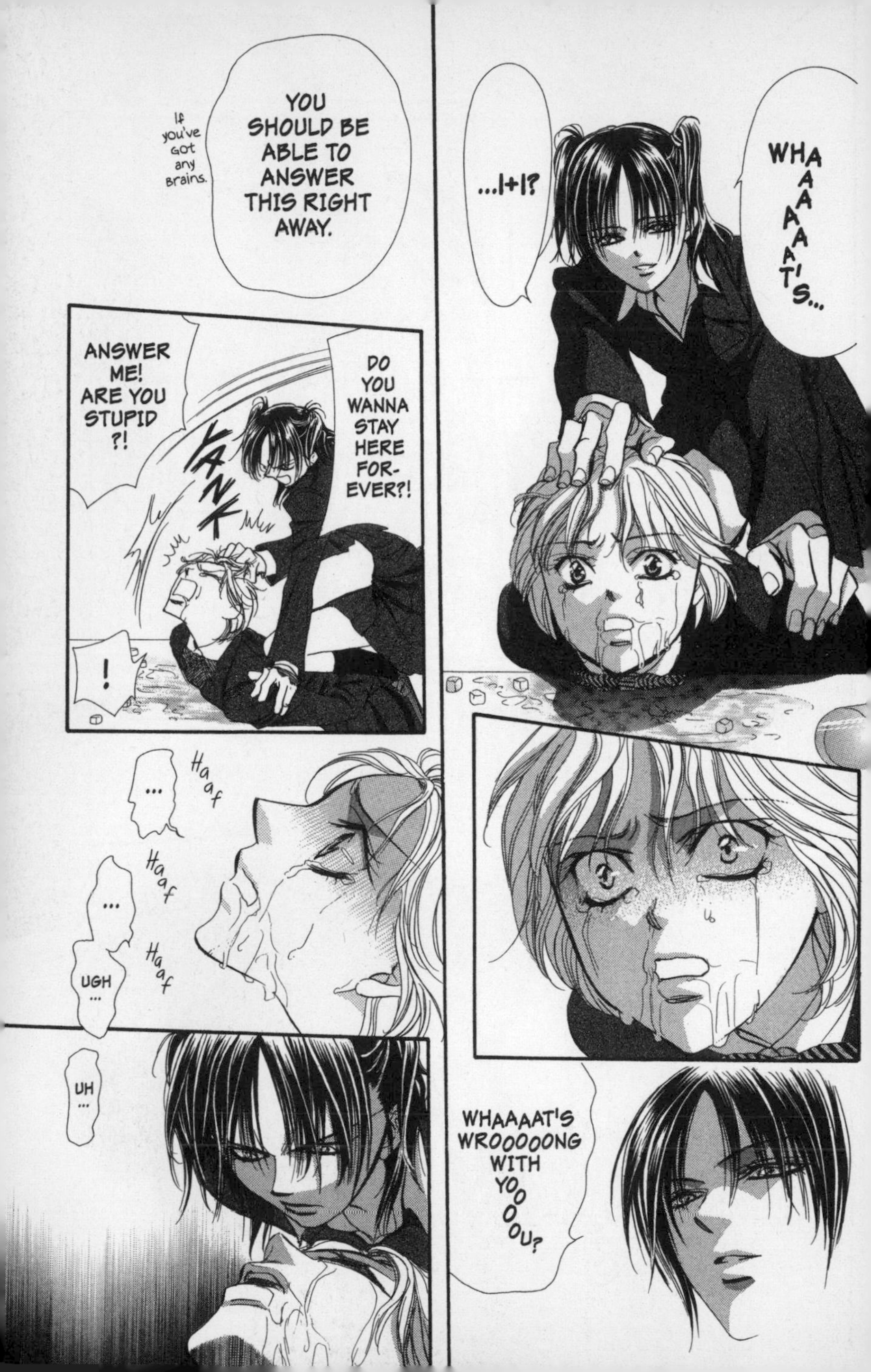
WHAAAAAT'S...
...1+1?
WHAAAAT'S WROOOOONG WITH YOOOOU?
YOU SHOULD BE ABLE TO ANSWER THIS RIGHT AWAY.
If you've got any Brains.
DO YOU WANNA STAY HERE FOR-EVER?!
ANSWER ME! ARE YOU STUPID ?!
YANK
!
Haaf
...
Haaf
...
Haaf
UGH ...
UH ...

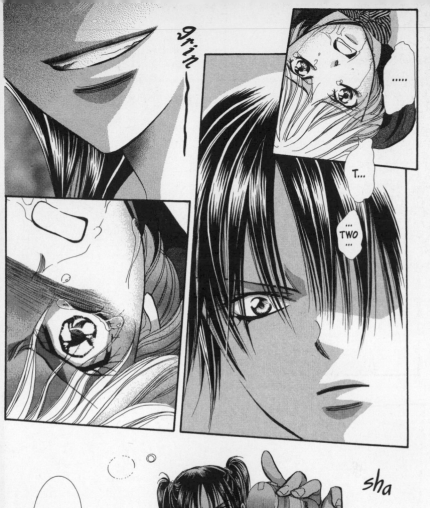

grin

.....

T....

...TWO...

sha

RIIII...

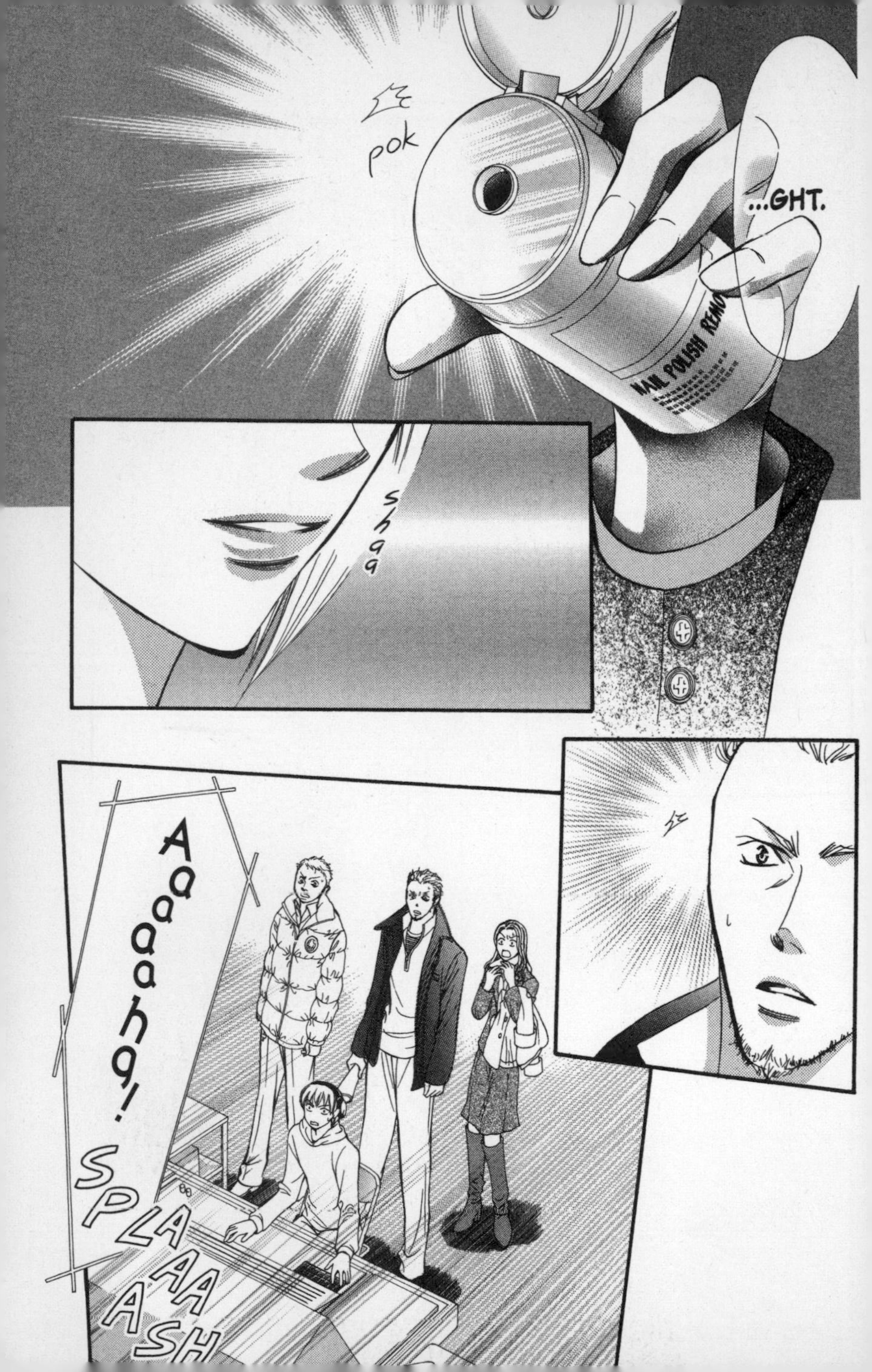
...GHT.
pok
NAIL POLISH REMO
shaa
Aaaaahg!
SPLAAAASH

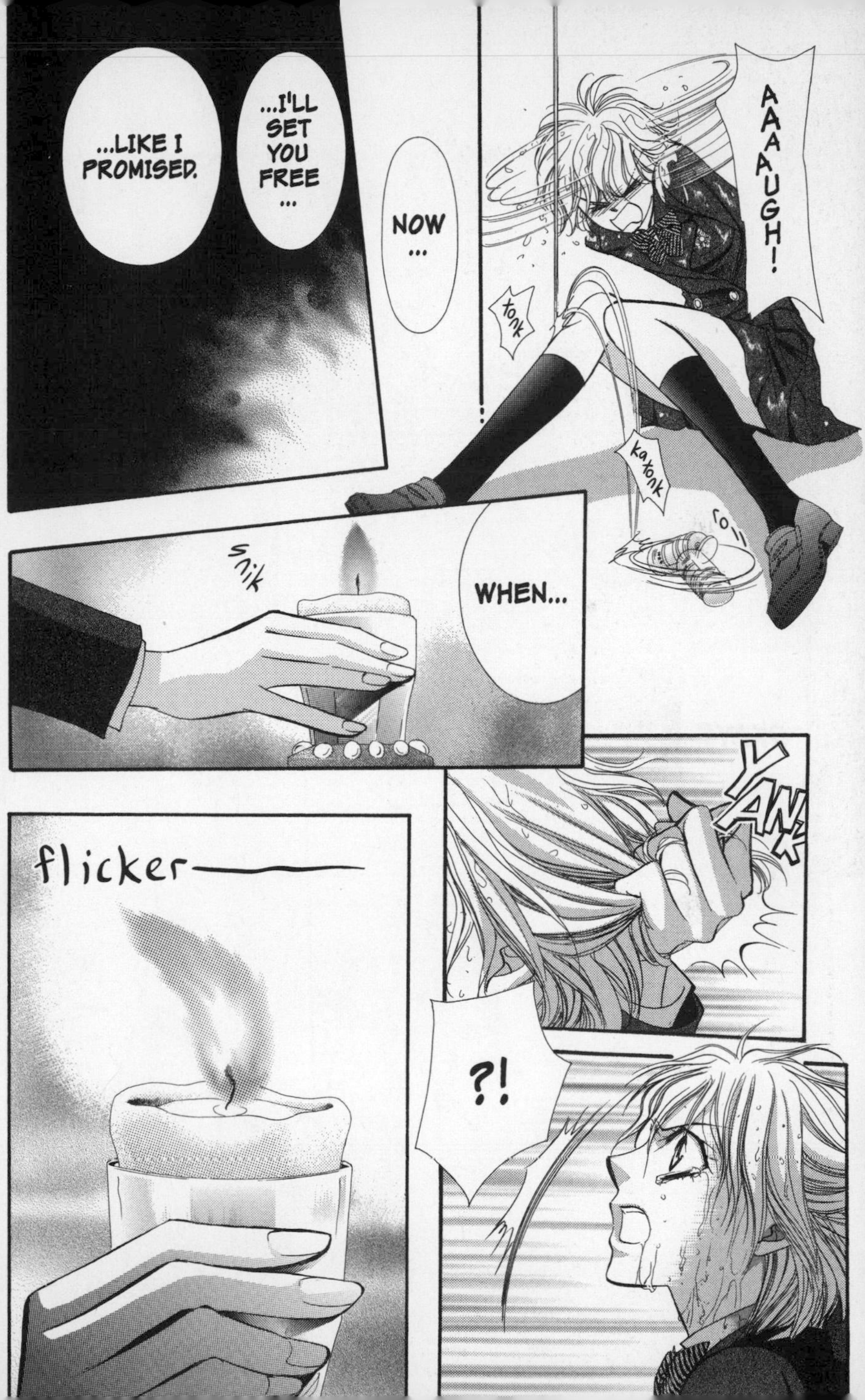

AAAAUGH!
xonk
kaxonk
roll
NOW ...
...I'LL SET YOU FREE ...
...LIKE I PROMISED.
WHEN...
snik
YANK
?!
flicker——

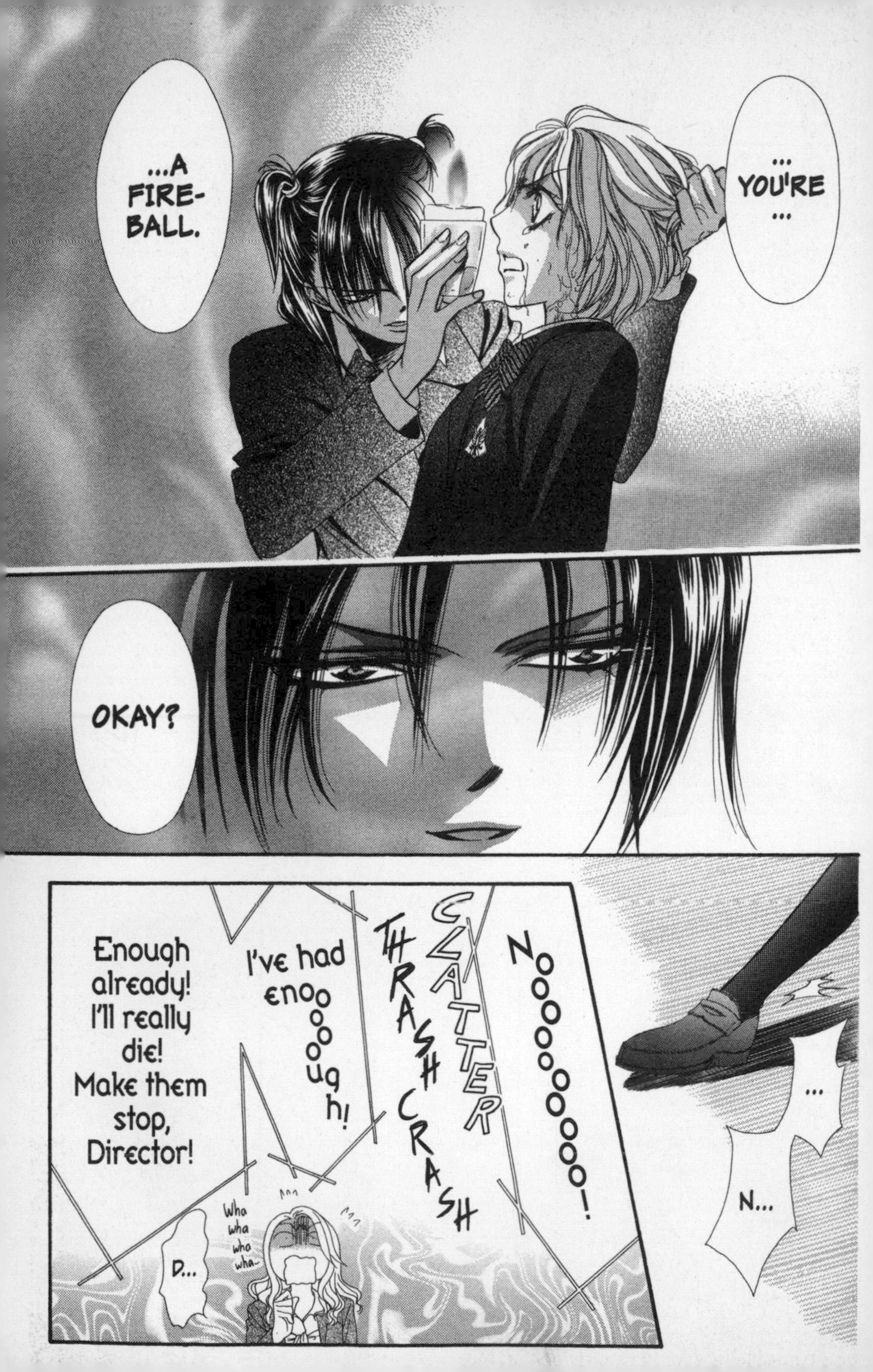
...YOU'RE...
...A FIRE-BALL.
OKAY?
...
N...
NOOOOOOOOOOO!
CLATTER
THRASH CRASH
I've had enoooooough!
Enough already! I'll really die! Make them stop, Director!
Wha wha wha wha...
D...

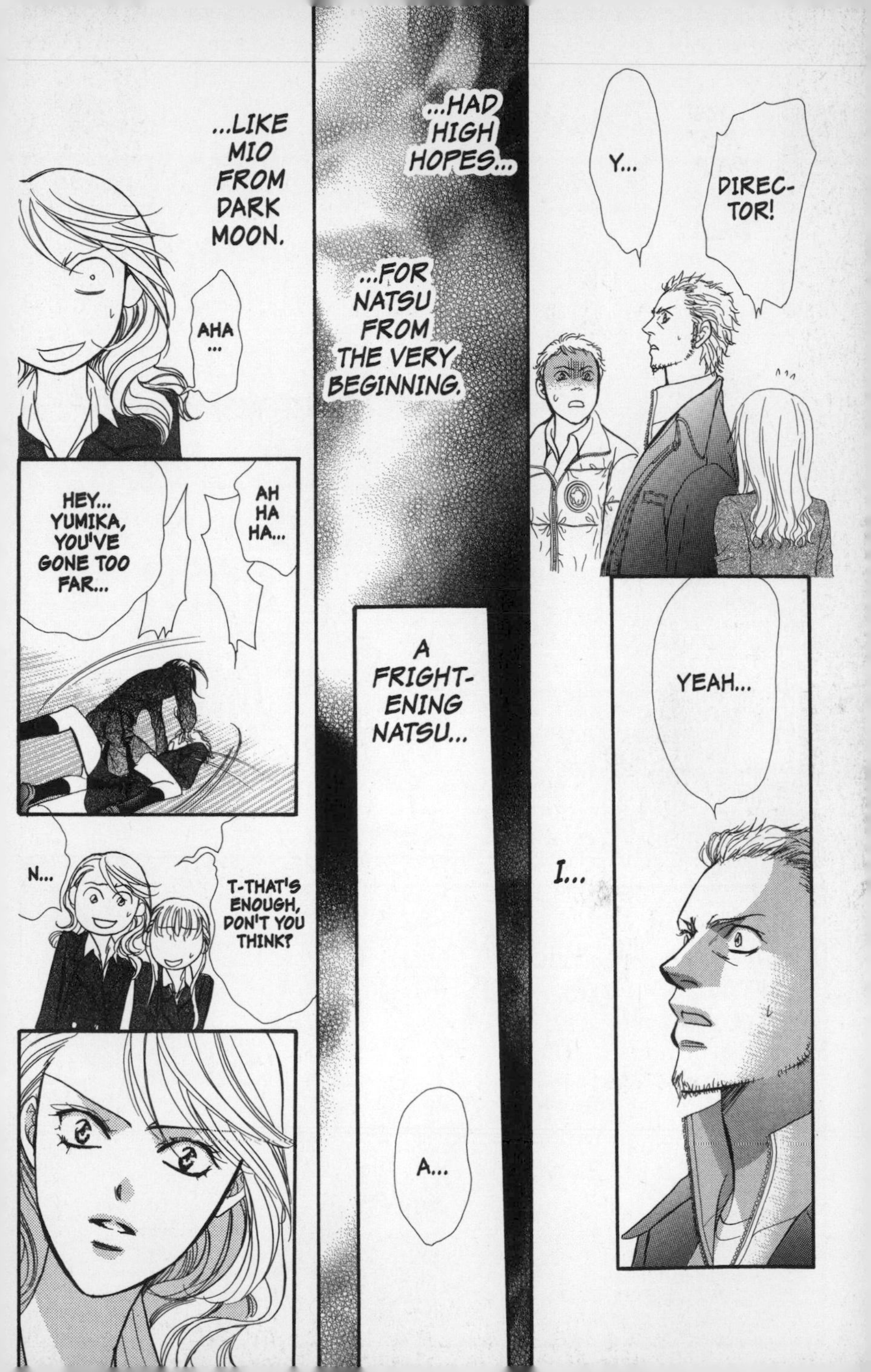
Y...
DIREC-TOR!
YEAH...
I...
...HAD HIGH HOPES...
...FOR NATSU FROM THE VERY BEGINNING.
A FRIGHT-ENING NATSU...
A...
...LIKE MIO FROM DARK MOON.
AHA ...
AH HA HA...
HEY... YUMIKA, YOU'VE GONE TOO FAR...
T-THAT'S ENOUGH, DON'T YOU THINK?
N...

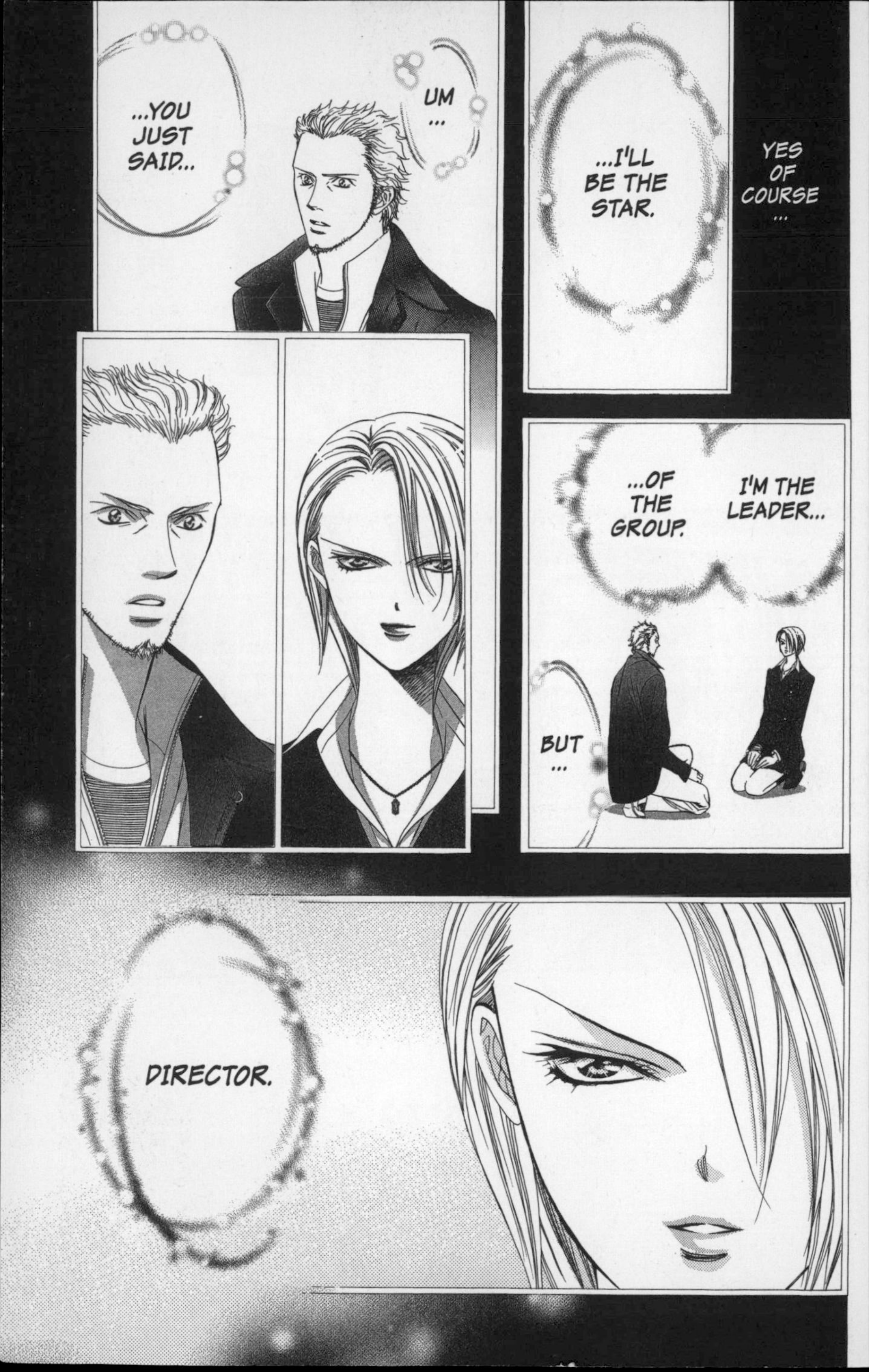
YES OF COURSE ...
...I'LL BE THE STAR.
UM ...
...YOU JUST SAID...
I'M THE LEADER...
...OF THE GROUP.
BUT ...
DIRECTOR.

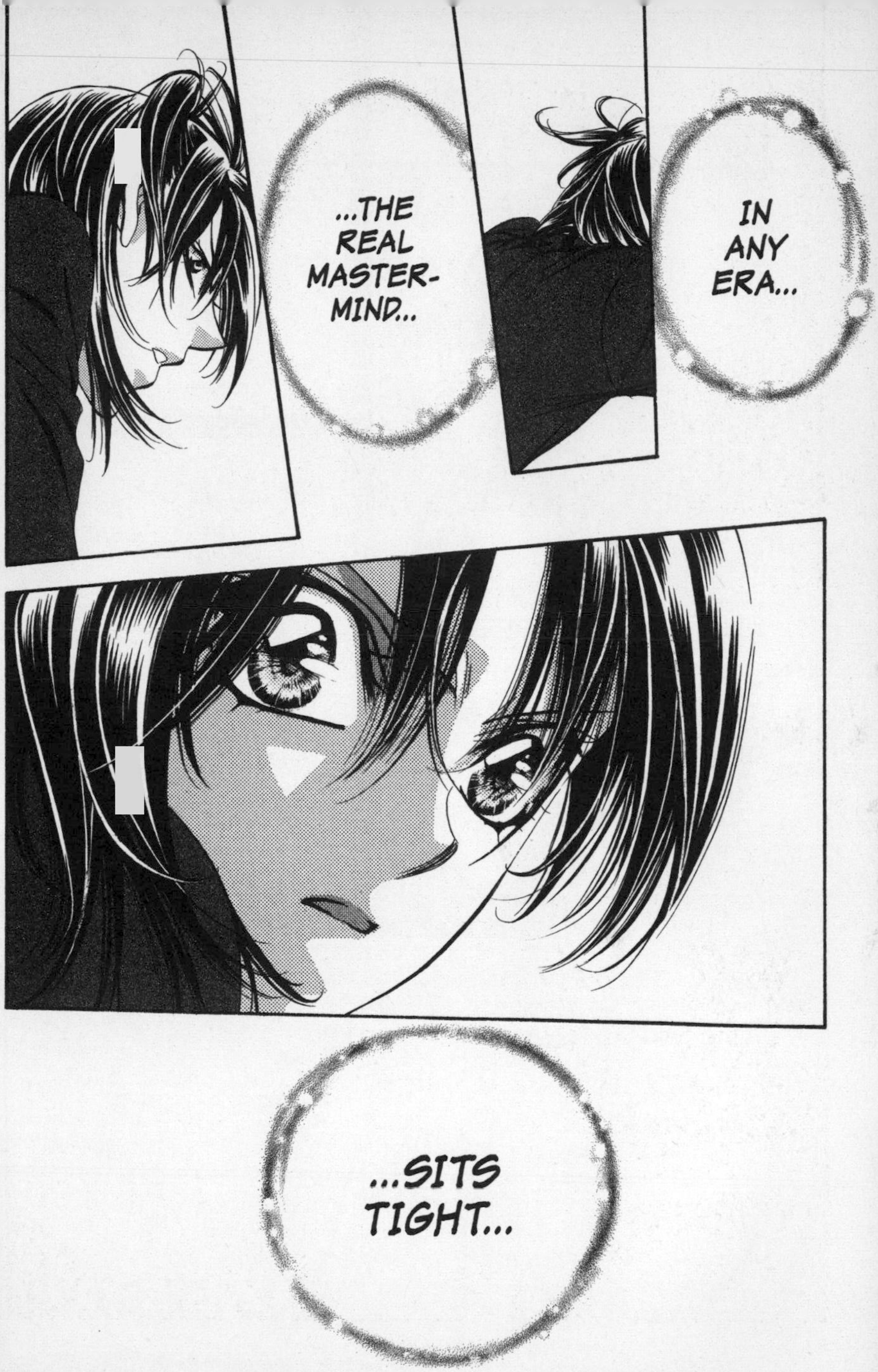
IN ANY ERA...
...THE REAL MASTER-MIND...
...SITS TIGHT...

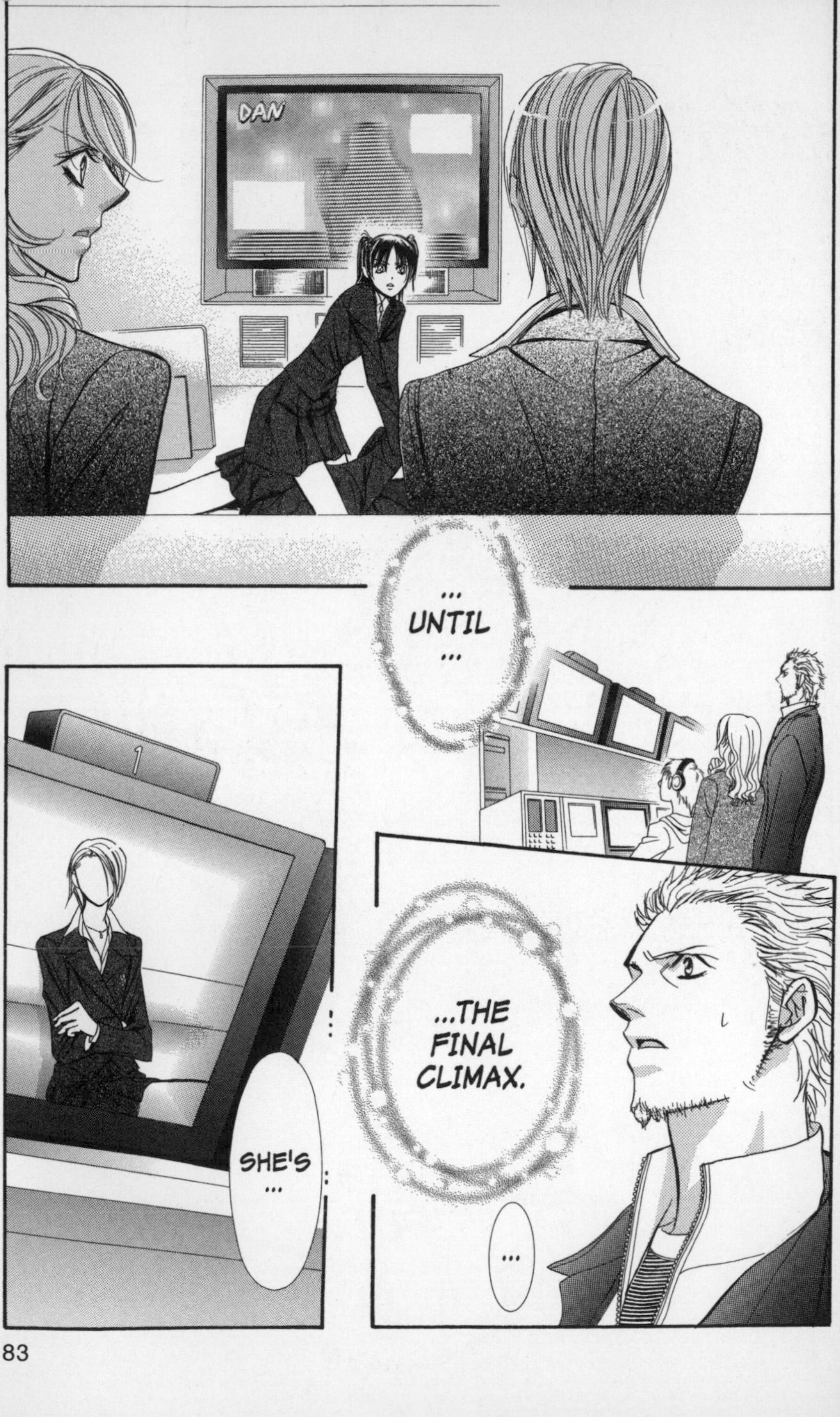
DAN
... UNTIL ...
...THE FINAL CLIMAX.
...
SHE'S ...

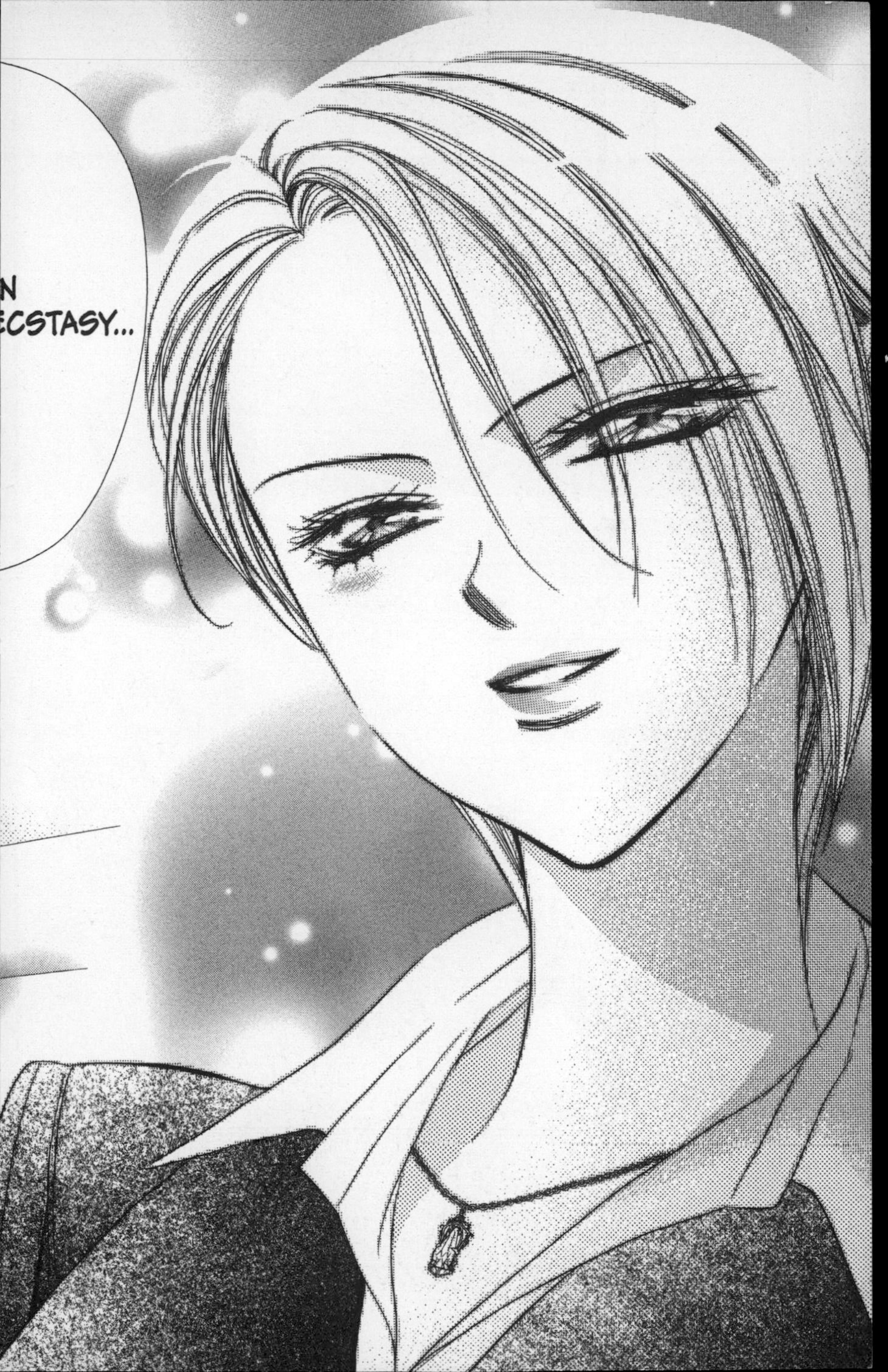
N
ECSTASY...

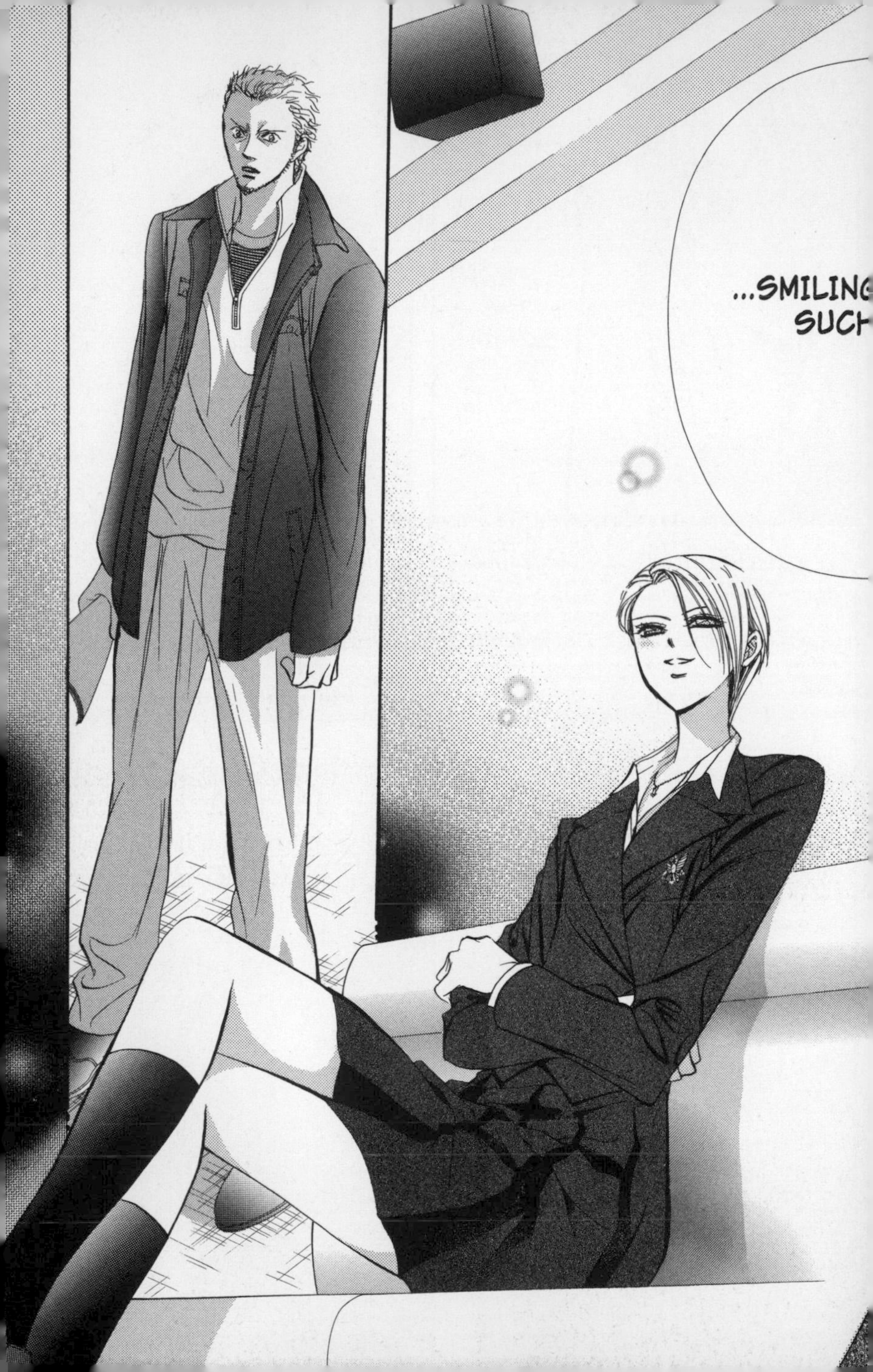
...SMILING SUCH

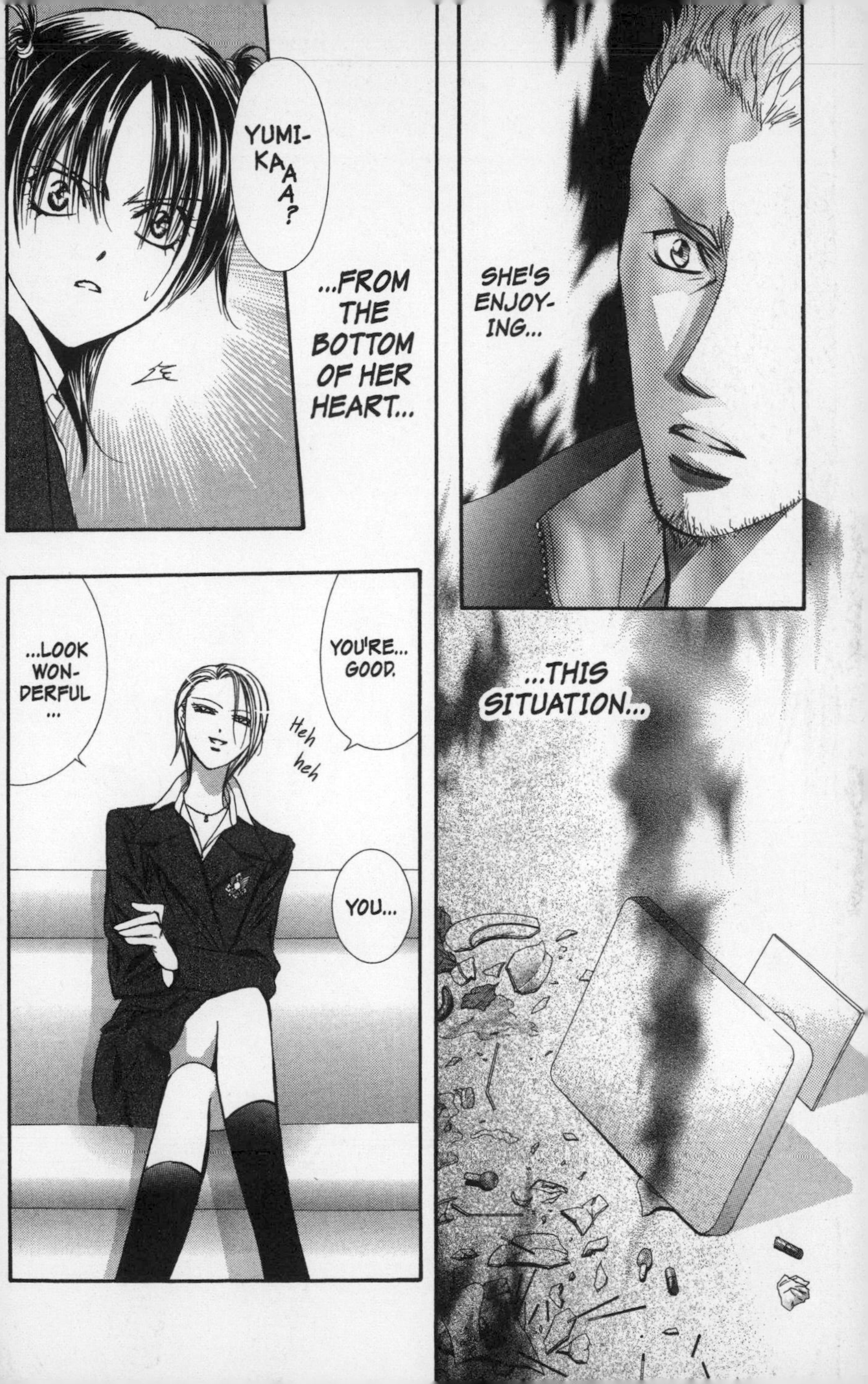
SHE'S ENJOY-ING...
YUMI-KAAAA?
...FROM THE BOTTOM OF HER HEART...
...THIS SITUATION...
YOU'RE... GOOD.
Heh heh
...LOOK WON-DERFUL...
YOU...

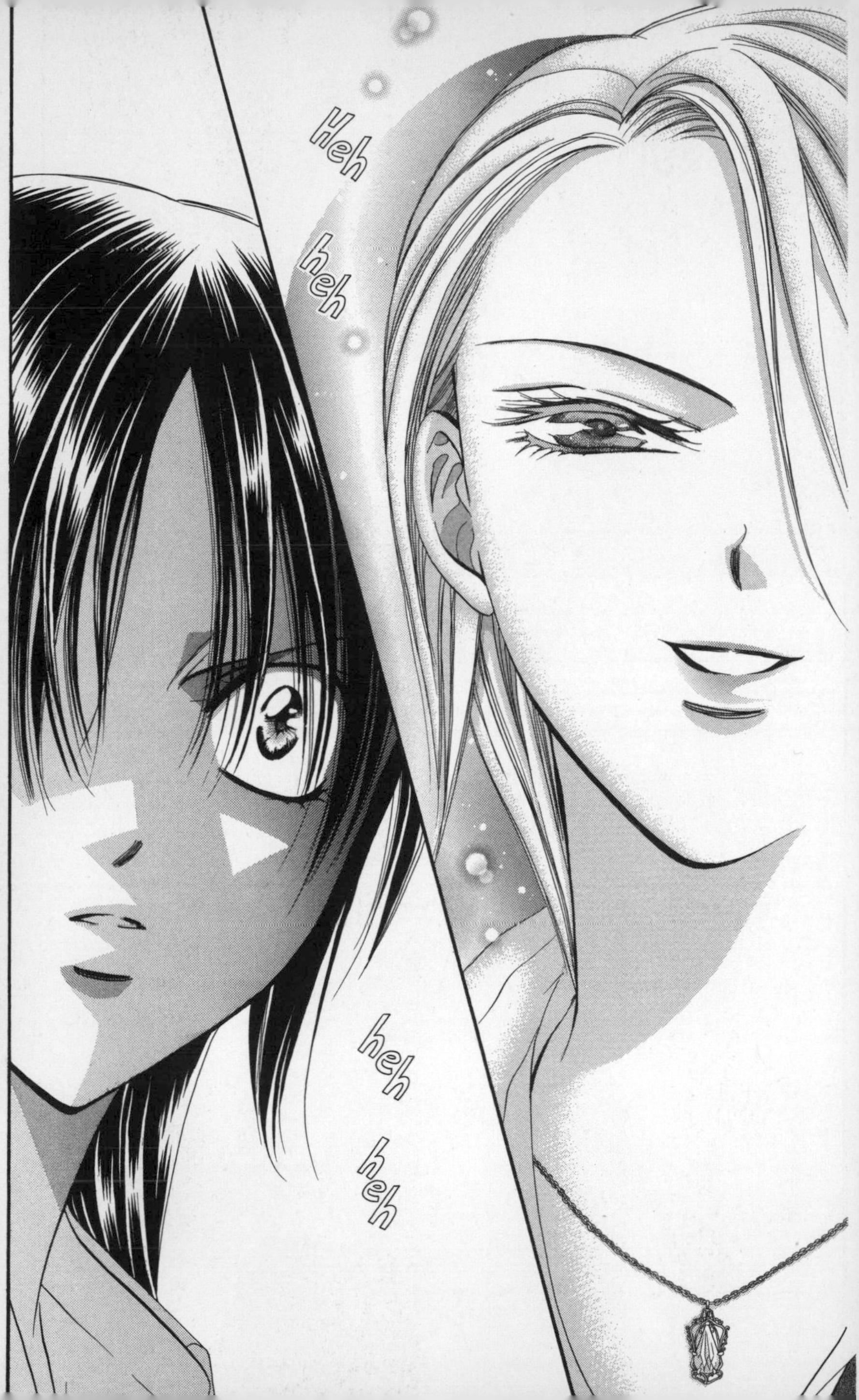
Heh
heh
heh
heh

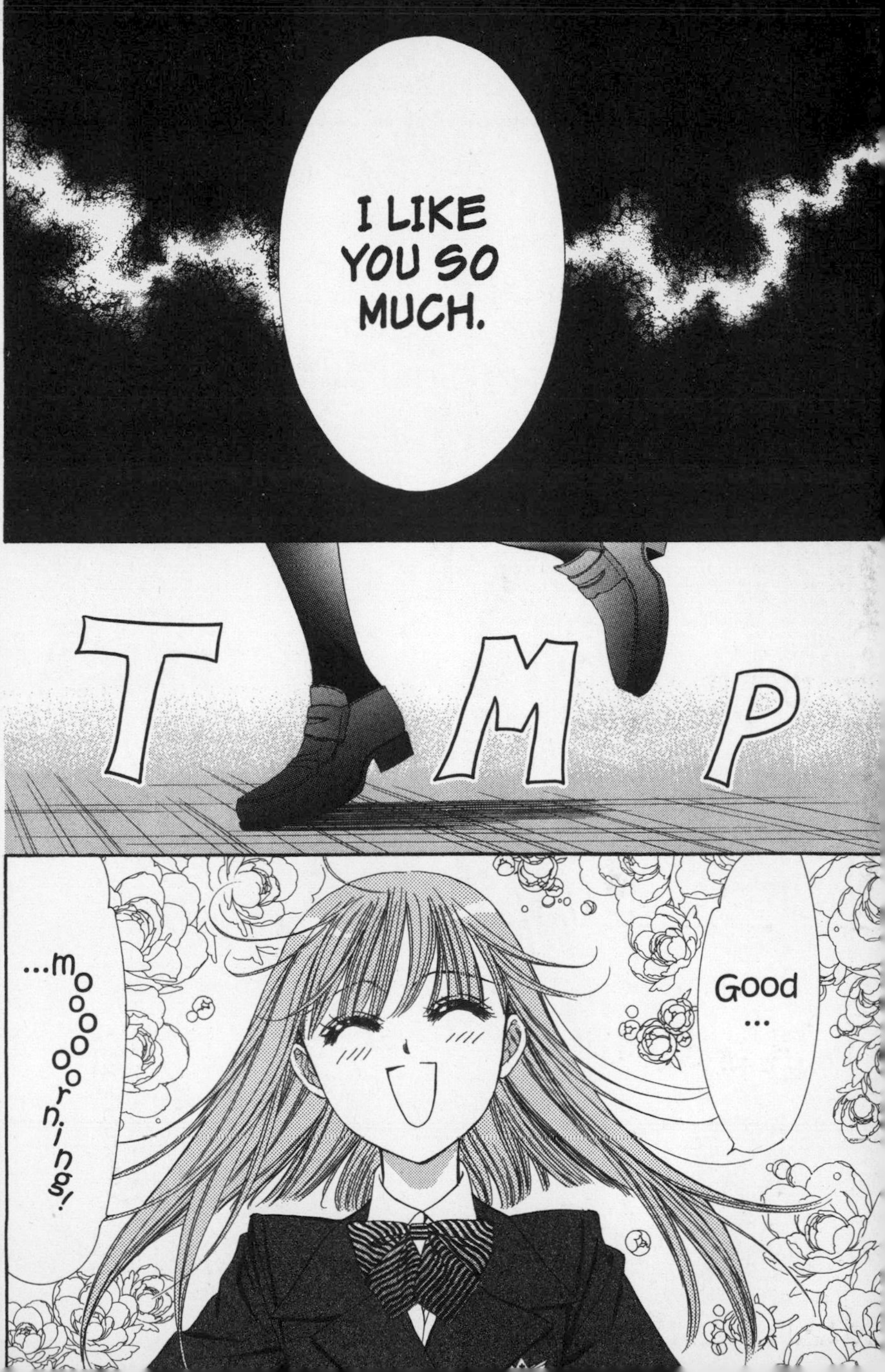
I LIKE YOU SO MUCH.
TMP
Good ...
...mooooooorning!

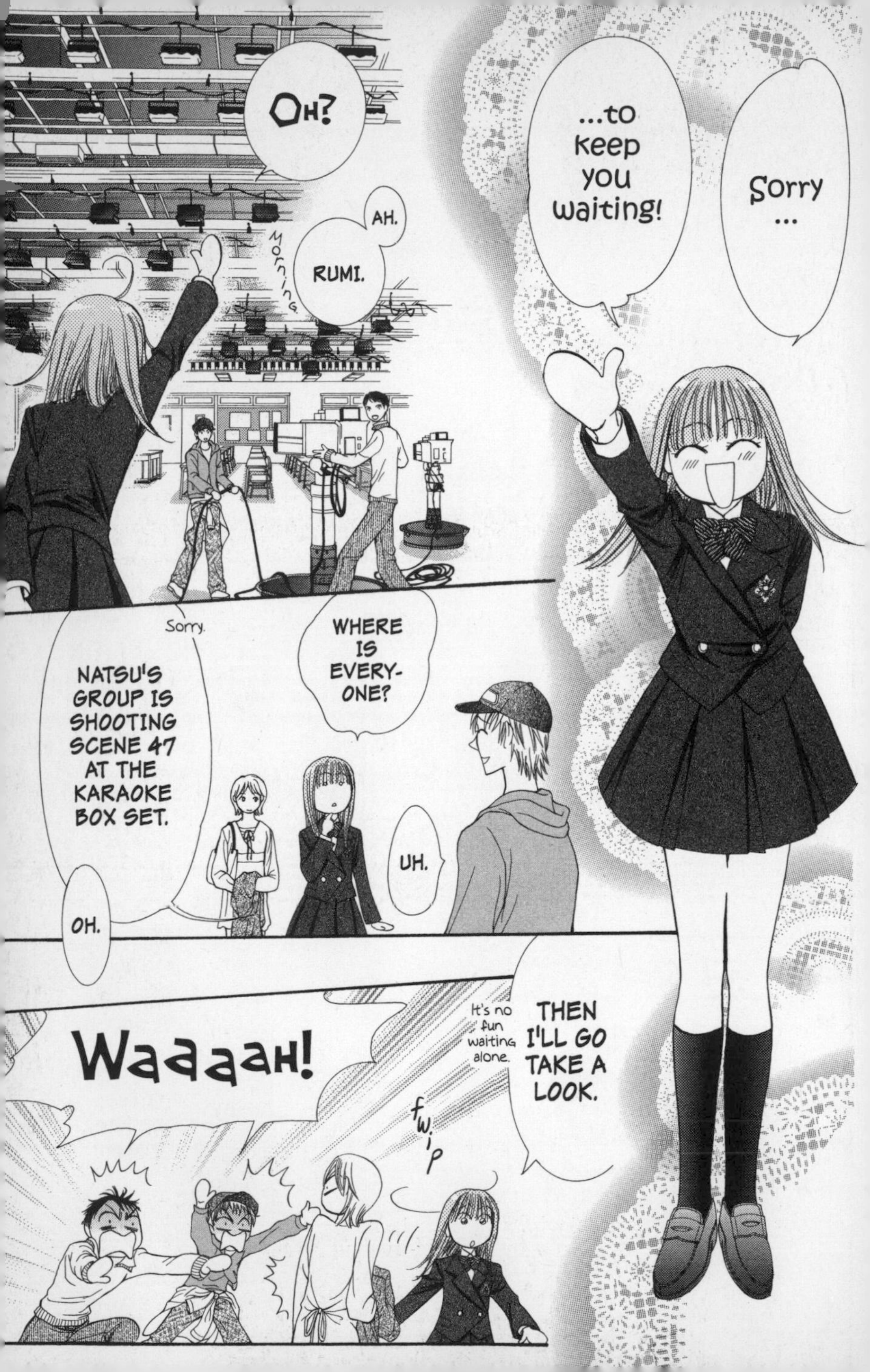
Sorry ...
...to keep you waiting!
OH?
AH.
RUMI.
Morning.
WHERE IS EVERY-ONE?
UH.
Sorry.
NATSU'S GROUP IS SHOOTING SCENE 47 AT THE KARAOKE BOX SET.
OH.
THEN I'LL GO TAKE A LOOK.
It's no fun waiting alone.
fwip
Waaaah!

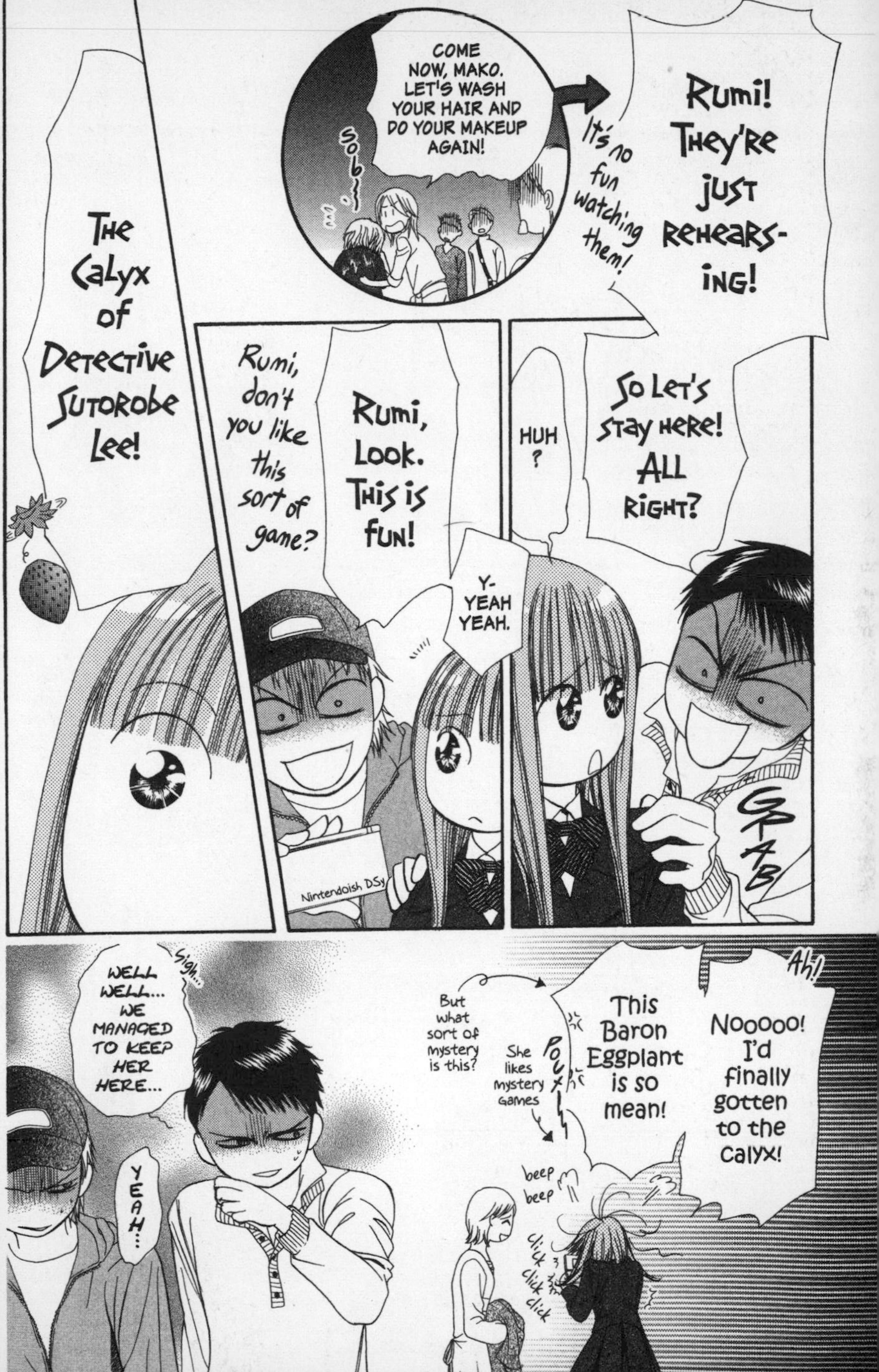

COME NOW, MAKO. LET'S WASH YOUR HAIR AND DO YOUR MAKEUP AGAIN!
Sob~
Rumi! They're just rehears-ing!
It's no fun watching them!
So let's stay here! All right?
HUH?
GRAB
Rumi, look. This is fun!
Rumi, don't you like this sort of game?
Y-YEAH YEAH.
Nintendoish DSy
The Calyx of Detective Sutorobe Lee!
Ah!
Nooooo! I'd finally gotten to the calyx!
This Baron Eggplant is so mean!
POUT
But what sort of mystery is this?
She likes mystery games
beep beep
click click click
WELL WELL... WE MANAGED TO KEEP HER HERE...
Sigh...
YEAH...

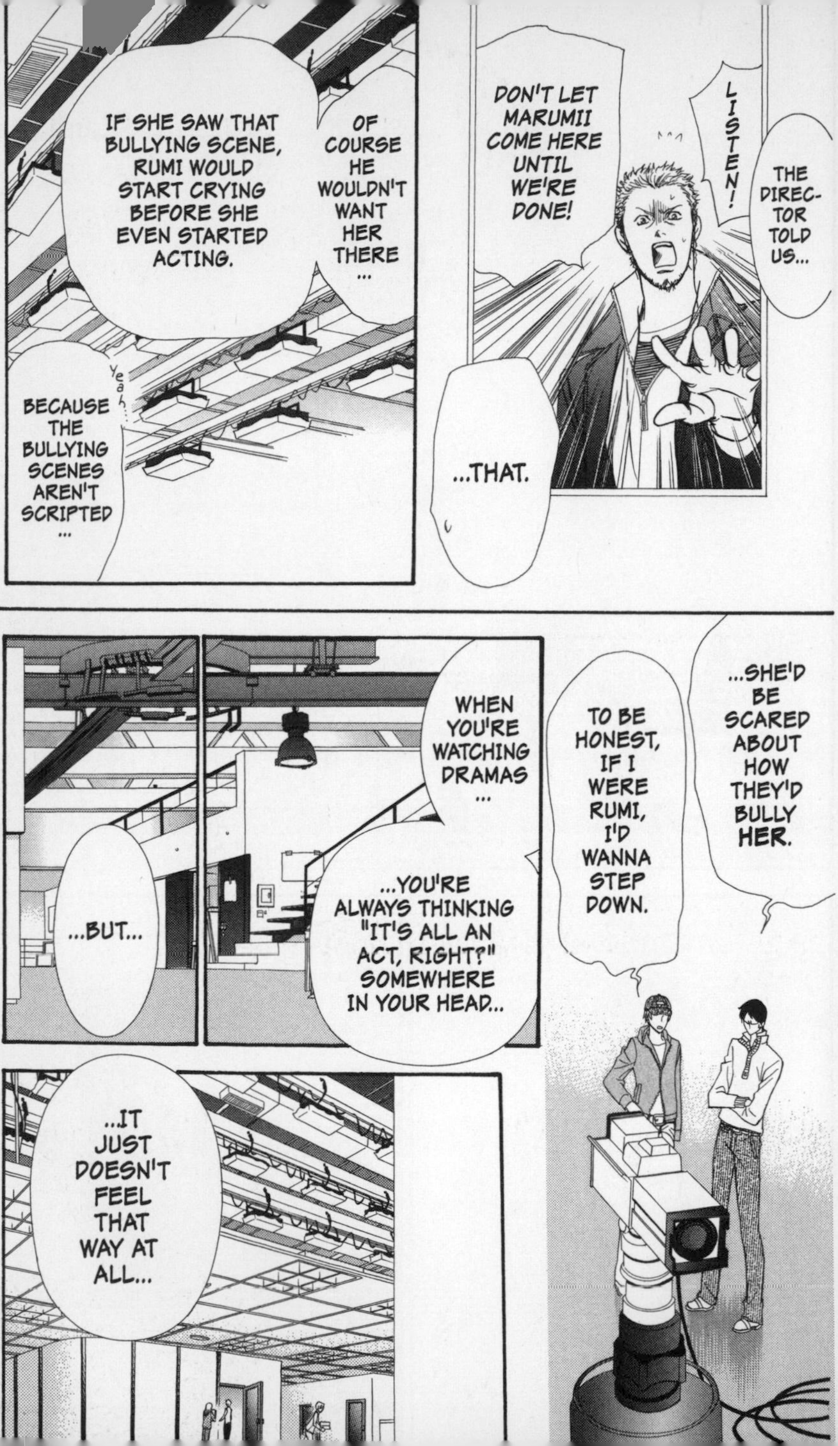
THE DIRECTOR TOLD US...
LISTEN!
DON'T LET MARUMII COME HERE UNTIL WE'RE DONE!
...THAT.
OF COURSE HE WOULDN'T WANT HER THERE...
IF SHE SAW THAT BULLYING SCENE, RUMI WOULD START CRYING BEFORE SHE EVEN STARTED ACTING.
Yeah...
BECAUSE THE BULLYING SCENES AREN'T SCRIPTED...
...SHE'D BE SCARED ABOUT HOW THEY'D BULLY HER.
TO BE HONEST, IF I WERE RUMI, I'D WANNA STEP DOWN.
WHEN YOU'RE WATCHING DRAMAS...
...YOU'RE ALWAYS THINKING "IT'S ALL AN ACT, RIGHT?" SOMEWHERE IN YOUR HEAD...
...BUT...
...IT JUST DOESN'T FEEL THAT WAY AT ALL...

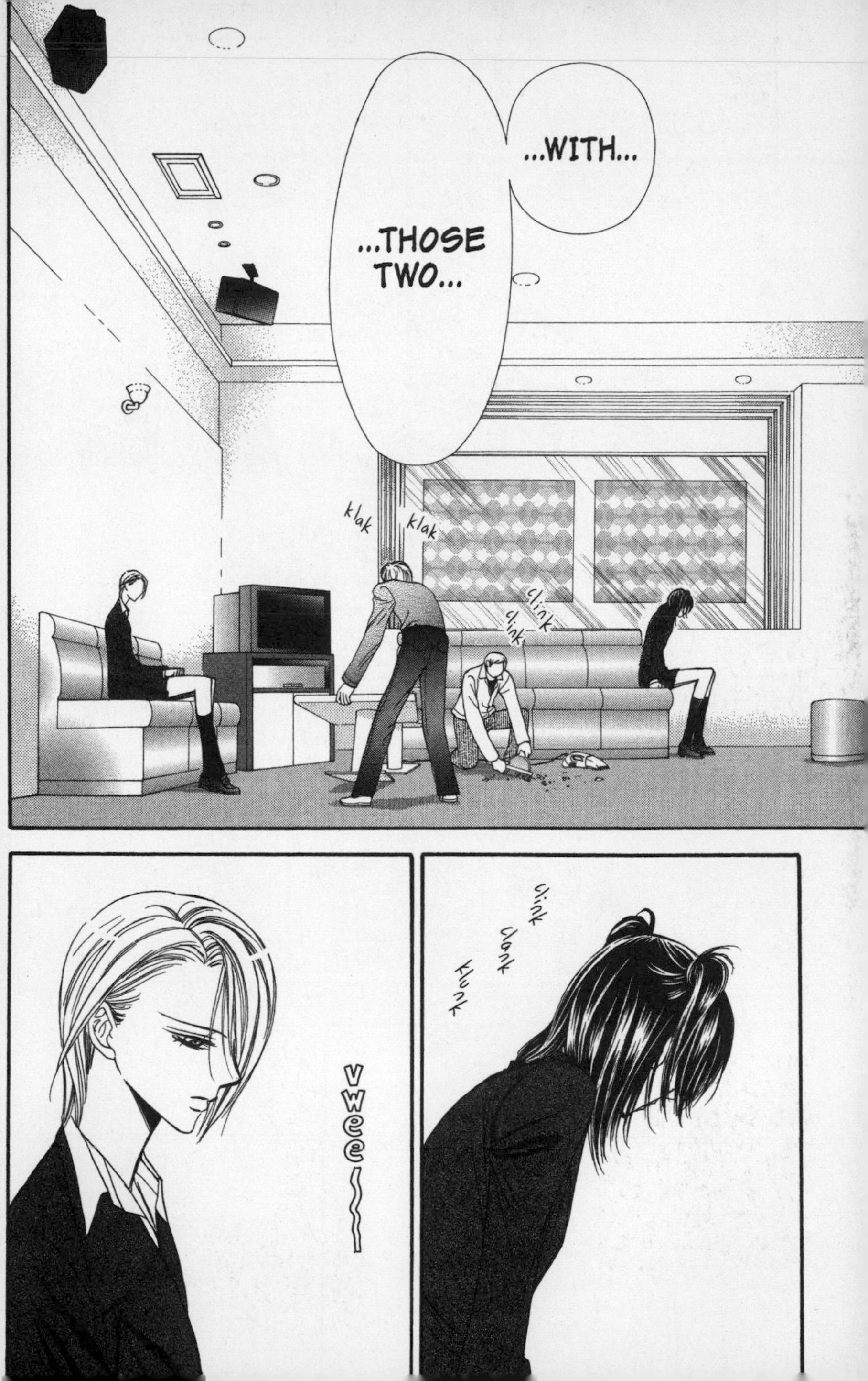
...WITH...
...THOSE TWO...
klak
klak
clink
clink
clink
clank
klunk
vwee~~~

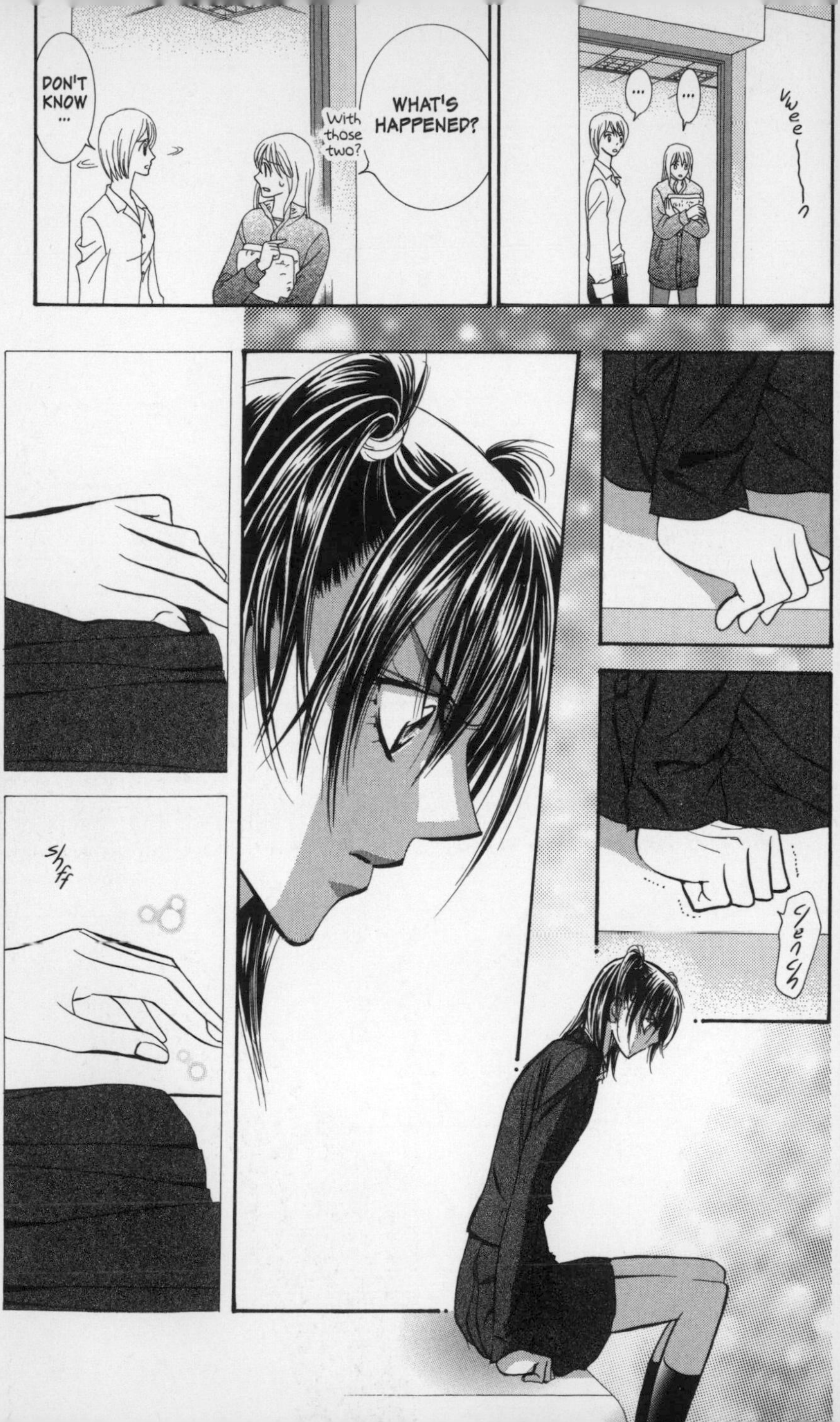
vwee——n
...
...
WHAT'S HAPPENED?
With those two?
DON'T KNOW ...
clench
shff

End of Act 135

Skip·Beat!

Act 136: Kiss and Cry

klak

klak

Blah
Blah
Blah Blah

tmp

tmp

tmp

I
FEEL
LIKE
I'VE
LOST...

...

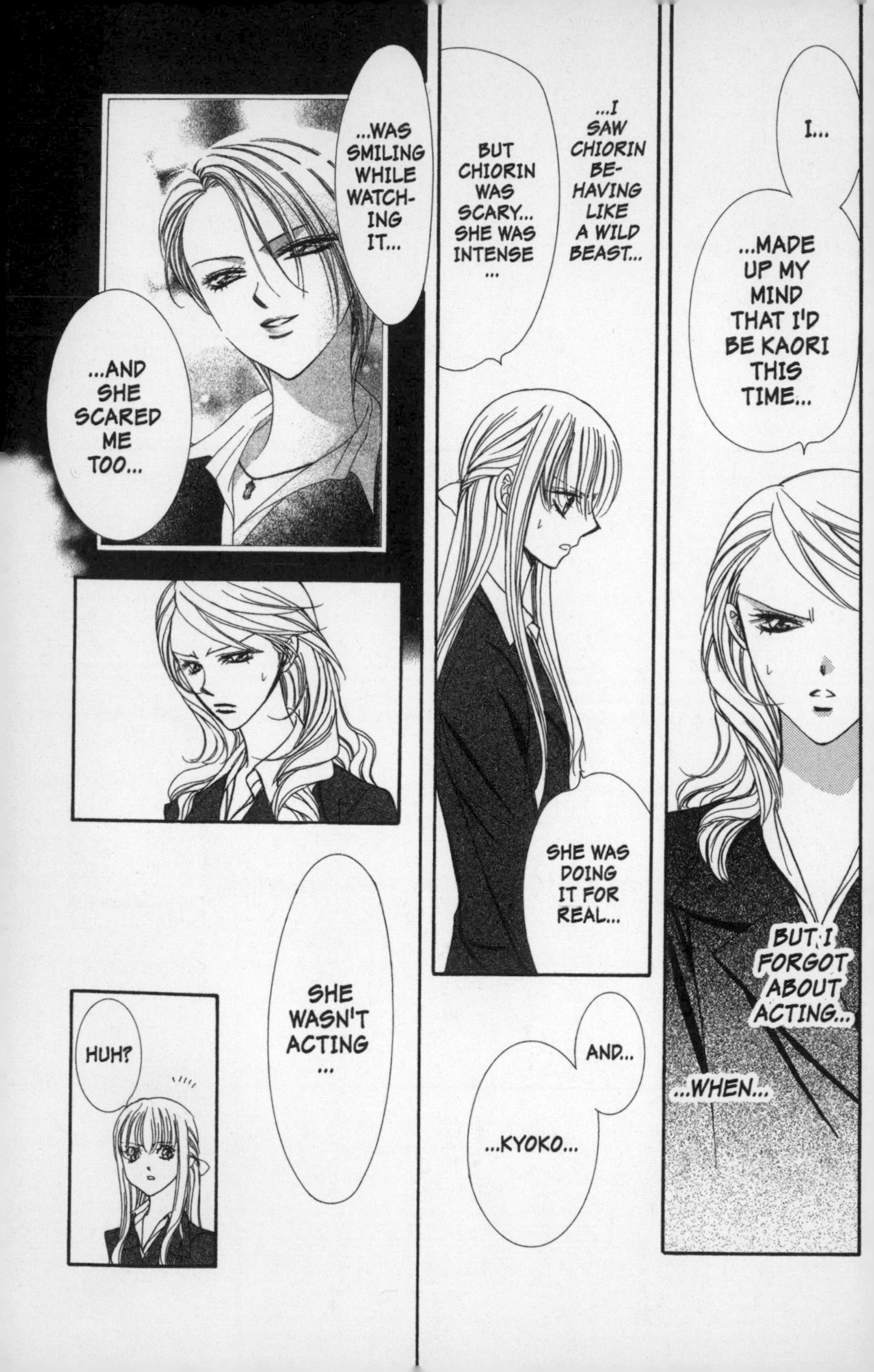
I...
...MADE UP MY MIND THAT I'D BE KAORI THIS TIME...
BUT I FORGOT ABOUT ACTING...
...WHEN...
...I SAW CHIORIN BE-HAVING LIKE A WILD BEAST...
BUT CHIORIN WAS SCARY... SHE WAS INTENSE...
SHE WAS DOING IT FOR REAL...
AND...
...KYOKO...
...WAS SMILING WHILE WATCH-ING IT...
...AND SHE SCARED ME TOO...
SHE WASN'T ACTING...
HUH?

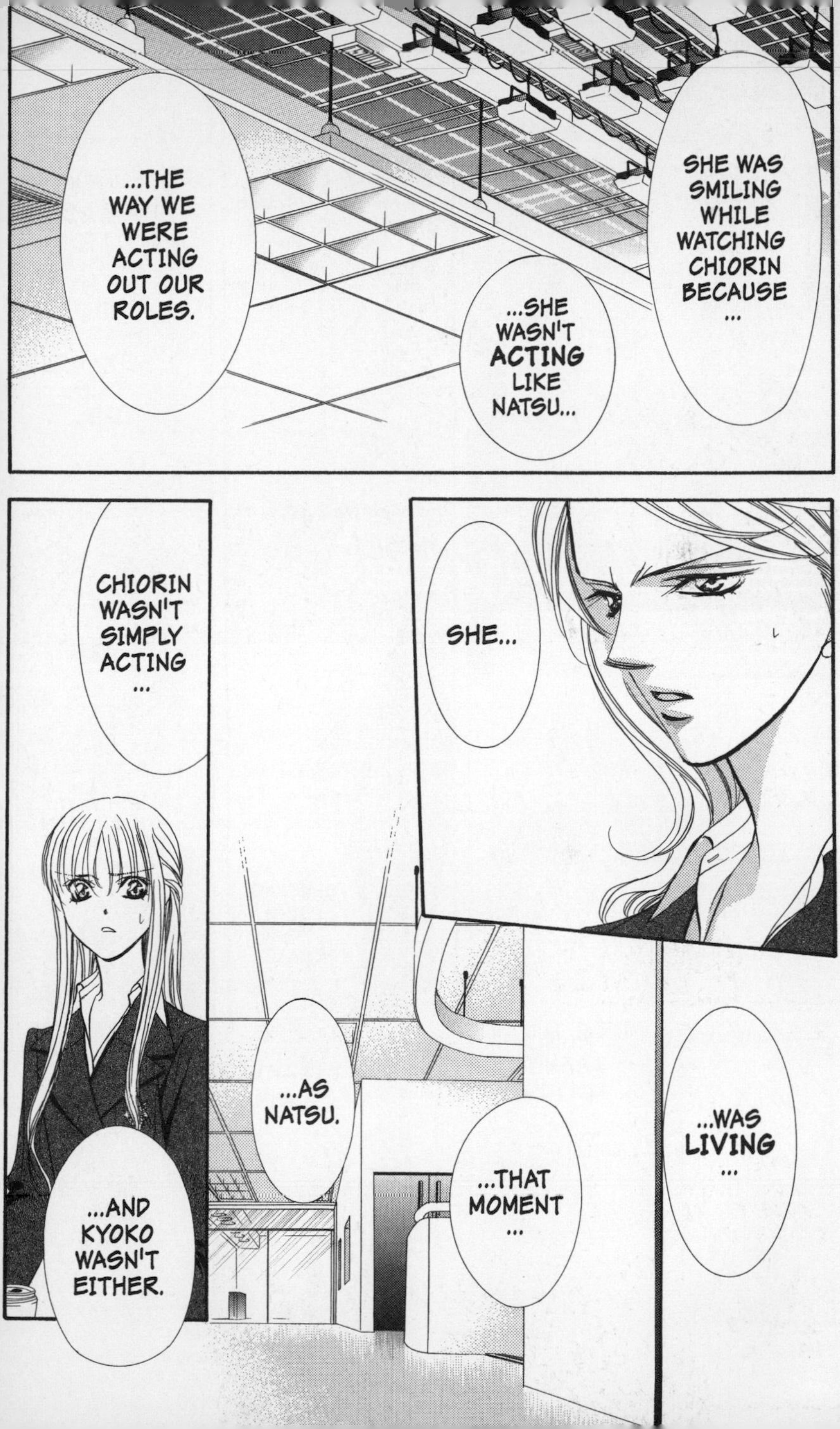
SHE WAS SMILING WHILE WATCHING CHIORIN BECAUSE ...
...SHE WASN'T ACTING LIKE NATSU...
...THE WAY WE WERE ACTING OUT OUR ROLES.
SHE...
...WAS LIVING ...
...THAT MOMENT ...
...AS NATSU.
CHIORIN WASN'T SIMPLY ACTING ...
...AND KYOKO WASN'T EITHER.

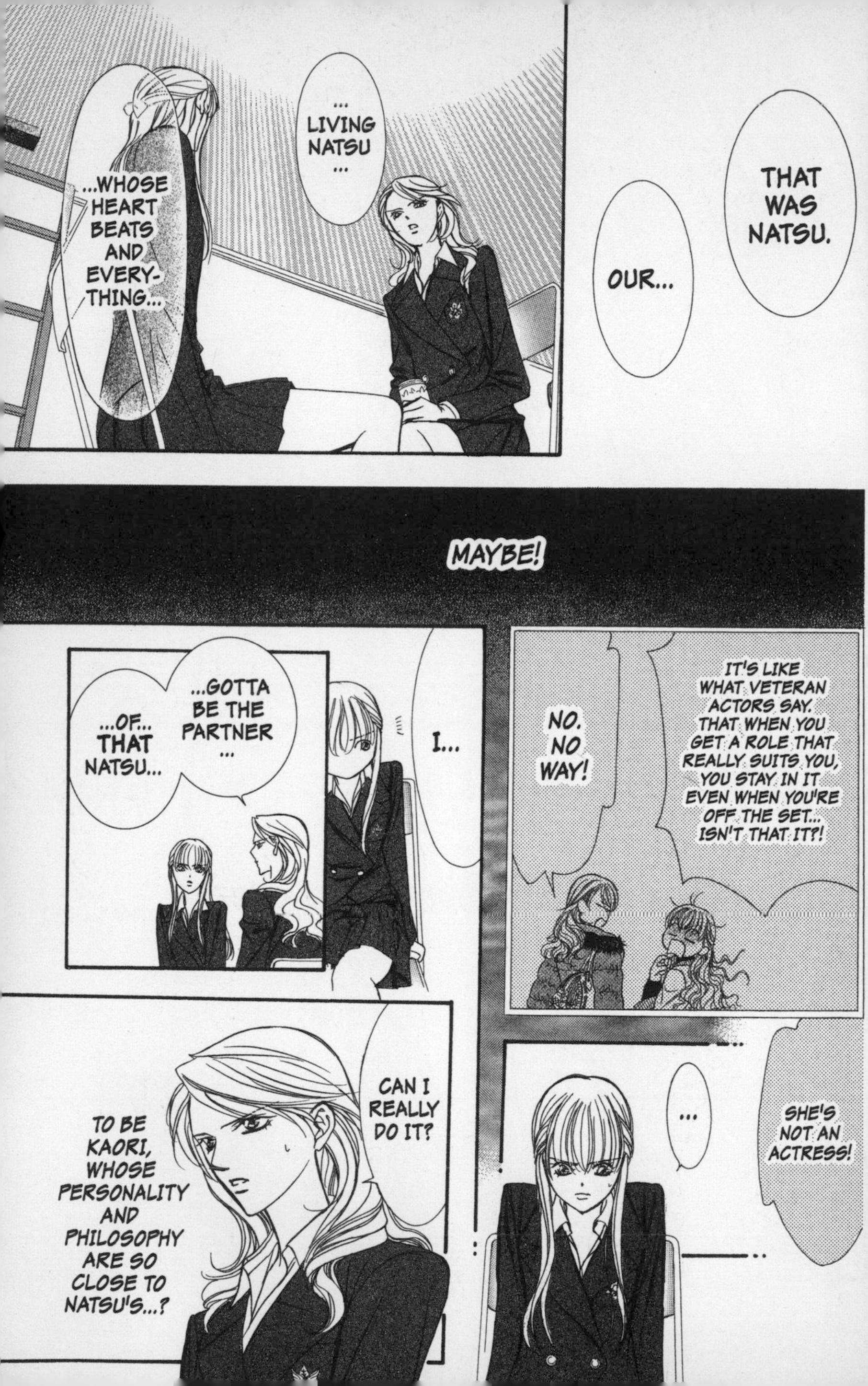
THAT WAS NATSU.
OUR...
... LIVING NATSU ...
...WHOSE HEART BEATS AND EVERY-THING...
MAYBE!
IT'S LIKE WHAT VETERAN ACTORS SAY. THAT WHEN YOU GET A ROLE THAT REALLY SUITS YOU, YOU STAY IN IT EVEN WHEN YOU'RE OFF THE SET... ISN'T THAT IT?!
NO. NO WAY!
I...
...GOTTA BE THE PARTNER ...
...OF... THAT NATSU...
SHE'S NOT AN ACTRESS!
...
CAN I REALLY DO IT?
TO BE KAORI, WHOSE PERSONALITY AND PHILOSOPHY ARE SO CLOSE TO NATSU'S...?

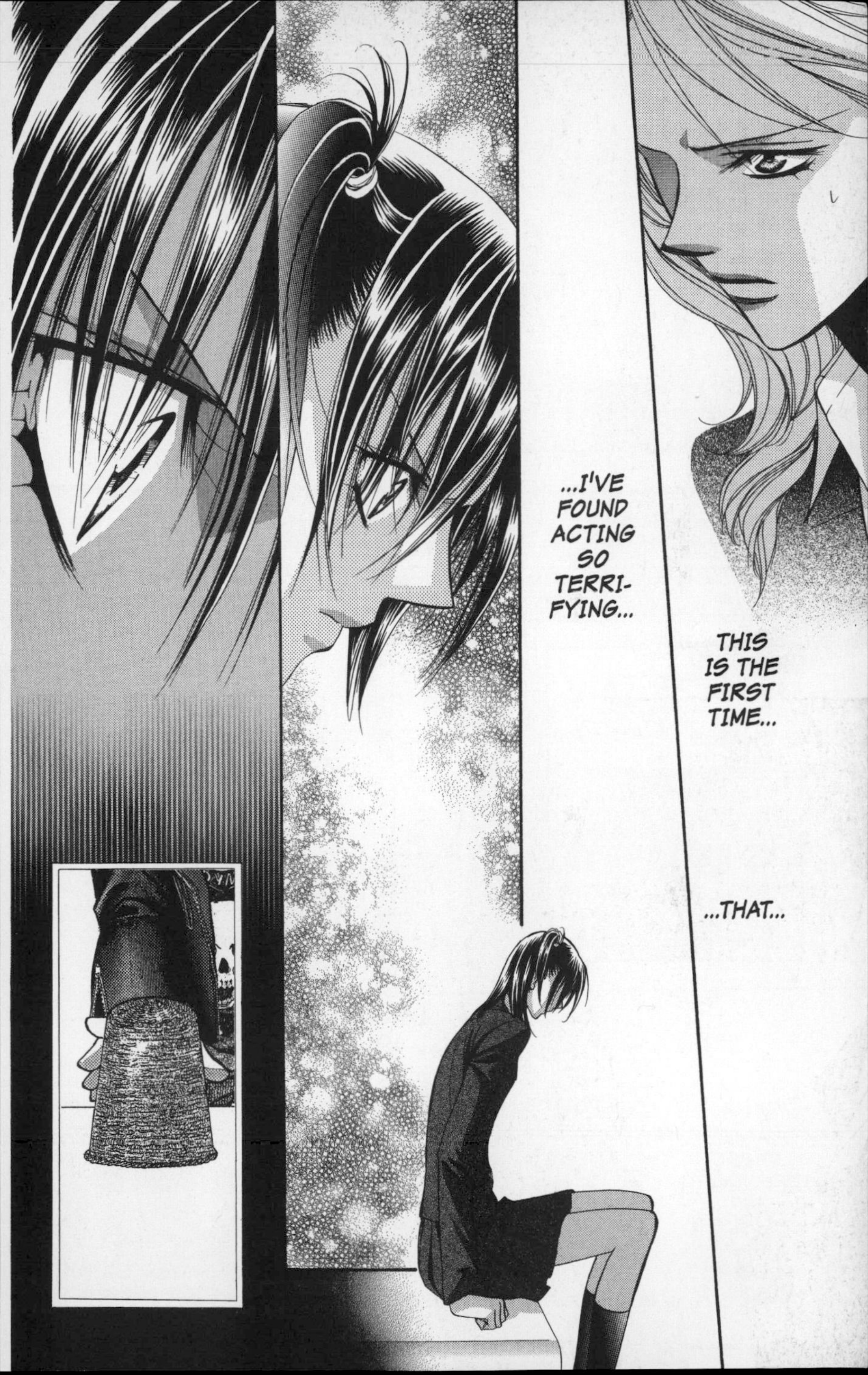
THIS IS THE FIRST TIME...
...THAT...
...I'VE FOUND ACTING SO TERRIFYING...

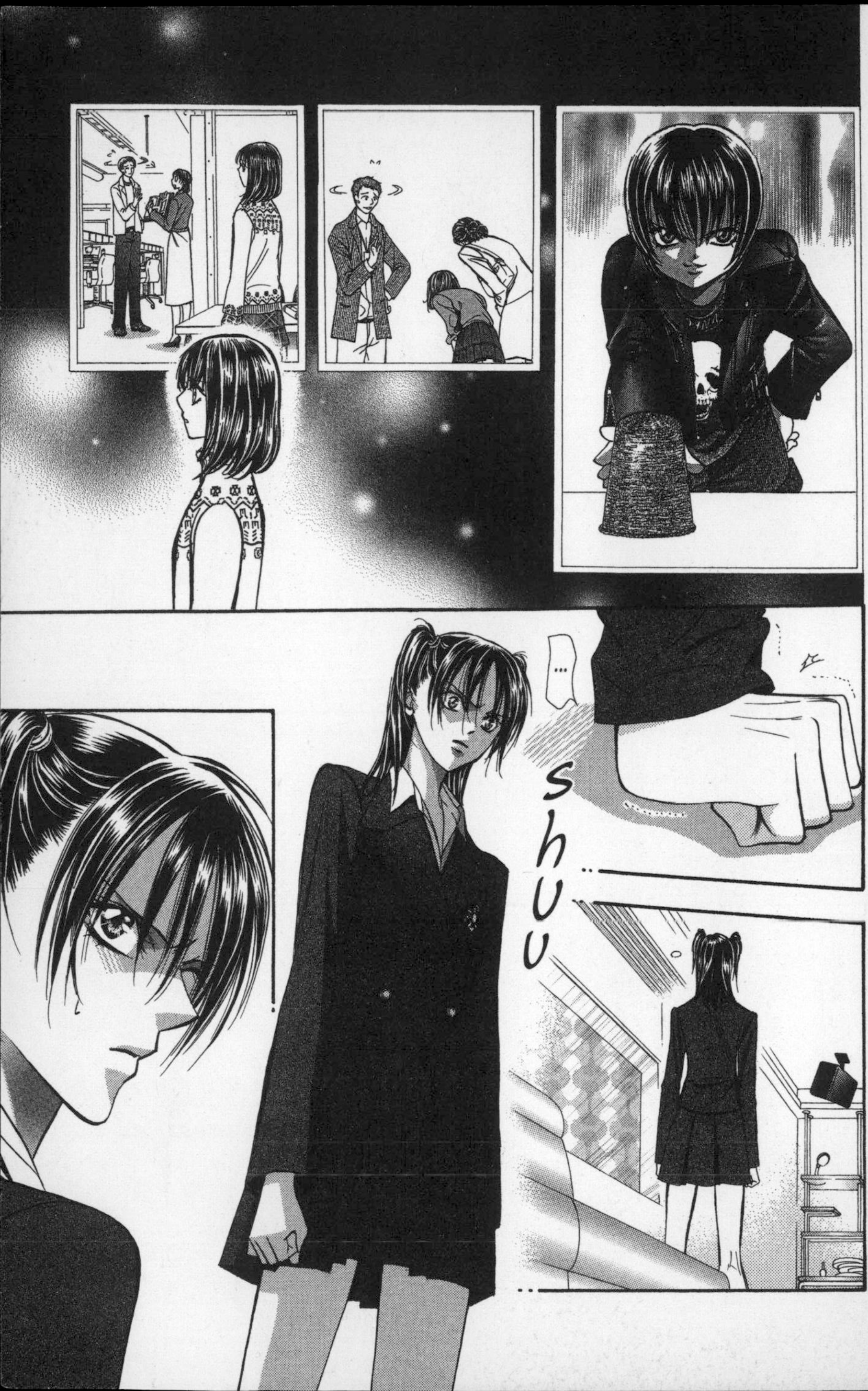
...
SHUUU

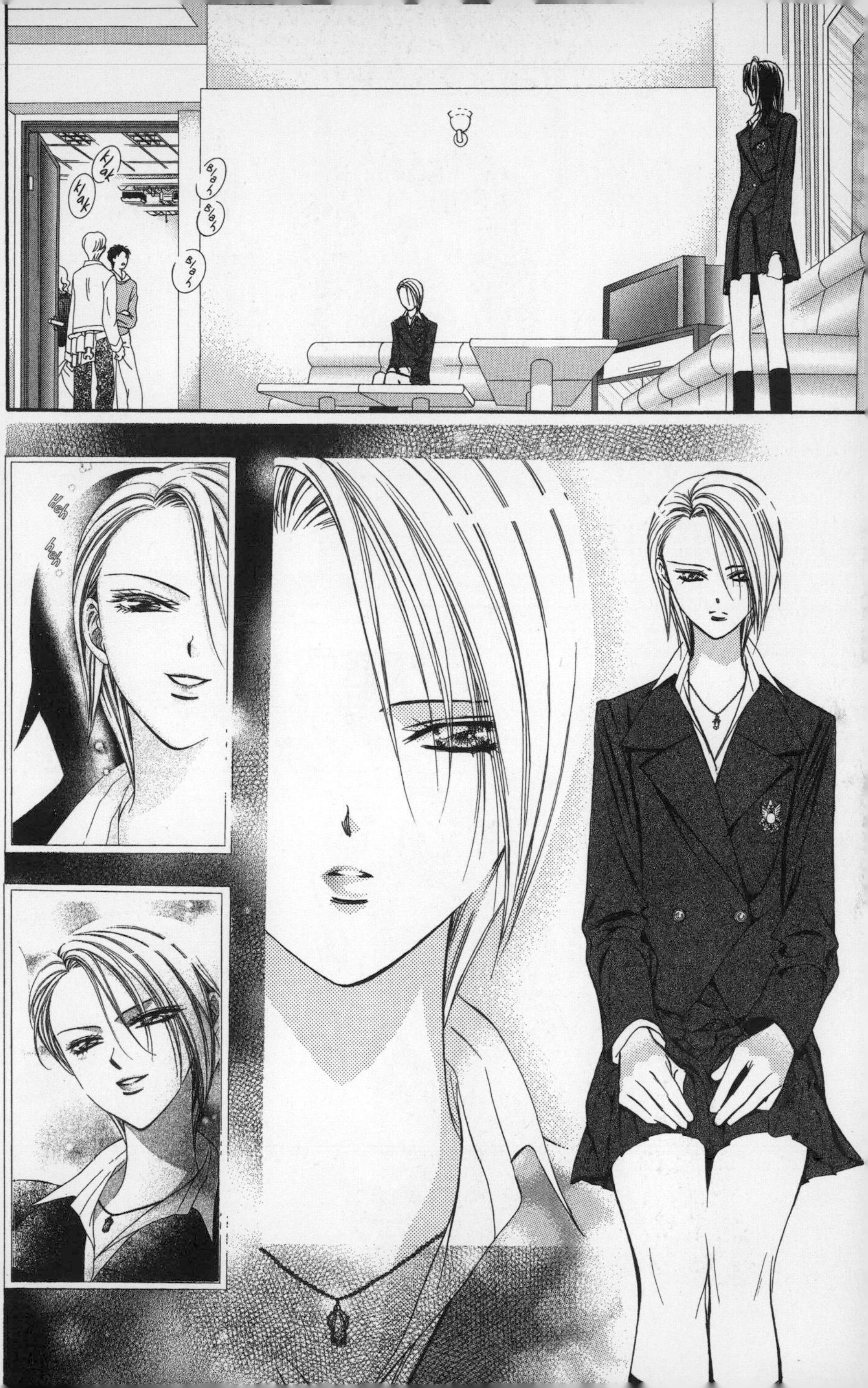
Blah
Blah
Blah
klak
klak
Heh
heh

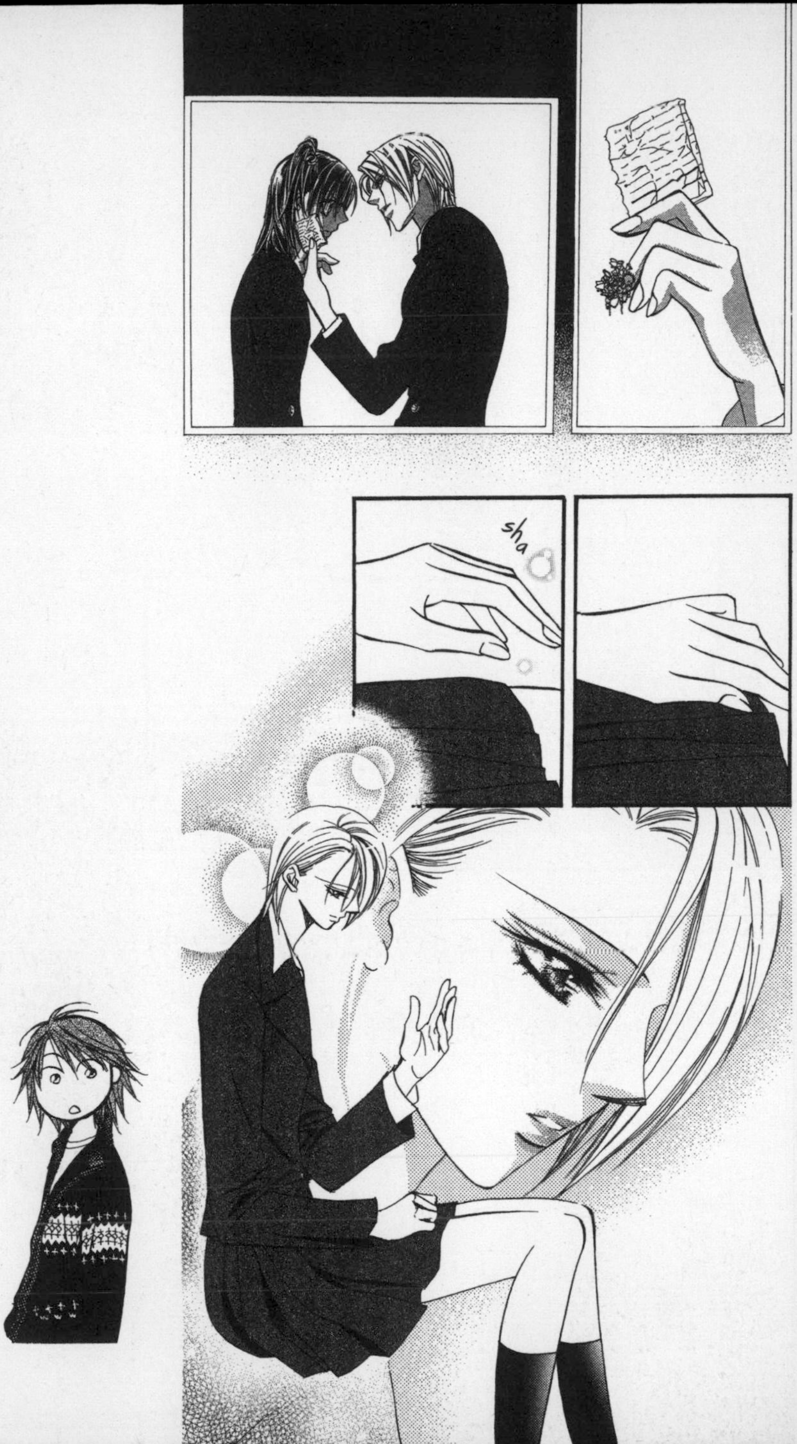
sha

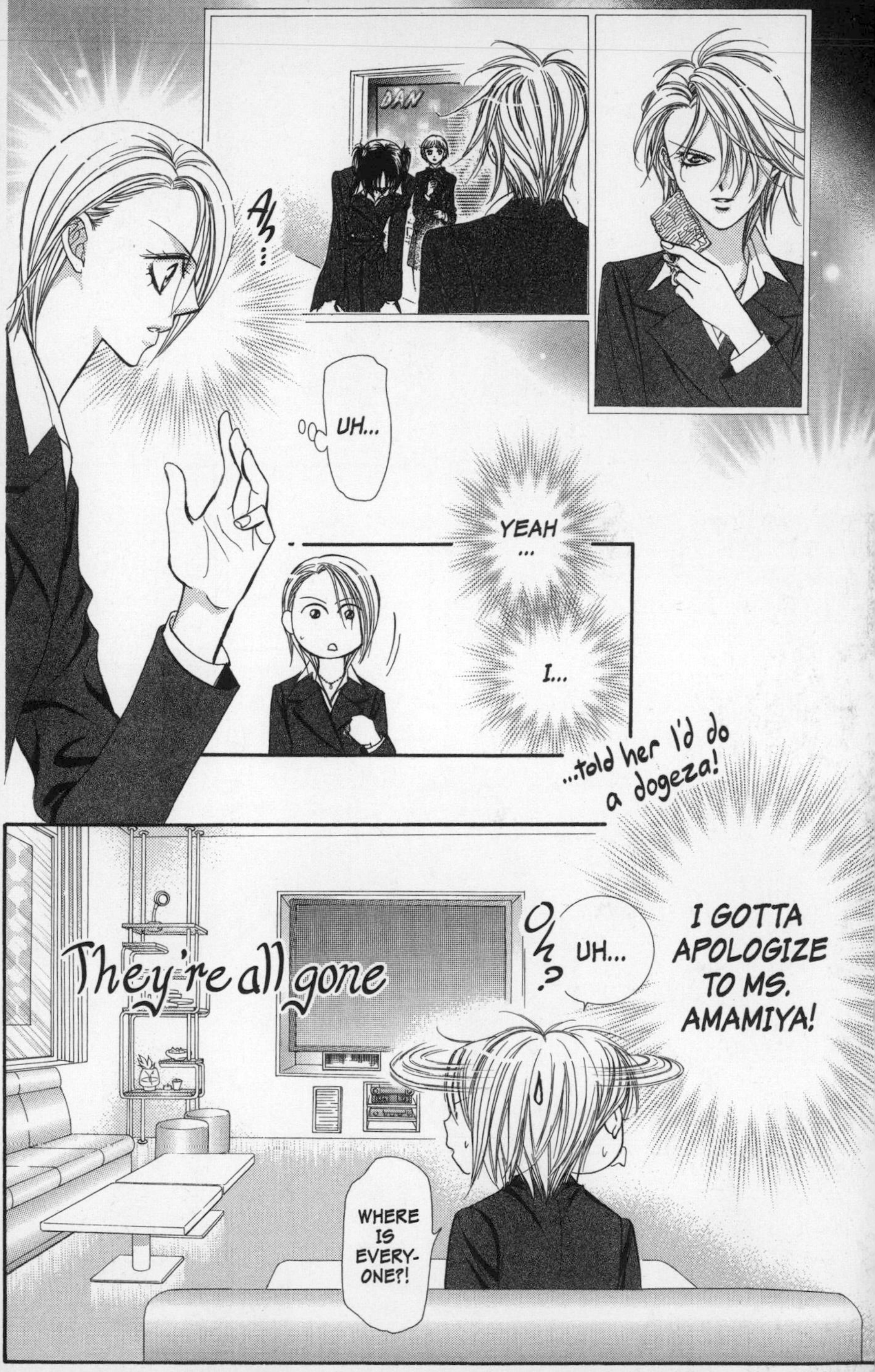
DAN
Ah...
UH...
YEAH ...
I...
...told her I'd do a dogeza!
I GOTTA APOLOGIZE TO MS. AMAMIYA!
Oh?
UH...
They're all gone
WHERE IS EVERY-ONE?!

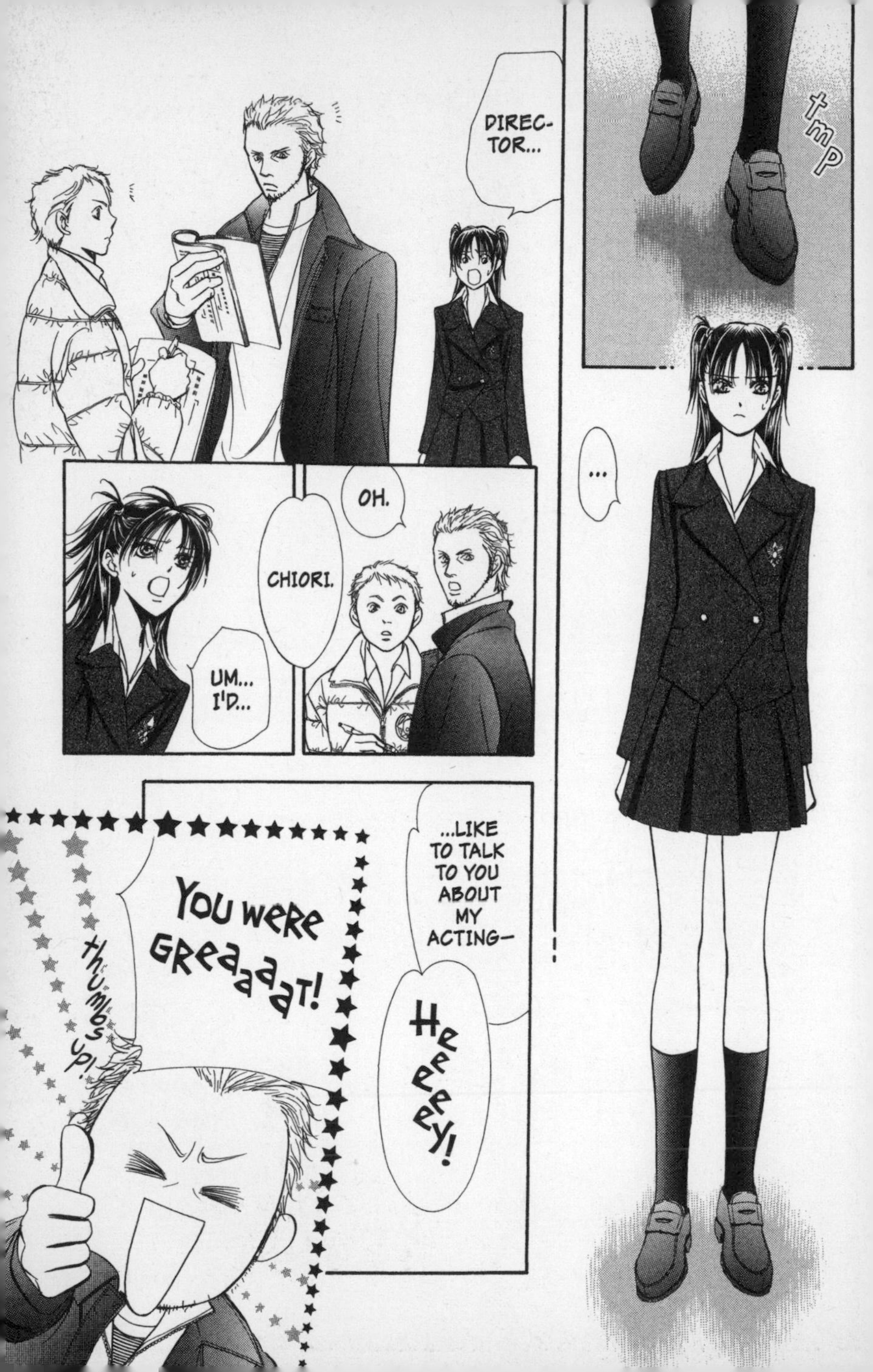
tmp
...
DIREC-TOR...
OH.
CHIORI.
UM... I'D...
...LIKE TO TALK TO YOU ABOUT MY ACTING—
Heeeeey!
You were Greaaaat!
thumbs up!

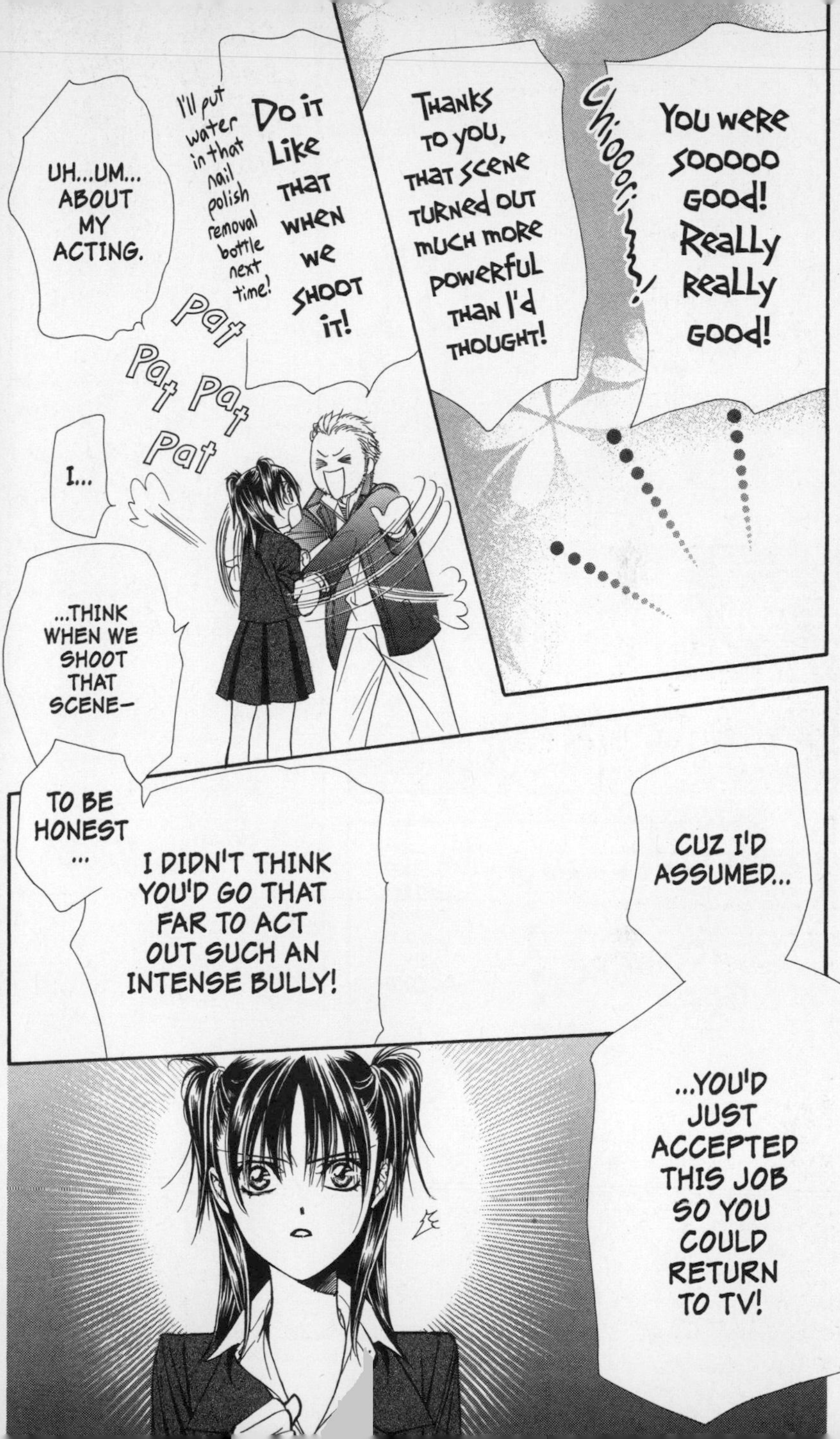
Chiooori~~~!
You were sooooo good! Really really good!
Thanks to you, that scene turned out much more powerful than I'd thought!
Do it like that when we shoot it!
I'll put water in that nail polish removal bottle next time!
Pat Pat Pat Pat
Uh...um... about my acting.
I...
...think when we shoot that scene—
To be honest...
I didn't think you'd go that far to act out such an intense bully!
Cuz I'd assumed...
...you'd just accepted this job so you could return to TV!

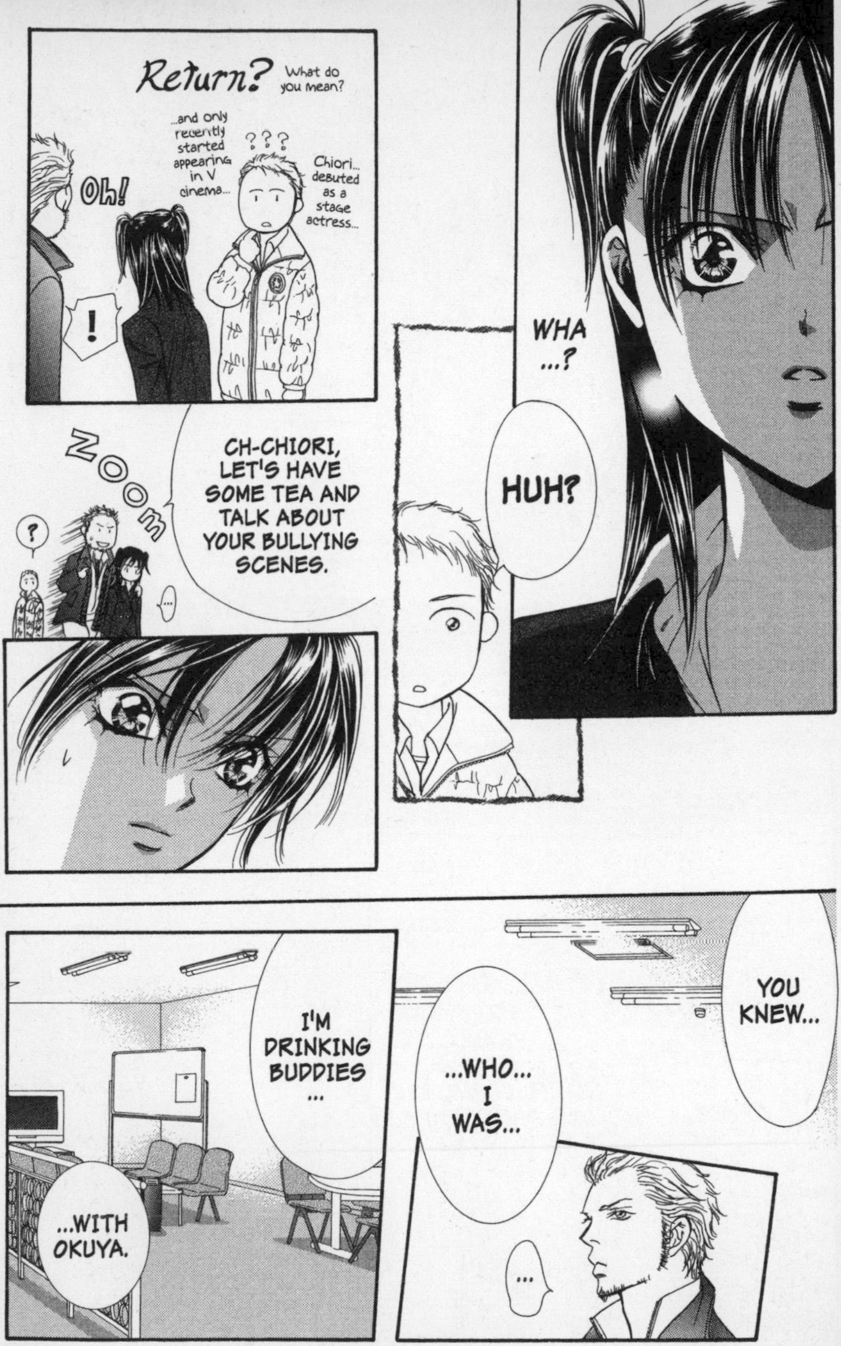
WHA ...?
HUH?
Return?
What do you mean?
Chiori... debuted as a stage actress...
...and only recently started appearing in V cinema...
???
Oh!
!
ZOOM
CH-CHIORI, LET'S HAVE SOME TEA AND TALK ABOUT YOUR BULLYING SCENES.
?
...
YOU KNEW...
...WHO... I WAS...
...
I'M DRINKING BUDDIES ...
...WITH OKUYA.

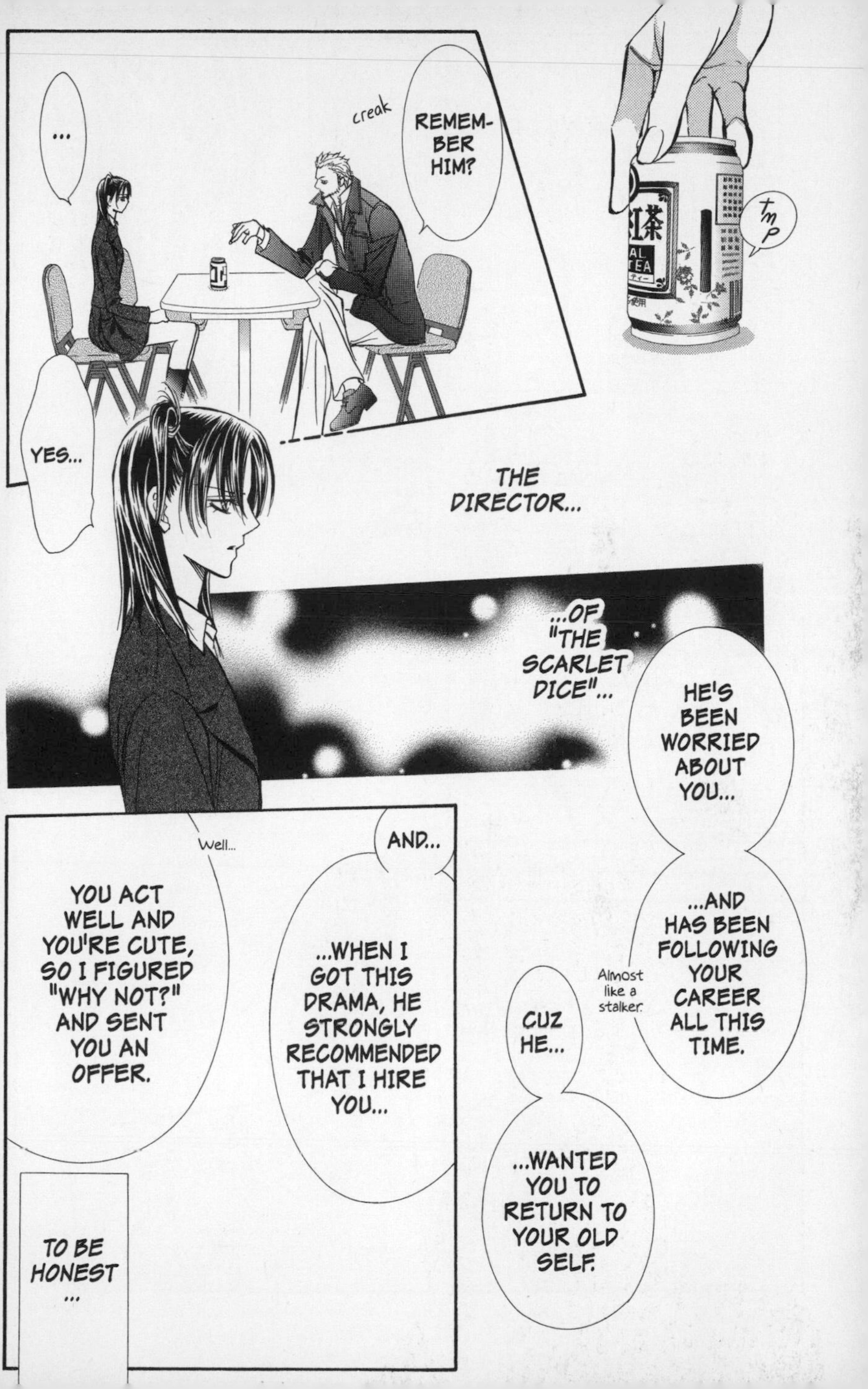
tmp
creak
REMEMBER HIM?
...
YES...
THE DIRECTOR...
...OF "THE SCARLET DICE"...
HE'S BEEN WORRIED ABOUT YOU...
...AND HAS BEEN FOLLOWING YOUR CAREER ALL THIS TIME.
Almost like a stalker.
CUZ HE...
...WANTED YOU TO RETURN TO YOUR OLD SELF.
AND...
...WHEN I GOT THIS DRAMA, HE STRONGLY RECOMMENDED THAT I HIRE YOU...
Well...
YOU ACT WELL AND YOU'RE CUTE, SO I FIGURED "WHY NOT?" AND SENT YOU AN OFFER.
TO BE HONEST...

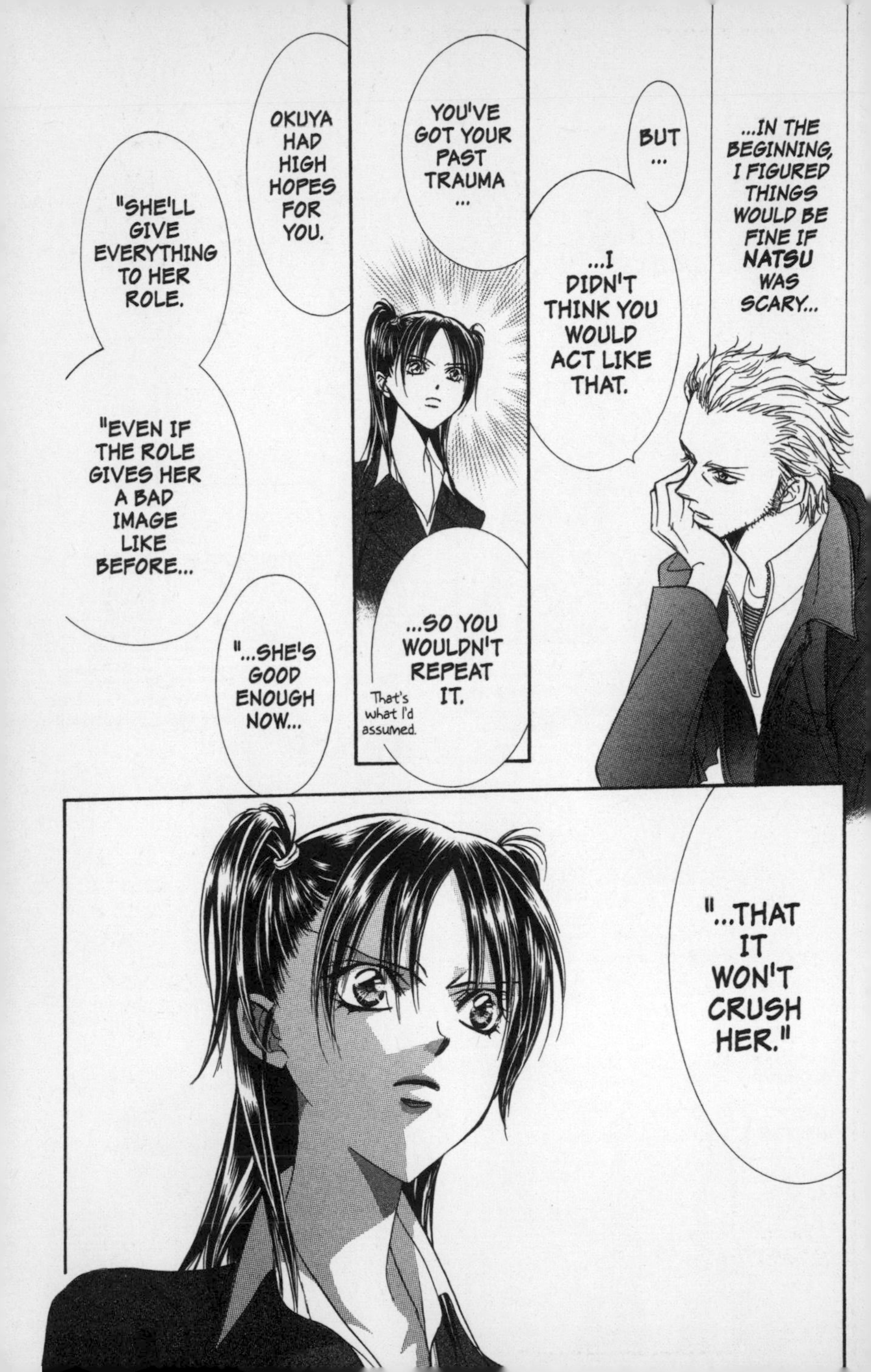
...IN THE BEGINNING, I FIGURED THINGS WOULD BE FINE IF NATSU WAS SCARY...
BUT ...
...I DIDN'T THINK YOU WOULD ACT LIKE THAT.
YOU'VE GOT YOUR PAST TRAUMA ...
...SO YOU WOULDN'T REPEAT IT.
That's what I'd assumed.
OKUYA HAD HIGH HOPES FOR YOU.
"SHE'LL GIVE EVERYTHING TO HER ROLE.
"EVEN IF THE ROLE GIVES HER A BAD IMAGE LIKE BEFORE...
"...SHE'S GOOD ENOUGH NOW...
"...THAT IT WON'T CRUSH HER."

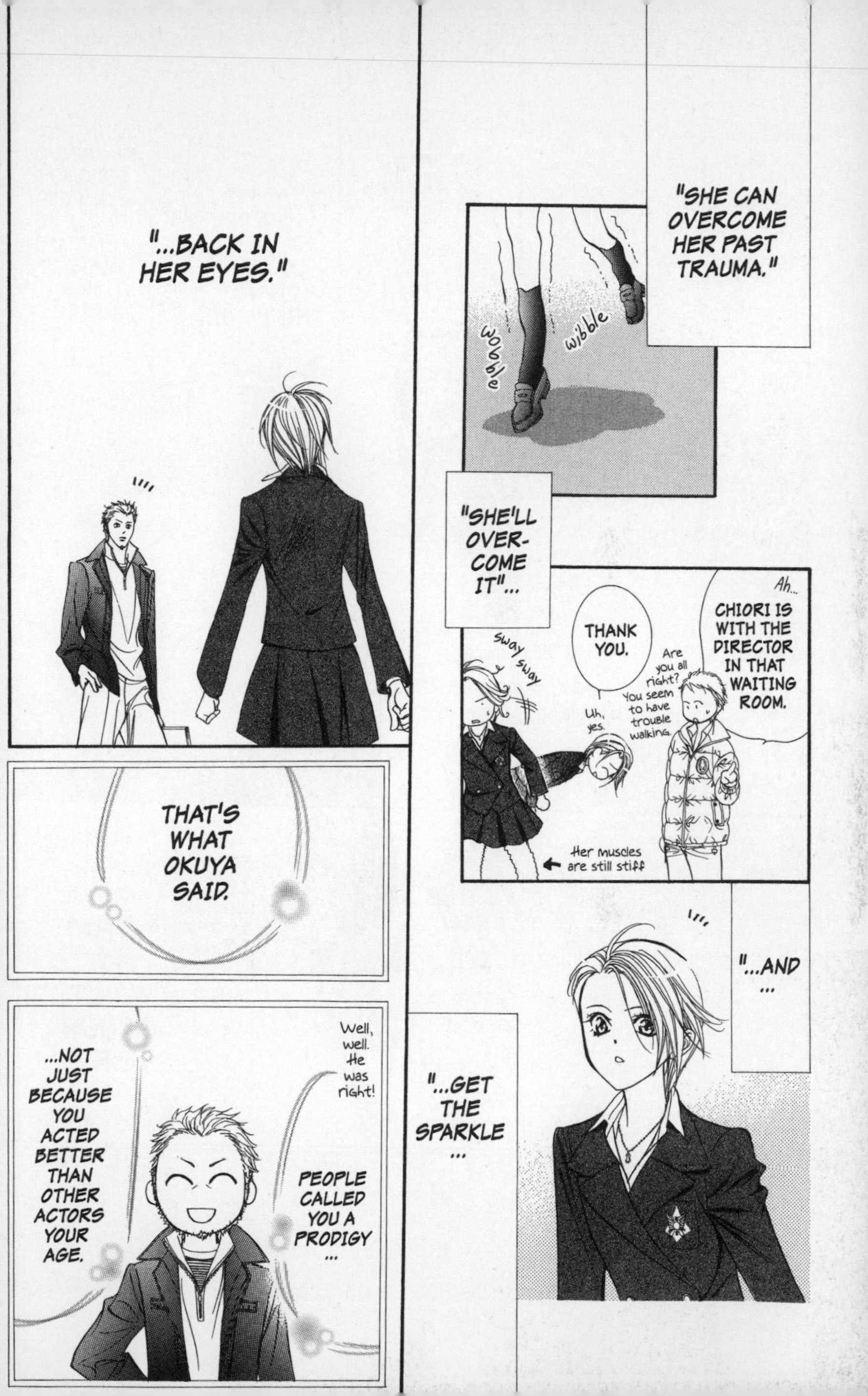
"SHE CAN OVERCOME HER PAST TRAUMA."
wibble
wobble
"SHE'LL OVER-COME IT"...
Ah...
CHIORI IS WITH THE DIRECTOR IN THAT WAITING ROOM.
Are you all right? You seem to have trouble walking.
THANK YOU.
Uh, yes.
sway sway
Her muscles are still stiff
"...AND ...
"...GET THE SPARKLE ...
"...BACK IN HER EYES."
THAT'S WHAT OKUYA SAID.
Well, well. He was right!
PEOPLE CALLED YOU A PRODIGY ...
...NOT JUST BECAUSE YOU ACTED BETTER THAN OTHER ACTORS YOUR AGE.

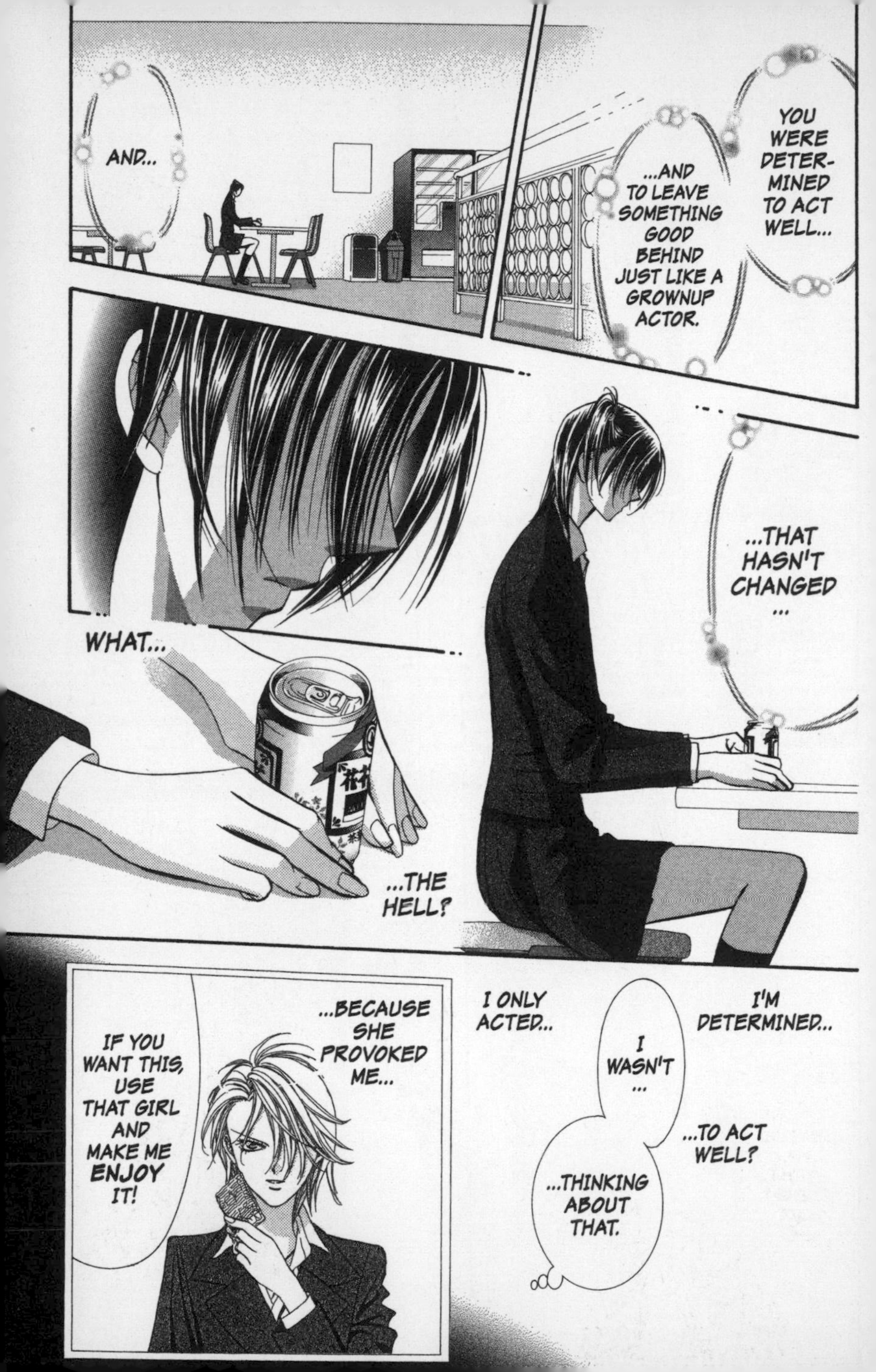
YOU WERE DETERMINED TO ACT WELL...
...AND TO LEAVE SOMETHING GOOD BEHIND JUST LIKE A GROWNUP ACTOR.
AND...
...THAT HASN'T CHANGED...
WHAT...
...THE HELL?
I'M DETERMINED...
...TO ACT WELL?
I WASN'T...
...THINKING ABOUT THAT.
I ONLY ACTED...
...BECAUSE SHE PROVOKED ME...
IF YOU WANT THIS, USE THAT GIRL AND MAKE ME ENJOY IT!

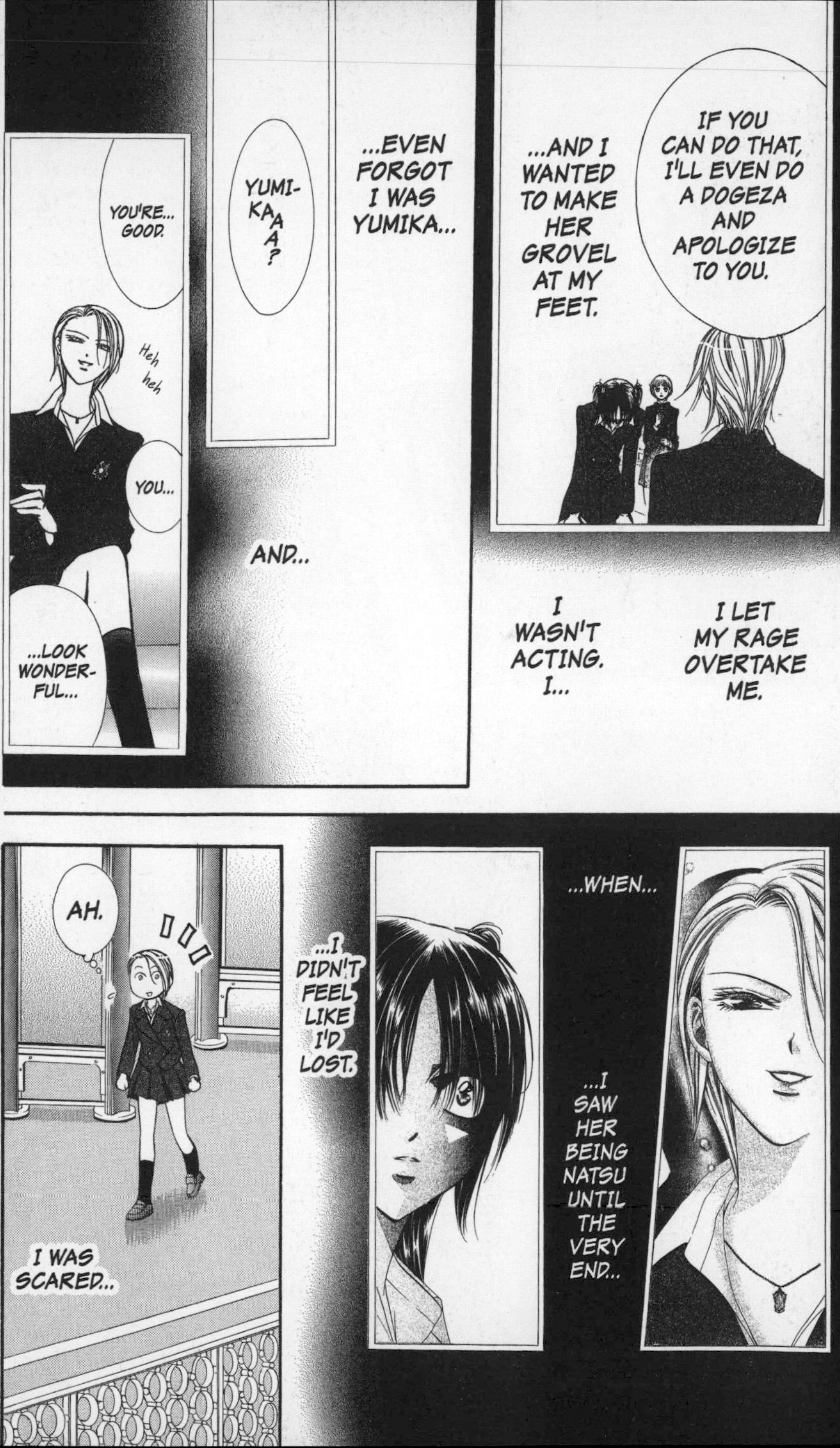
IF YOU CAN DO THAT, I'LL EVEN DO A DOGEZA AND APOLOGIZE TO YOU.
...AND I WANTED TO MAKE HER GROVEL AT MY FEET.
...EVEN FORGOT I WAS YUMIKA...
YUMI-KAAA?
I LET MY RAGE OVERTAKE ME.
I WASN'T ACTING. I...
AND...
YOU'RE... GOOD.
Heh heh
YOU...
...LOOK WONDERFUL...
...WHEN...
...I SAW HER BEING NATSU UNTIL THE VERY END...
...I DIDN'T FEEL LIKE I'D LOST.
AH.
I WAS SCARED...

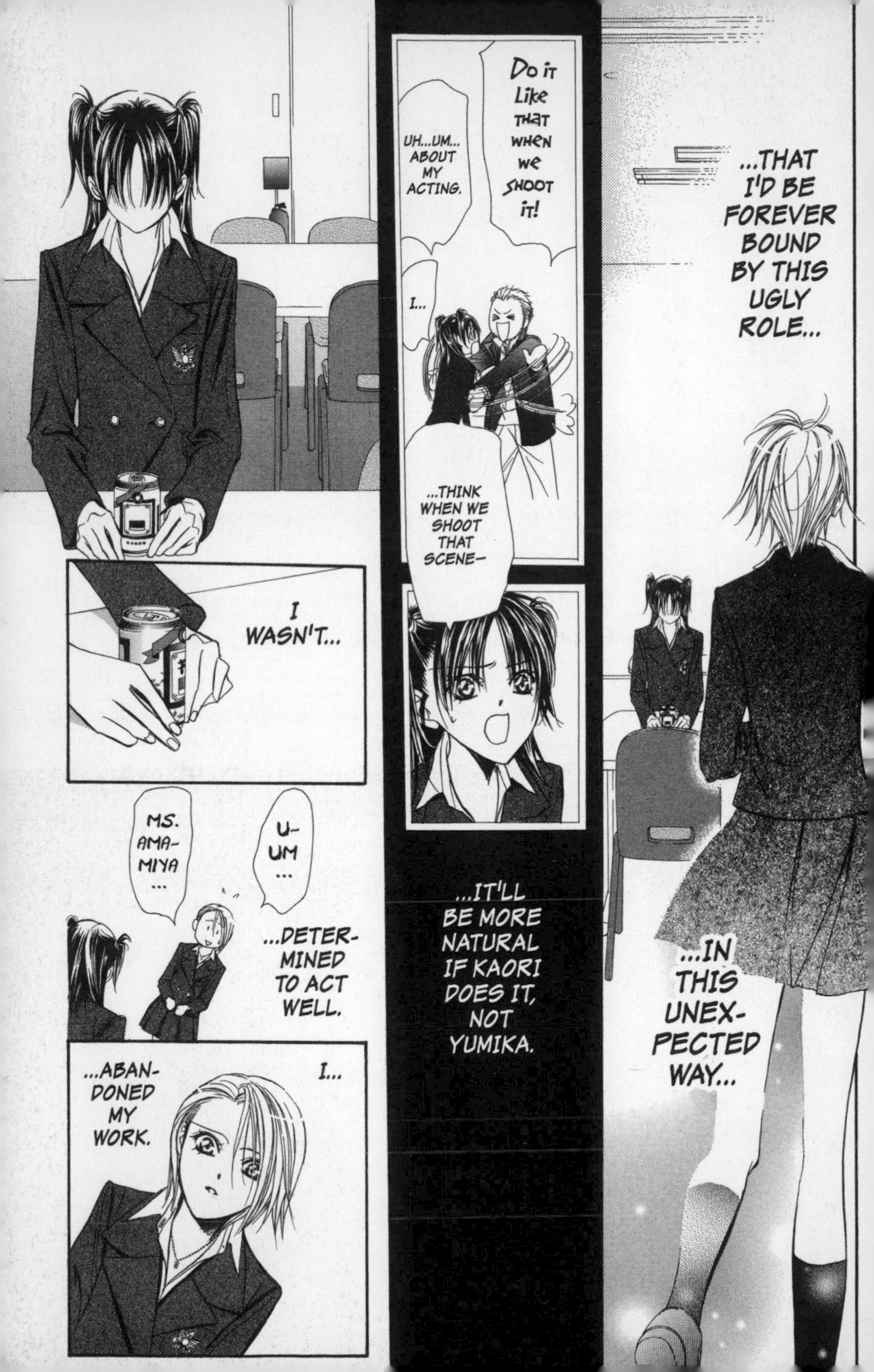
...THAT I'D BE FOREVER BOUND BY THIS UGLY ROLE...
...IN THIS UNEX-PECTED WAY...
Do it Like that when we shoot it!
UH...UM... ABOUT MY ACTING.
I...
...THINK WHEN WE SHOOT THAT SCENE—
...IT'LL BE MORE NATURAL IF KAORI DOES IT, NOT YUMIKA.
I WASN'T...
U-UM ...
MS. AMA-MIYA ...
...DETER-MINED TO ACT WELL.
I...
...ABAN-DONED MY WORK.

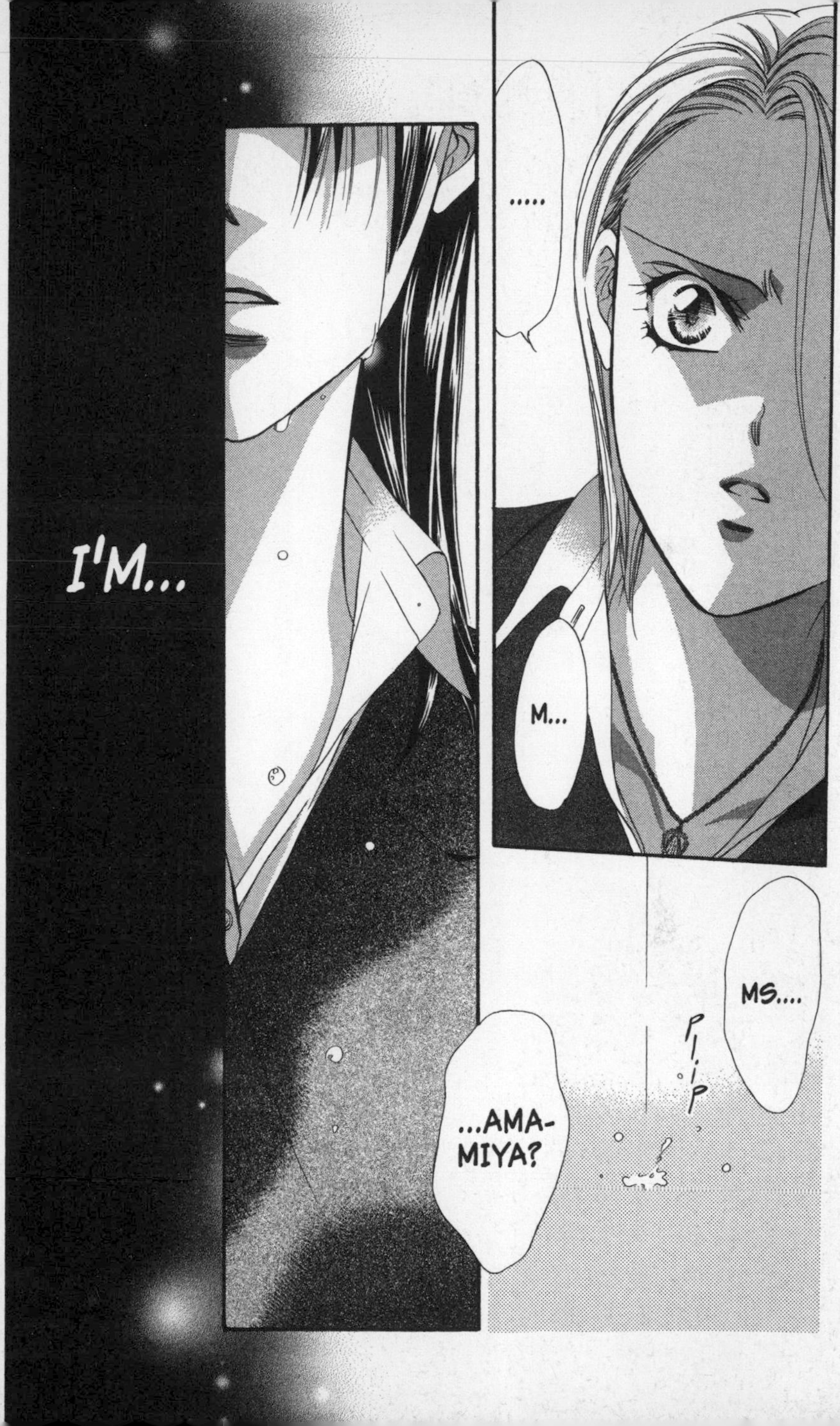
.....
M...
I'M...
MS....
PLIP
...AMA-
MIYA?

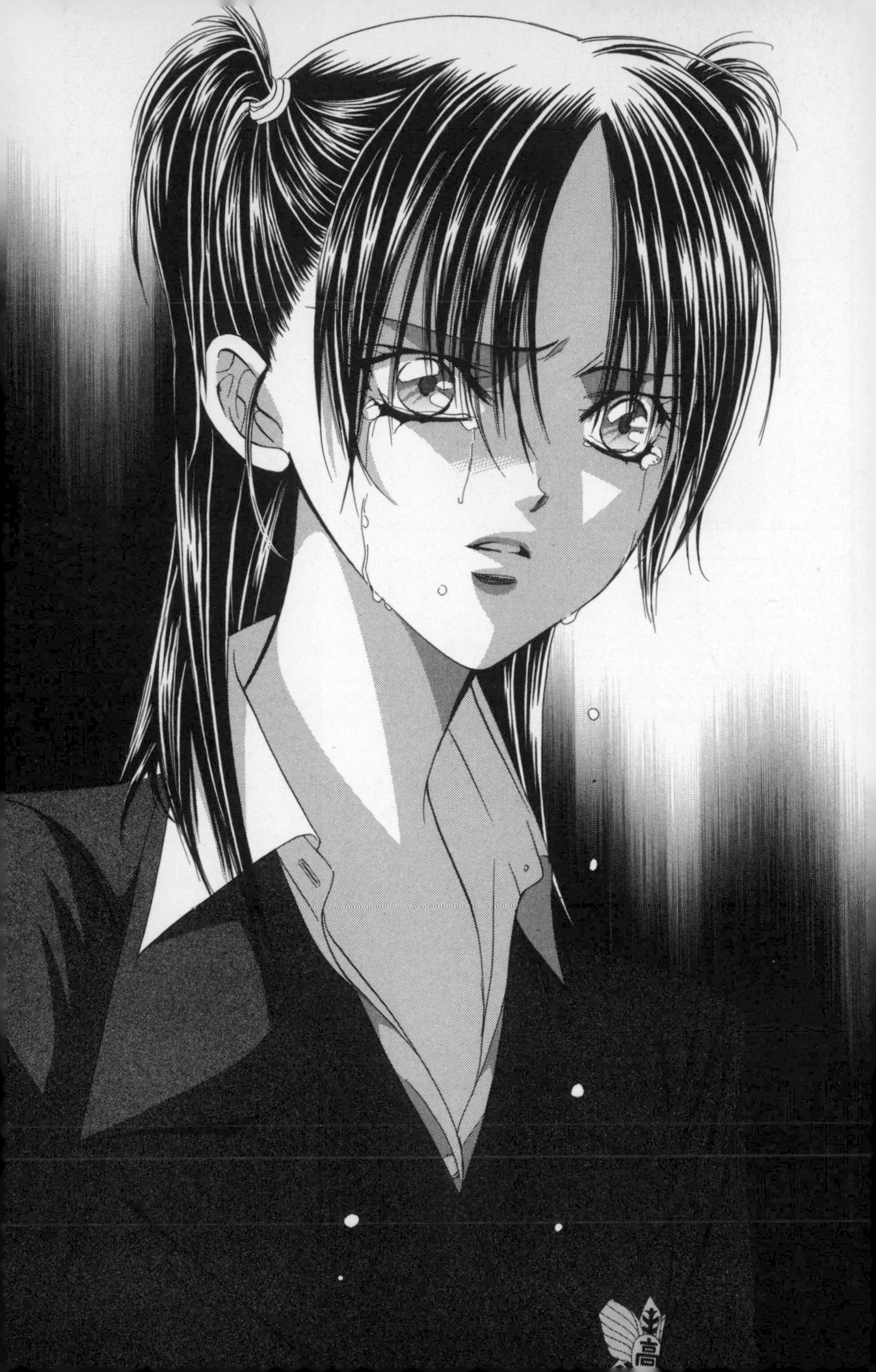

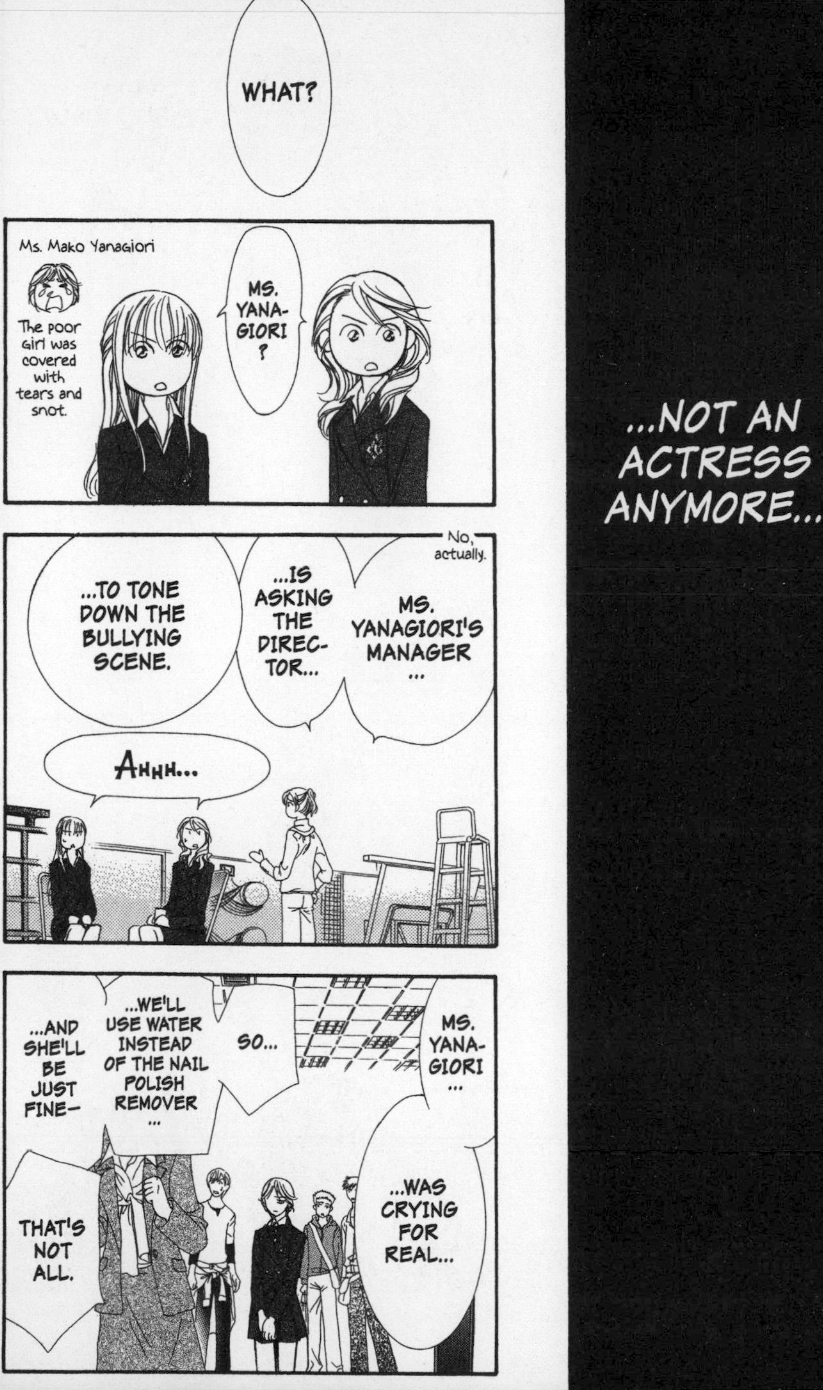
...NOT AN ACTRESS ANYMORE...
WHAT?
MS. YANAGIORI?
Ms. Mako Yanagiori
The poor girl was covered with tears and snot.
No, actually.
MS. YANAGIORI'S MANAGER ...
...IS ASKING THE DIRECTOR...
...TO TONE DOWN THE BULLYING SCENE.
AHHH...
MS. YANAGIORI ...
SO...
...WE'LL USE WATER INSTEAD OF THE NAIL POLISH REMOVER ...
...AND SHE'LL BE JUST FINE—
...WAS CRYING FOR REAL...
THAT'S NOT ALL.

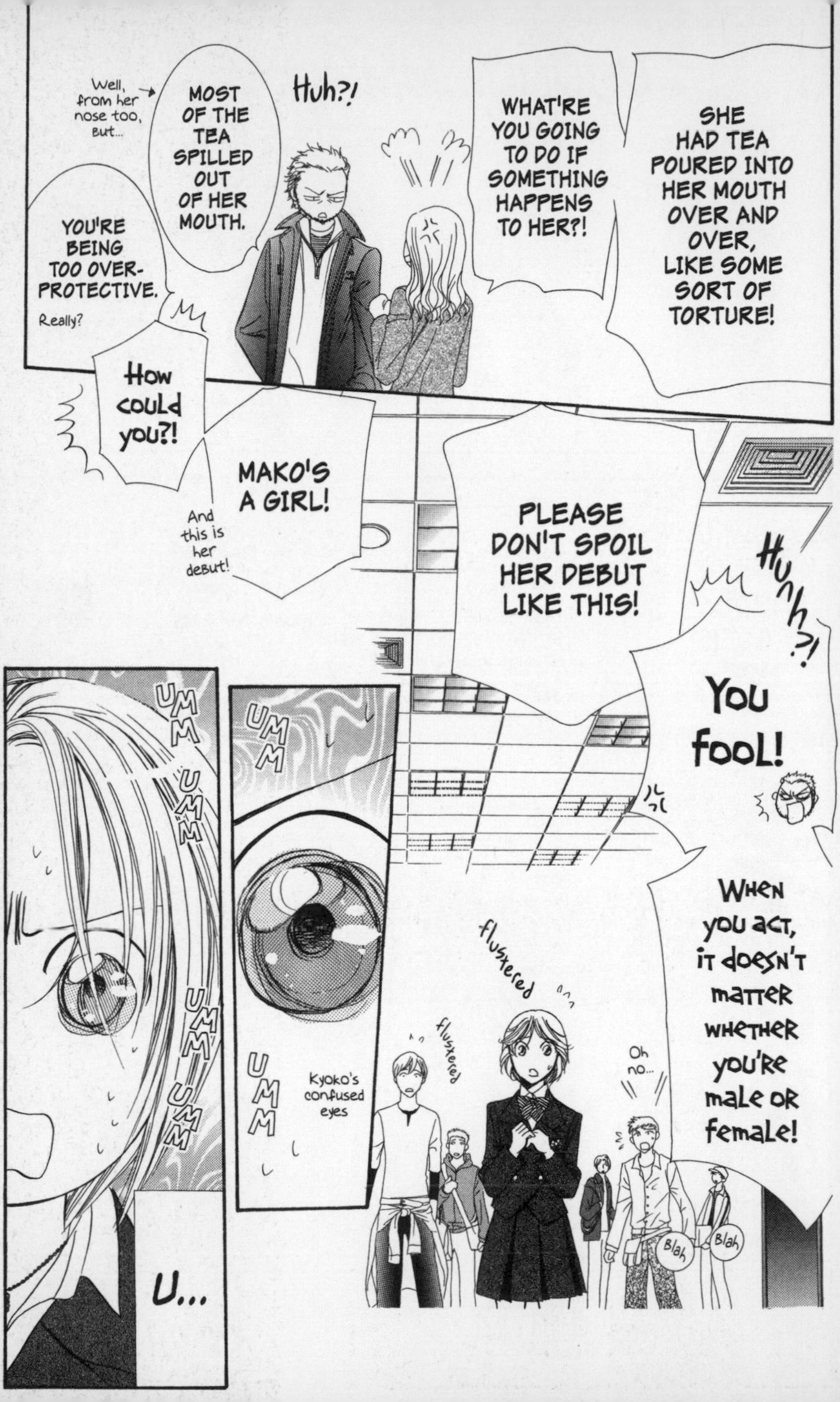
SHE HAD TEA POURED INTO HER MOUTH OVER AND OVER, LIKE SOME SORT OF TORTURE!
WHAT'RE YOU GOING TO DO IF SOMETHING HAPPENS TO HER?!
Huh?!
MOST OF THE TEA SPILLED OUT OF HER MOUTH.
Well, from her nose too, but...
YOU'RE BEING TOO OVER-PROTECTIVE.
Really?
PLEASE DON'T SPOIL HER DEBUT LIKE THIS!
MAKO'S A GIRL!
And this is her debut!
How could you?!
Huuh?!
You fool!
When you act, it doesn't matter whether you're male or female!
Oh no...
Blah
Blah
flustered
flustered
UMM
UMM
Kyoko's confused eyes
UMM
UMM
UMM
UMM
U...

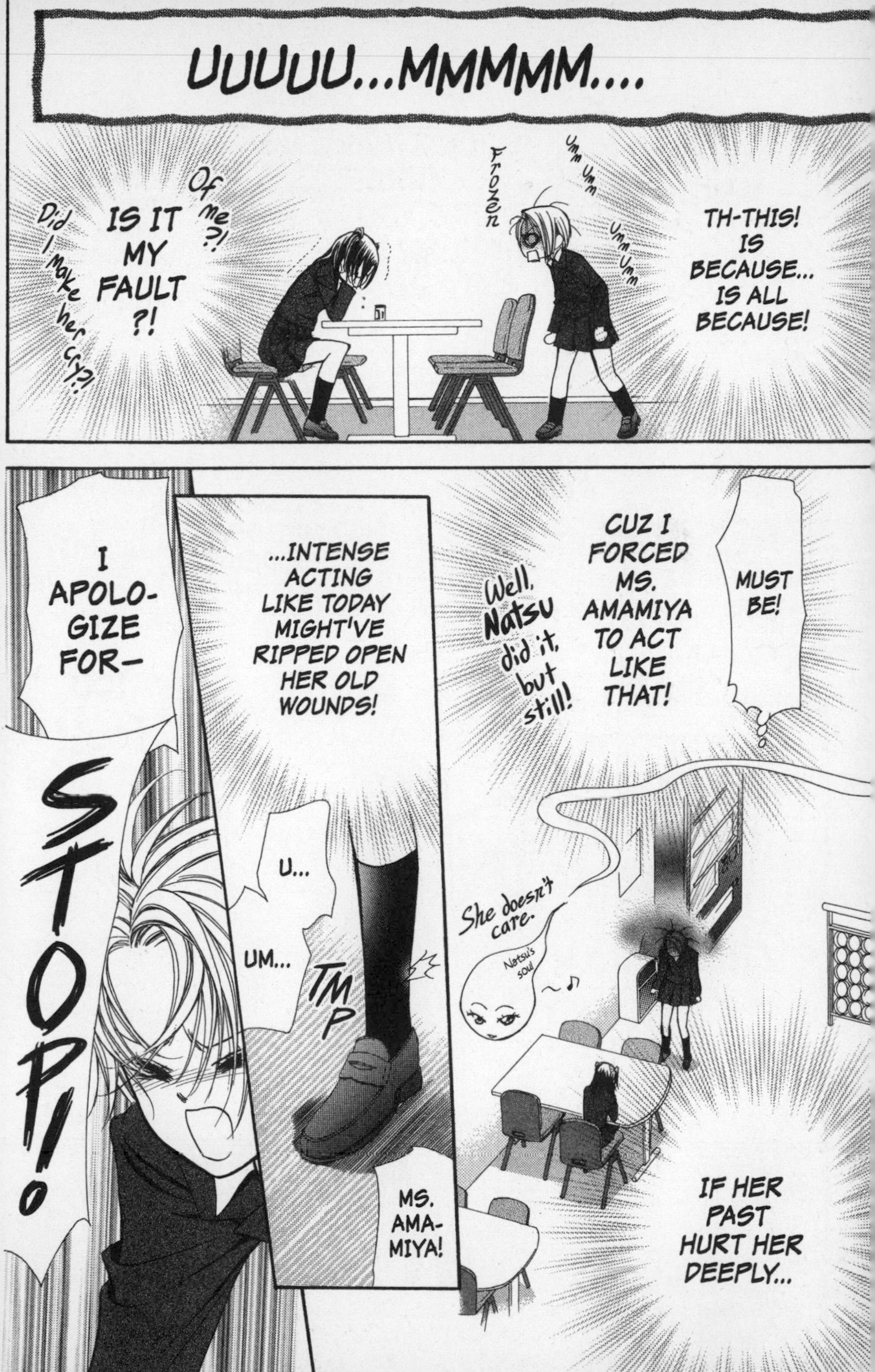
UUUUU...MMMMM....
TH-THIS! IS BECAUSE... IS ALL BECAUSE!
Umm Umm
Umm Umm
Frozen
Of me?!
IS IT MY FAULT ?!
Did I make her cry?!
MUST BE!
CUZ I FORCED MS. AMAMIYA TO ACT LIKE THAT!
Well, Natsu did it, but still!
She doesn't care.
Natsu's soul
~♪
IF HER PAST HURT HER DEEPLY...
...INTENSE ACTING LIKE TODAY MIGHT'VE RIPPED OPEN HER OLD WOUNDS!
U...
UM...
TMP
MS. AMAMIYA!
I APOLOGIZE FOR—
STOP!

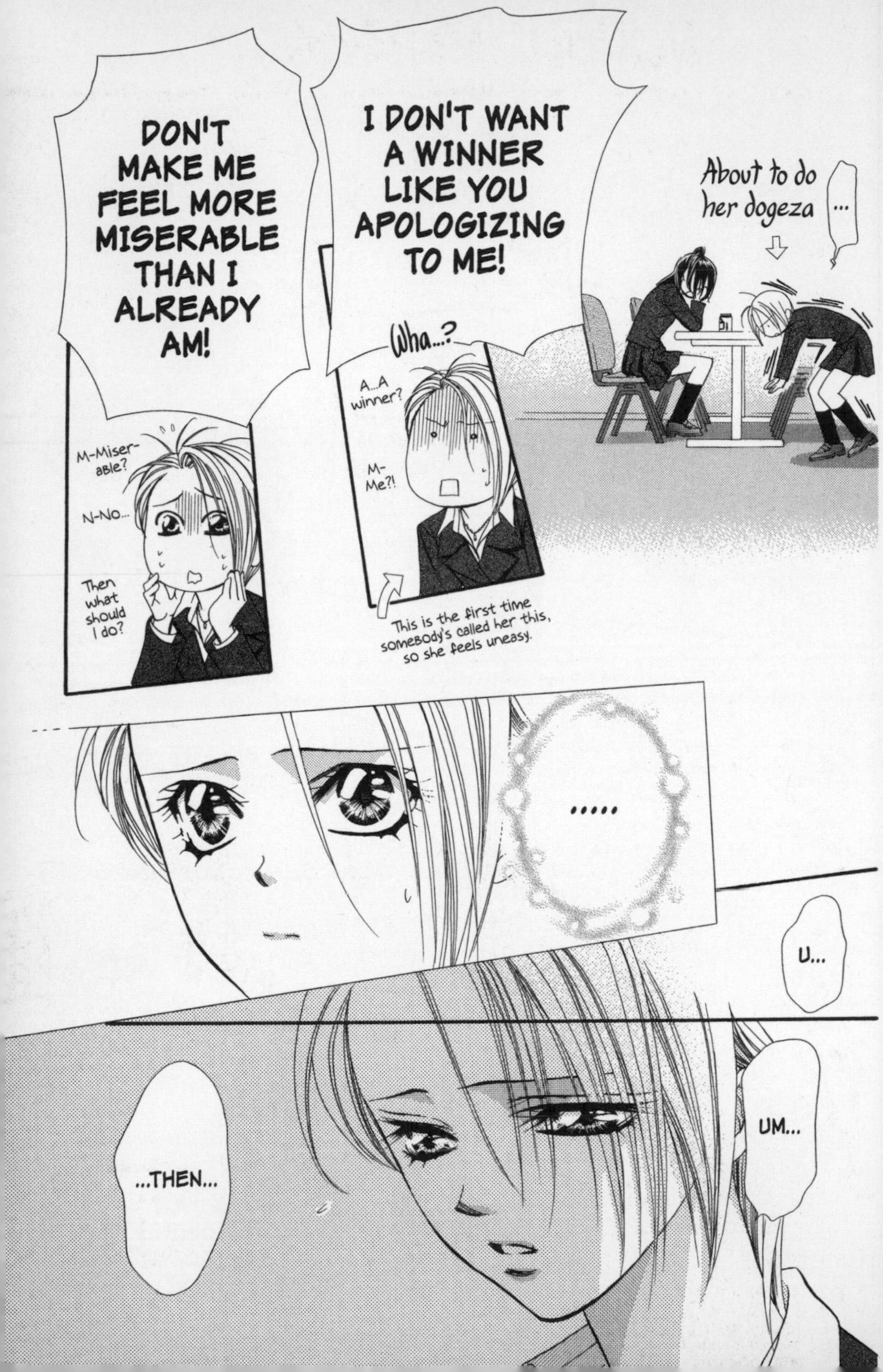
About to do her dogeza
...
I DON'T WANT A WINNER LIKE YOU APOLOGIZING TO ME!
Wha...?
A...A winner?
M-Me?!
This is the first time somebody's called her this, so she feels uneasy.
DON'T MAKE ME FEEL MORE MISERABLE THAN I ALREADY AM!
M-Miserable?
N-No...
Then what should I do?
.....
U...
UM...
...THEN...

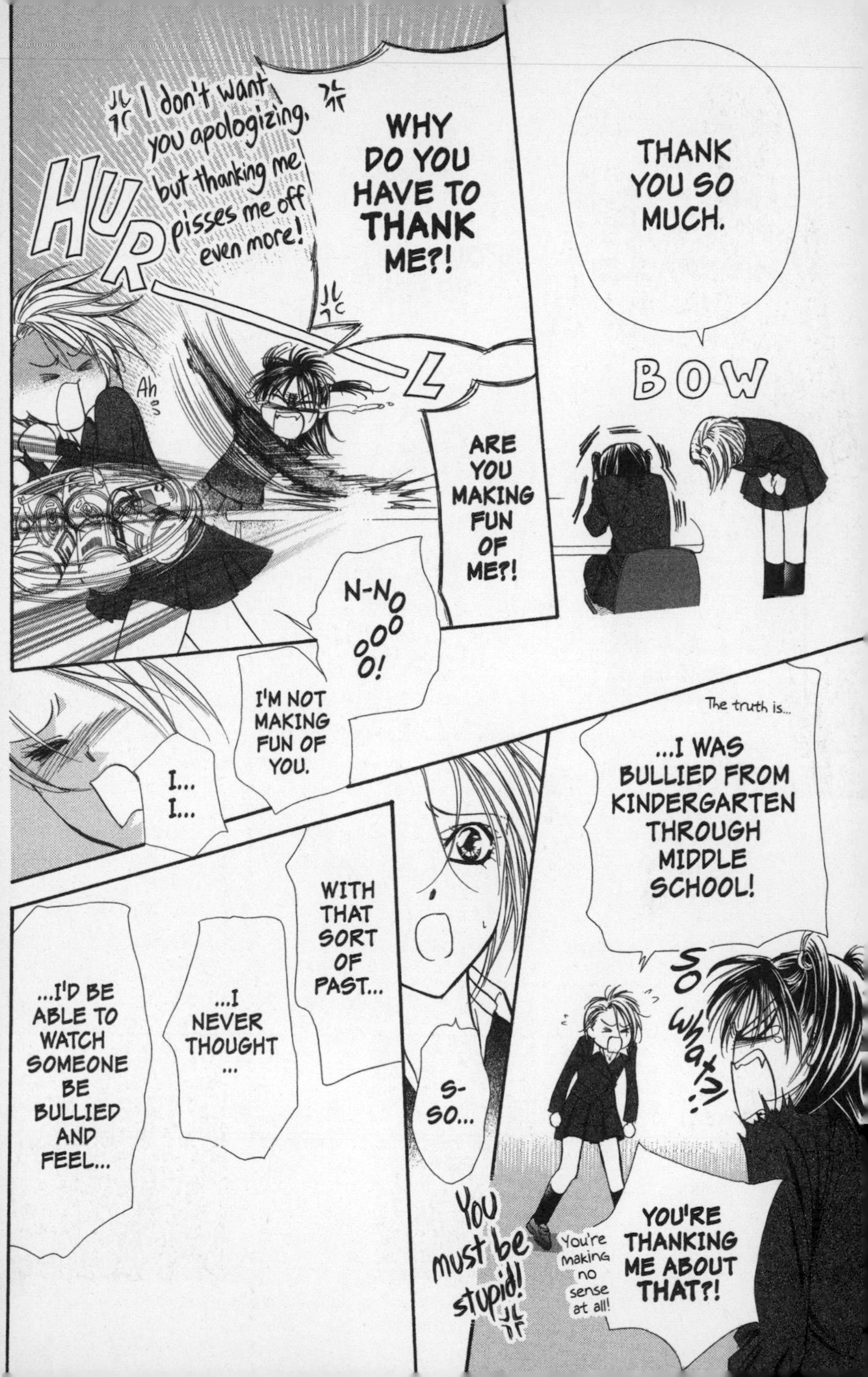
THANK YOU SO MUCH.
BOW
WHY DO YOU HAVE TO THANK ME?!
I don't want you apologizing, but thanking me pisses me off even more!
HURL
Ah
ARE YOU MAKING FUN OF ME?!
N-NOOOOOO!
The truth is...
...I WAS BULLIED FROM KINDERGARTEN THROUGH MIDDLE SCHOOL!
I'M NOT MAKING FUN OF YOU.
I... I...
SO what?!
YOU'RE THANKING ME ABOUT THAT?!
You're making no sense at all!
You must be stupid!
S-SO...
WITH THAT SORT OF PAST...
...I NEVER THOUGHT...
...I'D BE ABLE TO WATCH SOMEONE BE BULLIED AND FEEL...

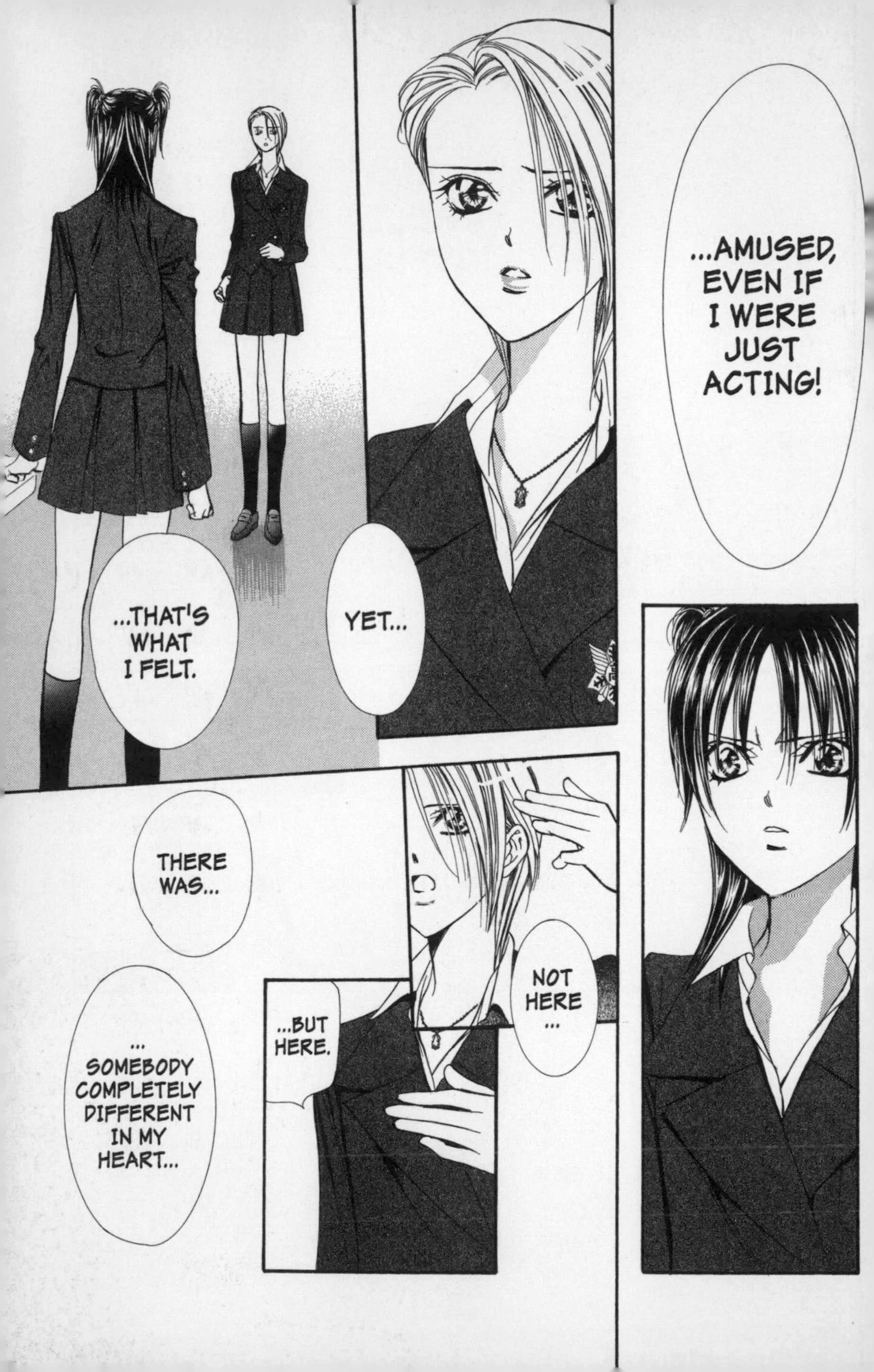
...AMUSED, EVEN IF I WERE JUST ACTING!
YET...
...THAT'S WHAT I FELT.
NOT HERE...
...BUT HERE.
THERE WAS...
...SOMEBODY COMPLETELY DIFFERENT IN MY HEART...

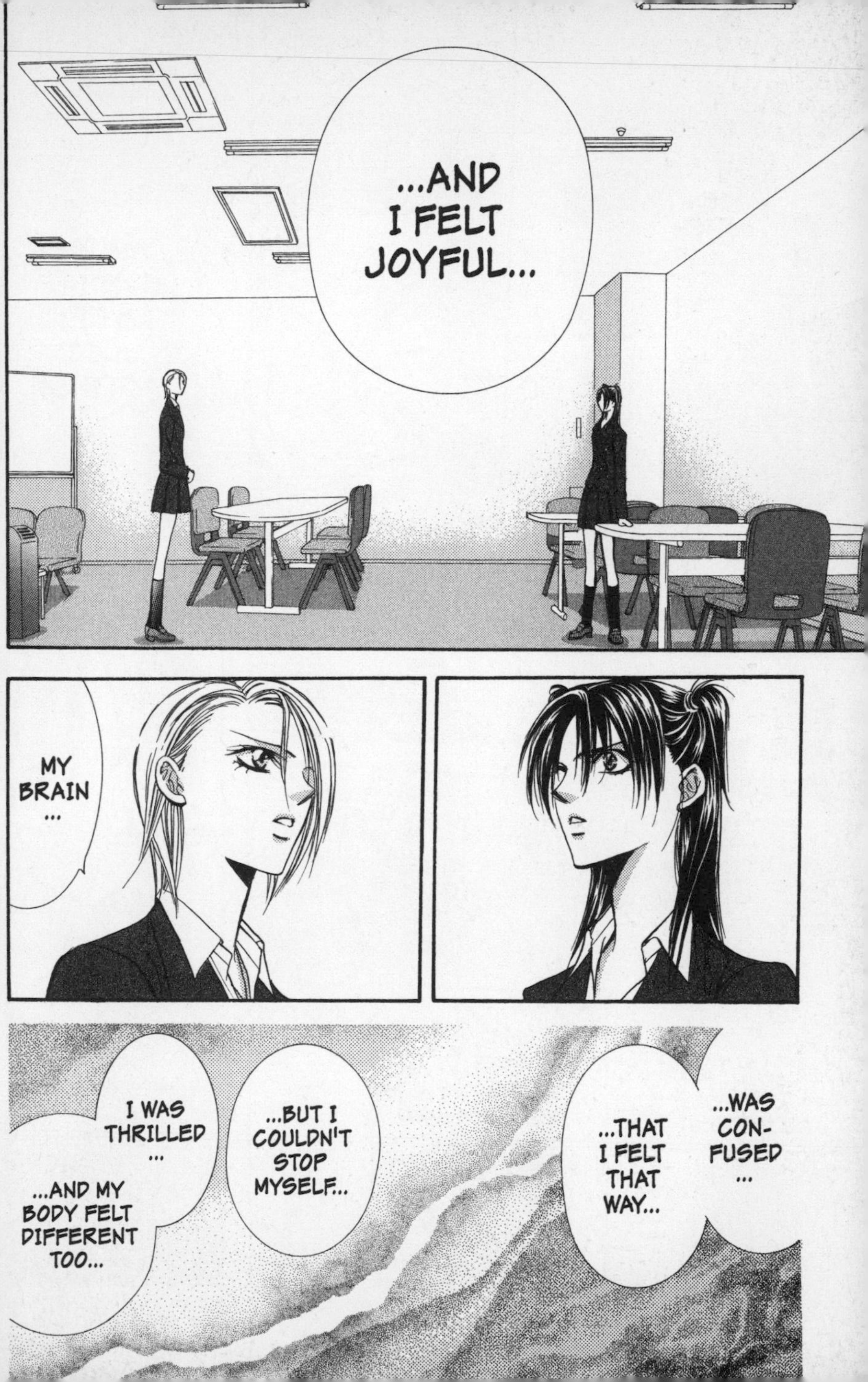
...AND I FELT JOYFUL...
MY BRAIN ...
...WAS CON-FUSED ...
...THAT I FELT THAT WAY...
...BUT I COULDN'T STOP MYSELF...
I WAS THRILLED ...
...AND MY BODY FELT DIFFERENT TOO...

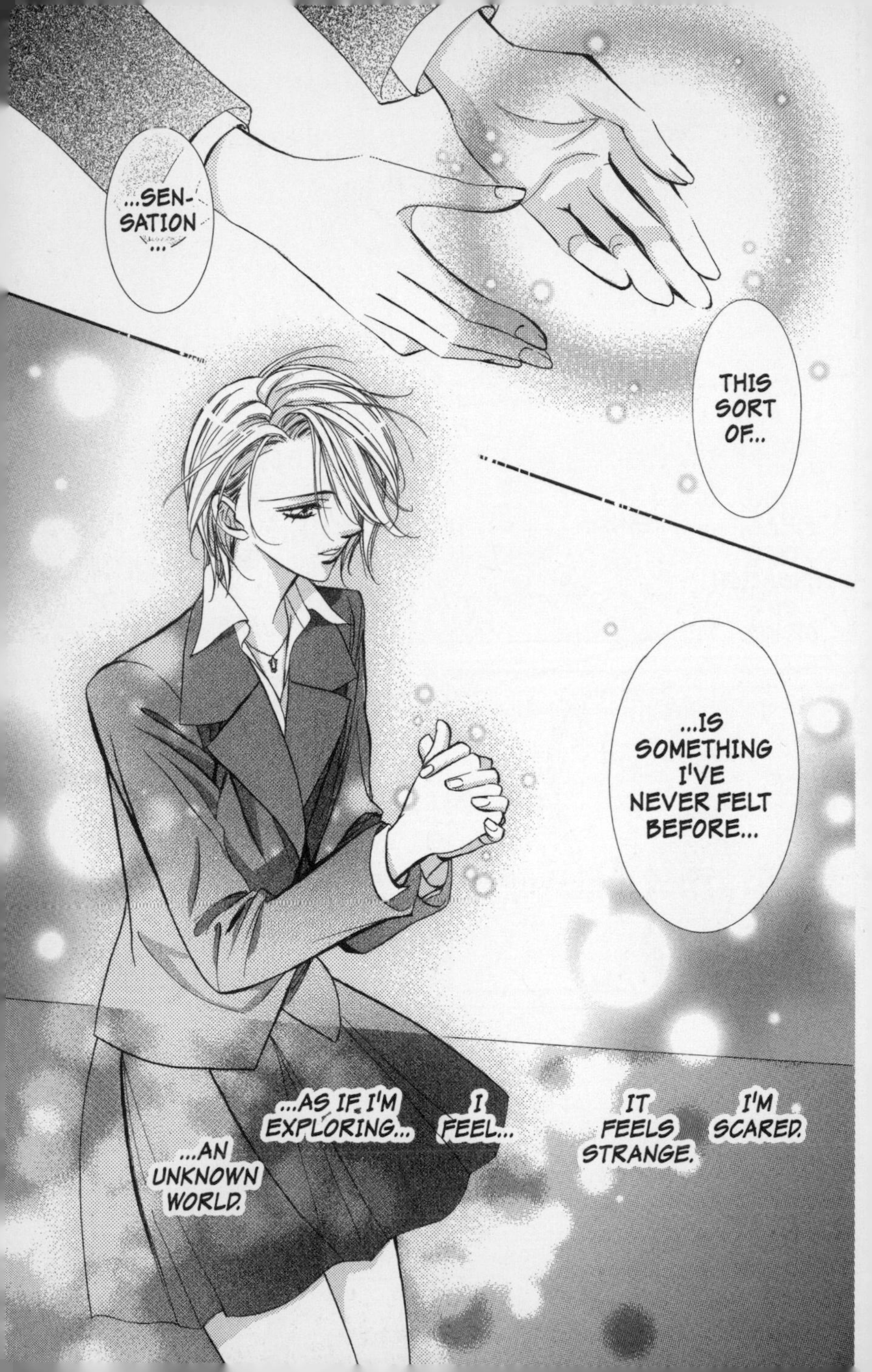
...SEN-SATION...
THIS SORT OF...
...IS SOMETHING I'VE NEVER FELT BEFORE...
I'M SCARED.
IT FEELS STRANGE.
I FEEL...
...AS IF I'M EXPLORING...
...AN UNKNOWN WORLD.

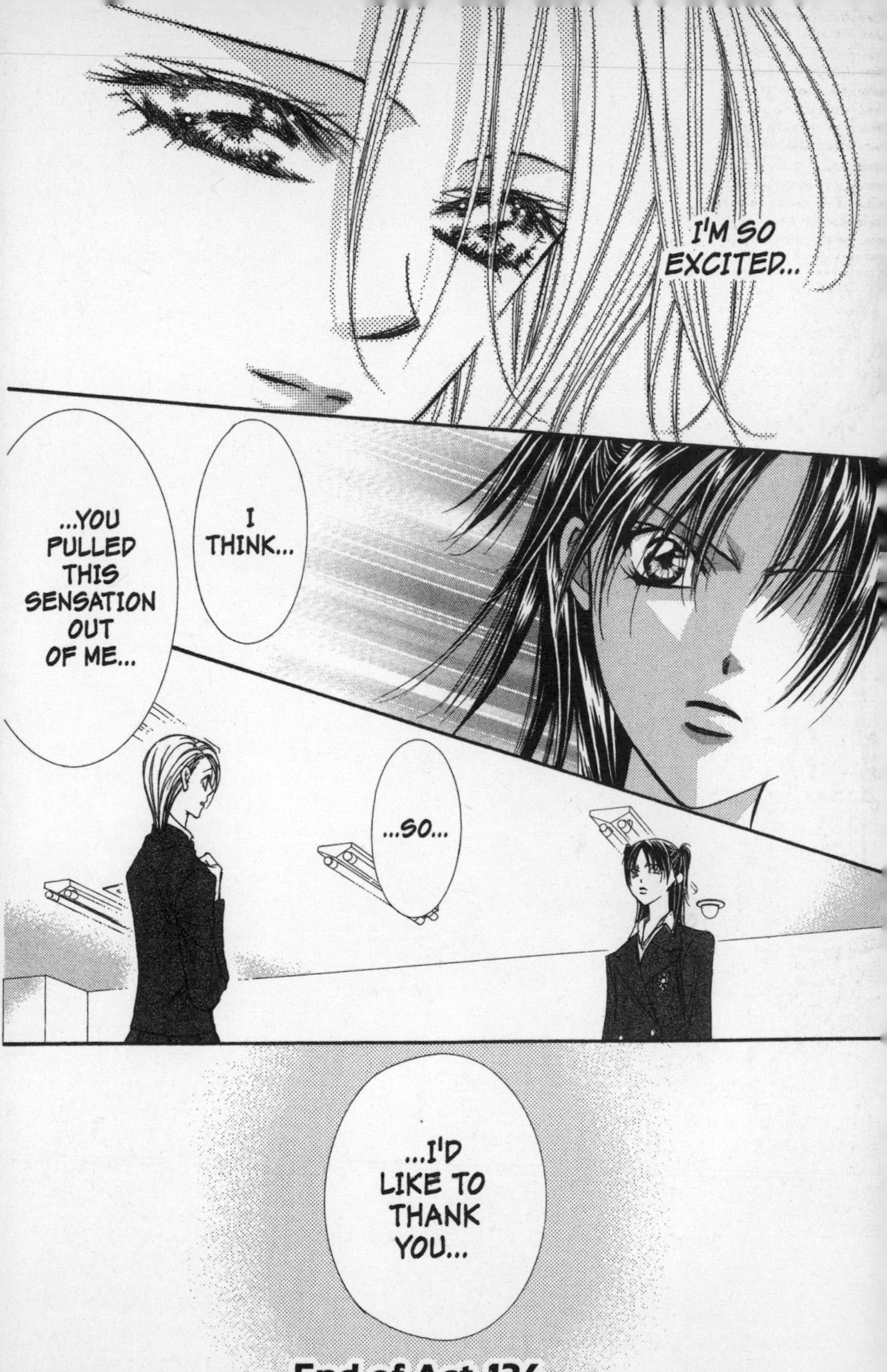
I'M SO EXCITED...
I THINK...
...YOU PULLED THIS SENSATION OUT OF ME...
...SO...
...I'D LIKE TO THANK YOU...

End of Act 136

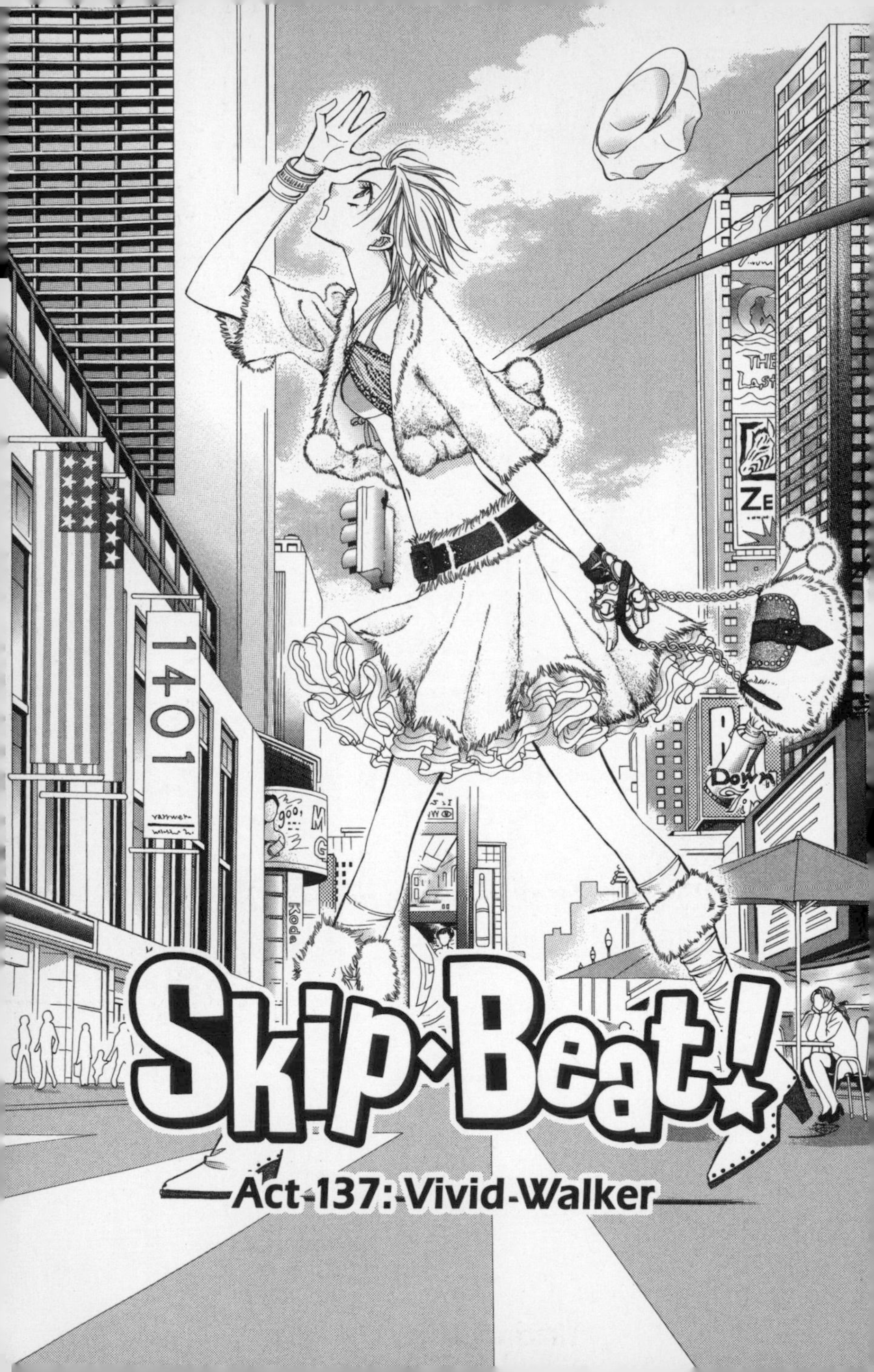
1401
THE Last
ZE
Down
Skip·Beat!
Act 137: Vivid Walker

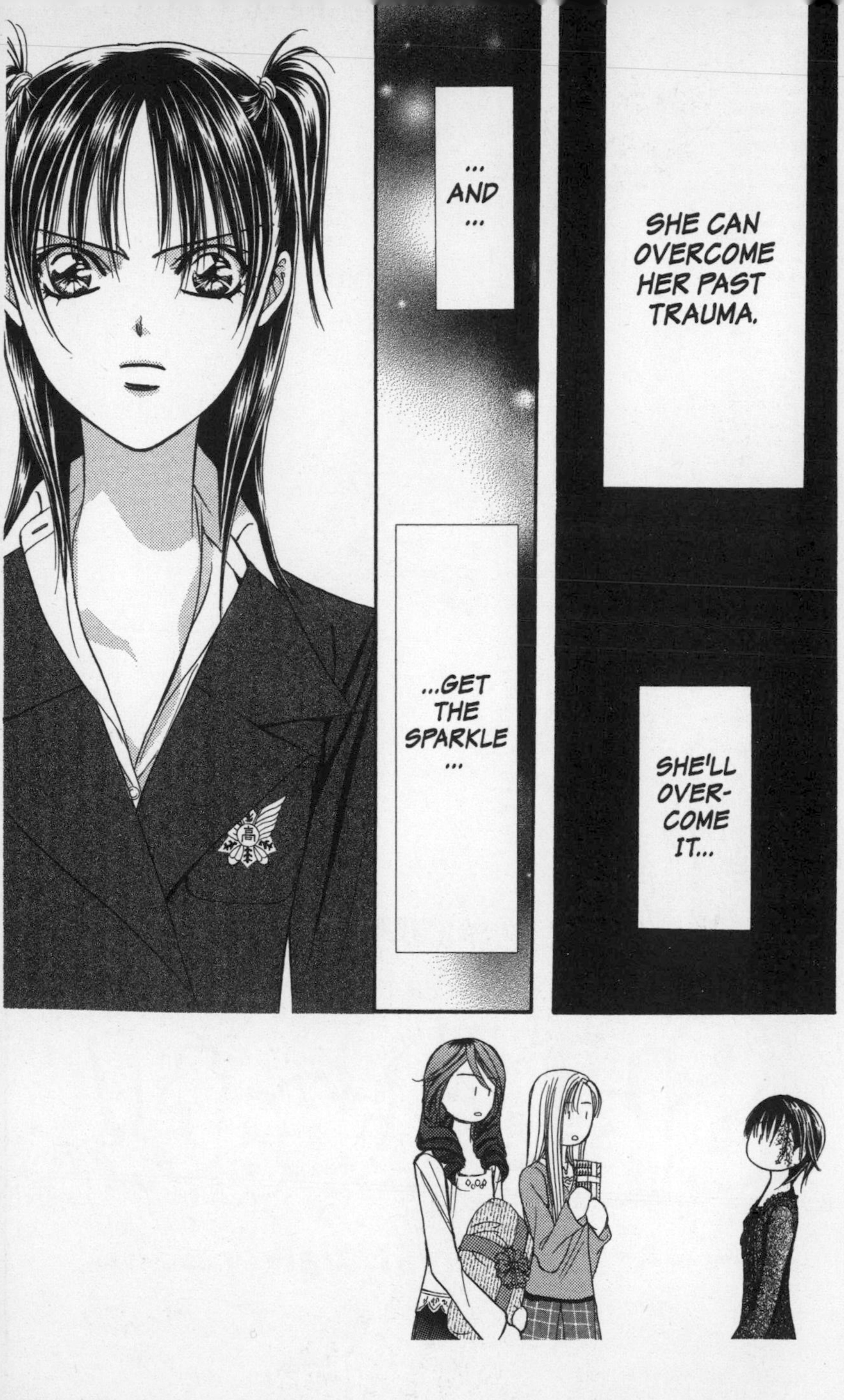
SHE CAN OVERCOME HER PAST TRAUMA.
SHE'LL OVER-COME IT...
... AND ...
...GET THE SPARKLE ...

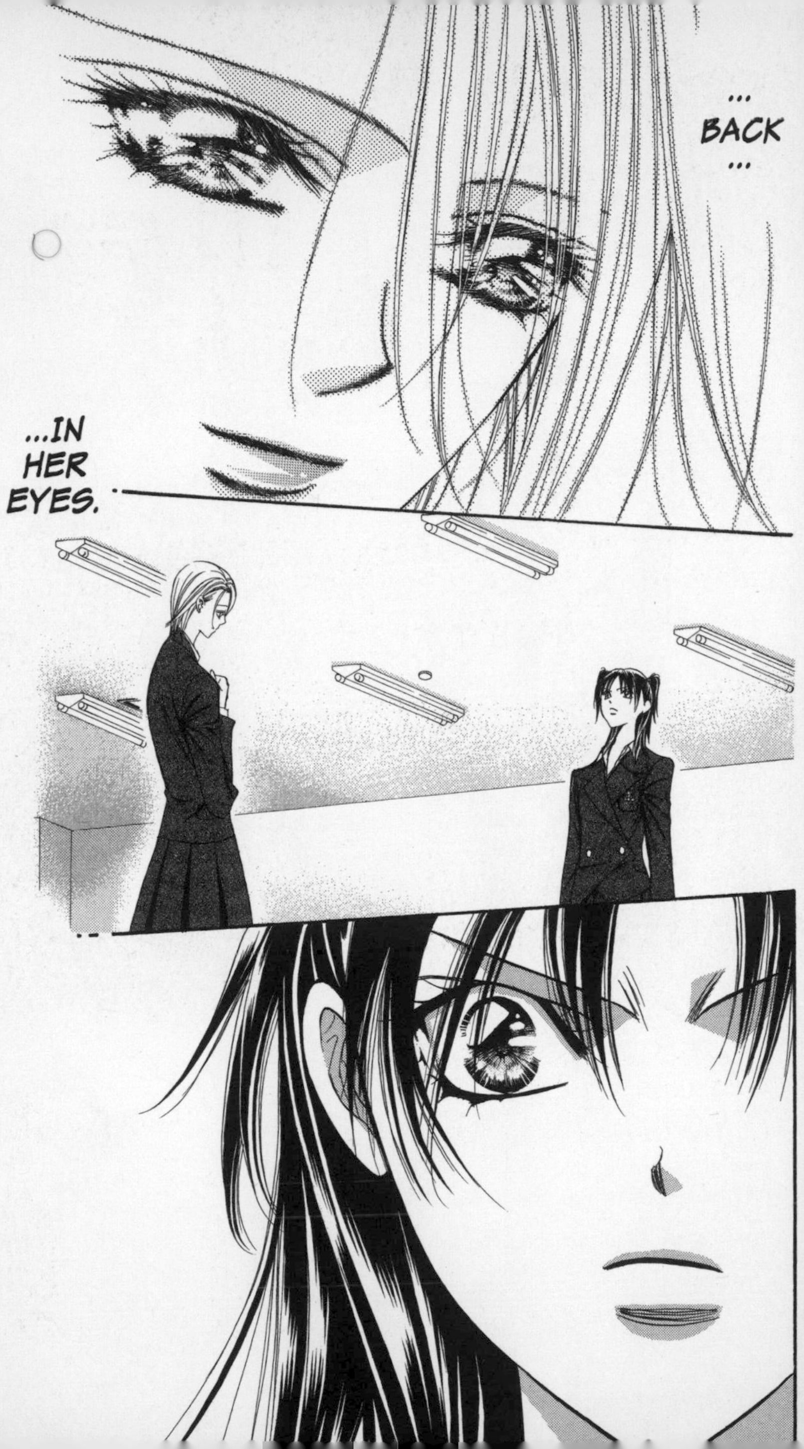
... BACK ...
...IN HER EYES.

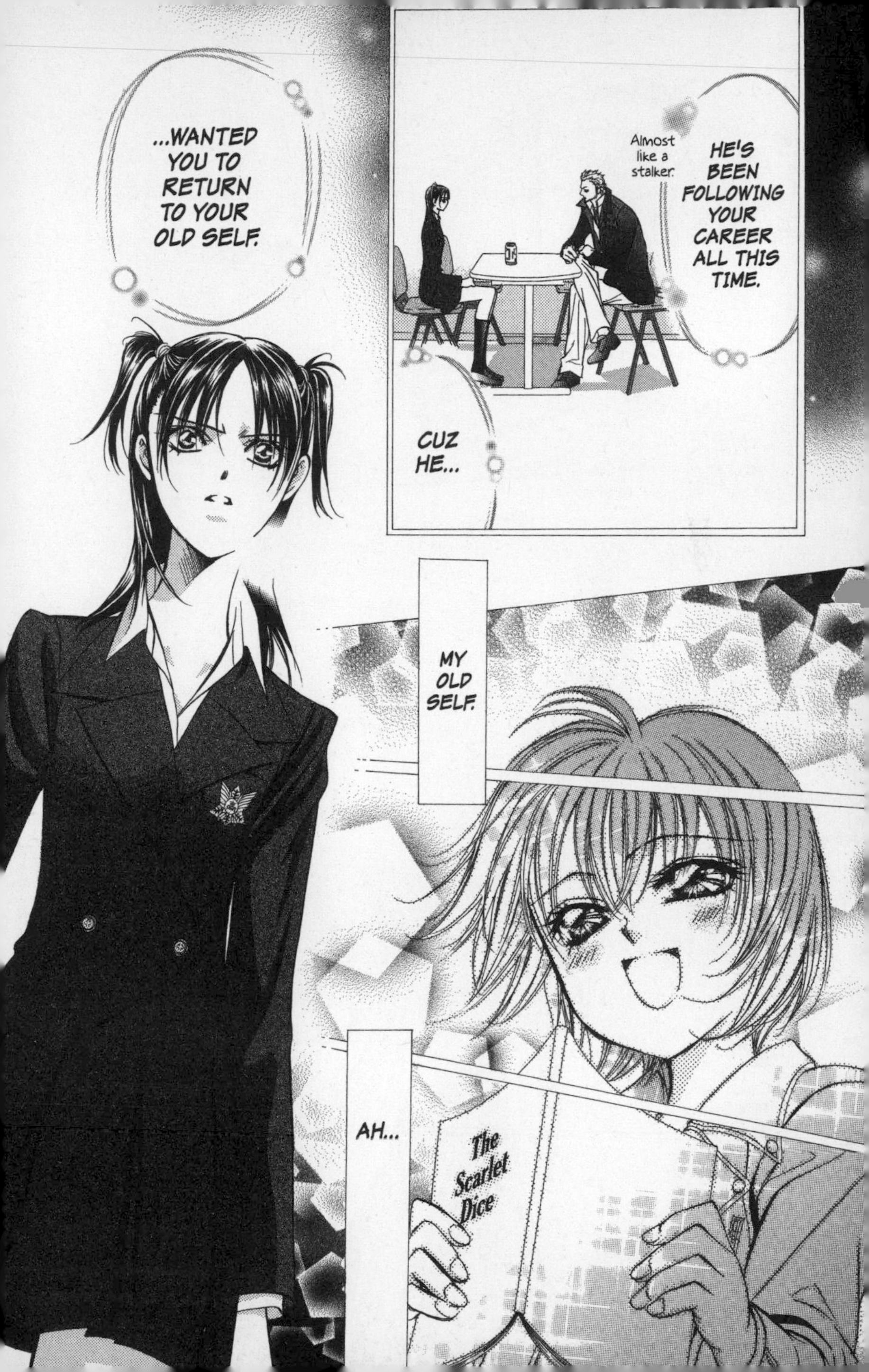
HE'S BEEN FOLLOWING YOUR CAREER ALL THIS TIME.
Almost like a stalker.
CUZ HE...
...WANTED YOU TO RETURN TO YOUR OLD SELF.
MY OLD SELF.
AH...
The Scarlet Dice

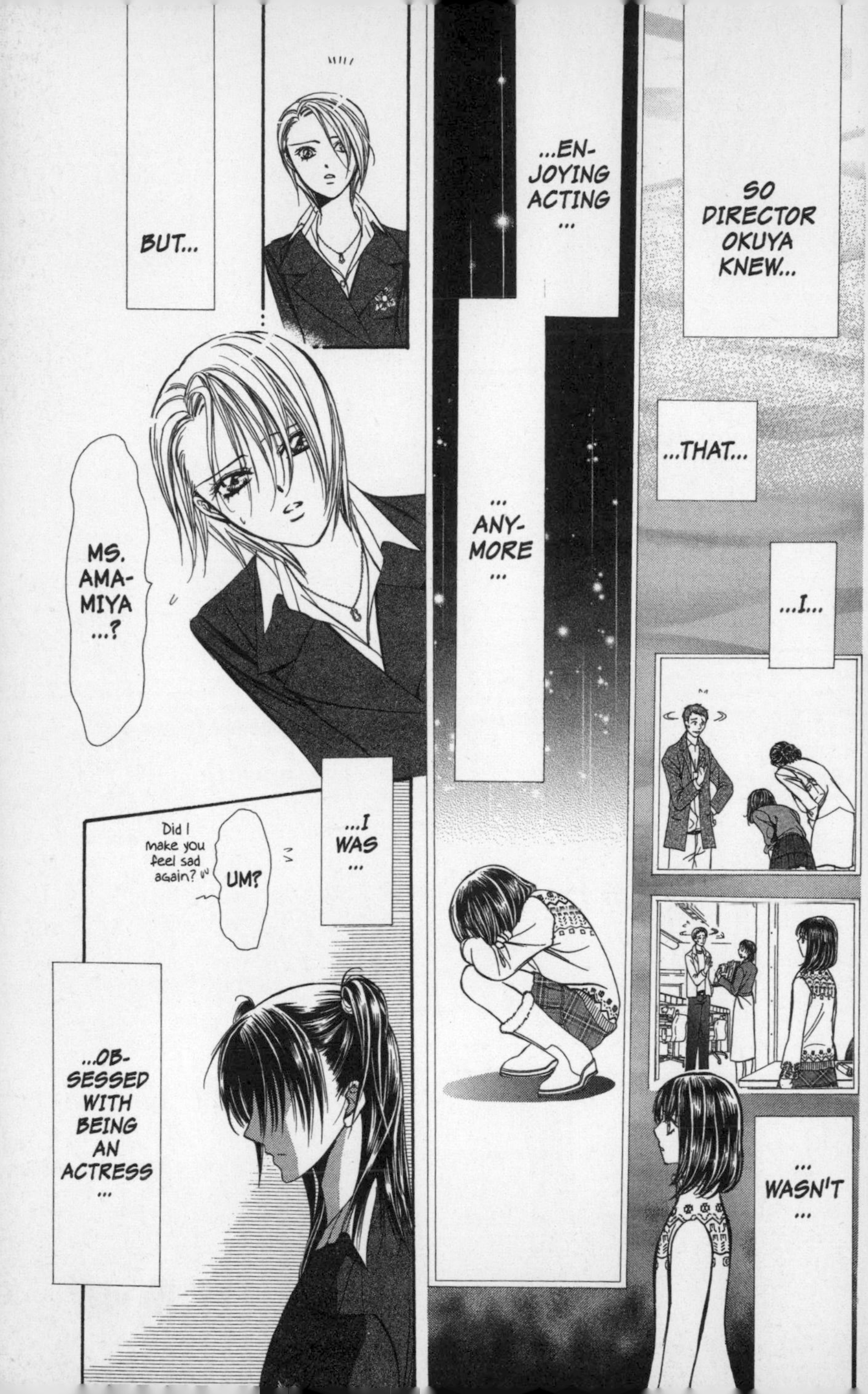
SO DIRECTOR OKUYA KNEW...
...THAT...
...I...
...WASN'T...
...EN-JOYING ACTING...
...ANY-MORE...
BUT...
MS. AMA-MIYA...?
...I WAS...
UM?
Did I make you feel sad again?
...OB-SESSED WITH BEING AN ACTRESS...

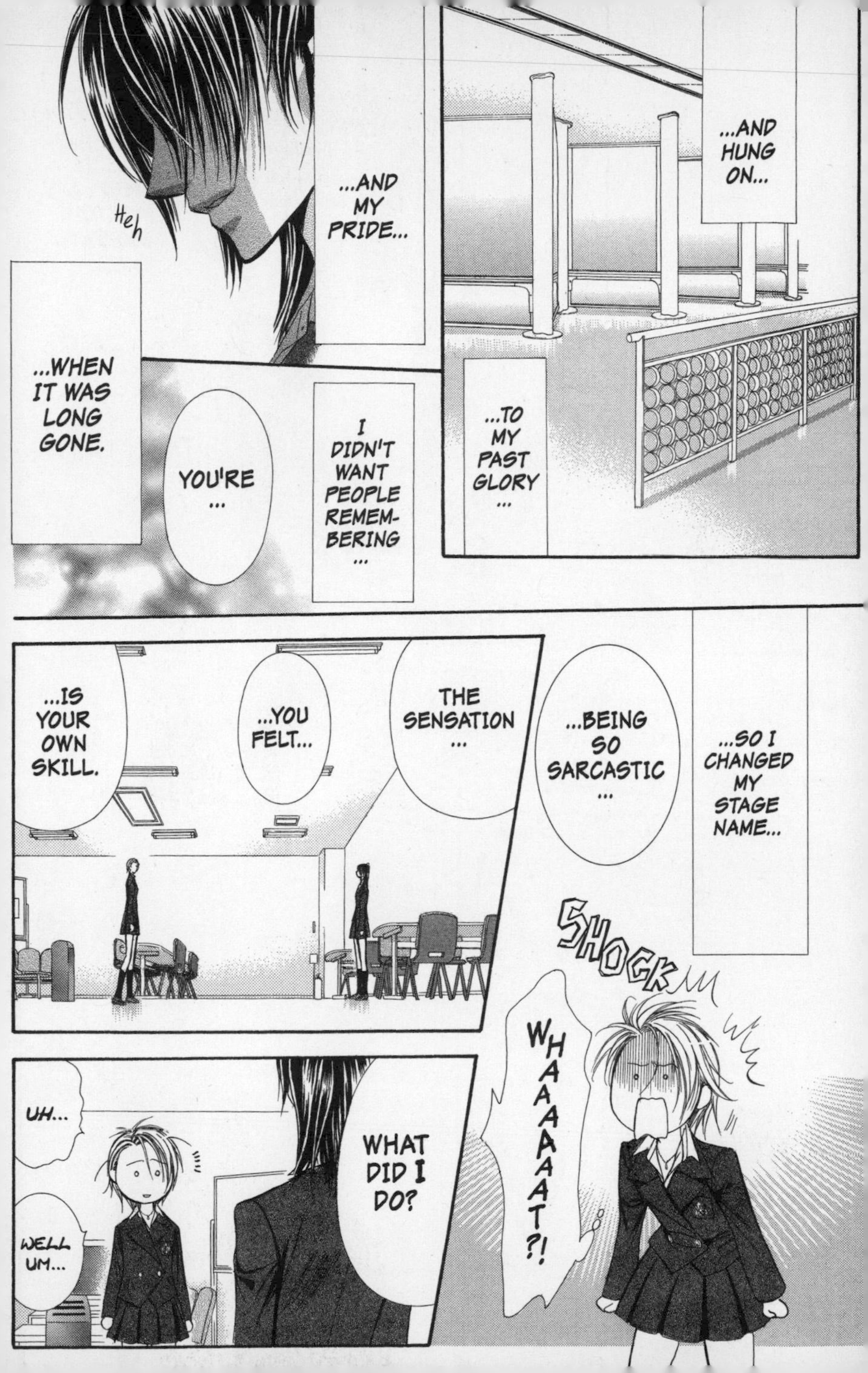
...AND HUNG ON...
...TO MY PAST GLORY...
...AND MY PRIDE...
Heh
I DIDN'T WANT PEOPLE REMEMBERING...
...WHEN IT WAS LONG GONE.
YOU'RE...
...SO I CHANGED MY STAGE NAME...
...BEING SO SARCASTIC...
SHOCK
WHAAAAAAT?!
THE SENSATION...
...YOU FELT...
...IS YOUR OWN SKILL.
WHAT DID I DO?
UH...
WELL UM...

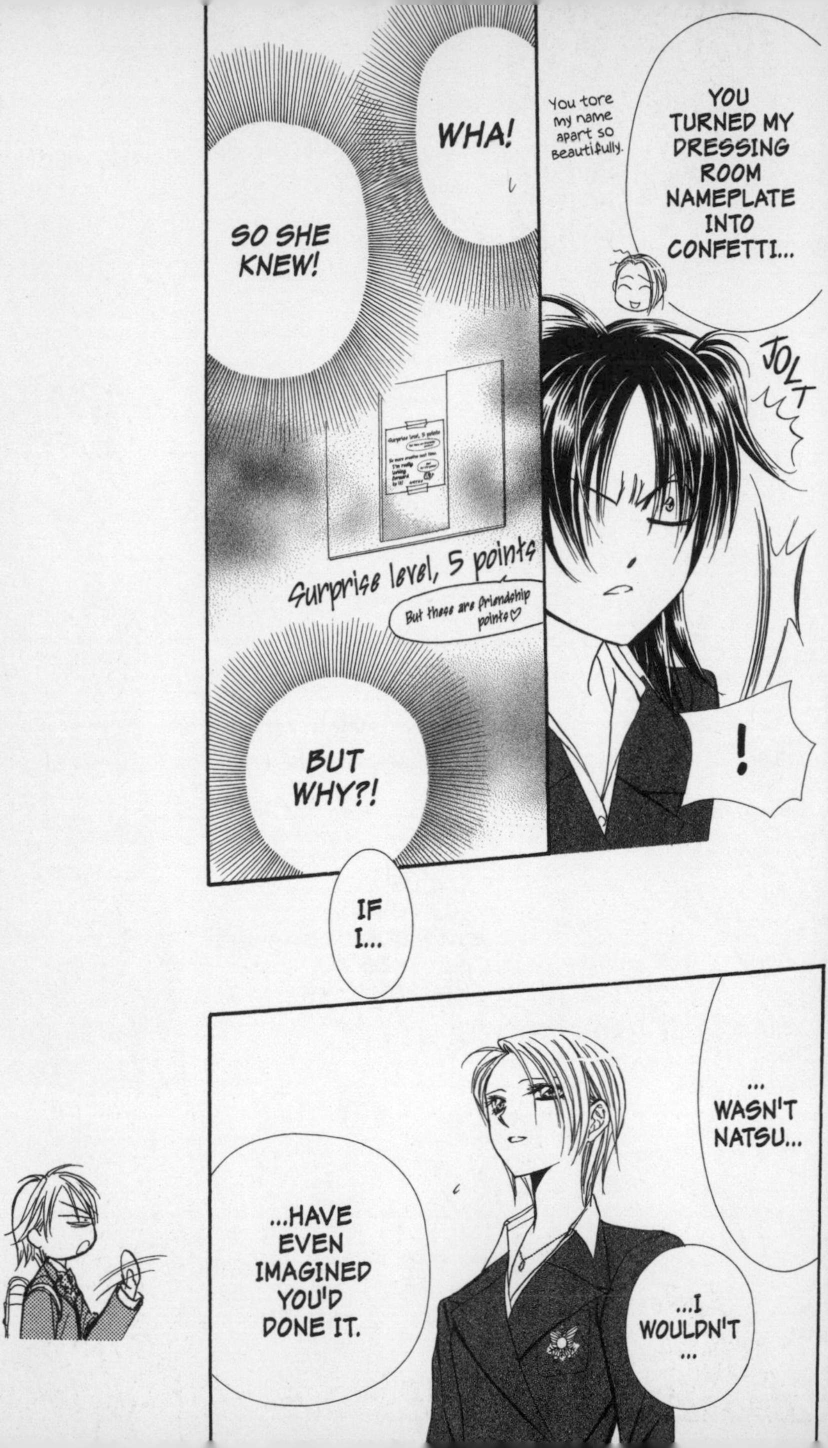
YOU TURNED MY DRESSING ROOM NAMEPLATE INTO CONFETTI...
You tore my name apart so beautifully.
JOLT
!
WHA!
SO SHE KNEW!
Surprise level, 5 points
But these are friendship points♡
BUT WHY?!
IF I...
...WASN'T NATSU...
...I WOULDN'T...
...HAVE EVEN IMAGINED YOU'D DONE IT.

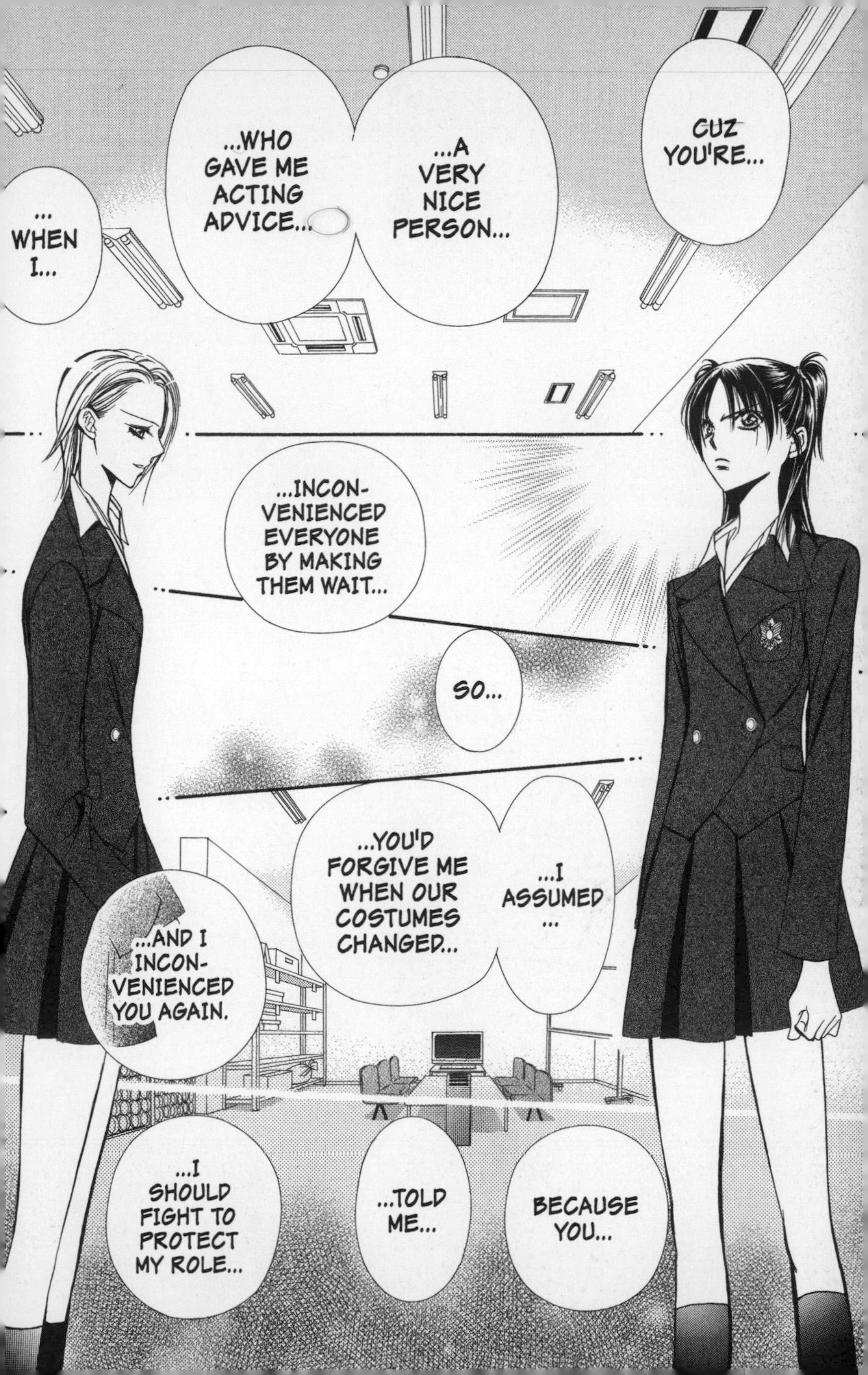
CUZ YOU'RE...
...A VERY NICE PERSON...
...WHO GAVE ME ACTING ADVICE...
... WHEN I...
...INCON-VENIENCED EVERYONE BY MAKING THEM WAIT...
SO...
...I ASSUMED...
...YOU'D FORGIVE ME WHEN OUR COSTUMES CHANGED...
...AND I INCON-VENIENCED YOU AGAIN.
BECAUSE YOU...
...TOLD ME...
...I SHOULD FIGHT TO PROTECT MY ROLE...

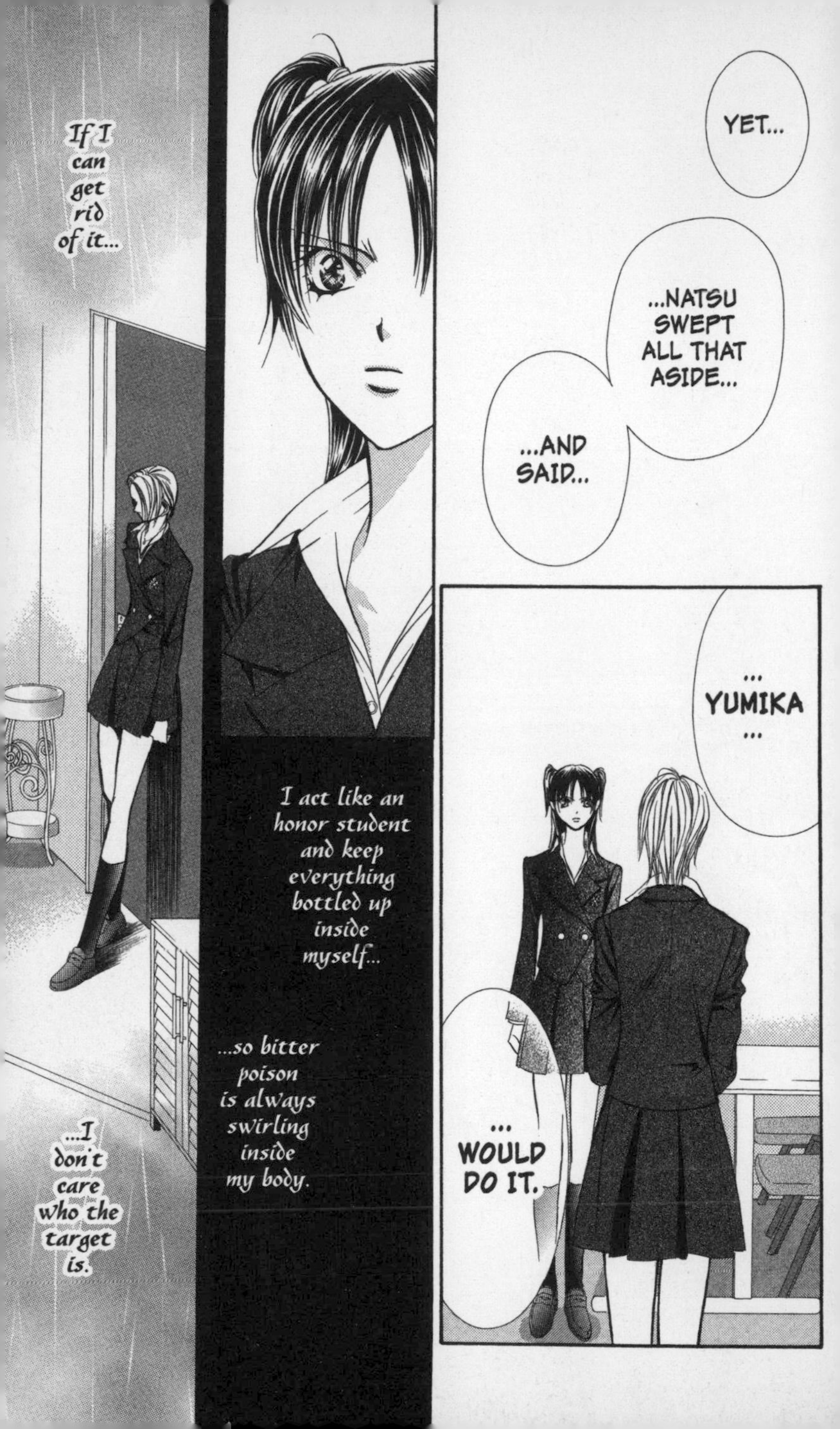
YET...
...NATSU SWEPT ALL THAT ASIDE...
...AND SAID...
...YUMIKA...
...WOULD DO IT.
I act like an honor student and keep everything bottled up inside myself...
...so bitter poison is always swirling inside my body.
If I can get rid of it...
...I don't care who the target is.

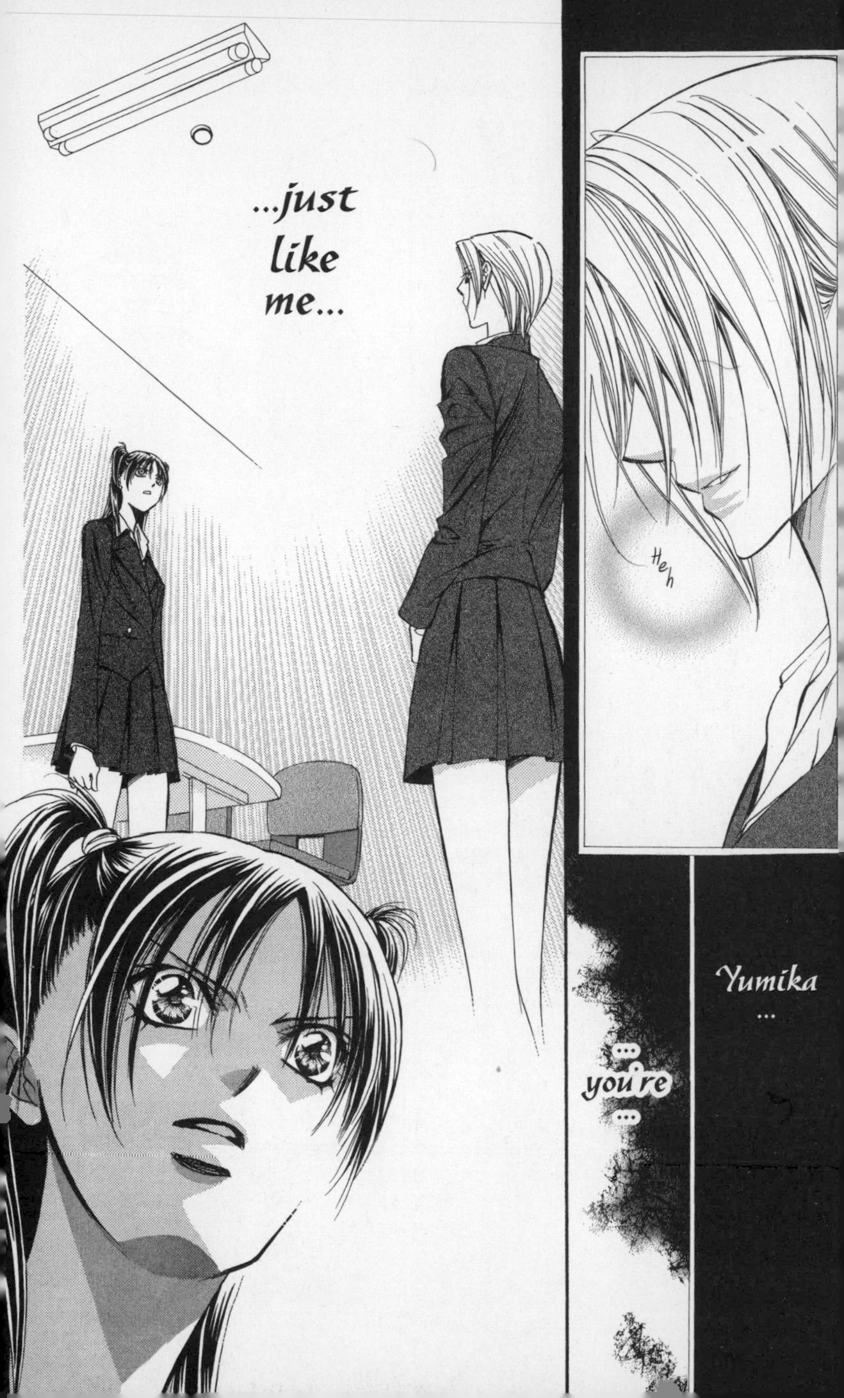
Heh
Yumika ...
...you're...
...just like me...

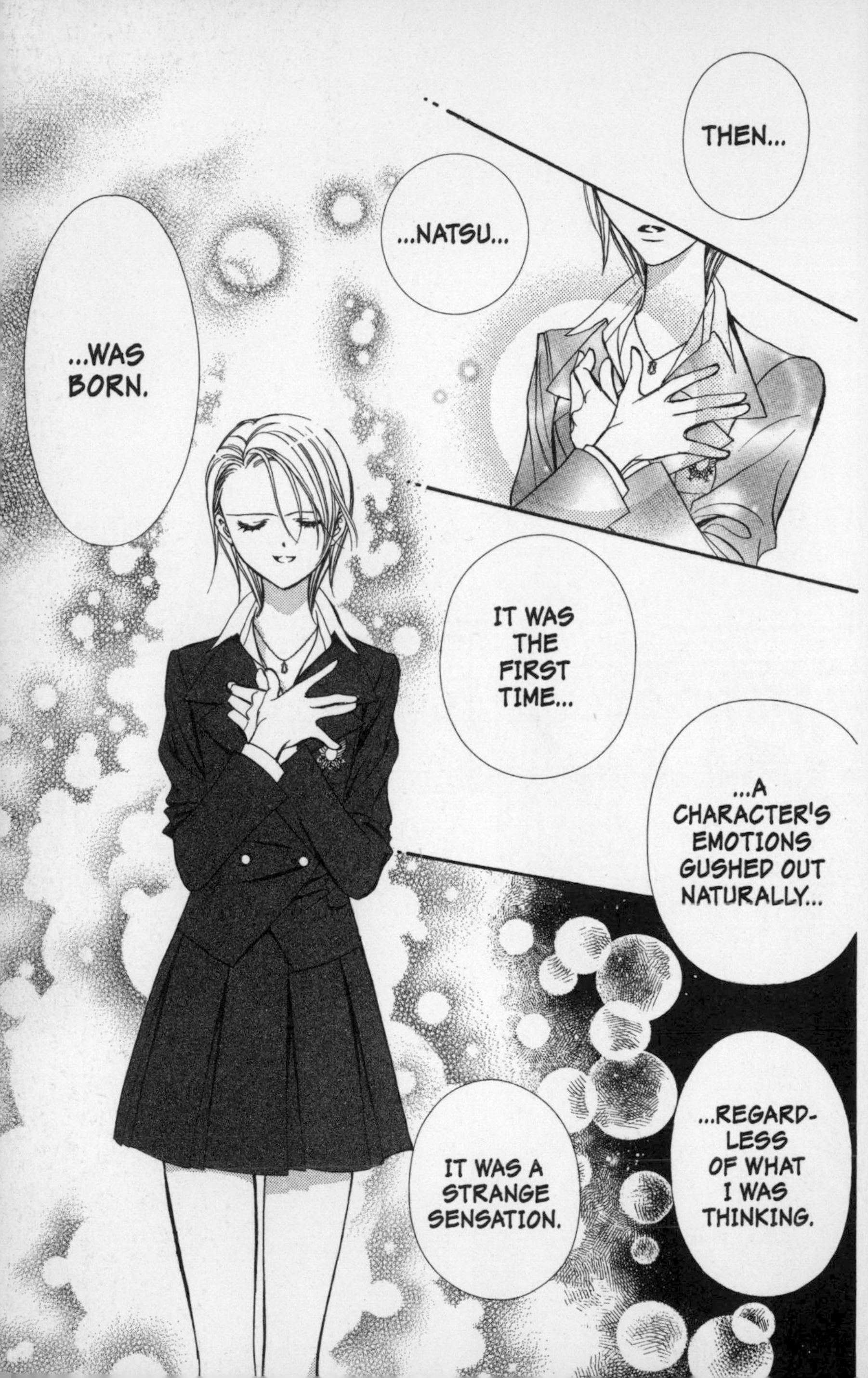
THEN...
...NATSU...
...WAS BORN.
IT WAS THE FIRST TIME...
...A CHARACTER'S EMOTIONS GUSHED OUT NATURALLY...
...REGARD-LESS OF WHAT I WAS THINKING.
IT WAS A STRANGE SENSATION.

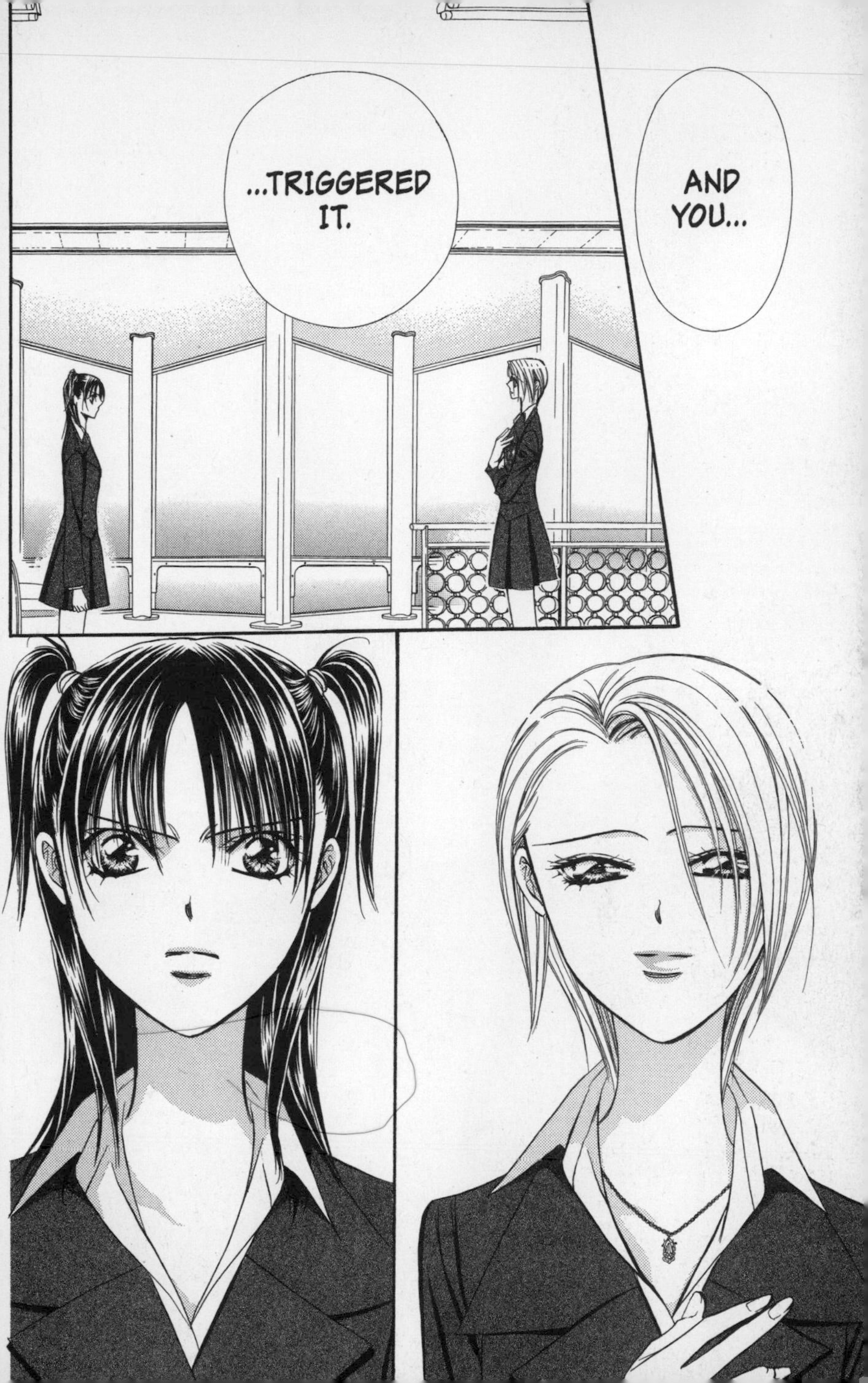
AND YOU...
...TRIGGERED IT.

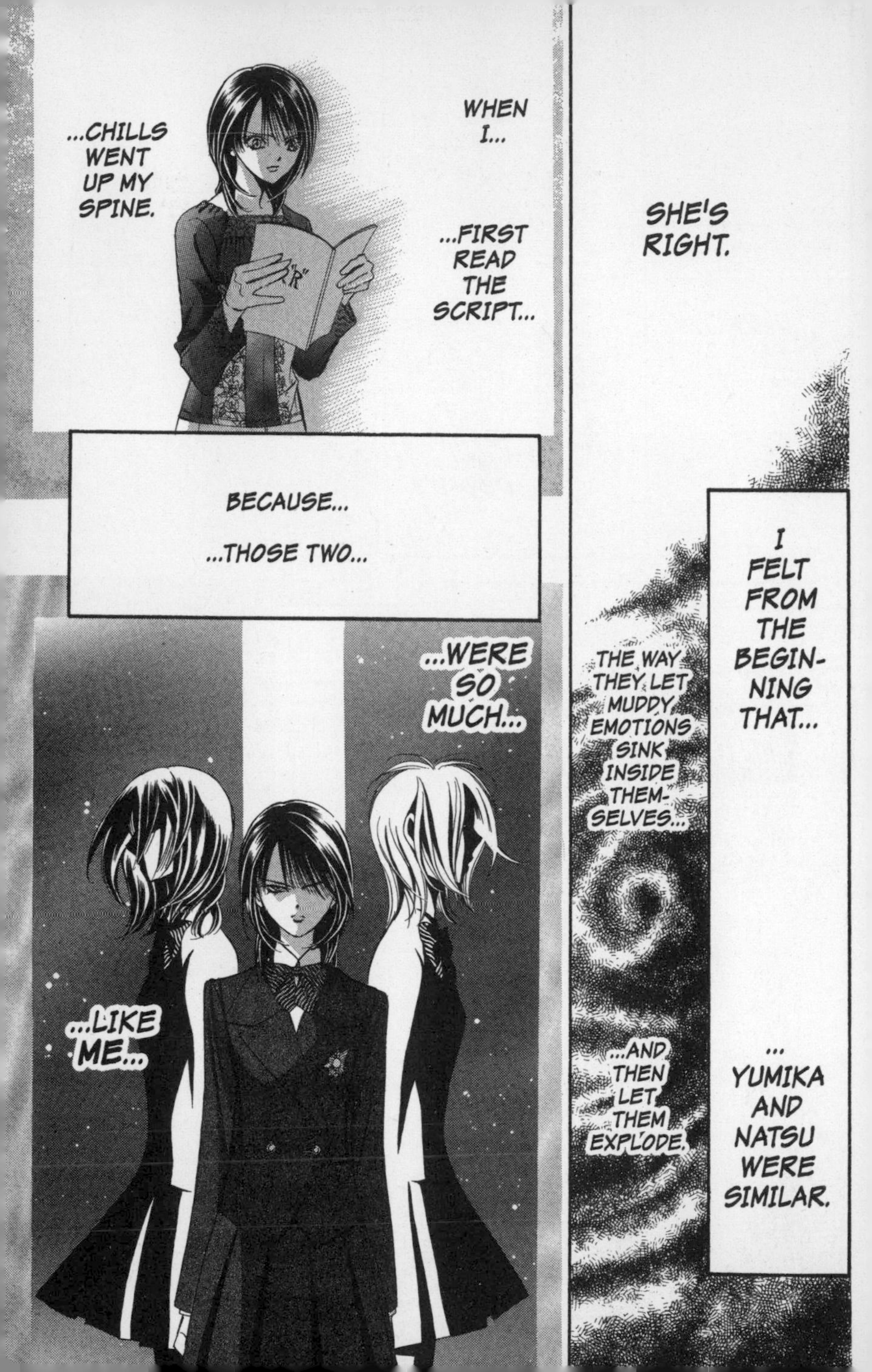
SHE'S RIGHT.
I FELT FROM THE BEGIN-NING THAT...
THE WAY THEY LET MUDDY EMOTIONS SINK INSIDE THEM-SELVES...
...AND THEN LET THEM EXPLODE.
... YUMIKA AND NATSU WERE SIMILAR.
WHEN I...
...FIRST READ THE SCRIPT...
...CHILLS WENT UP MY SPINE.
BECAUSE...
...THOSE TWO...
...WERE SO MUCH...
...LIKE ME...

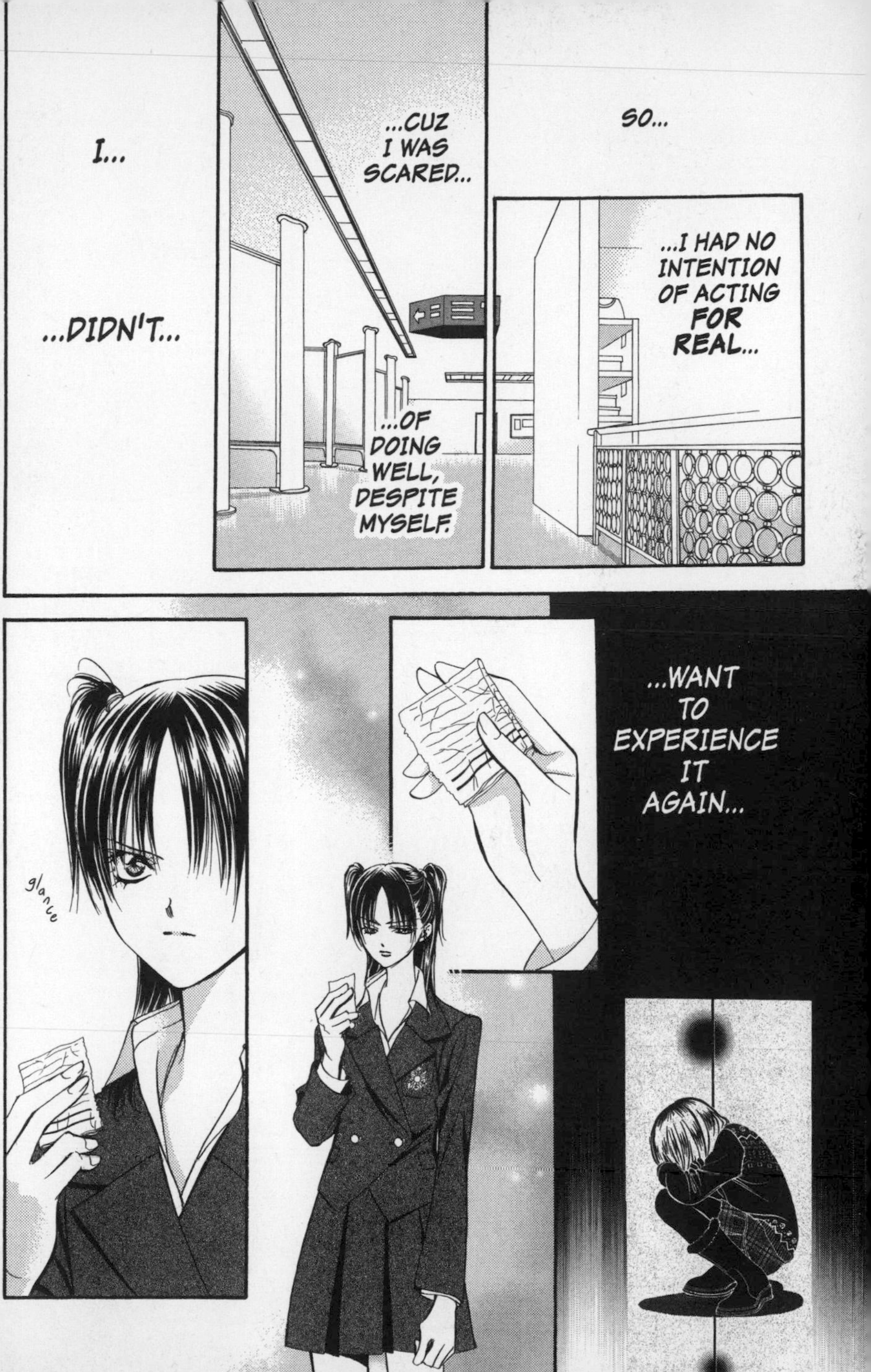
SO...
...I HAD NO INTENTION OF ACTING FOR REAL...
...CUZ I WAS SCARED...
...OF DOING WELL, DESPITE MYSELF.
I...
...DIDN'T...
...WANT TO EXPERIENCE IT AGAIN...
glance

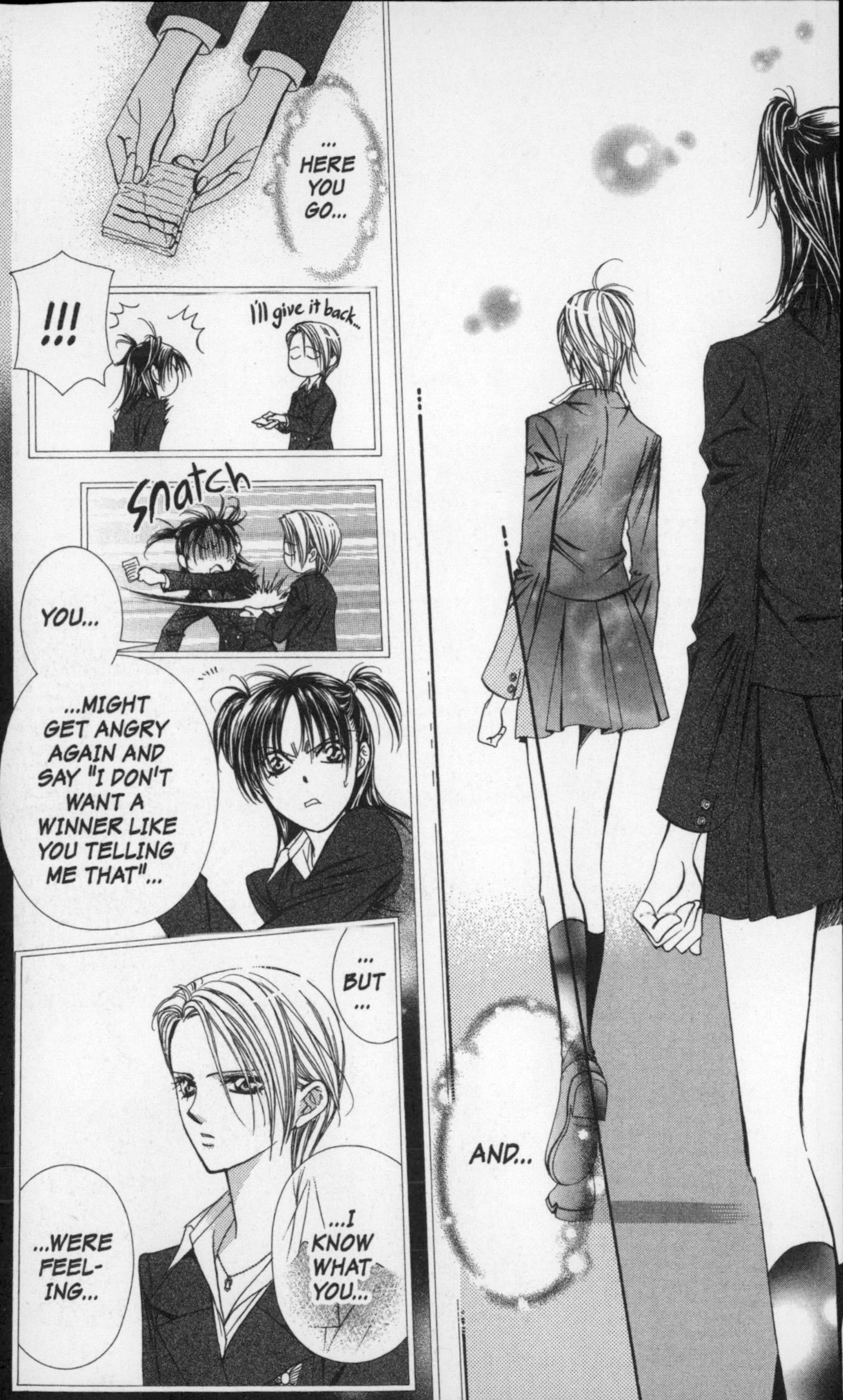
AND...
... HERE YOU GO...
I'll give it back...
!!!
Snatch
YOU...
...MIGHT GET ANGRY AGAIN AND SAY "I DON'T WANT A WINNER LIKE YOU TELLING ME THAT"...
... BUT ...
...I KNOW WHAT YOU...
...WERE FEEL-ING...

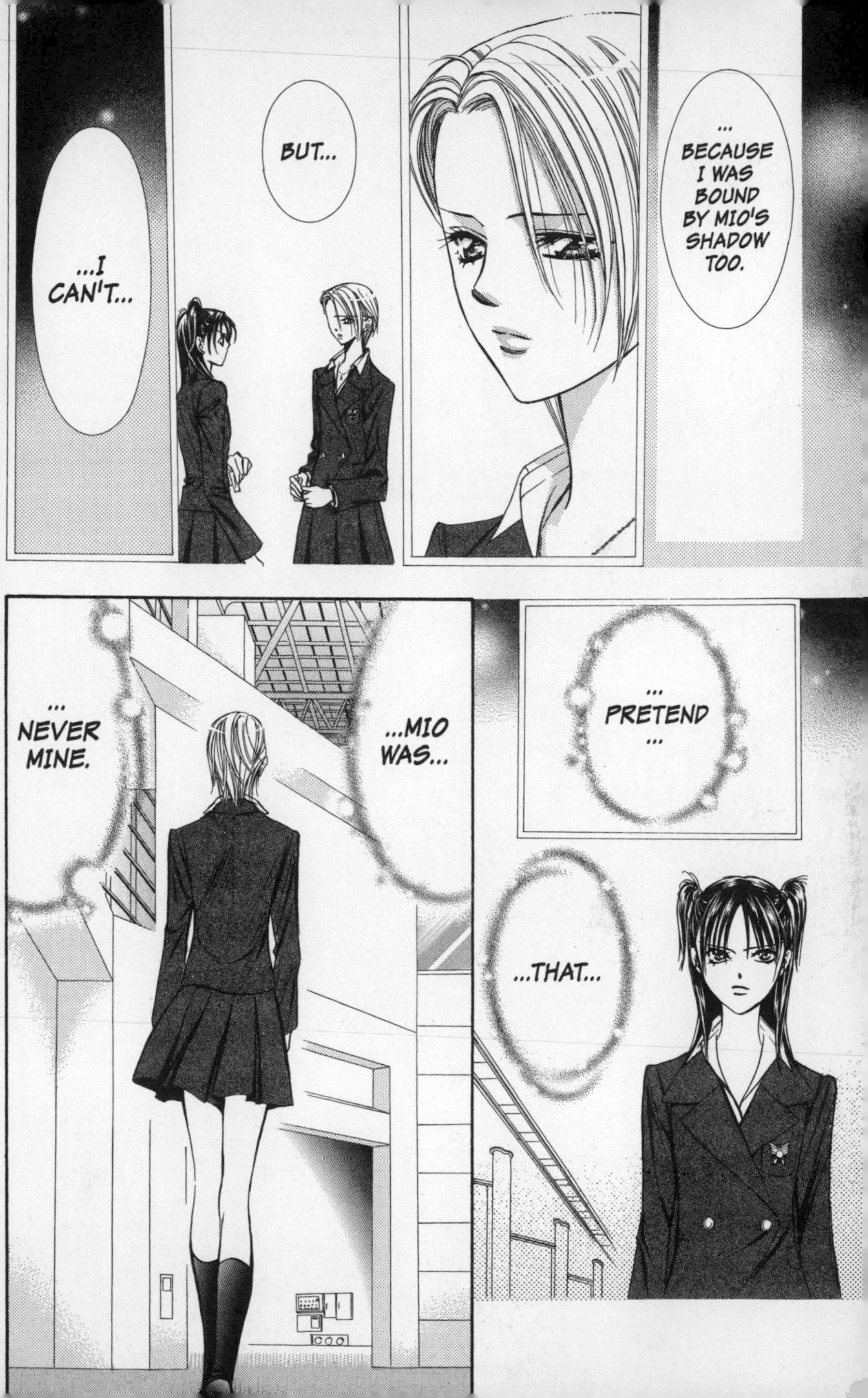
... BECAUSE I WAS BOUND BY MIO'S SHADOW TOO.
BUT...
...I CAN'T...
... PRETEND ...
...THAT...
...MIO WAS...
... NEVER MINE.

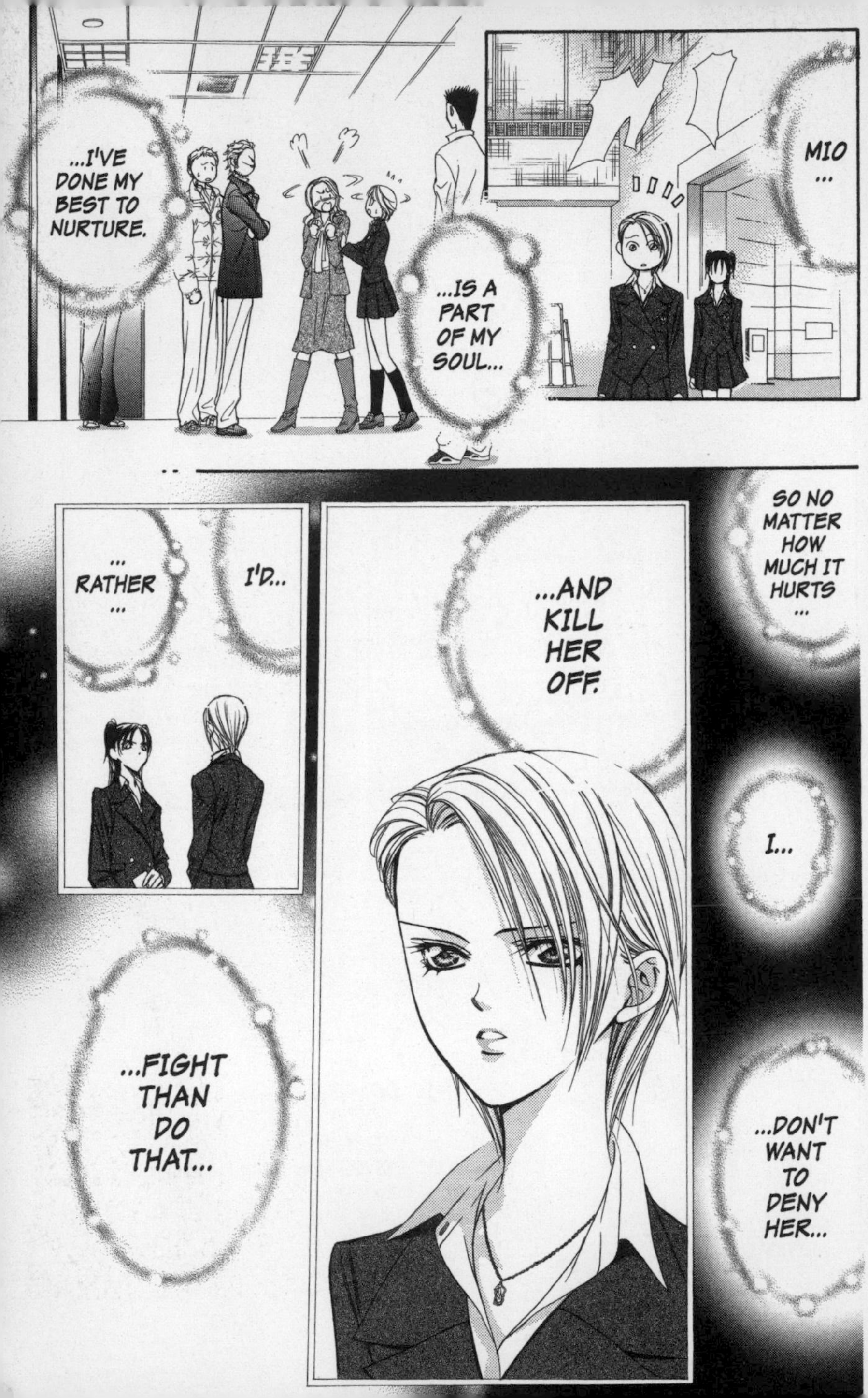
MIO...
...I'VE DONE MY BEST TO NURTURE.
...IS A PART OF MY SOUL...
SO NO MATTER HOW MUCH IT HURTS...
I...
...DON'T WANT TO DENY HER...
...AND KILL HER OFF.
I'D...
...RATHER...
...FIGHT THAN DO THAT...

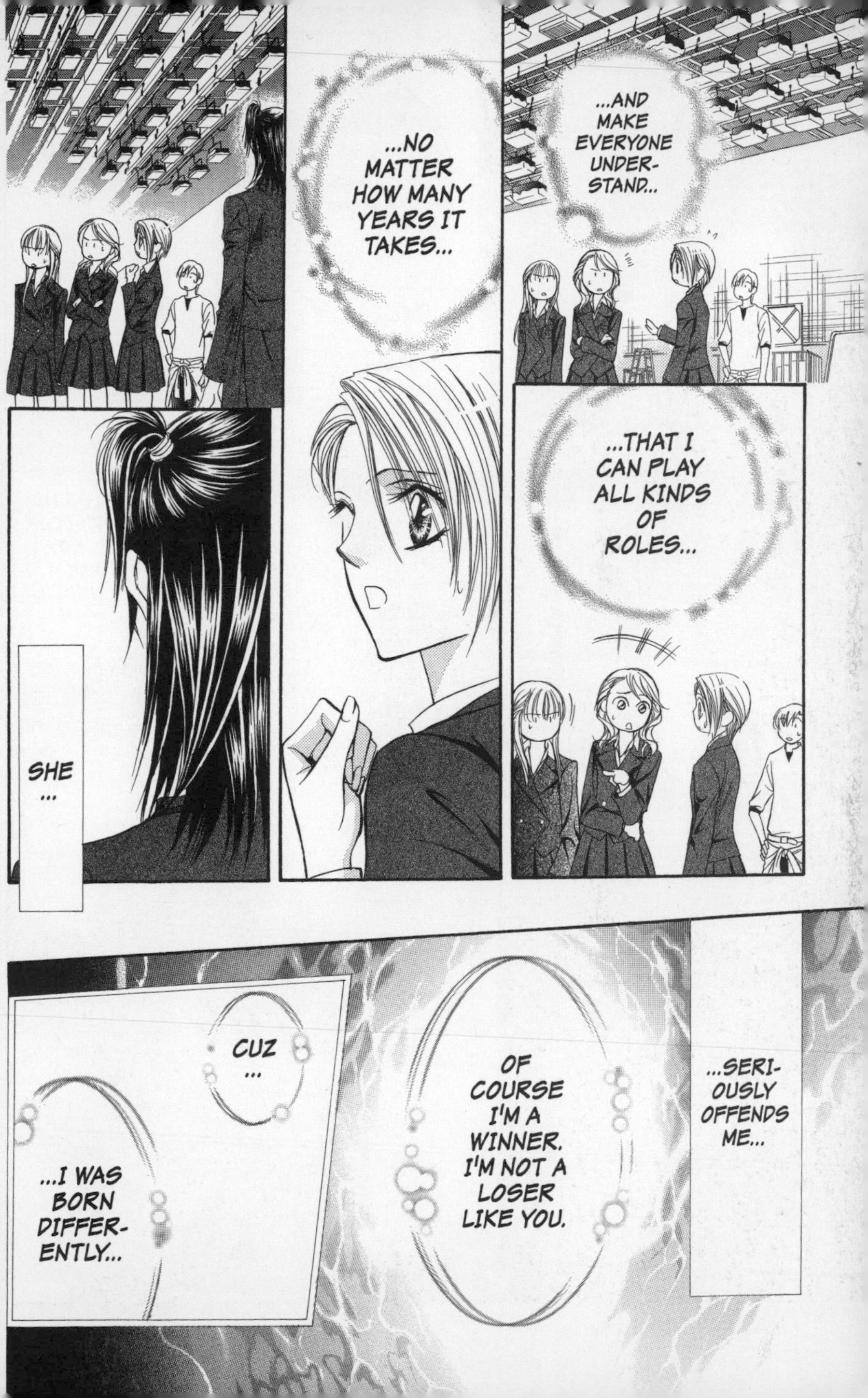
...AND MAKE EVERYONE UNDER-STAND...
...THAT I CAN PLAY ALL KINDS OF ROLES...
...NO MATTER HOW MANY YEARS IT TAKES...
SHE ...
...SERI-OUSLY OFFENDS ME...
OF COURSE I'M A WINNER. I'M NOT A LOSER LIKE YOU.
CUZ ...
...I WAS BORN DIFFER-ENTLY...

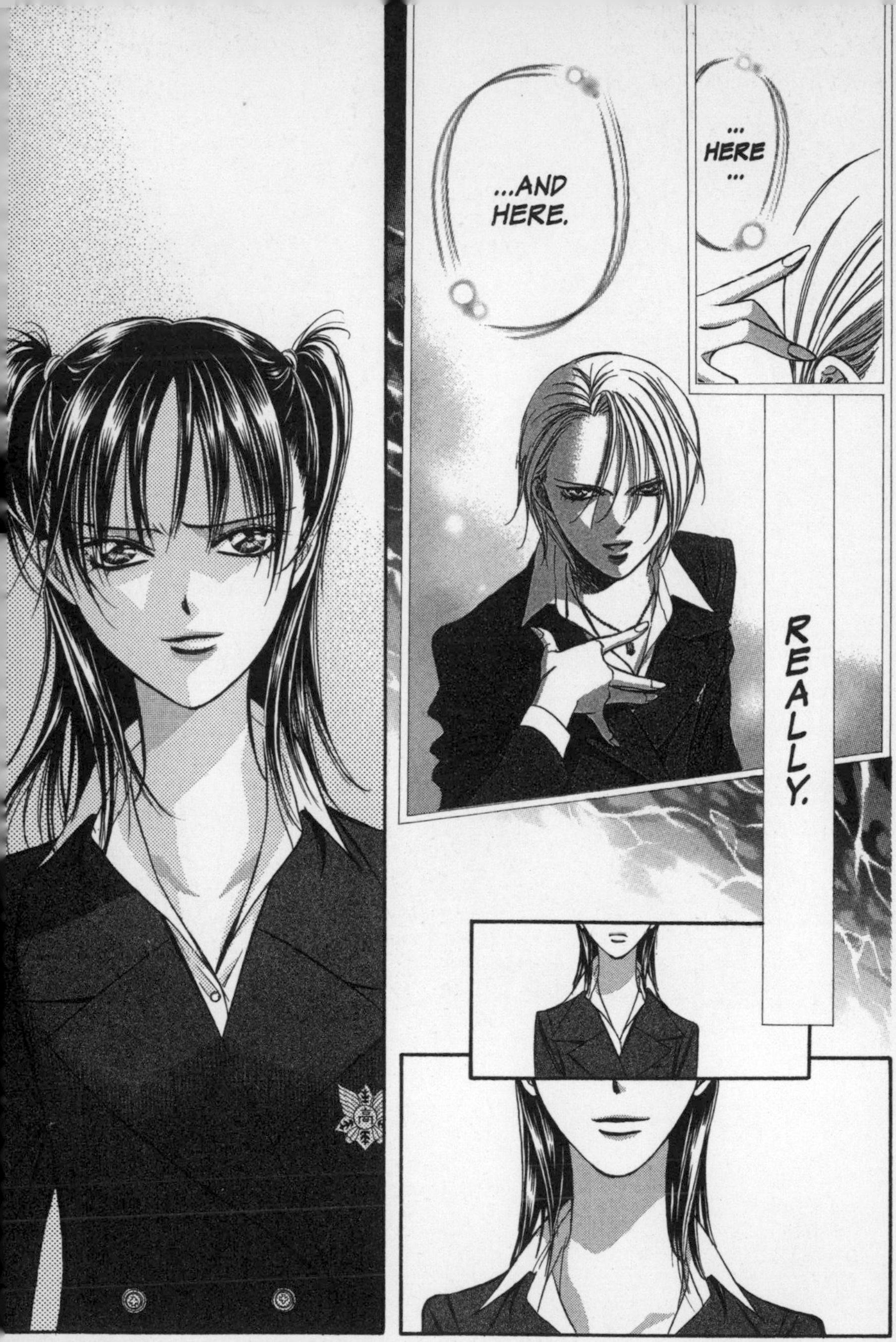
...
HERE
...
...AND HERE.
REALLY.

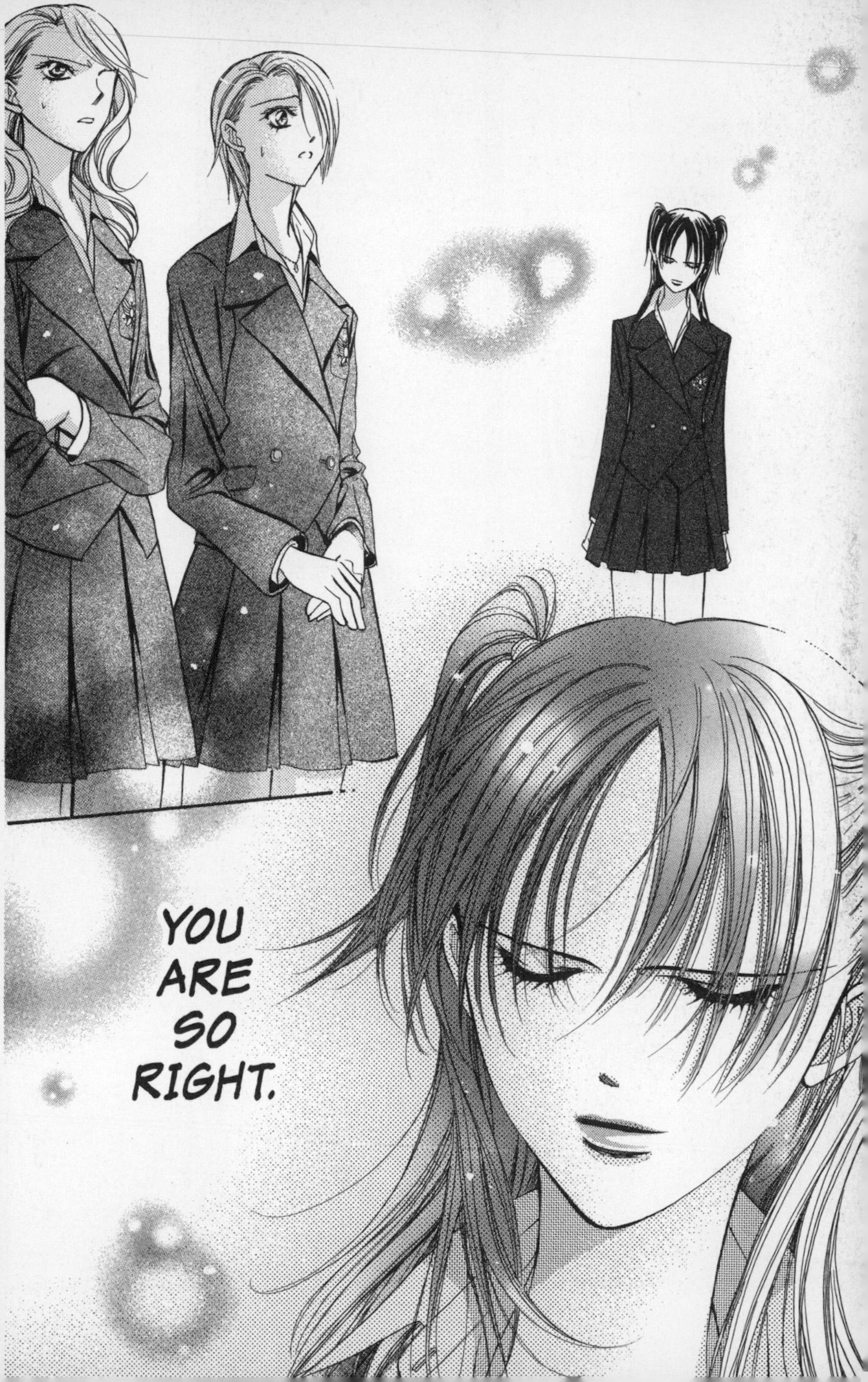
YOU ARE SO RIGHT.

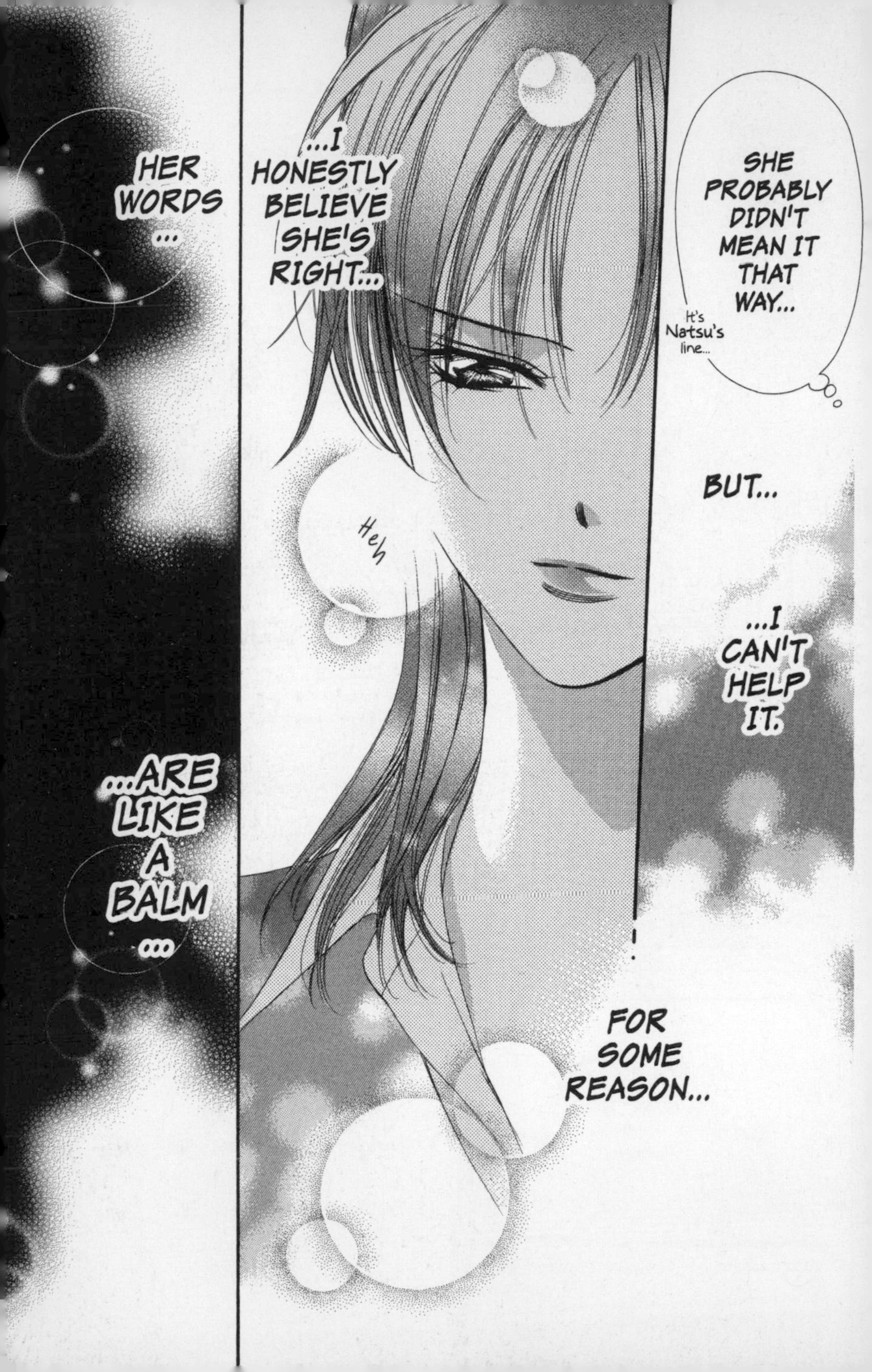

SHE PROBABLY DIDN'T MEAN IT THAT WAY...
It's Natsu's line...
BUT...
...I CAN'T HELP IT.
FOR SOME REASON...
...I HONESTLY BELIEVE SHE'S RIGHT...
Heh
HER WORDS...
...ARE LIKE A BALM...

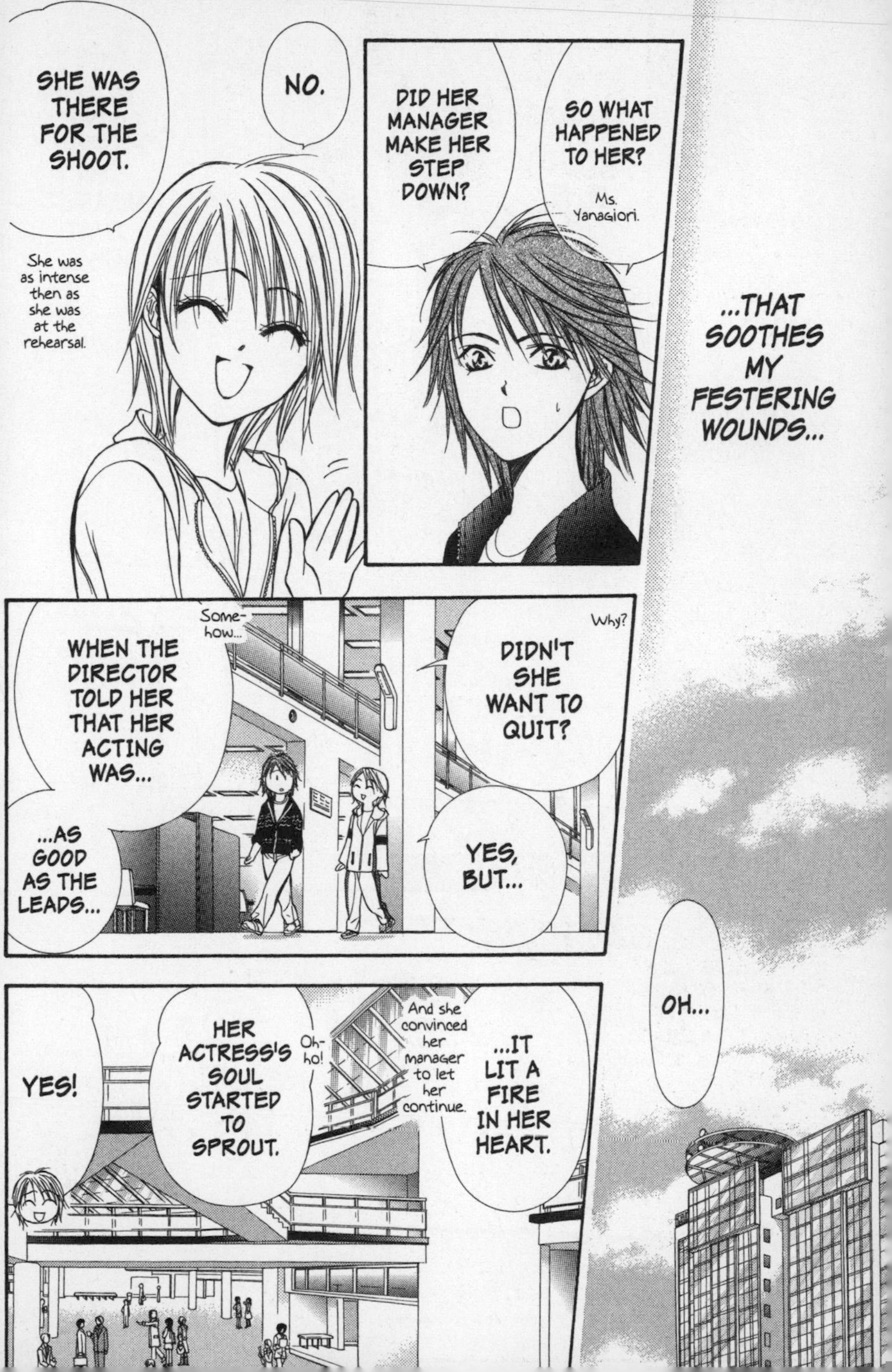
...THAT SOOTHES MY FESTERING WOUNDS...
OH...
SO WHAT HAPPENED TO HER?
Ms. Yanagiori.
DID HER MANAGER MAKE HER STEP DOWN?
NO.
SHE WAS THERE FOR THE SHOOT.
She was as intense then as she was at the rehearsal.
Why?
DIDN'T SHE WANT TO QUIT?
YES, BUT...
Some-how...
WHEN THE DIRECTOR TOLD HER THAT HER ACTING WAS...
...AS GOOD AS THE LEADS...
...IT LIT A FIRE IN HER HEART.
And she convinced her manager to let her continue.
Oh-ho!
HER ACTRESS'S SOUL STARTED TO SPROUT.
YES!

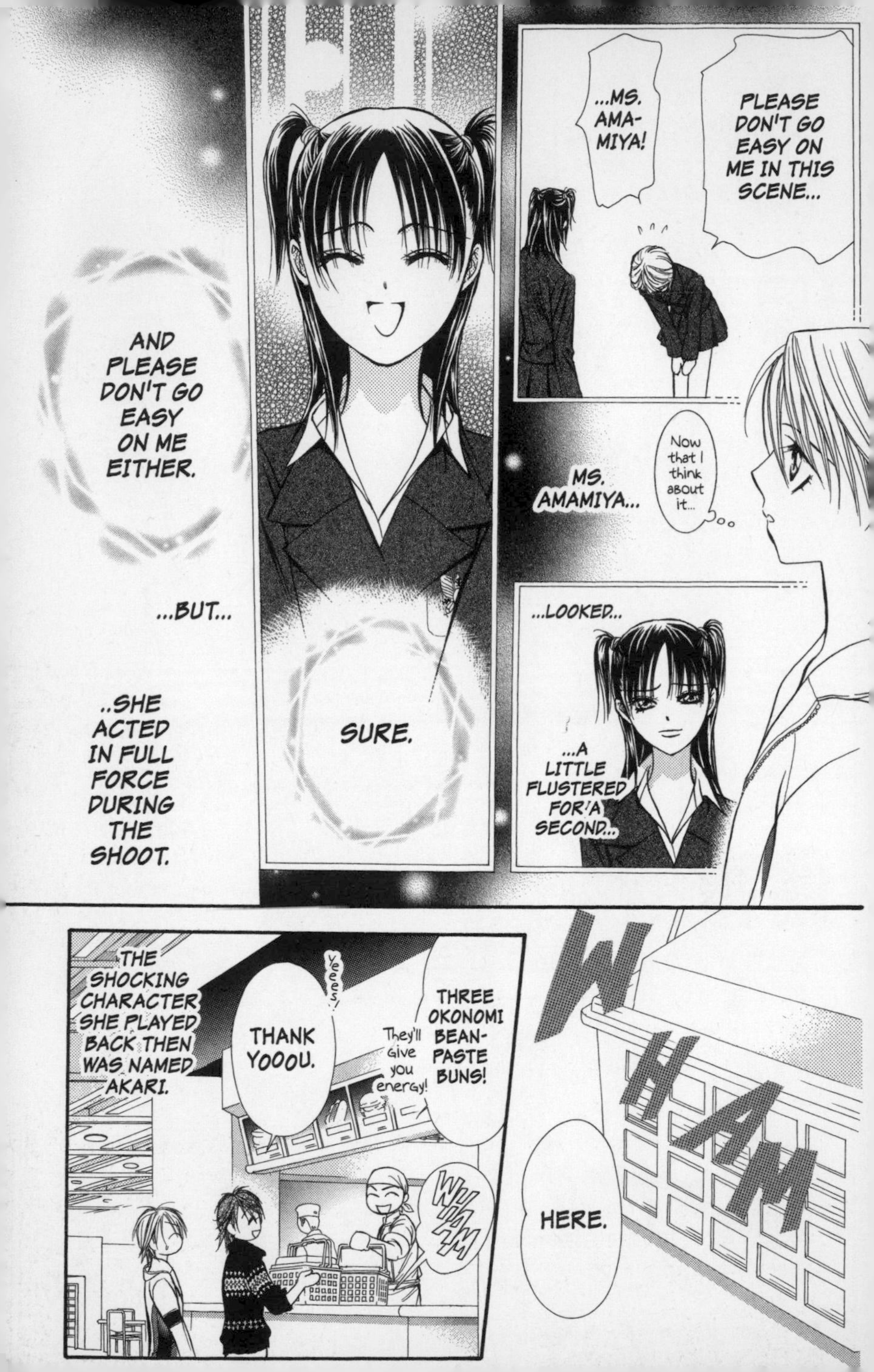
PLEASE DON'T GO EASY ON ME IN THIS SCENE...
...MS. AMA-MIYA!
Now that I think about it...
MS. AMAMIYA...
...LOOKED...
...A LITTLE FLUSTERED FOR A SECOND...
SURE.
AND PLEASE DON'T GO EASY ON ME EITHER.
...BUT...
..SHE ACTED IN FULL FORCE DURING THE SHOOT.
WHAM
HERE.
THREE OKONOMI BEAN-PASTE BUNS!
They'll Give you energy!
Yeeees!
THANK YOOOU.
WHAM
THE SHOCKING CHARACTER SHE PLAYED BACK THEN WAS NAMED AKARI.

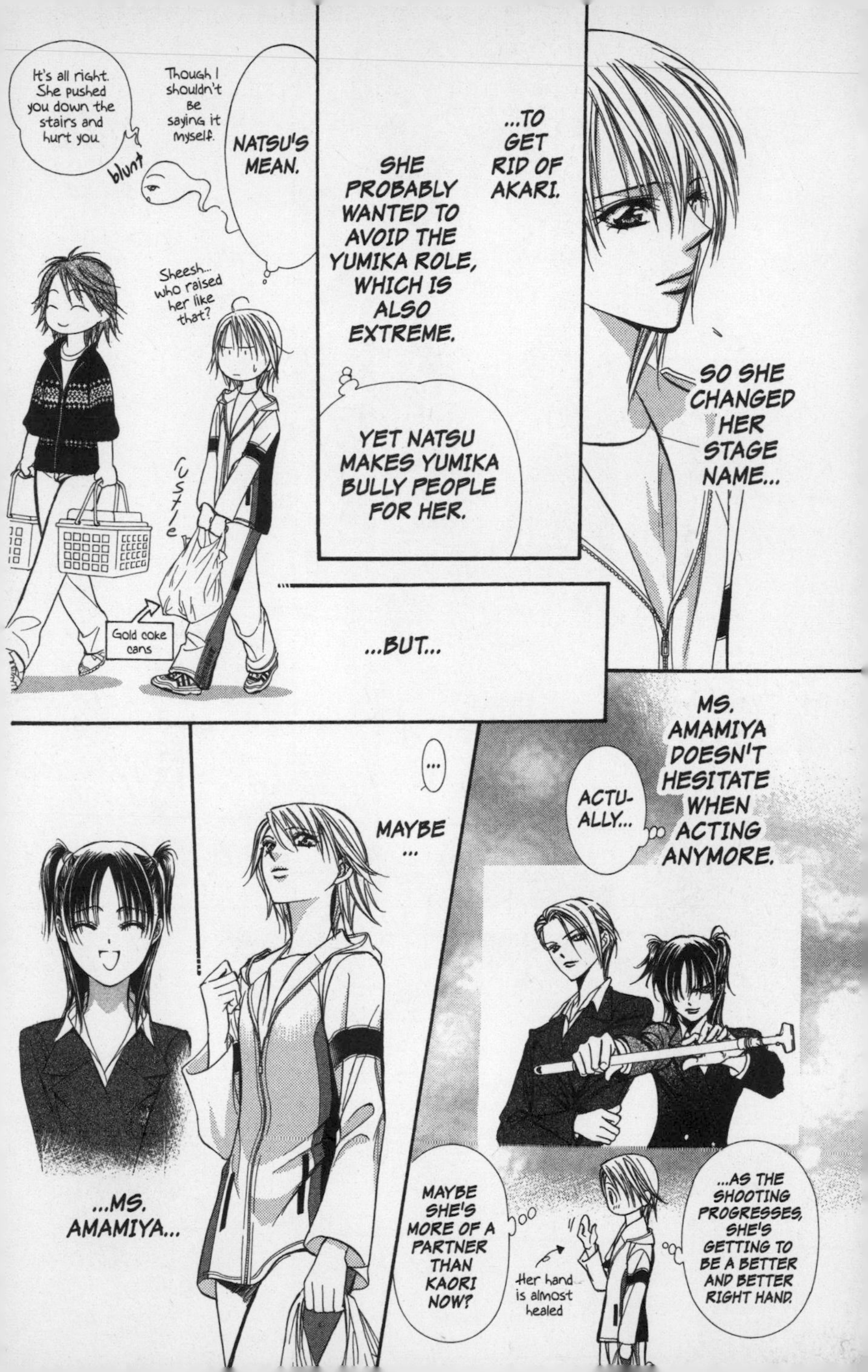
SO SHE CHANGED HER STAGE NAME...
...TO GET RID OF AKARI.
SHE PROBABLY WANTED TO AVOID THE YUMIKA ROLE, WHICH IS ALSO EXTREME.
YET NATSU MAKES YUMIKA BULLY PEOPLE FOR HER.
NATSU'S MEAN.
Though I shouldn't be saying it myself.
It's all right. She pushed you down the stairs and hurt you.
blunt
Sheesh... who raised her like that?
rustle
Gold coke cans
...BUT...
MS. AMAMIYA DOESN'T HESITATE WHEN ACTING ANYMORE.
ACTU-ALLY...
...AS THE SHOOTING PROGRESSES, SHE'S GETTING TO BE A BETTER AND BETTER RIGHT HAND.
MAYBE SHE'S MORE OF A PARTNER THAN KAORI NOW?
Her hand is almost healed
...
MAYBE...
...MS. AMAMIYA...

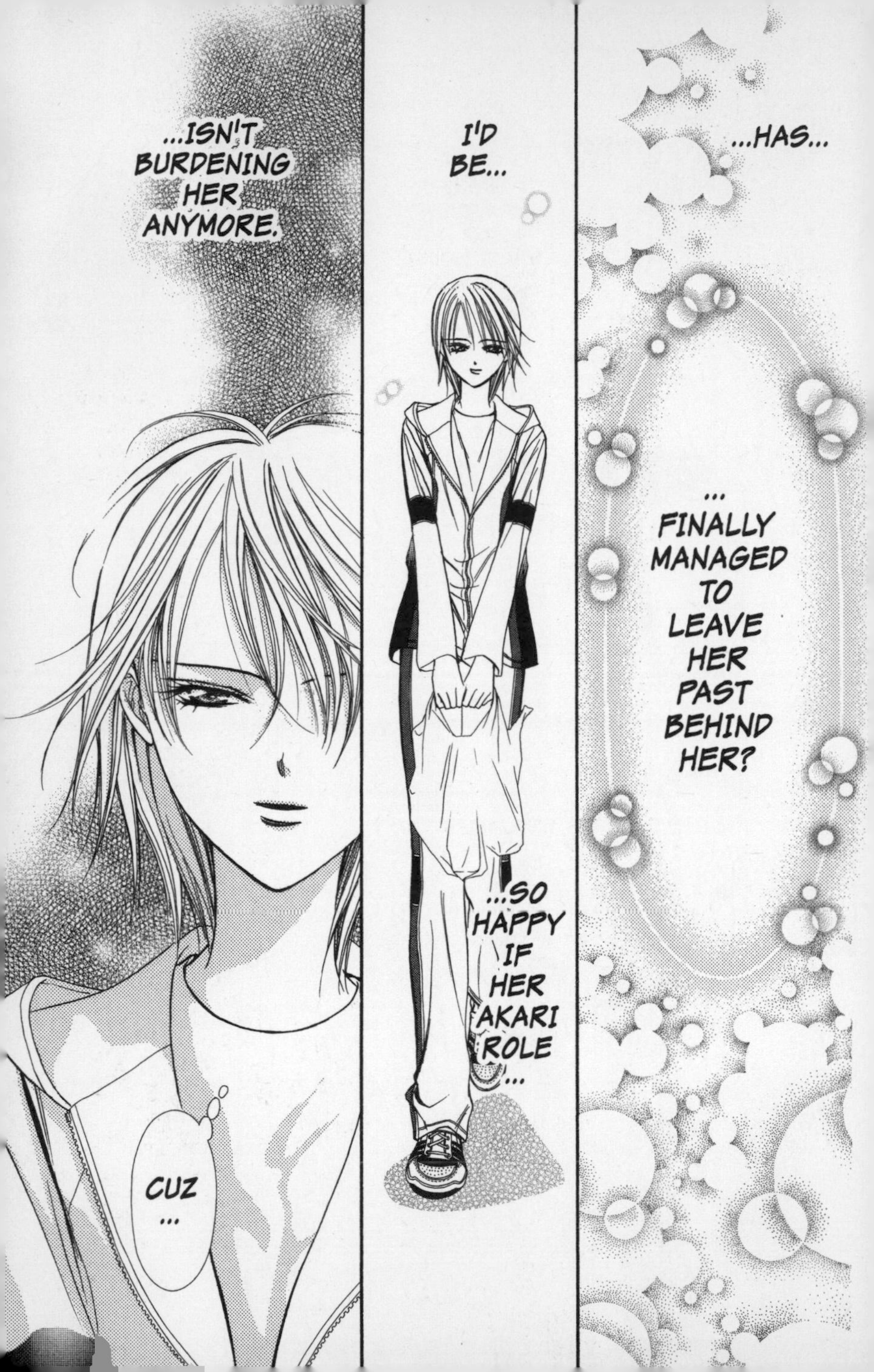
...HAS...
... FINALLY MANAGED TO LEAVE HER PAST BEHIND HER?
I'D BE...
...SO HAPPY IF HER AKARI ROLE...
...ISN'T BURDENING HER ANYMORE.
CUZ ...

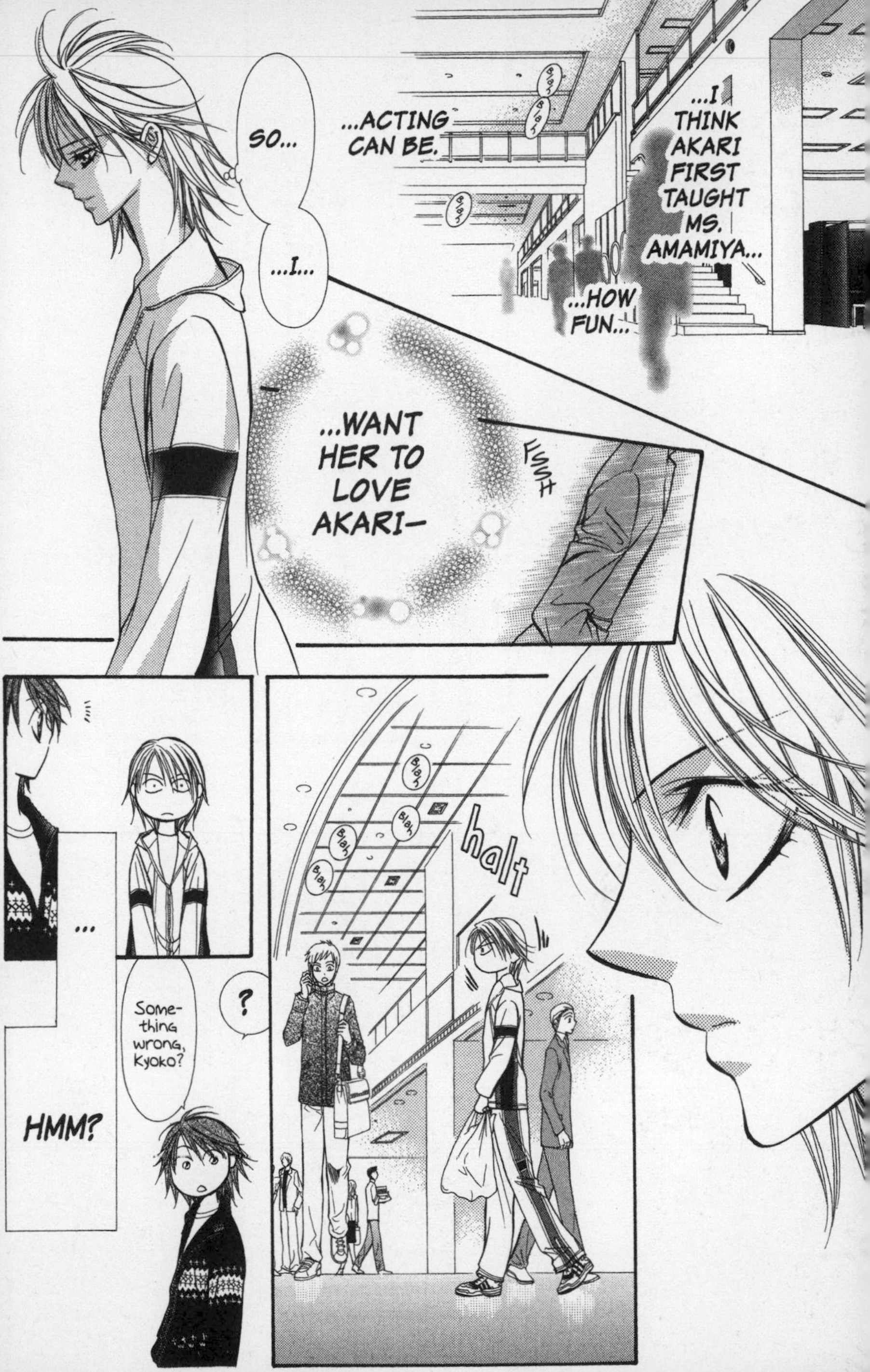
...I THINK AKARI FIRST TAUGHT MS. AMAMIYA...
...HOW FUN...
...ACTING CAN BE.
SO...
...I...
...WANT HER TO LOVE AKARI—
FSSH
halt
Blah
Blah
Blah
Blah
...
?
Something wrong, Kyoko?
HMM?

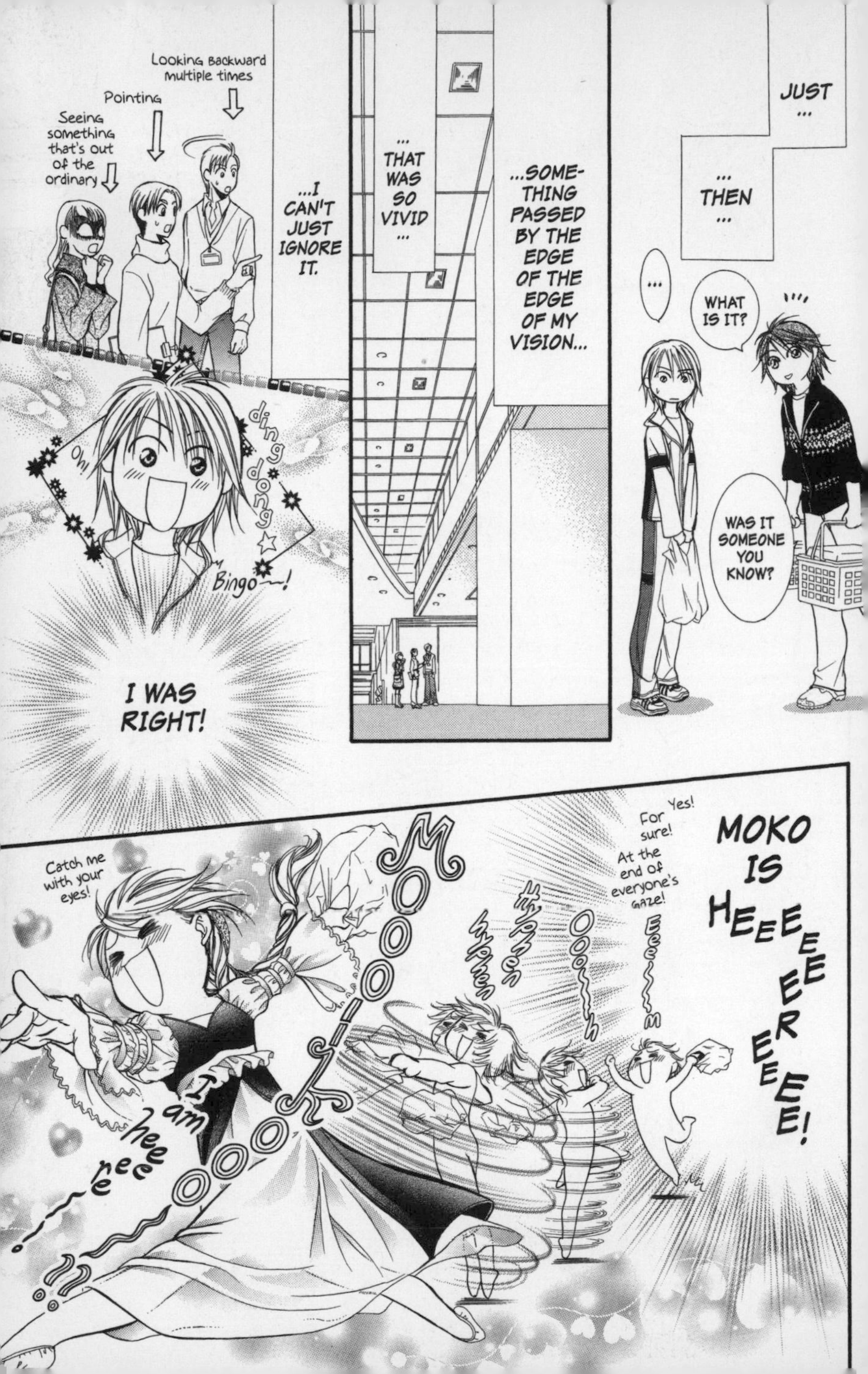
JUST...
...THEN...
WHAT IS IT?
...
WAS IT SOMEONE YOU KNOW?
...SOMETHING PASSED BY THE EDGE OF THE EDGE OF MY VISION...
...THAT WAS SO VIVID...
...I CAN'T JUST IGNORE IT.
Looking Backward multiple times
Pointing
Seeing something that's out of the ordinary
Oh!
ding dong☆
Bingo~~!
I WAS RIGHT!
MOKO IS HEEEEEEREEEEE!
Yes! For sure! At the end of everyone's GAZE!
Eee~~m
Oooo~~h
hyper hyper
MOOOOOH!
Catch me with your eyes!
I am heeeree~~!
OOOOO~~??

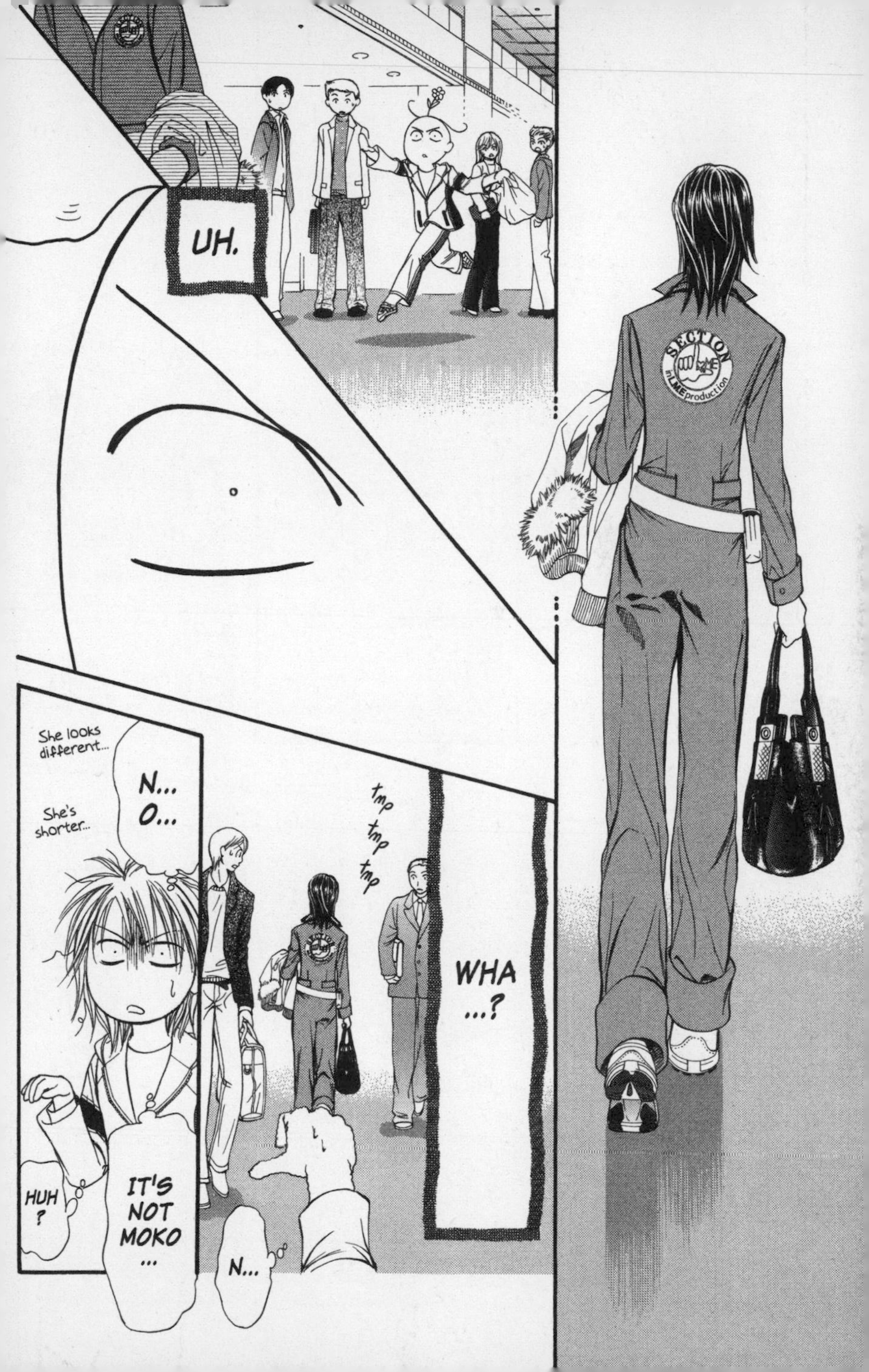
UH.
tmp tmp tmp
WHA ...?
N... O...
She looks different...
She's shorter...
N...
IT'S NOT MOKO ...
HUH ?

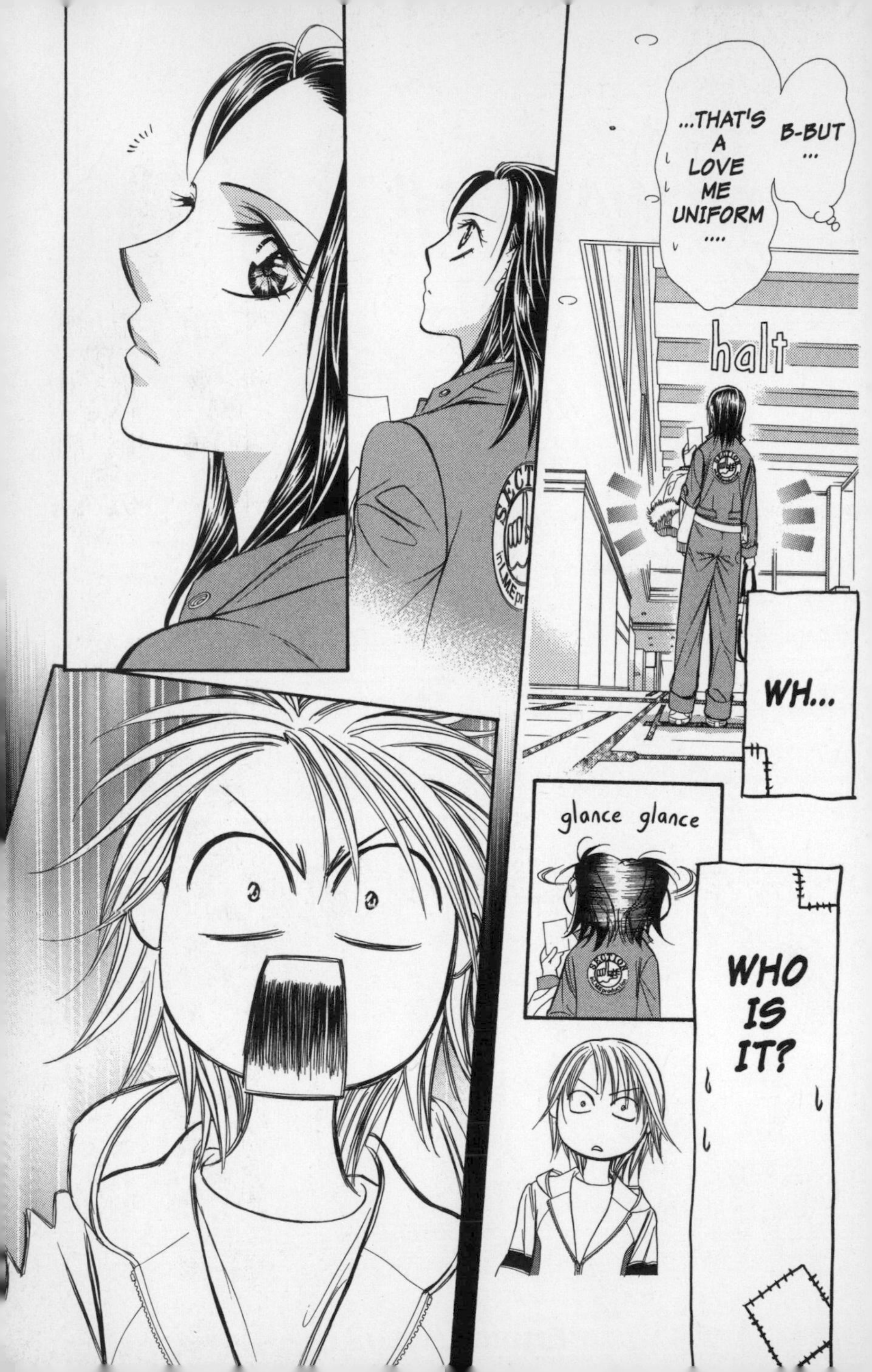
B-BUT ...
...THAT'S A LOVE ME UNIFORM ....
halt
WH...
glance glance
WHO IS IT?

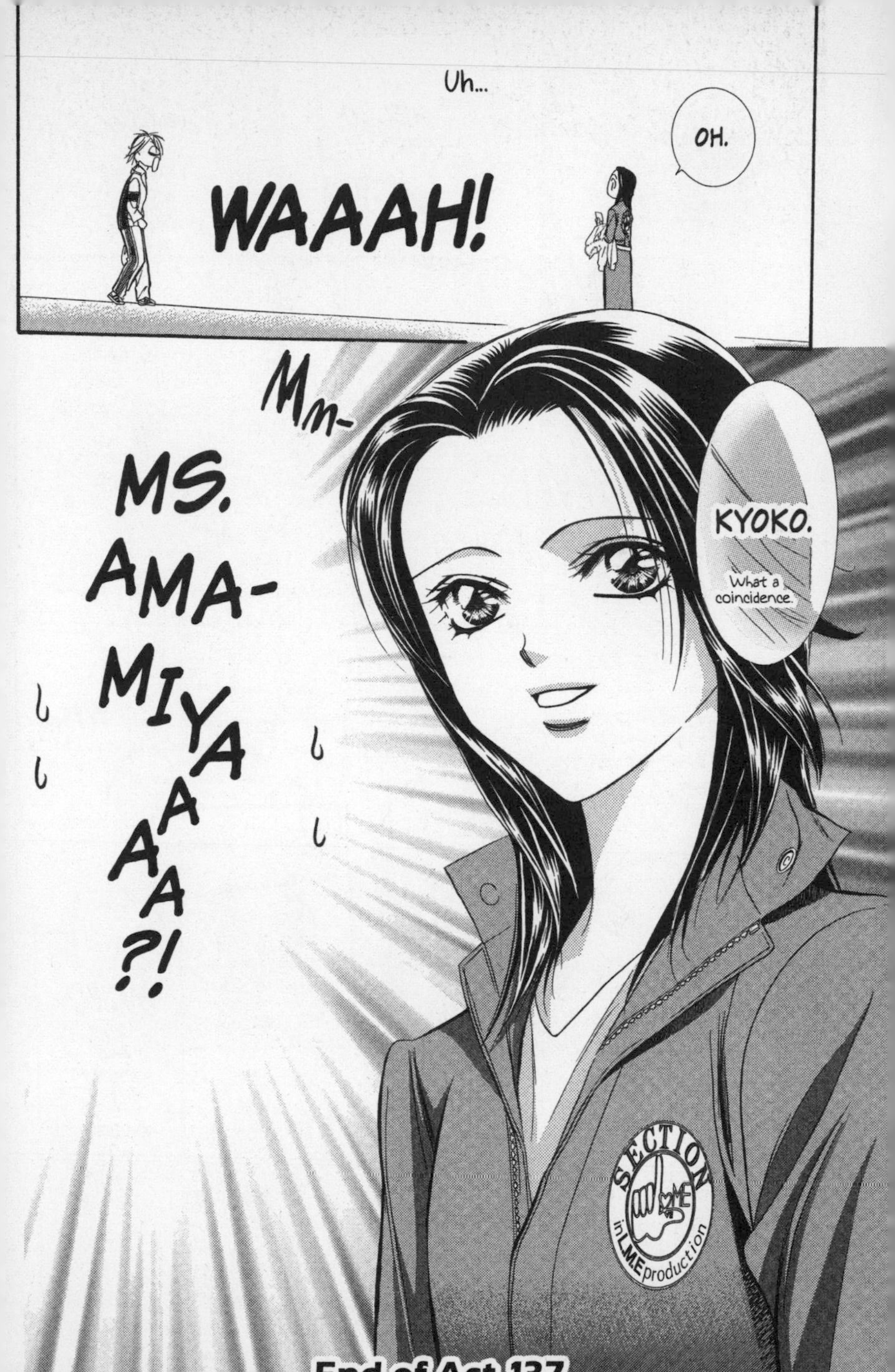
Uh...
OH.
WAAAH!
KYOKO.
What a coincidence.
Mn-
MS. AMA-MIYAAAAA?!
End of Act 137

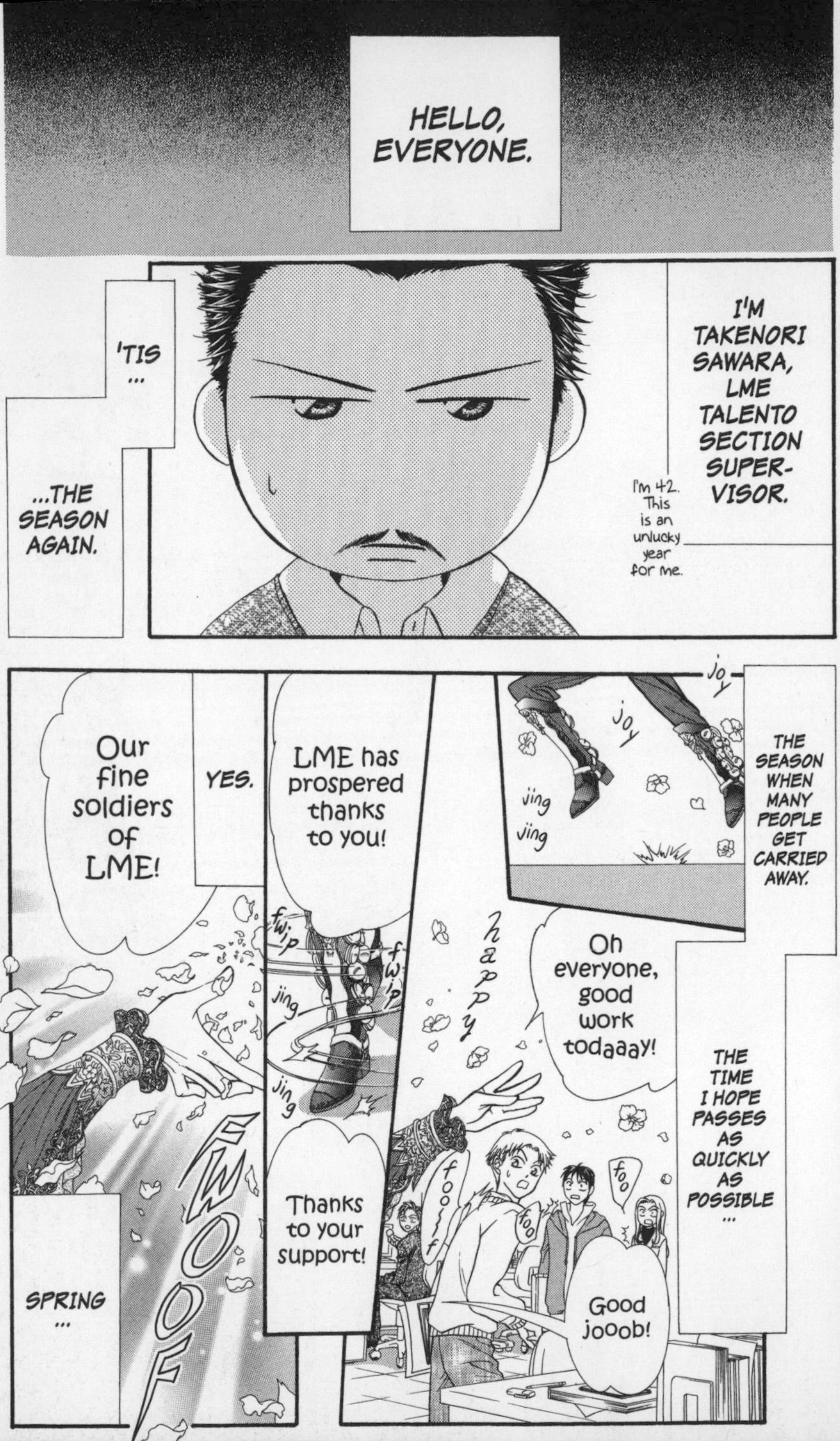
HELLO, EVERYONE.
I'M TAKENORI SAWARA, LME TALENTO SECTION SUPER-VISOR.
I'm 42. This is an unlucky year for me.
'TIS ...
...THE SEASON AGAIN.
THE SEASON WHEN MANY PEOPLE GET CARRIED AWAY.
joy
joy
jing
jing
Oh everyone, good work todaaay!
happy
THE TIME I HOPE PASSES AS QUICKLY AS POSSIBLE ...
foo
foo--f
foo
Good jooob!
LME has prospered thanks to you!
fwip
fwip
jing
jing
Thanks to your support!
YES.
Our fine soldiers of LME!
FWOOOF
SPRING ...

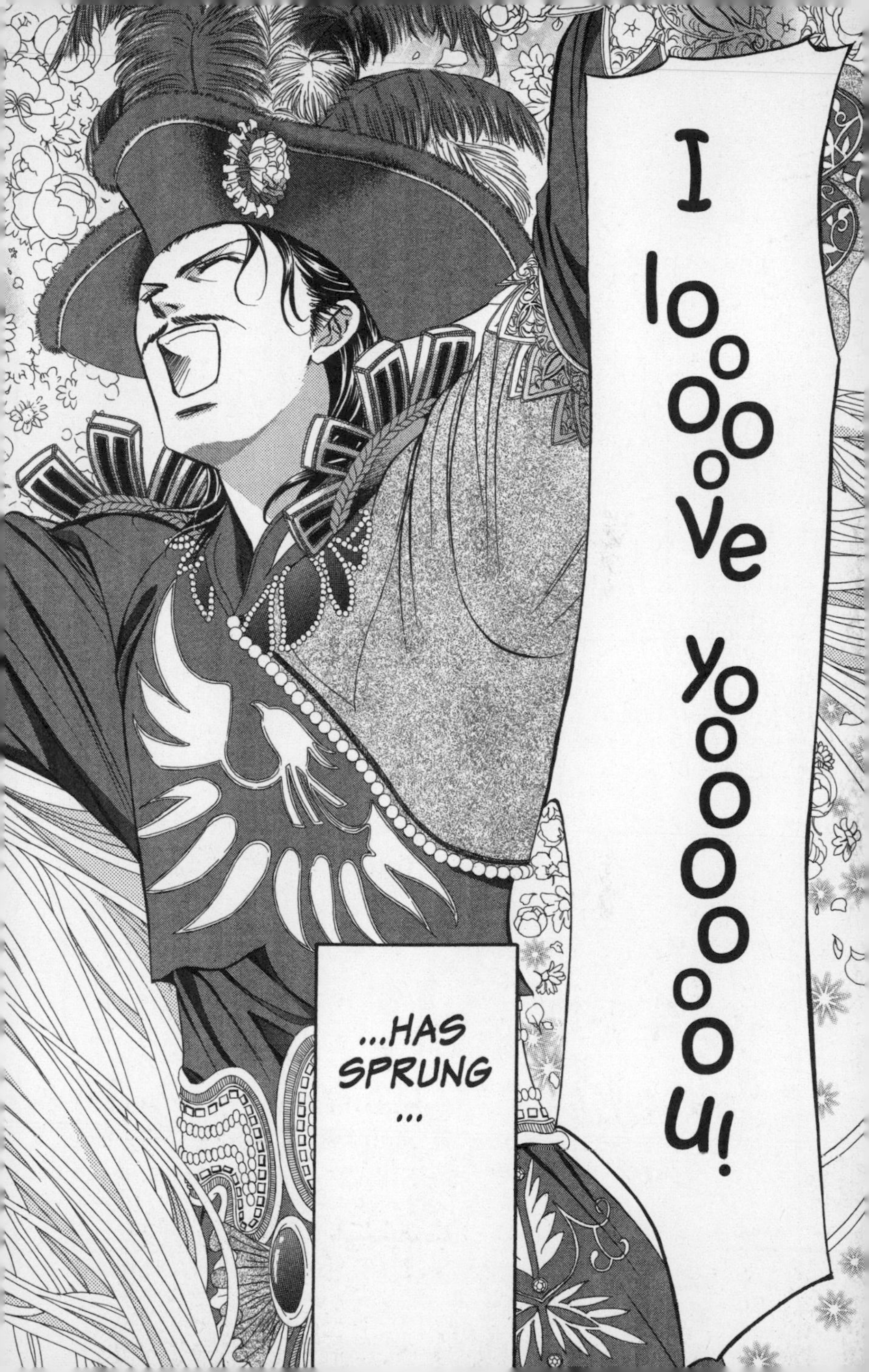
I loooove yooooooou!
...HAS SPRUNG ...

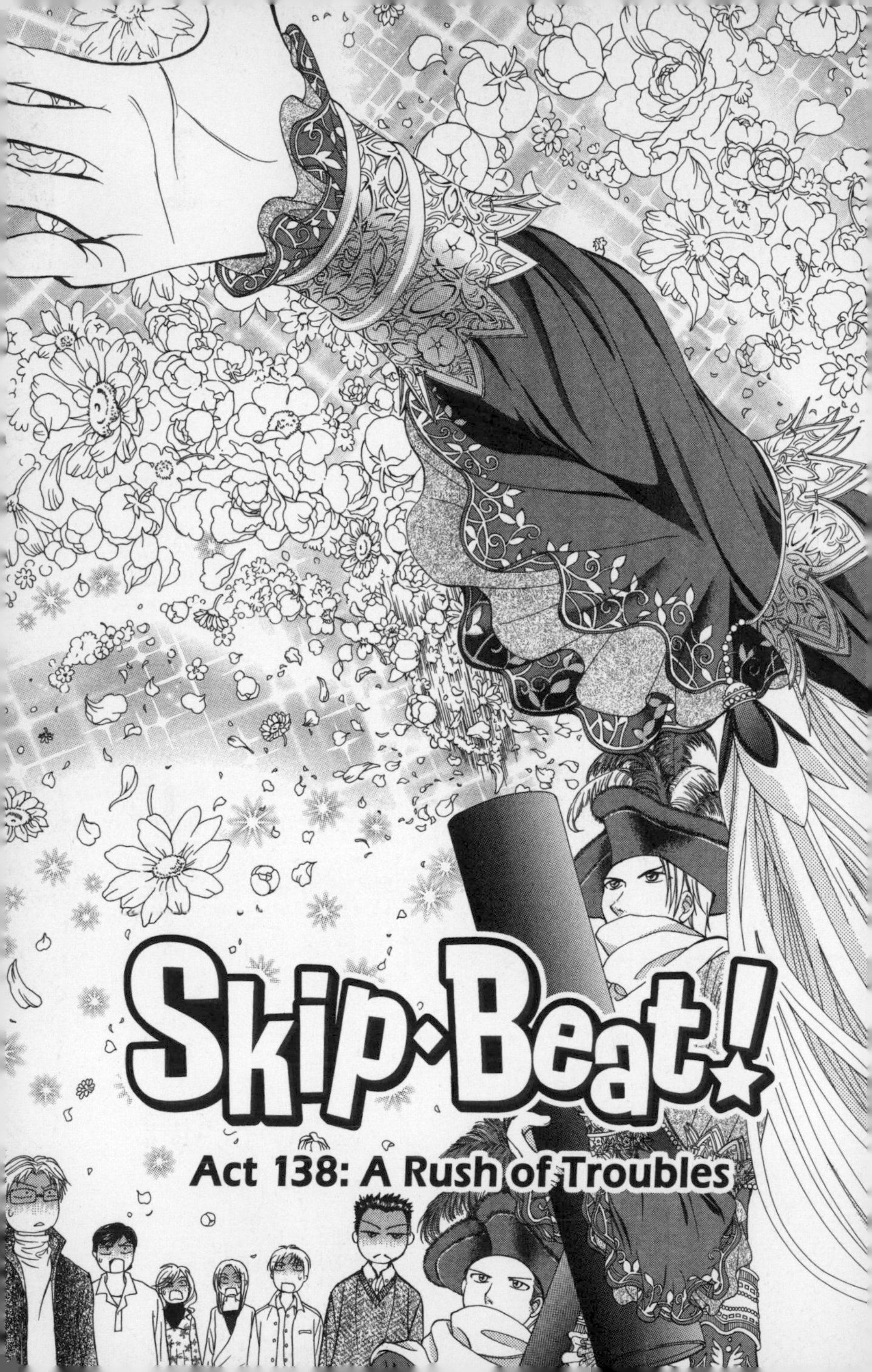
Skip·Beat!
Act 138: A Rush of Troubles

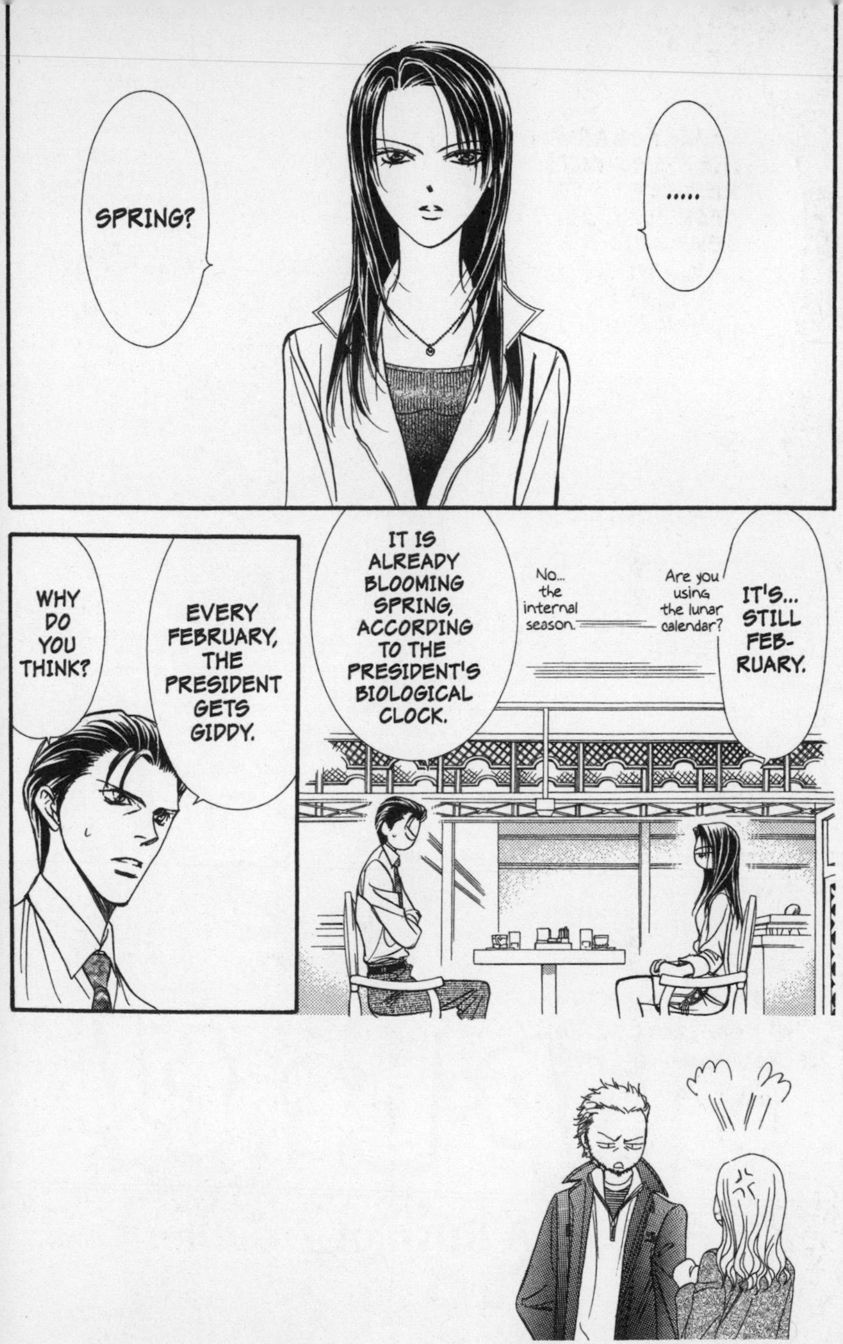
.....
SPRING?
IT'S... STILL FEB-RUARY.
Are you using the lunar calendar?
No... the internal season.
IT IS ALREADY BLOOMING SPRING, ACCORDING TO THE PRESIDENT'S BIOLOGICAL CLOCK.
EVERY FEBRUARY, THE PRESIDENT GETS GIDDY.
WHY DO YOU THINK?

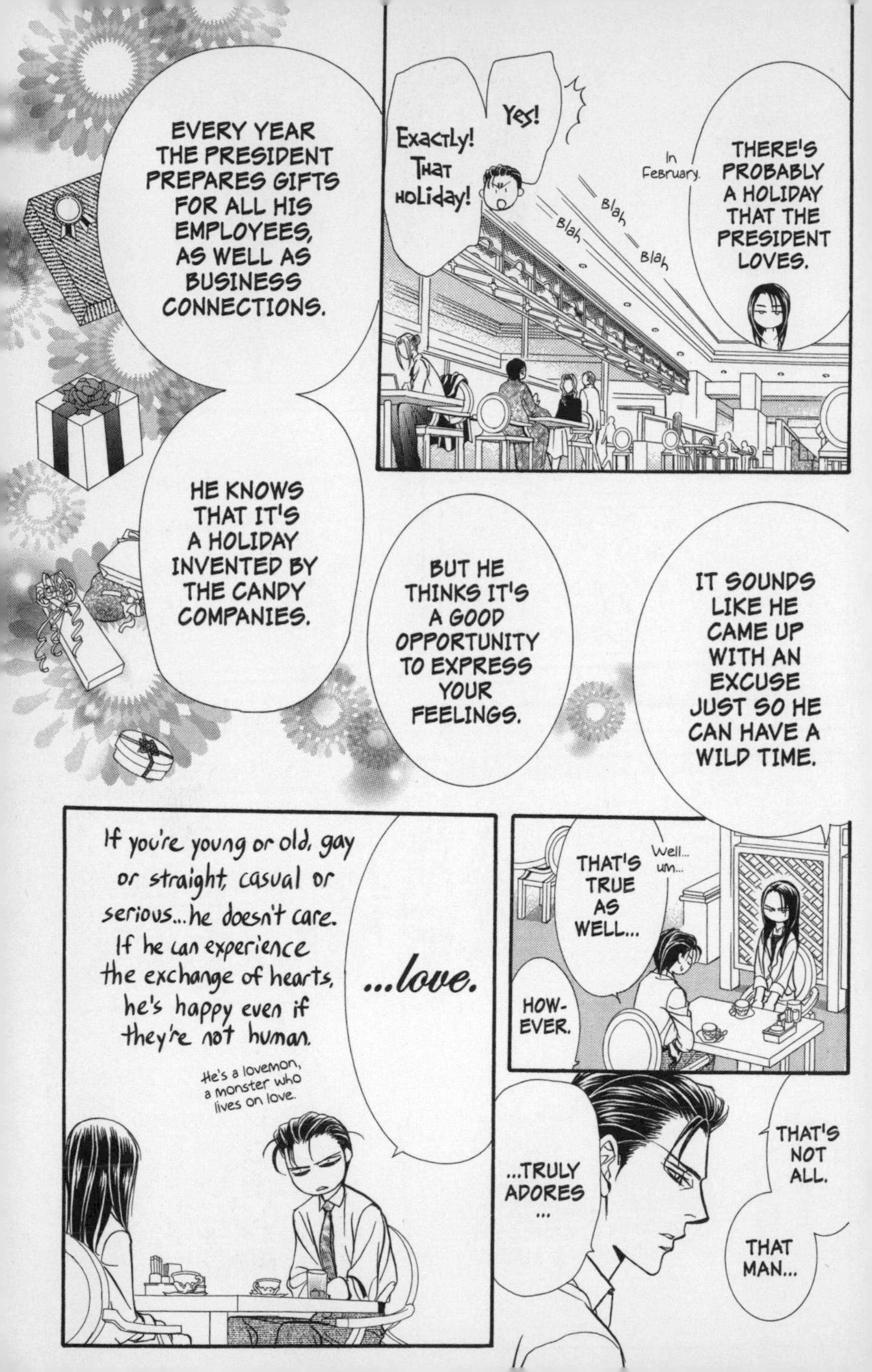

THERE'S PROBABLY A HOLIDAY THAT THE PRESIDENT LOVES.
In February.
Blah
Blah
Blah
Yes!
Exactly! That holiday!
EVERY YEAR THE PRESIDENT PREPARES GIFTS FOR ALL HIS EMPLOYEES, AS WELL AS BUSINESS CONNECTIONS.
HE KNOWS THAT IT'S A HOLIDAY INVENTED BY THE CANDY COMPANIES.
BUT HE THINKS IT'S A GOOD OPPORTUNITY TO EXPRESS YOUR FEELINGS.
IT SOUNDS LIKE HE CAME UP WITH AN EXCUSE JUST SO HE CAN HAVE A WILD TIME.
THAT'S TRUE AS WELL...
Well... um...
HOW-EVER.
THAT'S NOT ALL.
THAT MAN...
...TRULY ADORES...
...love.
If you're young or old, gay or straight, casual or serious...he doesn't care. If he can experience the exchange of hearts, he's happy even if they're not human.
He's a lovemon, a monster who lives on love.

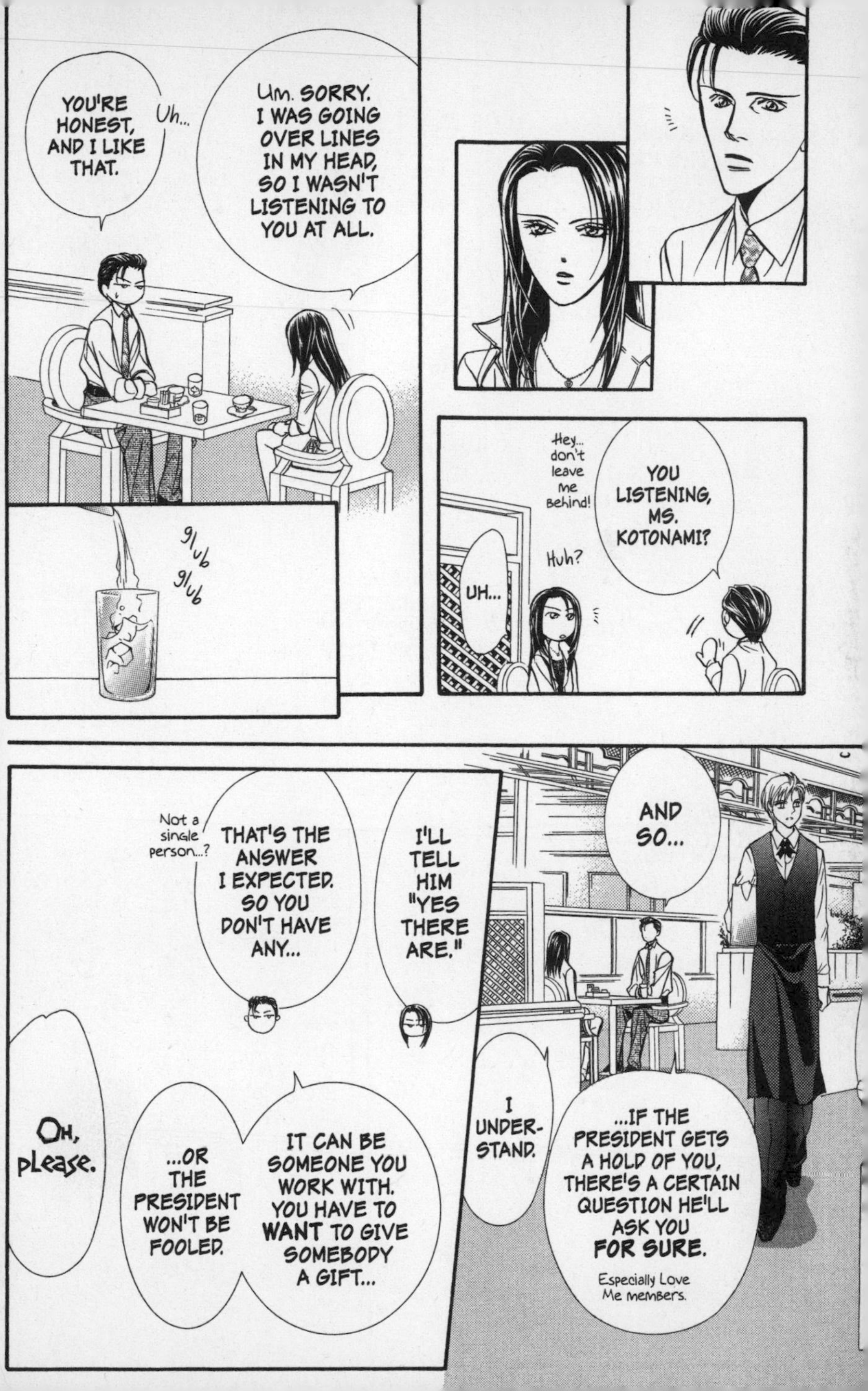

YOU LISTENING, MS. KOTONAMI?
Huh?
UH...
Hey... don't leave me behind!
Um. SORRY. I WAS GOING OVER LINES IN MY HEAD, SO I WASN'T LISTENING TO YOU AT ALL.
Uh...
YOU'RE HONEST, AND I LIKE THAT.
glub glub
AND SO...
...IF THE PRESIDENT GETS A HOLD OF YOU, THERE'S A CERTAIN QUESTION HE'LL ASK YOU FOR SURE.
Especially Love Me members.
I UNDER-STAND.
I'LL TELL HIM "YES THERE ARE."
THAT'S THE ANSWER I EXPECTED. SO YOU DON'T HAVE ANY...
Not a single person...?
IT CAN BE SOMEONE YOU WORK WITH. YOU HAVE TO WANT TO GIVE SOMEBODY A GIFT...
...OR THE PRESIDENT WON'T BE FOOLED.
Oh, please.

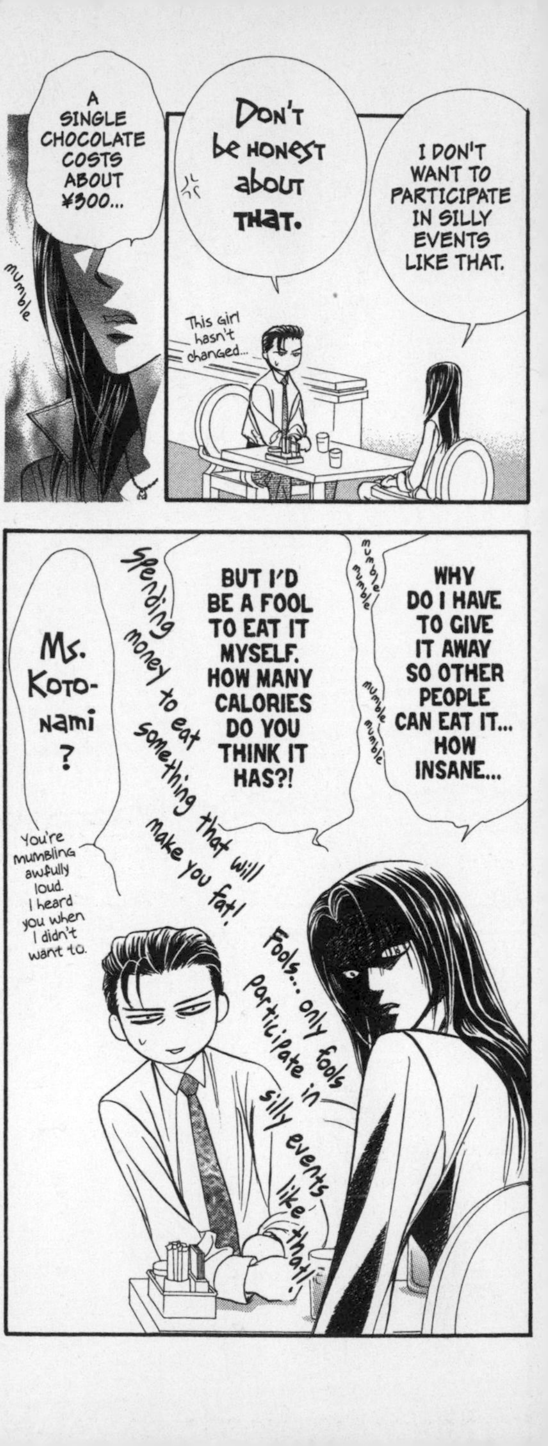
I DON'T WANT TO PARTICIPATE IN SILLY EVENTS LIKE THAT.
Don't be honest about that.
This girl hasn't changed...
A SINGLE CHOCOLATE COSTS ABOUT ¥300...
mumble
WHY DO I HAVE TO GIVE IT AWAY SO OTHER PEOPLE CAN EAT IT... HOW INSANE...
mumble mumble
mumble mumble
BUT I'D BE A FOOL TO EAT IT MYSELF. HOW MANY CALORIES DO YOU THINK IT HAS?!
Spending money to eat something that will make you fat!
Ms. Koto-nami?
You're mumbling awfully loud. I heard you when I didn't want to.
Fools... only fools participate in silly events like that!
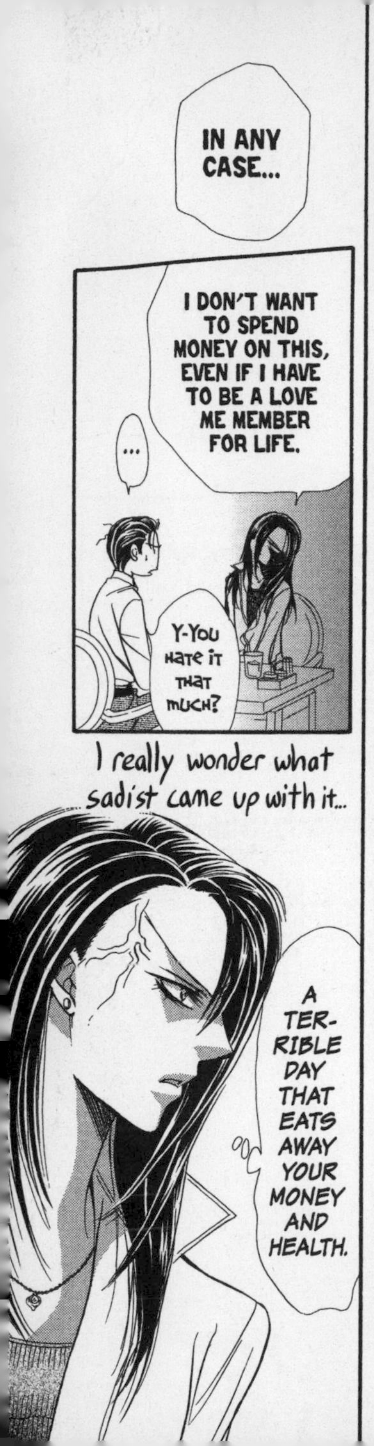
IN ANY CASE...
I DON'T WANT TO SPEND MONEY ON THIS, EVEN IF I HAVE TO BE A LOVE ME MEMBER FOR LIFE.
...
Y-YOU HATE IT THAT MUCH?
I really wonder what sadist came up with it...
A TER-RIBLE DAY THAT EATS AWAY YOUR MONEY AND HEALTH.

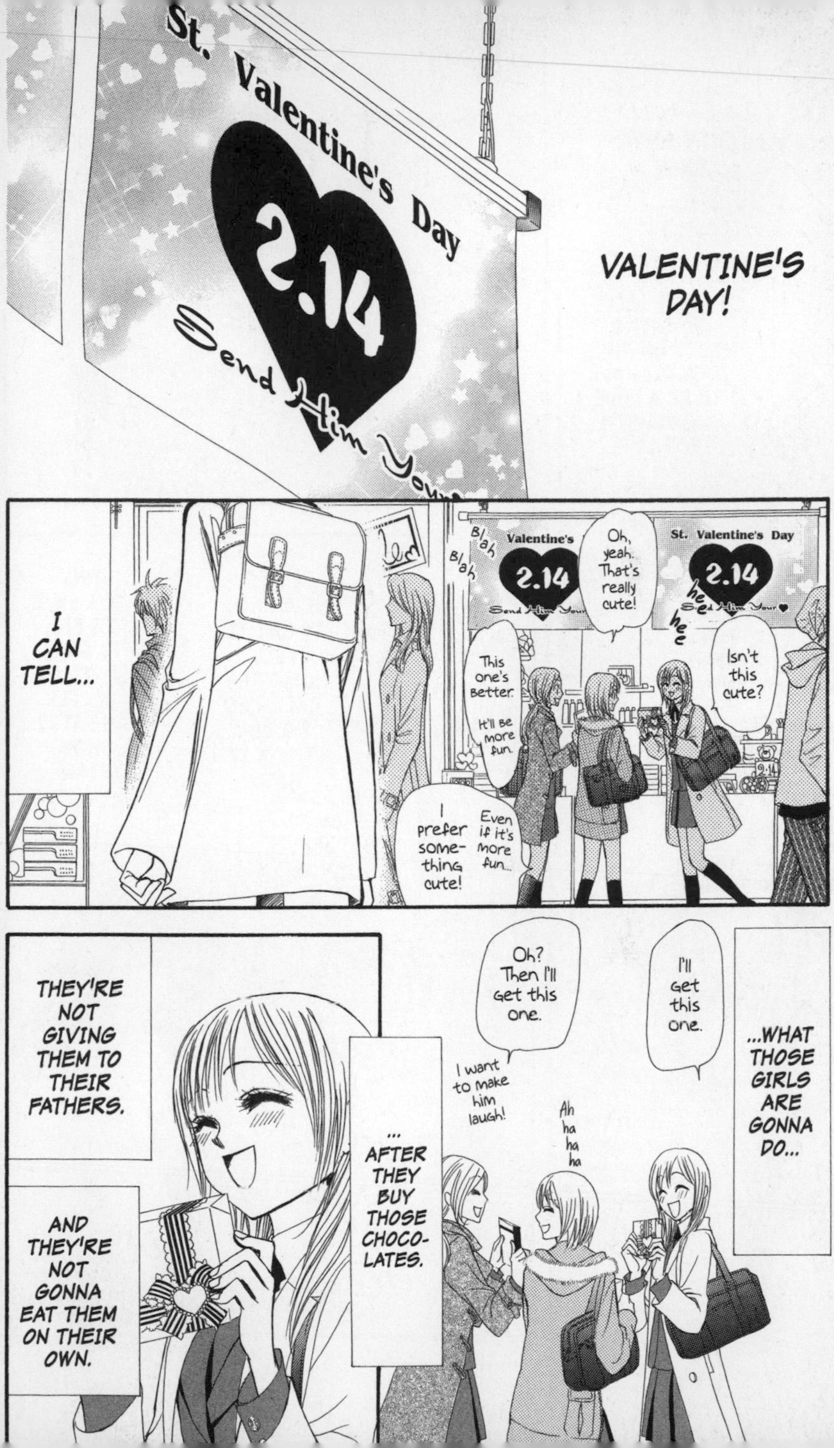
VALENTINE'S DAY!
St. Valentine's Day
2.14
Send Him Your
Isn't this cute?
hee hee
St. Valentine's Day
2.14
Send Him Your♥
Oh, yeah. That's really cute!
Valentine's
2.14
Blah Blah
This one's better.
It'll be more fun.
Even if it's more fun...
I prefer some-thing cute!
I CAN TELL...
...WHAT THOSE GIRLS ARE GONNA DO...
I'll get this one.
Oh? Then I'll get this one.
Ah ha ha ha
I want to make him laugh!
... AFTER THEY BUY THOSE CHOCO-LATES.
THEY'RE NOT GIVING THEM TO THEIR FATHERS.
AND THEY'RE NOT GONNA EAT THEM ON THEIR OWN.

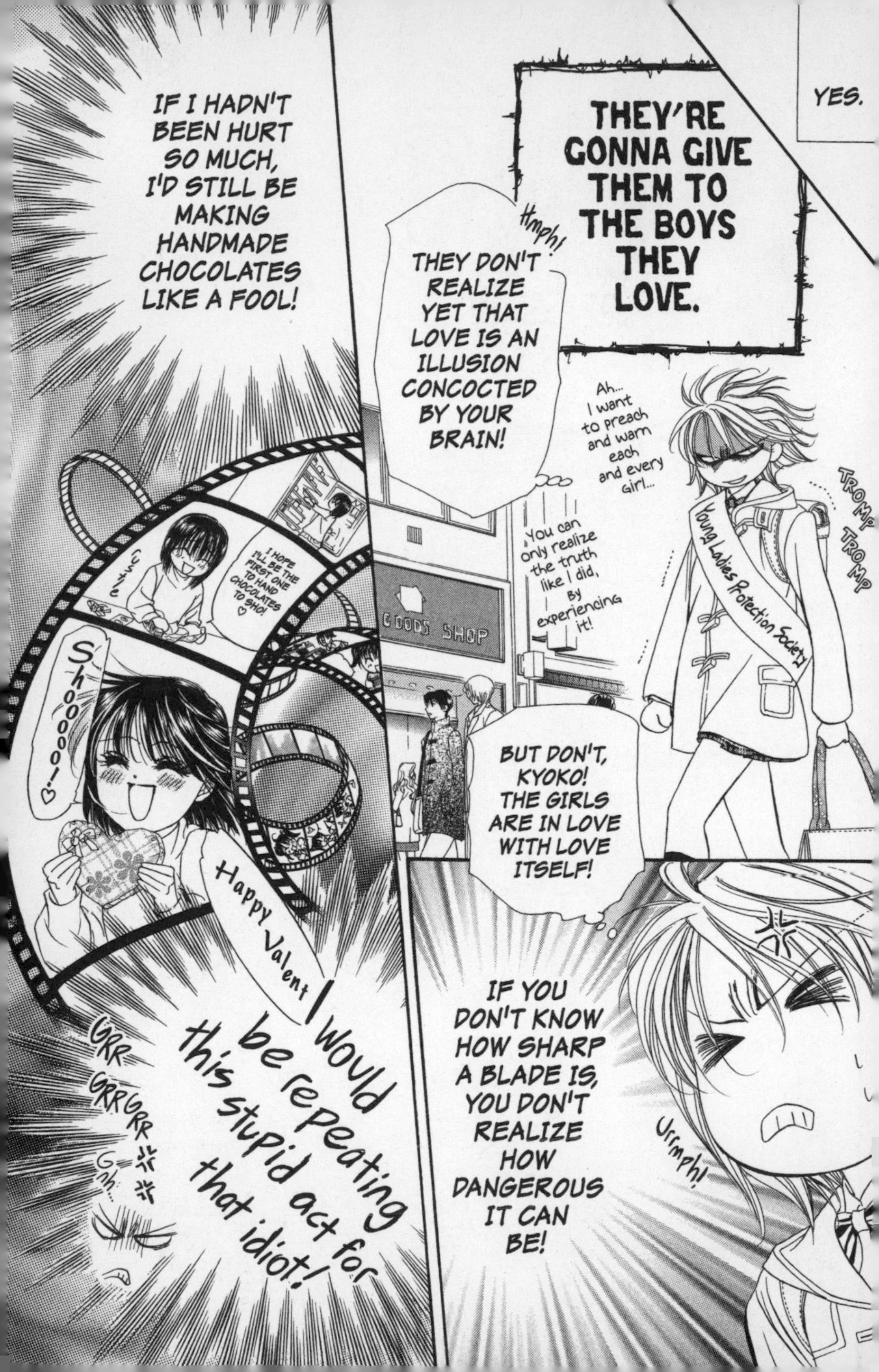
YES.
THEY'RE GONNA GIVE THEM TO THE BOYS THEY LOVE.
Hmph!
THEY DON'T REALIZE YET THAT LOVE IS AN ILLUSION CONCOCTED BY YOUR BRAIN!
Ah... I want to preach and warn each and every girl...
You can only realize the truth like I did, By experiencing it!
TROMP TROMP
GOODS SHOP
Young Ladies Protection Society
BUT DON'T, KYOKO! THE GIRLS ARE IN LOVE WITH LOVE ITSELF!
IF YOU DON'T KNOW HOW SHARP A BLADE IS, YOU DON'T REALIZE HOW DANGEROUS IT CAN BE!
Urrmph!
IF I HADN'T BEEN HURT SO MUCH, I'D STILL BE MAKING HANDMADE CHOCOLATES LIKE A FOOL!
I HOPE I'LL BE THE FIRST ONE TO HAND CHOCOLATES TO SHO! ♡
Shooooooo!♡
Happy Valent
I would be repeating this stupid act for that idiot!
GRR GRRGRR
Gnh...

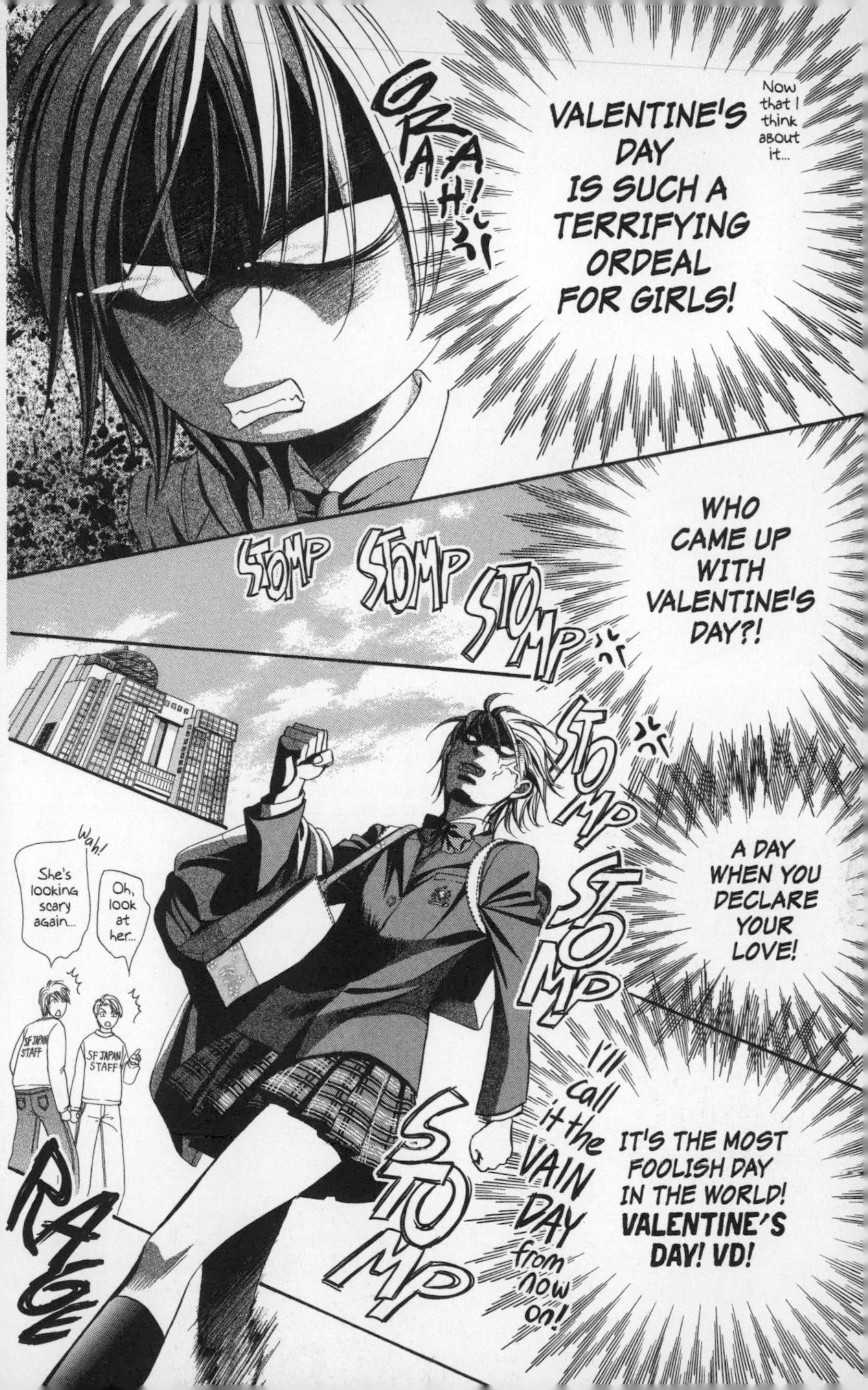
Now that I think about it...
VALENTINE'S DAY IS SUCH A TERRIFYING ORDEAL FOR GIRLS!
GRAAH!!
WHO CAME UP WITH VALENTINE'S DAY?!
STOMP
STOMP
STOMP
A DAY WHEN YOU DECLARE YOUR LOVE!
STOMP
STOMP
IT'S THE MOST FOOLISH DAY IN THE WORLD! VALENTINE'S DAY! VD!
I'll call it the VAIN DAY from now on!
STOMP
Wah!
Oh, look at her...
She's looking scary again...
SF JAPAN STAFF
SF JAPAN STAFF
RAGE

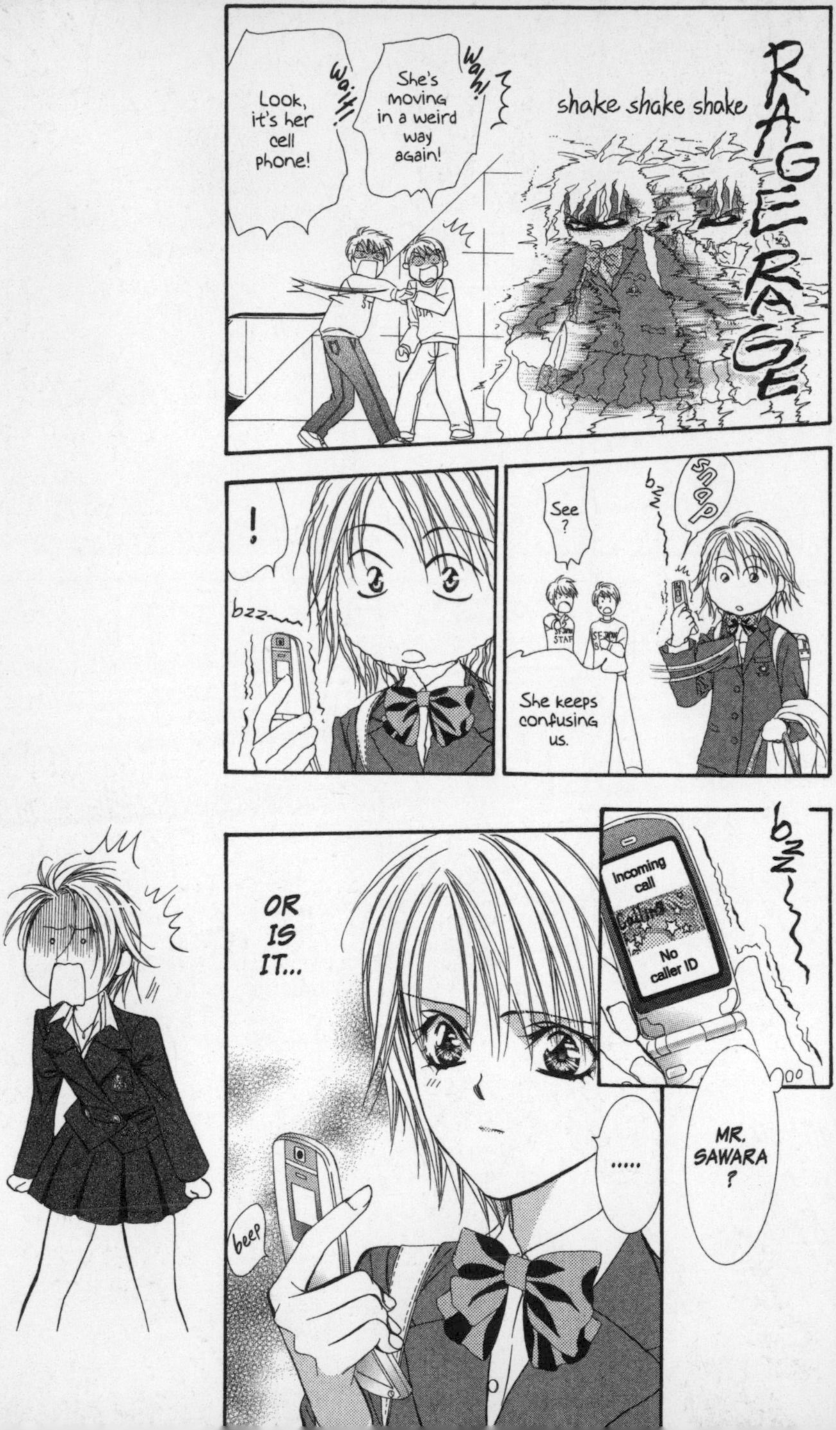

RAGE RAGE
shake shake shake
Wah!
She's moving in a weird way again!
Wait!
Look, it's her cell phone!
snap
bzz
See?
She keeps confusing us.
!
bzz
bzz
Incoming call
No caller ID
MR. SAWARA?
.....
OR IS IT...
beep

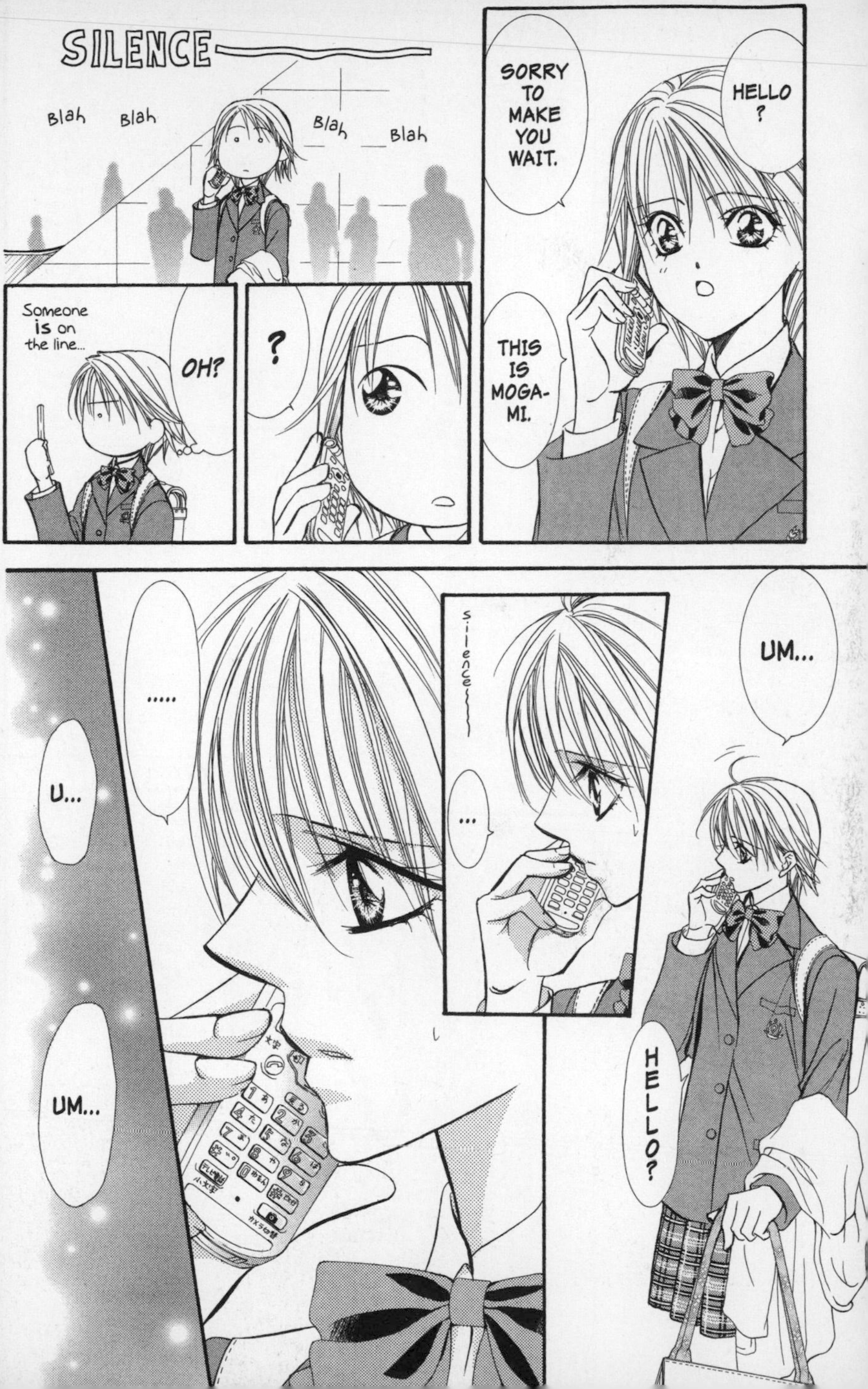
HELLO ?
SORRY TO MAKE YOU WAIT.
THIS IS MOGA-MI.
SILENCE
Blah
Blah
Blah
Blah
?
OH?
Someone is on the line...
UM...
HELLO?
silence
...
.....
U...
UM...

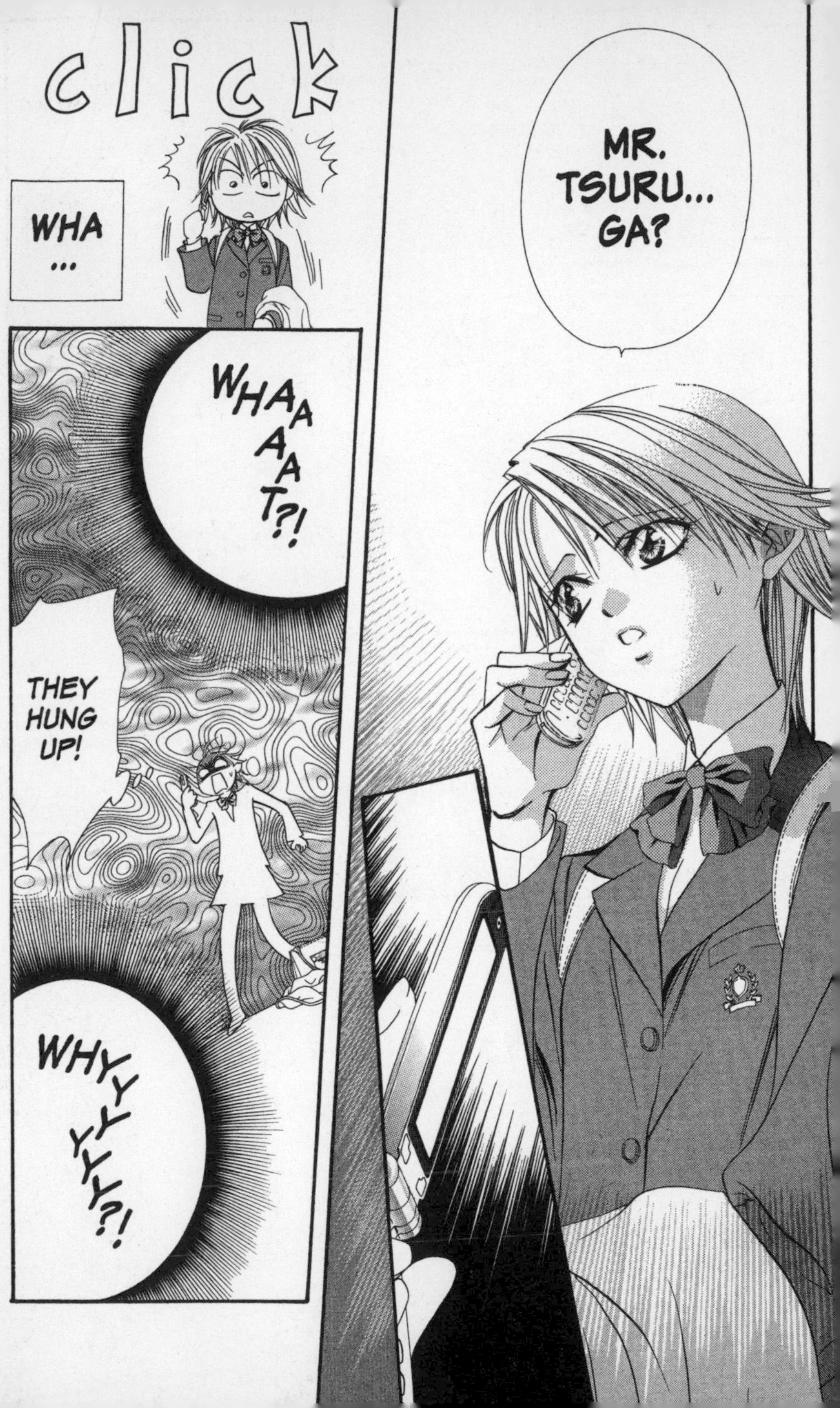
MR. TSURU... GA?
click
WHA ...
WHAAAAT?!
THEY HUNG UP!
WHYYYYYY?!

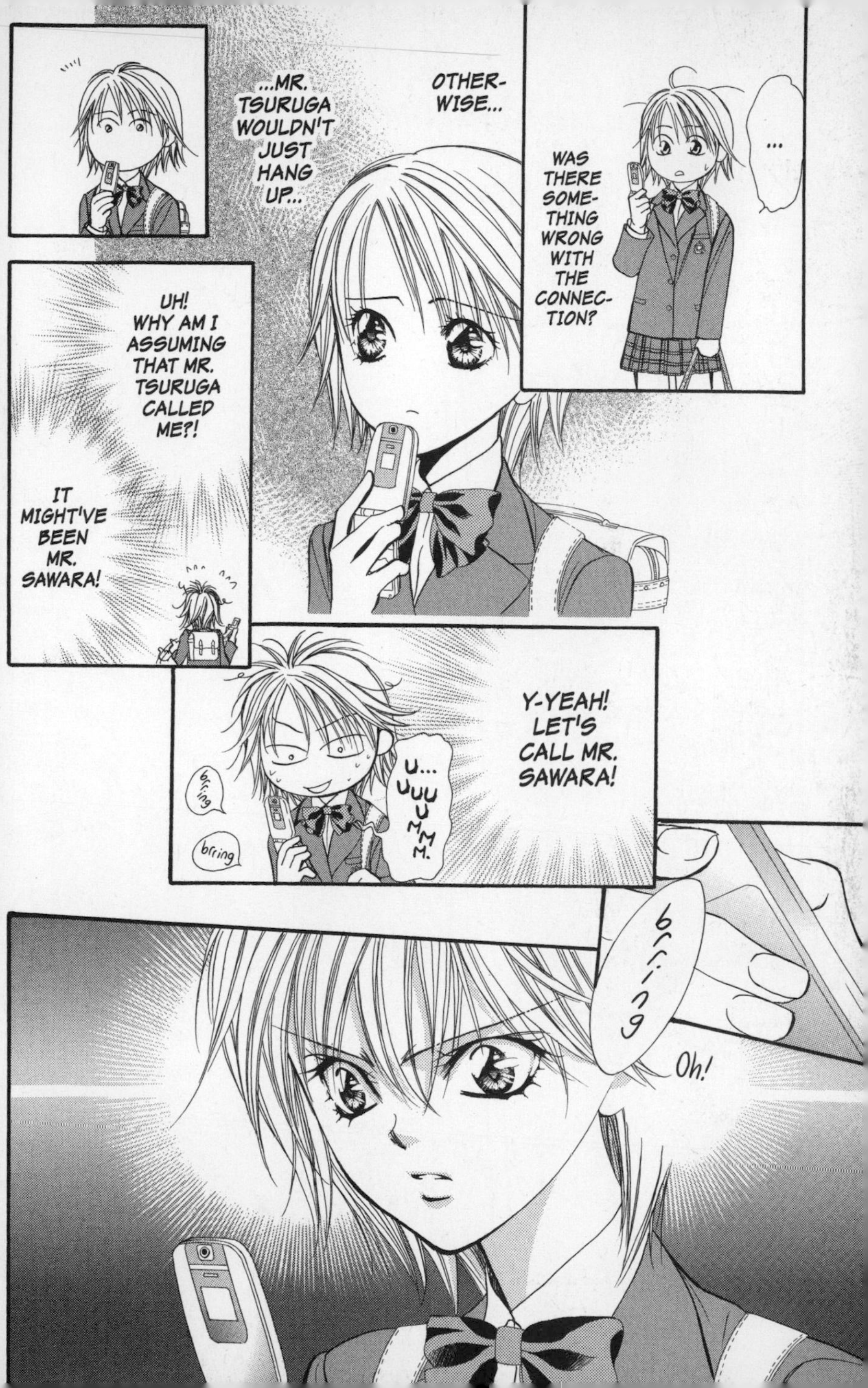
...
WAS THERE SOMETHING WRONG WITH THE CONNECTION?
OTHERWISE...
...MR. TSURUGA WOULDN'T JUST HANG UP...
UH! WHY AM I ASSUMING THAT MR. TSURUGA CALLED ME?!
IT MIGHT'VE BEEN MR. SAWARA!
Y-YEAH! LET'S CALL MR. SAWARA!
U... UUUUMMM.
brring
brring
brring
Oh!

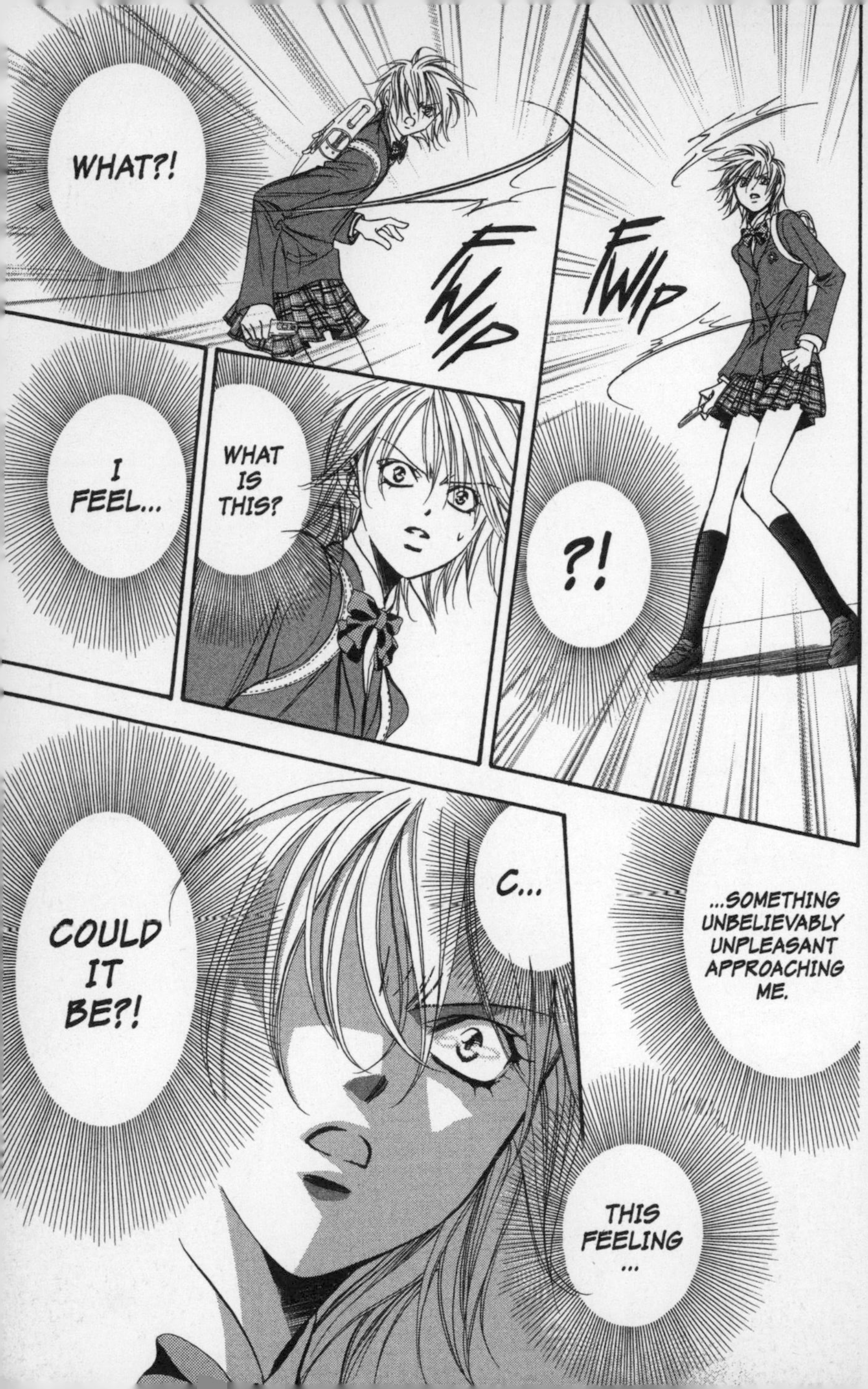
FWIP
?!
WHAT?!
FWIP
WHAT IS THIS?
I FEEL...
...SOMETHING UNBELIEVABLY UNPLEASANT APPROACHING ME.
C...
THIS FEELING ...
COULD IT BE?!

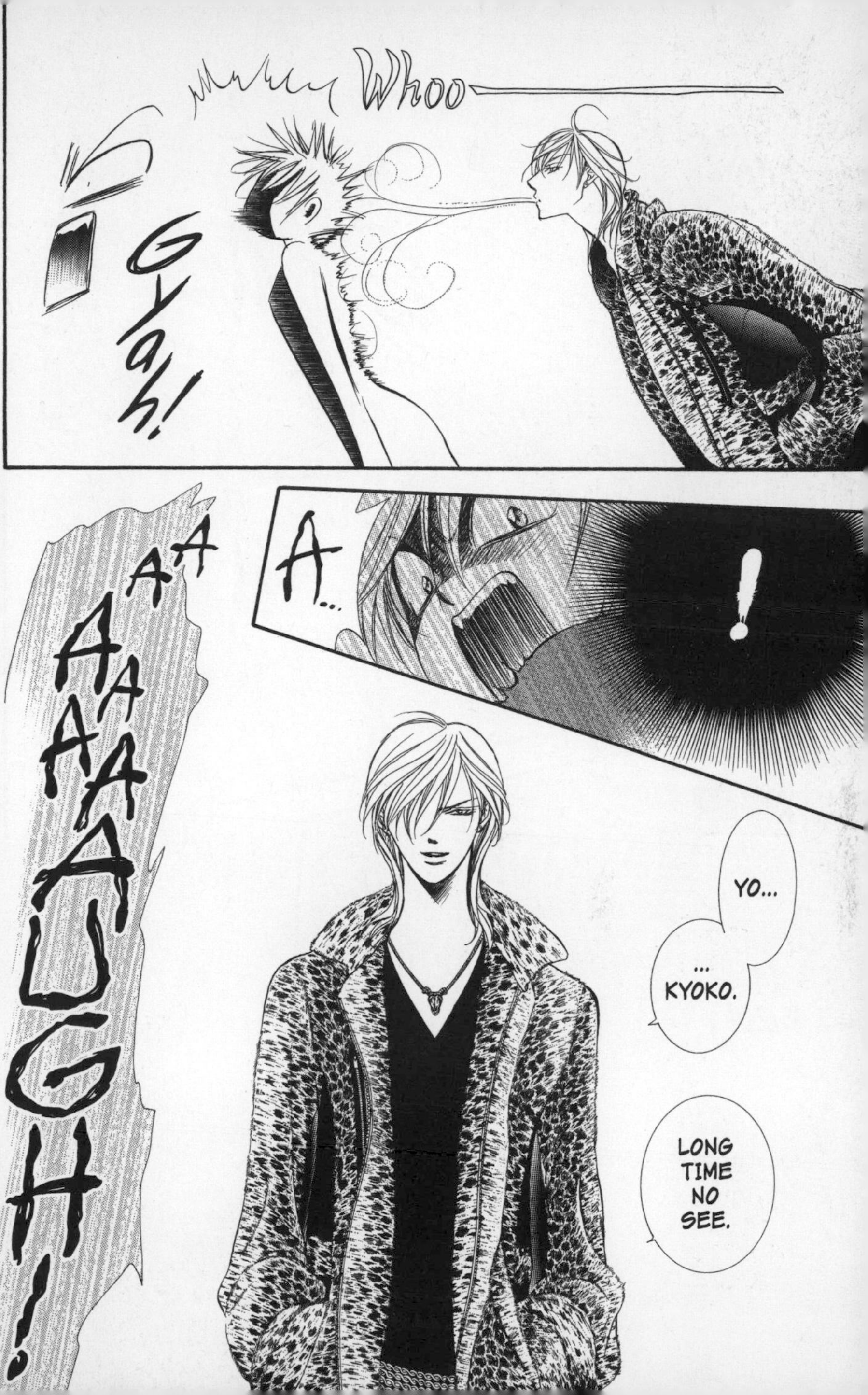
Whoo
Gyah!
A...
!
YO...
...KYOKO.
LONG TIME NO SEE.
AAAAAAAAAUGH!!

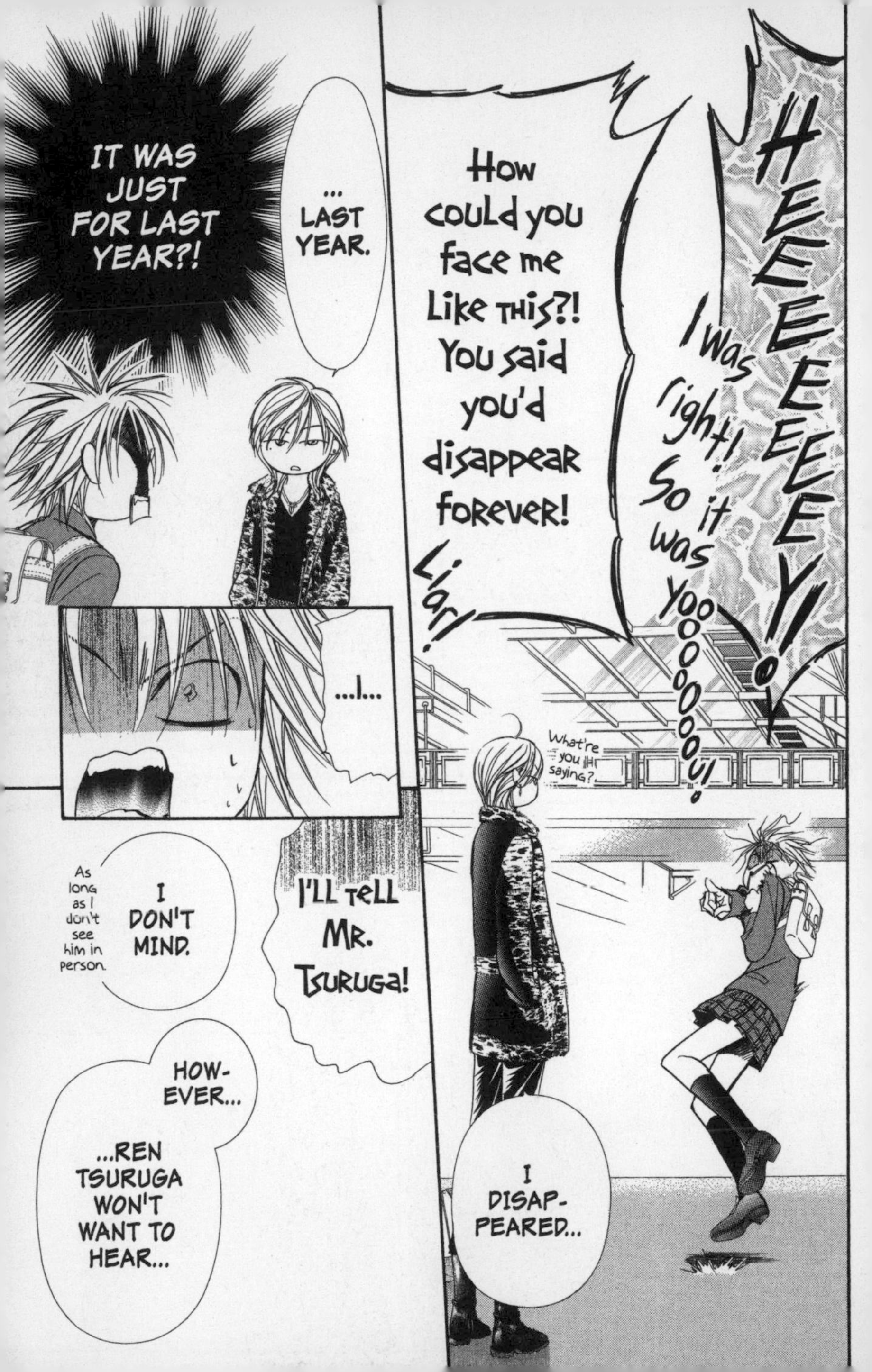
HEEEEEEEY!
I was right! So it was yoooooooou!
How could you face me like this?! You said you'd disappear forever!
Liar!
What're you saying?
I DISAP-PEARED...
...LAST YEAR.
IT WAS JUST FOR LAST YEAR?!
...I...
I'LL TELL MR. TSURUGA!
I DON'T MIND.
As long as I don't see him in person.
HOW-EVER...
...REN TSURUGA WON'T WANT TO HEAR...

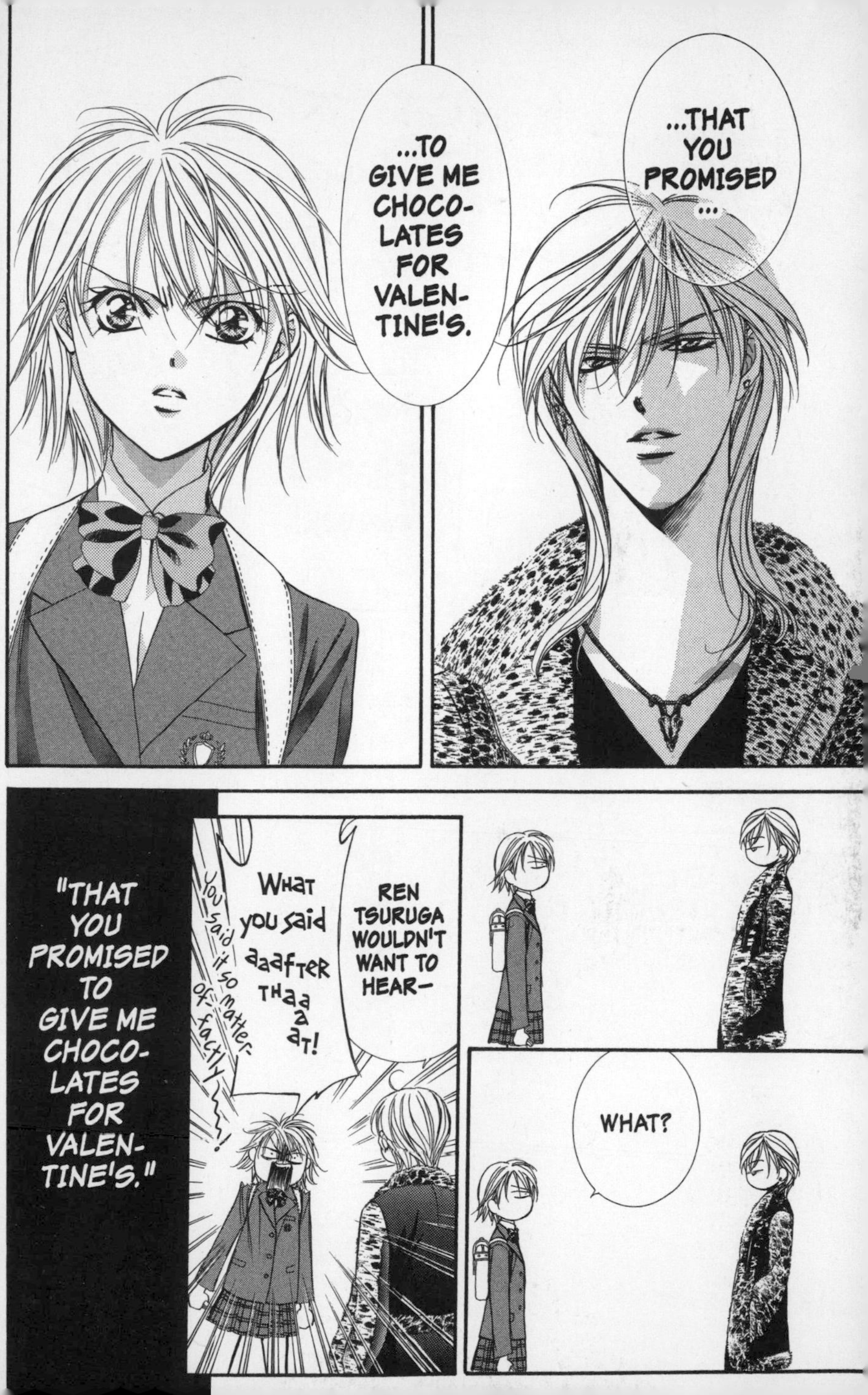
...THAT YOU PROMISED ...
...TO GIVE ME CHOCO-LATES FOR VALEN-TINE'S.
WHAT?
REN TSURUGA WOULDN'T WANT TO HEAR—
WHAT you said aaafter thaaaat!
You said it so matter-of-factly...!
"THAT YOU PROMISED TO GIVE ME CHOCO-LATES FOR VALEN-TINE'S."

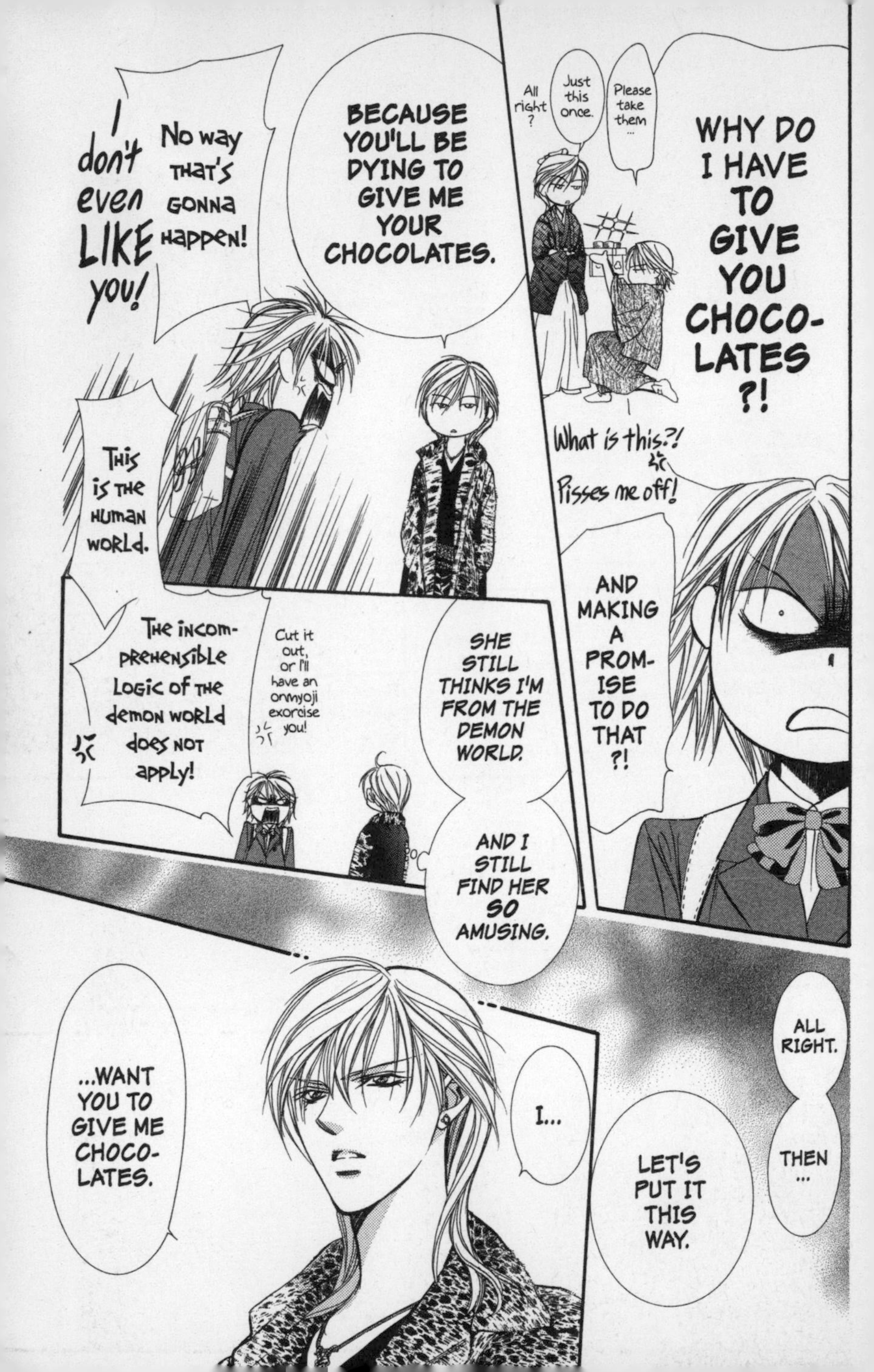
WHY DO I HAVE TO GIVE YOU CHOCOLATES?!
Please take them...
Just this once.
All right?
What is this?! Pisses me off!
AND MAKING A PROMISE TO DO THAT?!
BECAUSE YOU'LL BE DYING TO GIVE ME YOUR CHOCOLATES.
No way that's gonna happen!
I don't even LIKE you!
This is the human world.
SHE STILL THINKS I'M FROM THE DEMON WORLD.
AND I STILL FIND HER SO AMUSING.
Cut it out, or I'll have an onmyoji exorcise you!
The incomprehensible logic of the demon world does not apply!
ALL RIGHT.
THEN...
LET'S PUT IT THIS WAY.
I...
...WANT YOU TO GIVE ME CHOCOLATES.

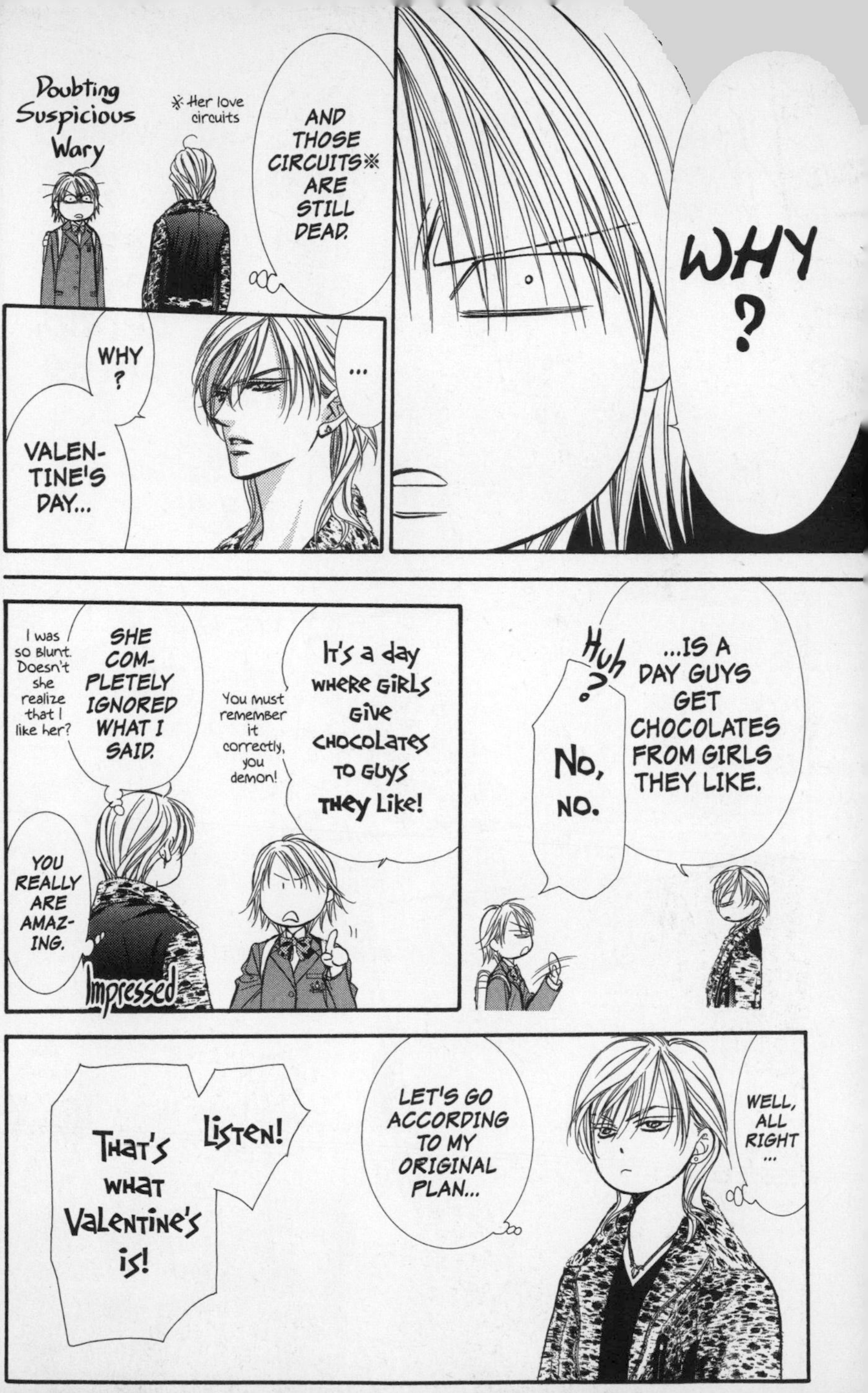
WHY ?
AND THOSE CIRCUITS※ ARE STILL DEAD.
※Her love circuits
Doubting Suspicious Wary
...
WHY ?
VALENTINE'S DAY...
...IS A DAY GUYS GET CHOCOLATES FROM GIRLS THEY LIKE.
Huh ?
No, no.
It's a day where girls give chocolates to guys they like!
You must remember it correctly, you demon!
SHE COMPLETELY IGNORED WHAT I SAID.
I was so blunt. Doesn't she realize that I like her?
YOU REALLY ARE AMAZING.
Impressed
WELL, ALL RIGHT...
LET'S GO ACCORDING TO MY ORIGINAL PLAN...
Listen!
That's what Valentine's is!

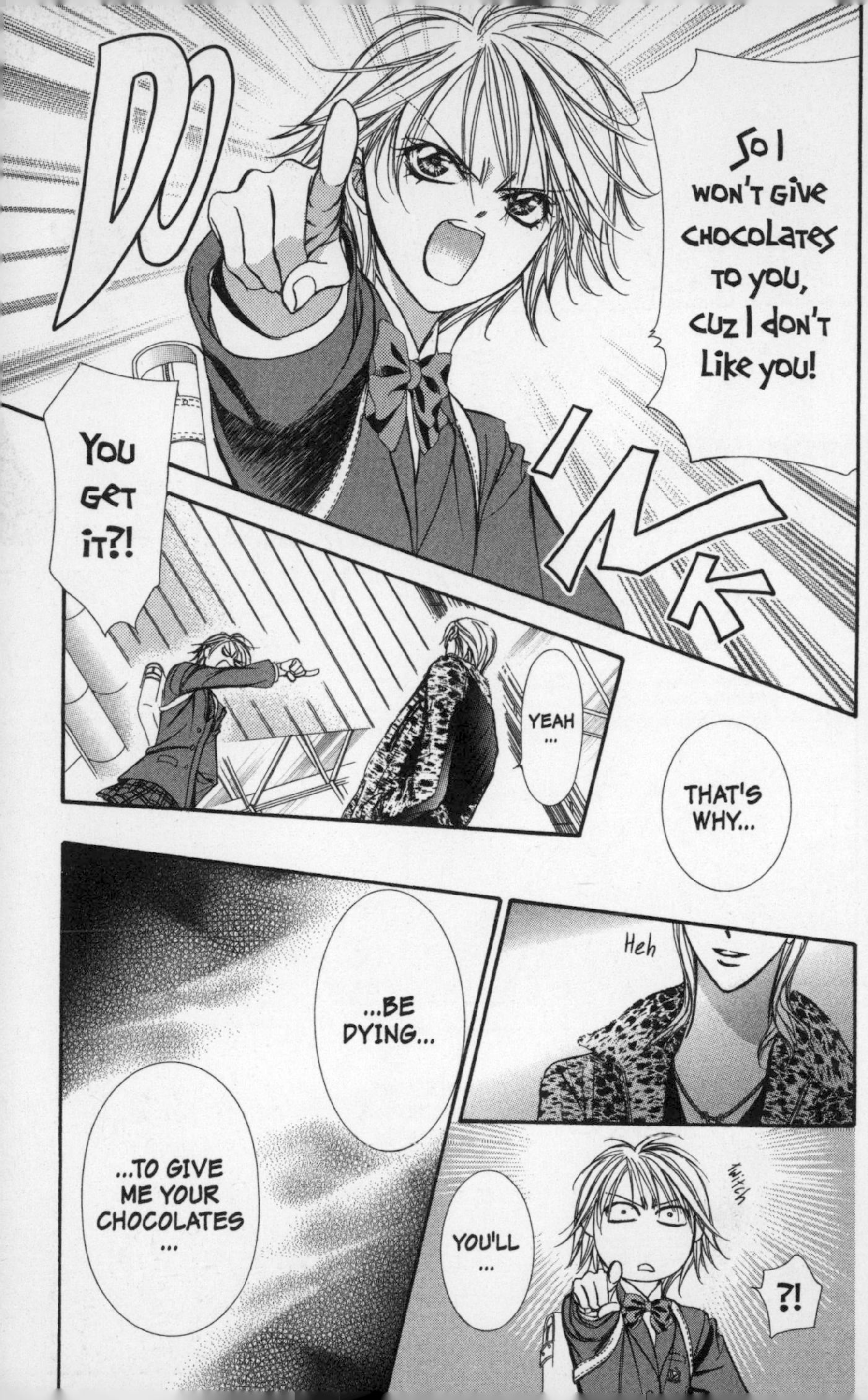
SO I WON'T GIVE CHOCOLATES TO YOU, CUZ I DON'T LIKE YOU!
DO
INK
YOU GET IT?!
YEAH ...
THAT'S WHY...
Heh
YOU'LL ...
twitch
?!
...BE DYING...
...TO GIVE ME YOUR CHOCOLATES ...

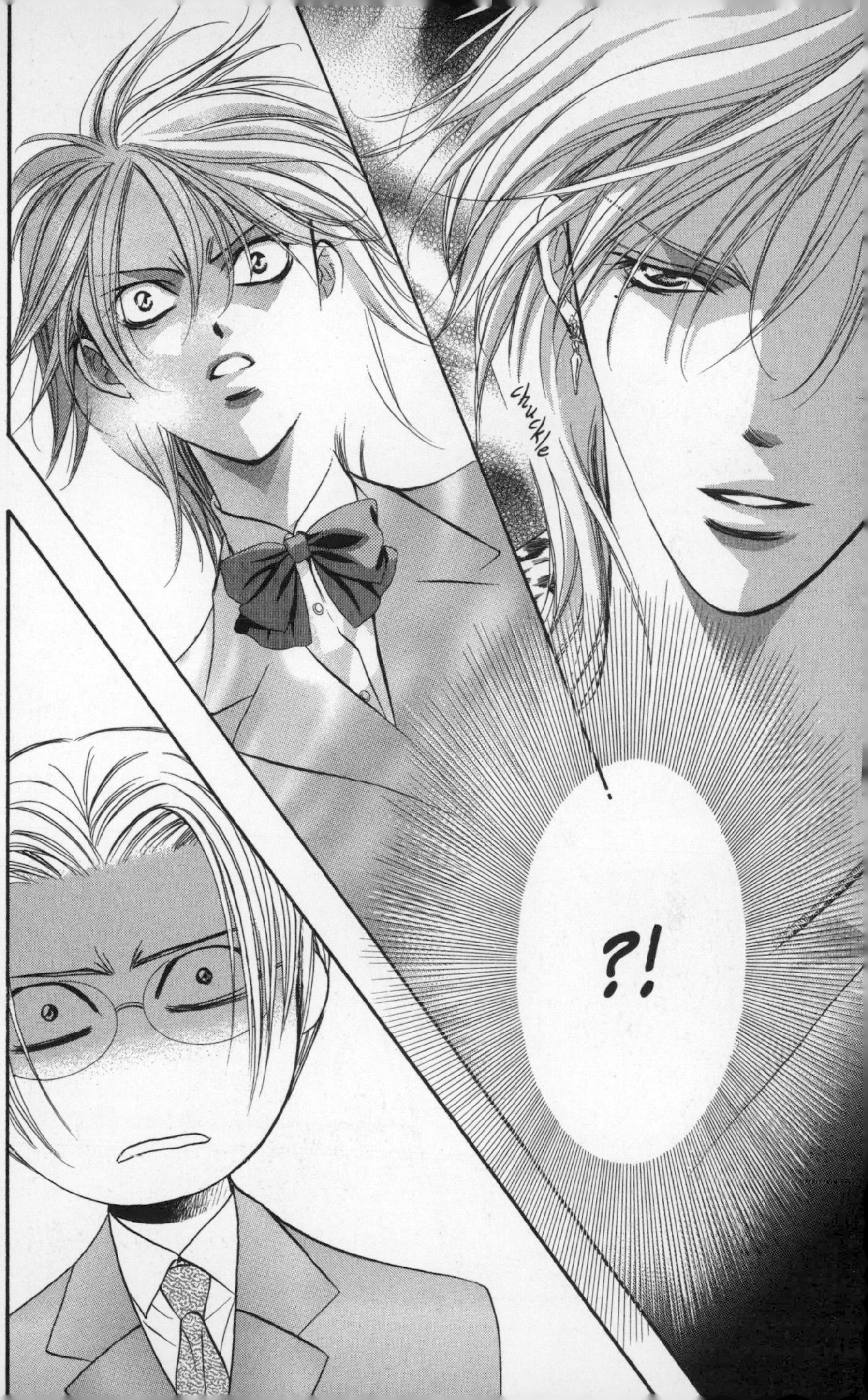
chuckle
?!

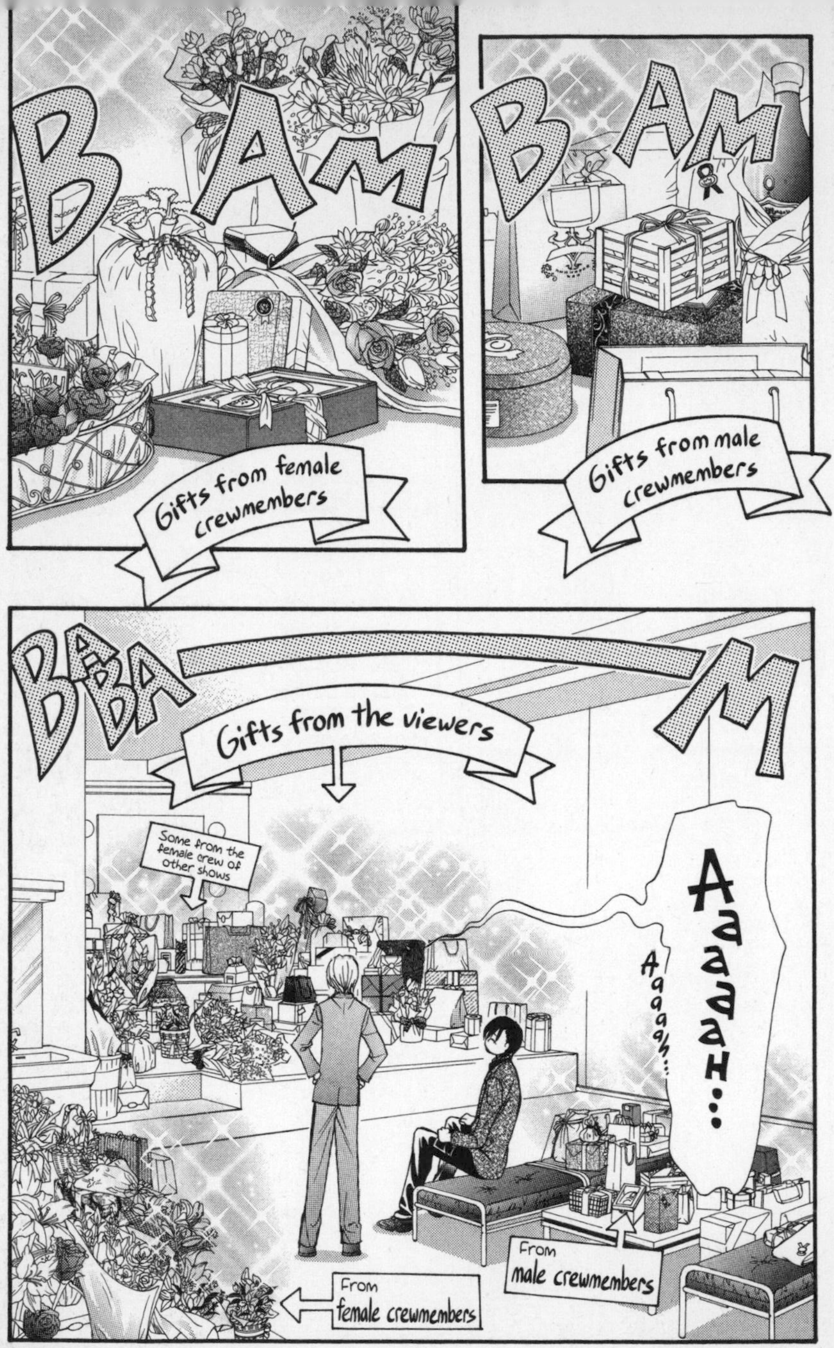
BAM
Gifts from male crewmembers
BAM
Gifts from female crewmembers
BABABA—M
Gifts from the viewers
Aaaaah...
Aaaah...
Some from the female crew of other shows
From male crewmembers
From female crewmembers

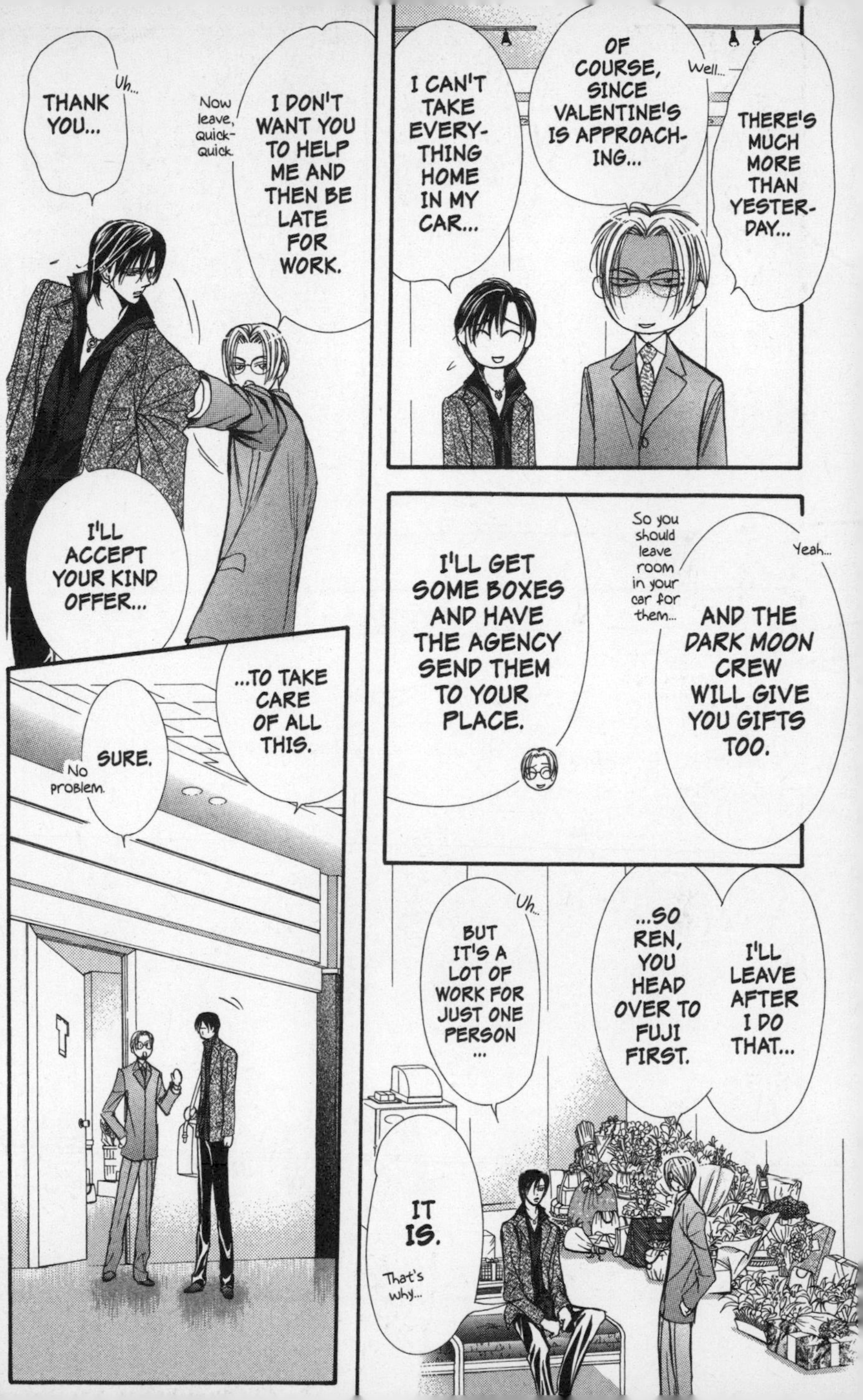
THERE'S MUCH MORE THAN YESTERDAY...
Well...
OF COURSE, SINCE VALENTINE'S IS APPROACHING...
I CAN'T TAKE EVERYTHING HOME IN MY CAR...
Yeah...
AND THE DARK MOON CREW WILL GIVE YOU GIFTS TOO.
So you should leave room in your car for them...
I'LL GET SOME BOXES AND HAVE THE AGENCY SEND THEM TO YOUR PLACE.
I'LL LEAVE AFTER I DO THAT...
...SO REN, YOU HEAD OVER TO FUJI FIRST.
Uh...
BUT IT'S A LOT OF WORK FOR JUST ONE PERSON...
IT IS.
That's why...
I DON'T WANT YOU TO HELP ME AND THEN BE LATE FOR WORK.
Now leave, quick-quick.
Uh...
THANK YOU...
I'LL ACCEPT YOUR KIND OFFER...
...TO TAKE CARE OF ALL THIS.
SURE.
No problem.

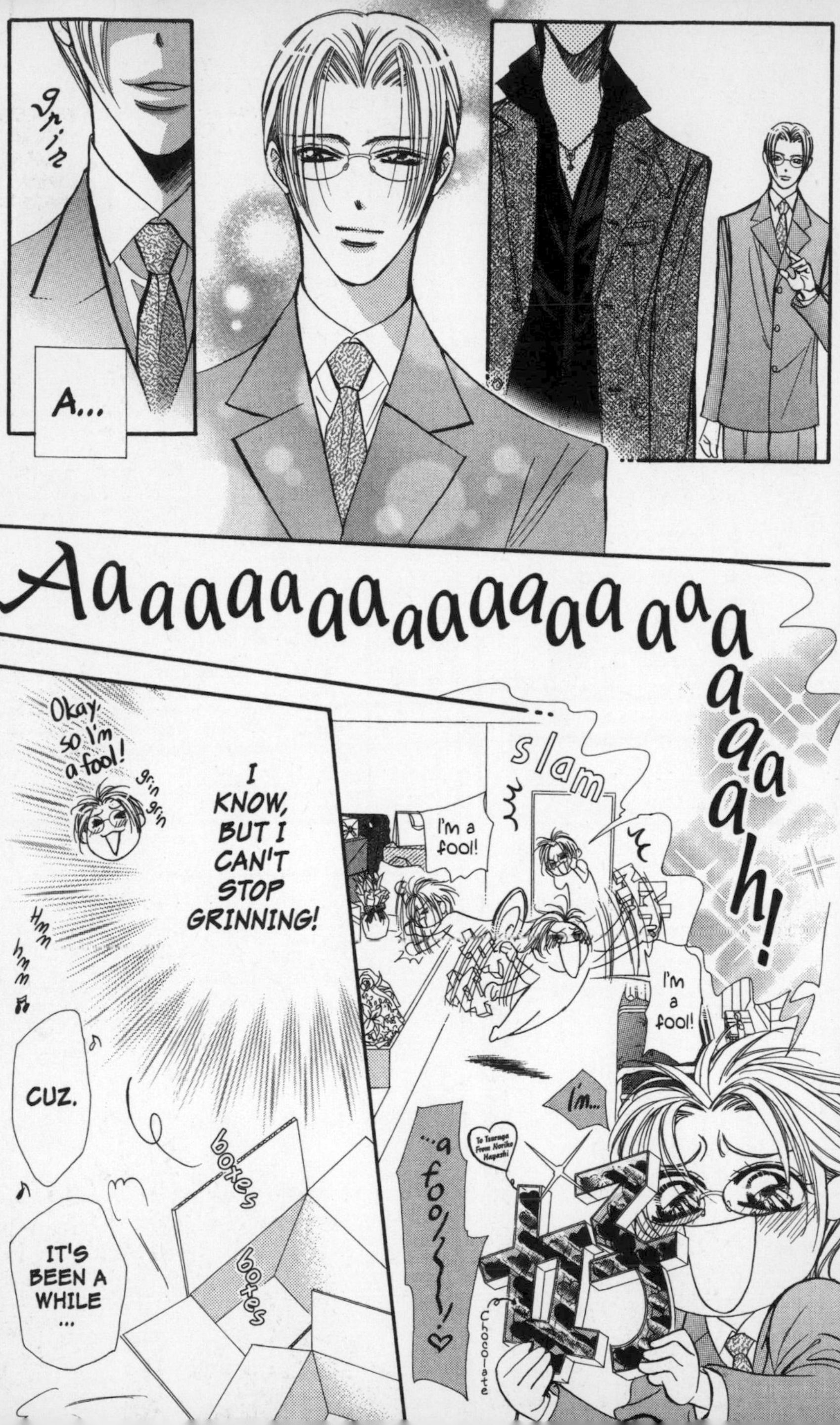
...
grin
A...
Aaaaaaaaaaaaaaaaaaaah!
slam
I'm a fool!
I'm a fool!
I'm...
...a fool~~!
To Tsuruga From Noriko Hayashi
Chocolate
Okay, so I'm a fool!
grin grin
I KNOW, BUT I CAN'T STOP GRINNING!
Hmm hmm
CUZ.
IT'S BEEN A WHILE ...
boxes
boxes

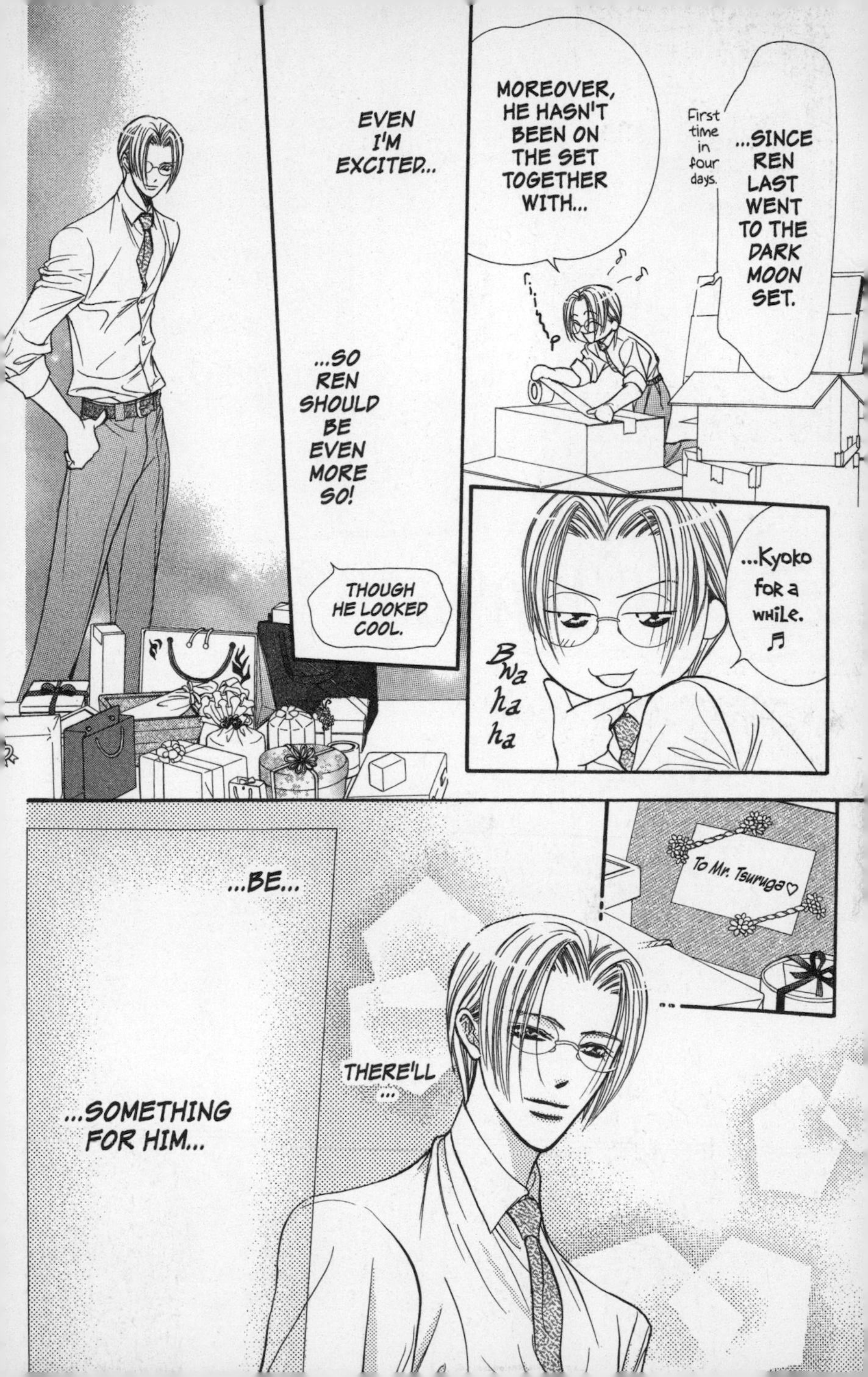
...SINCE REN LAST WENT TO THE DARK MOON SET.
First time in four days.
MOREOVER, HE HASN'T BEEN ON THE SET TOGETHER WITH...
...Kyoko for a while. ♬
Bwa ha ha
EVEN I'M EXCITED...
...SO REN SHOULD BE EVEN MORE SO!
THOUGH HE LOOKED COOL.
To Mr. Tsuruga♡
...
THERE'LL...
...BE...
...SOMETHING FOR HIM...

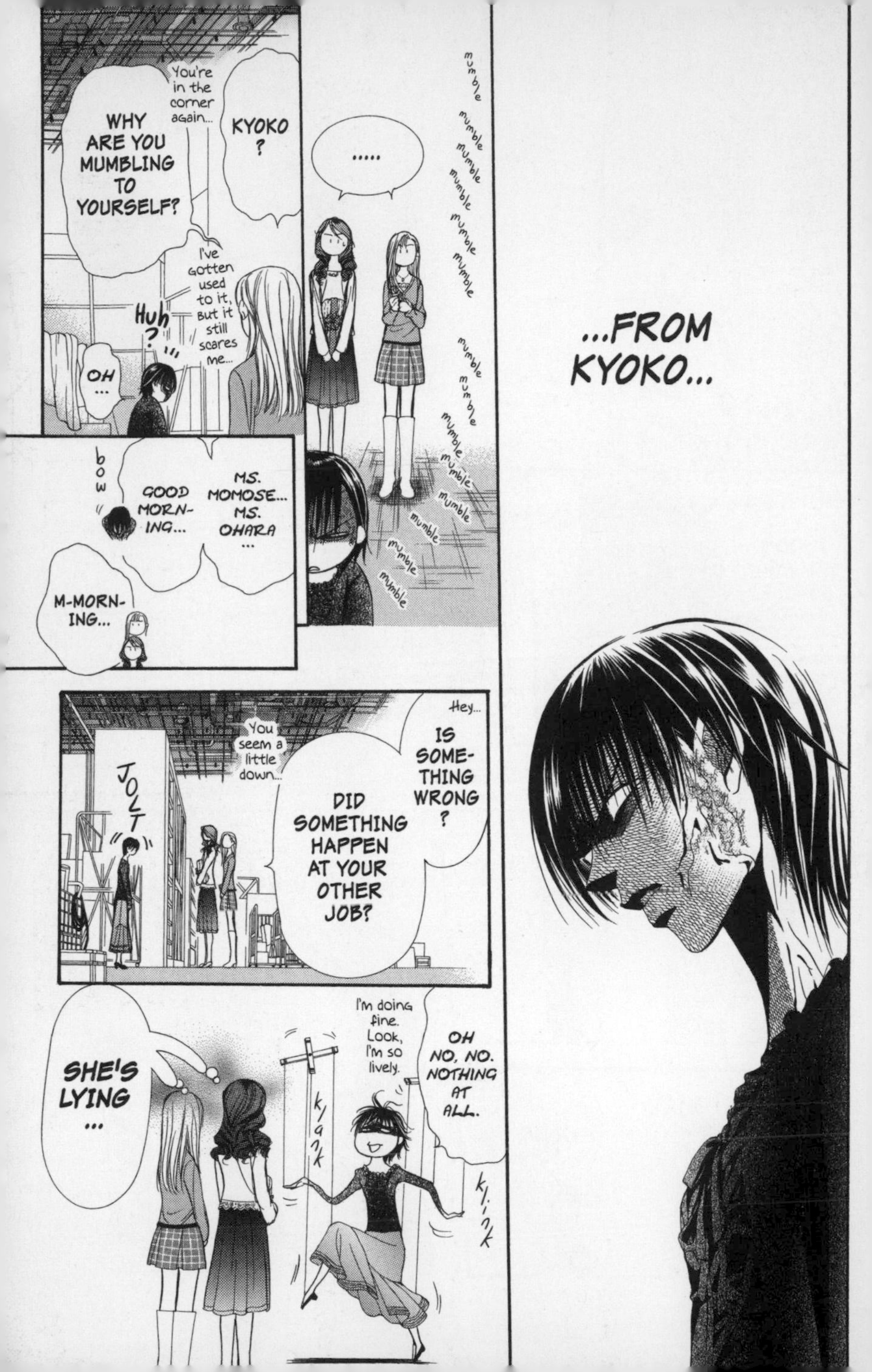
...FROM KYOKO...
mumble mumble mumble mumble mumble mumble
.....
mumble mumble mumble mumble mumble mumble mumble
KYOKO?
You're in the corner again...
WHY ARE YOU MUMBLING TO YOURSELF?
I've gotten used to it, but it still scares me...
Huh?
OH...
MS. MOMOSE... MS. OHARA...
GOOD MORNING...
bow
M-MORNING...
Hey...
IS SOMETHING WRONG?
You seem a little down...
DID SOMETHING HAPPEN AT YOUR OTHER JOB?
JOLT
OH NO, NO. NOTHING AT ALL.
I'm doing fine. Look, I'm so lively.
klink
klank
SHE'S LYING...

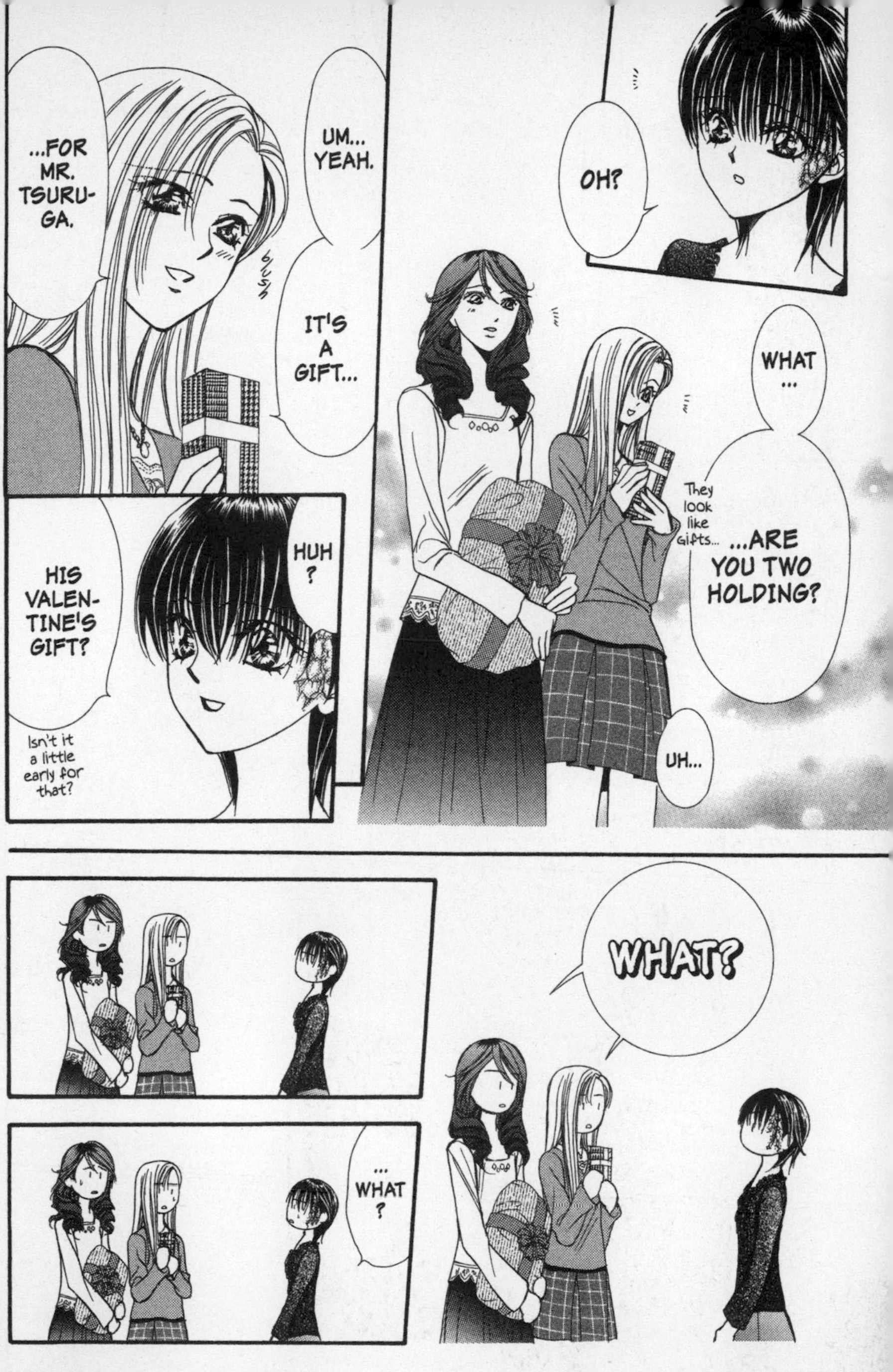
OH?
WHAT ... ...ARE YOU TWO HOLDING?
They look like gifts...
UH...
UM... YEAH.
IT'S A GIFT...
blush
...FOR MR. TSURUGA.
HUH?
HIS VALENTINE'S GIFT?
Isn't it a little early for that?
WHAT?
...WHAT?

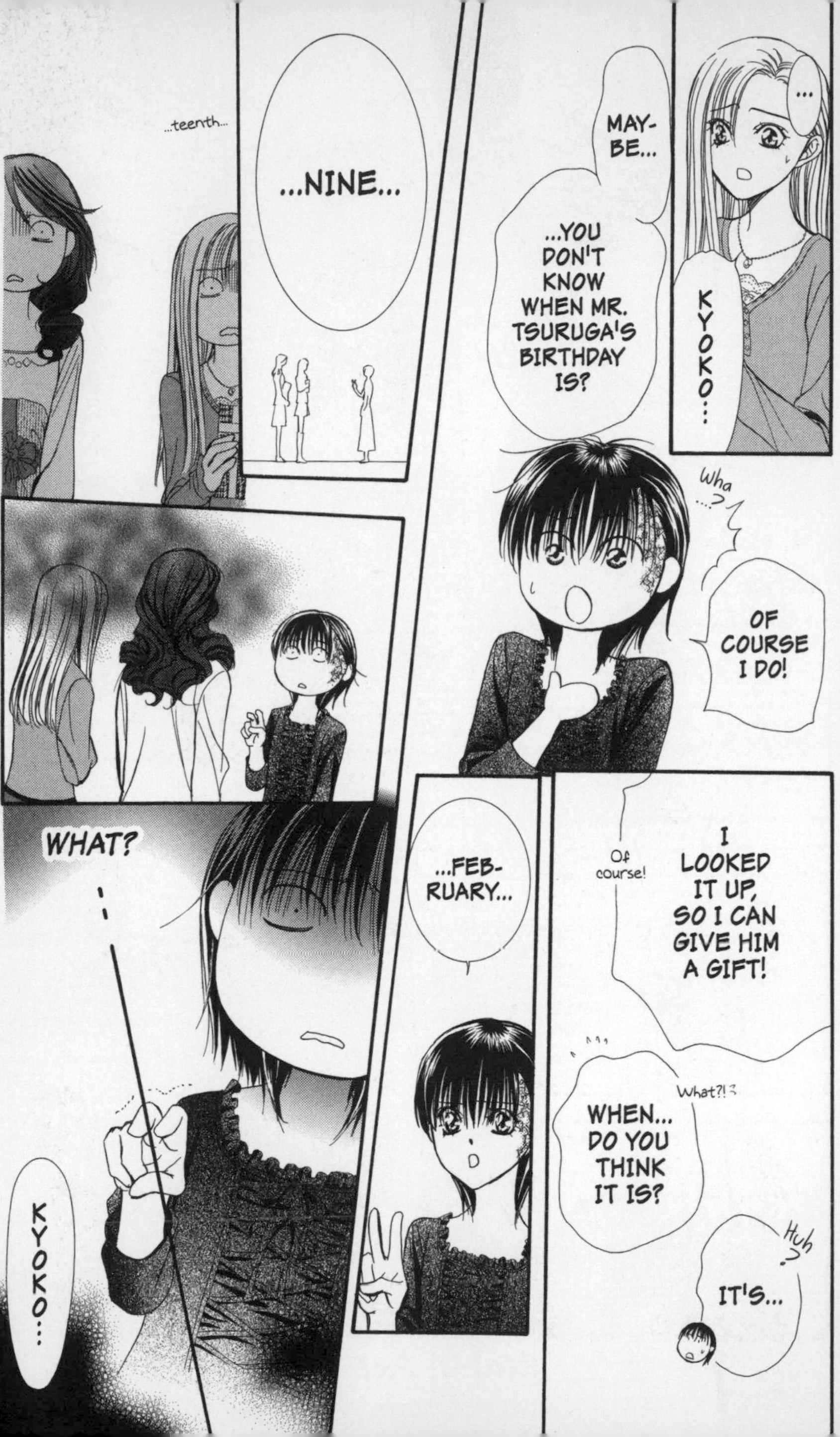
...
KYOKO...
MAY-BE...
...YOU DON'T KNOW WHEN MR. TSURUGA'S BIRTHDAY IS?
Wha...?
OF COURSE I DO!
I LOOKED IT UP, SO I CAN GIVE HIM A GIFT!
Of course!
WHEN... DO YOU THINK IT IS?
What?!
Huh?
IT'S...
...FEB-RUARY...
...NINE...
...teenth...
WHAT?
KYOKO...

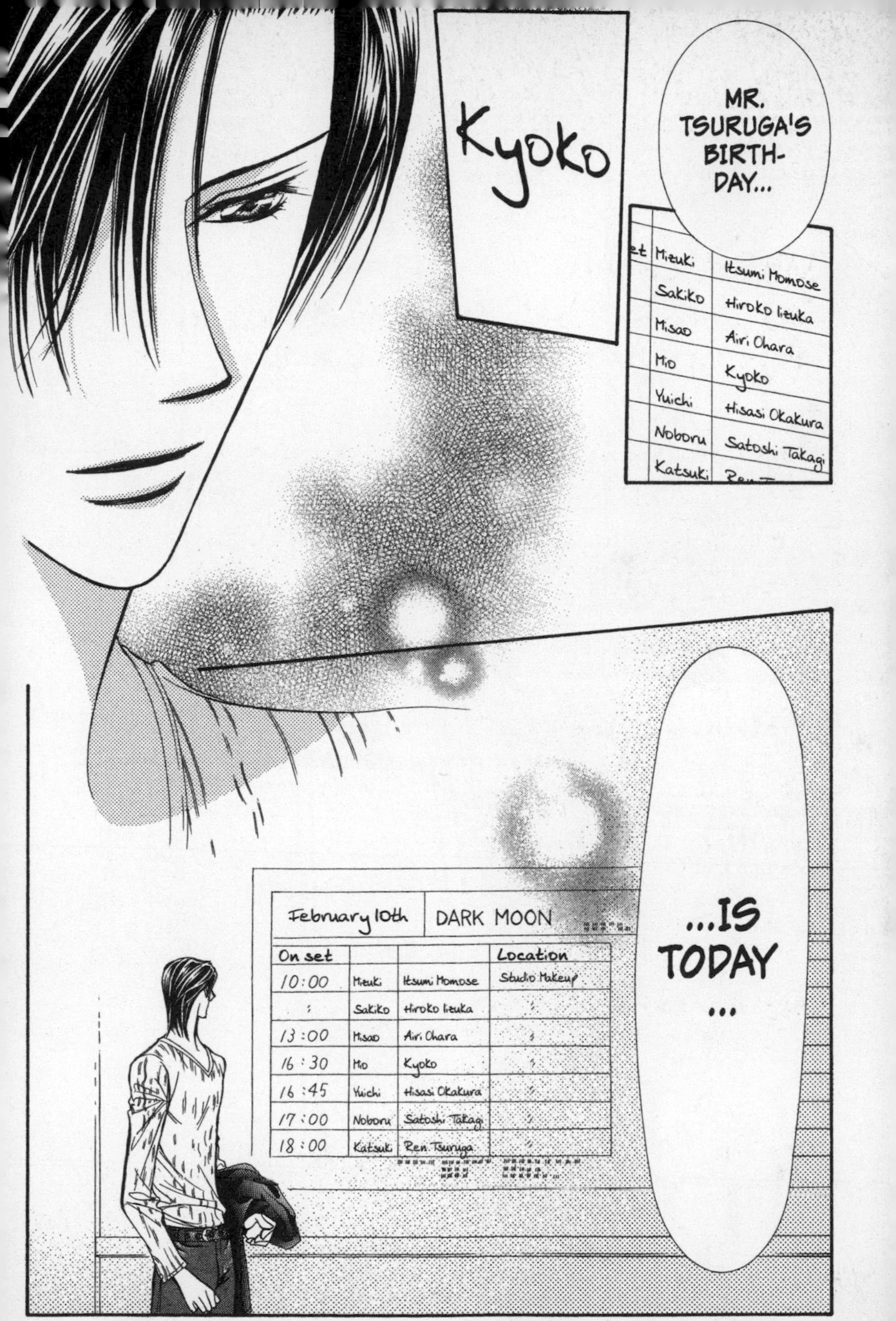
MR. TSURUGA'S BIRTHDAY...
Kyoko
Mizuki Itsumi Momose
Sakiko Hiroko Iizuka
Misao Airi Ohara
Mio Kyoko
Yuichi Hisasi Okakura
Noboru Satoshi Takagi
Katsuki
February 10th DARK MOON
On set Location
10:00 Mizuki Itsumi Momose Studio Makeup
Sakiko Hiroko Iizuka
13:00 Misao Airi Ohara
16:30 Mio Kyoko
16:45 Yuichi Hisasi Okakura
17:00 Noboru Satoshi Takagi
18:00 Katsuki Ren Tsuruga
...IS TODAY...

End of Act 138

Skip·Beat! End Notes
Everyone knows how to be a fan, but sometimes cool things from other cultures need a little help crossing the language barrier.

Page 63, panel 5: dogeza
Kneeling on the ground and bowing.

Page 68, panel 3: Let's make a good country, Kamakura Shogunate
"Good country" is *iikuni* in Japanese, which also sounds like "1192." The Kamakura Shogunate began in 1192.

Page 107, panel 3: V cinema
Similar to direct-to-video.

Page 155, panel 2: Unlucky year
In Japan certain ages are considered unlucky for men or women. For men ages 25, 42 and 61 are unlucky, with 42 being the most unlucky.

Page 161, panel 2: 300 yen
About $3.50 USD.

Page 173, panel 3: Onmyoji
A practitioner of yin-yang magic; a sorcerer.

Page 179, panel 4: Chocolate boxes
The boxes are in the shape of the kanji for "love."

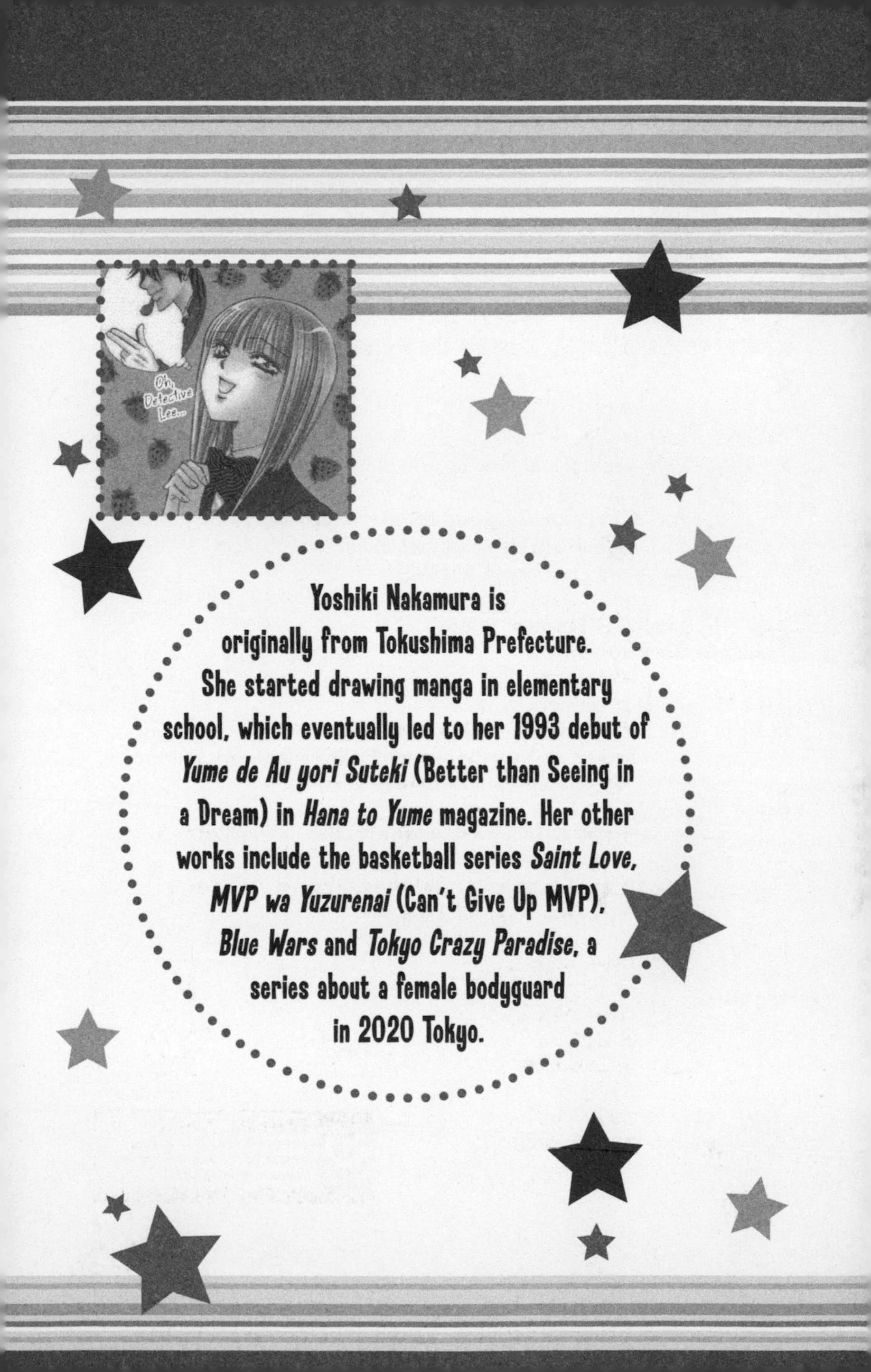
Oh, Detective Lee...

Yoshiki Nakamura is originally from Tokushima Prefecture. She started drawing manga in elementary school, which eventually led to her 1993 debut of *Yume de Au yori Suteki* (Better than Seeing in a Dream) in *Hana to Yume* magazine. Her other works include the basketball series *Saint Love*, *MVP wa Yuzurenai* (Can't Give Up MVP), *Blue Wars* and *Tokyo Crazy Paradise*, a series about a female bodyguard in 2020 Tokyo.

SKIP-BEAT!
Vol. 23
Shojo Beat Edition

STORY AND ART BY YOSHIKI NAKAMURA

English Translation & Adaptation/Tomo Kimura
Touch-up Art & Lettering/Sabrina Heep
Design/Ronnie Casson
Editor/Pancha Diaz

Skip-Beat! by Yoshiki Nakamura © Yoshiki Nakamura 2009.
All rights reserved. First published in Japan in 2009 by HAKUSENSHA, Inc., Tokyo.
English language translation rights arranged with HAKUSENSHA, Inc., Tokyo.

The stories, characters and incidents mentioned in this publication are entirely fictional.

Printed in the U.S.A.

Published by VIZ Media, LLC
P.O. Box 77010
San Francisco, CA 94107

10 9 8 7 6 5 4 3 2 1
First printing, April 2011

www.viz.com

www.shojobeat.com

PARENTAL ADVISORY
SKIP-BEAT! is rated T for Teen and is
recommended for ages 13 and up. This
volume contains a grudge.

ratings.viz.com

The secret the Day Class at Cross Academy doesn't know:

the Night Class is full of vampires!

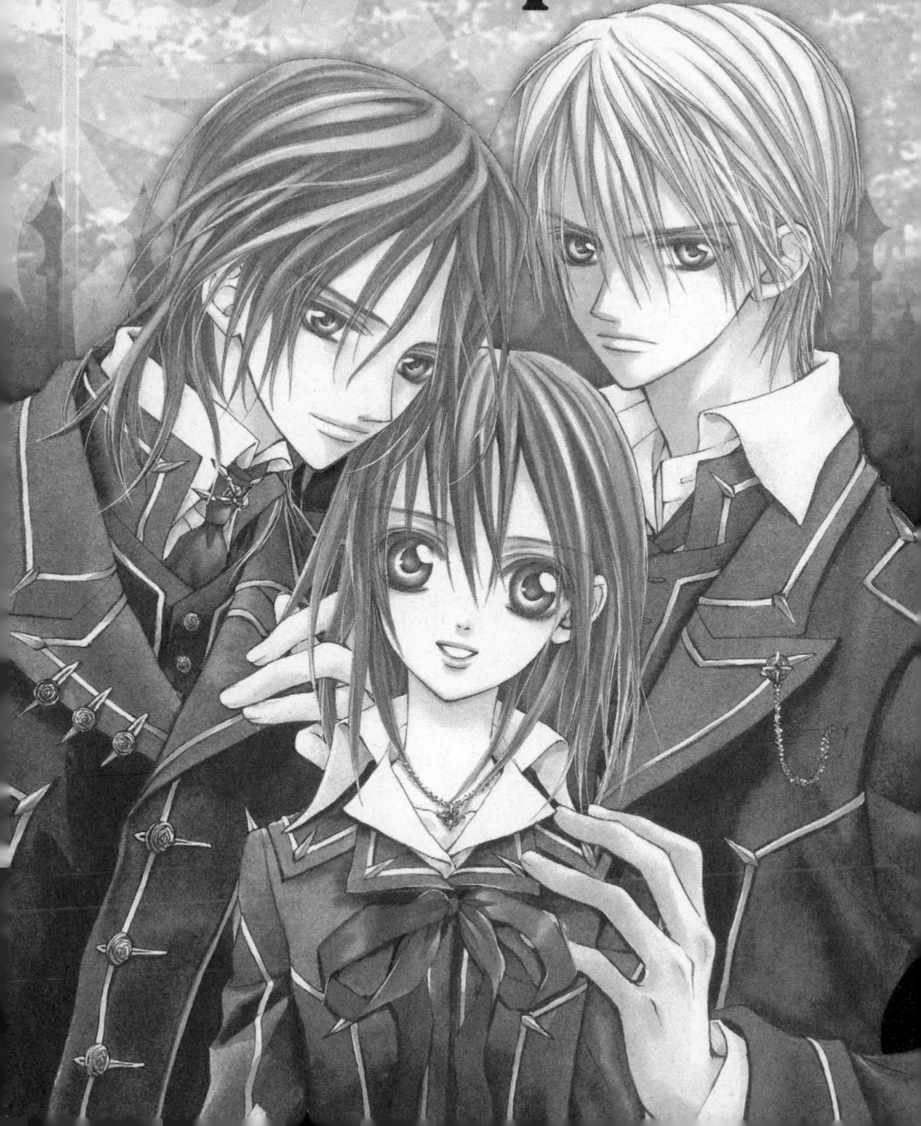

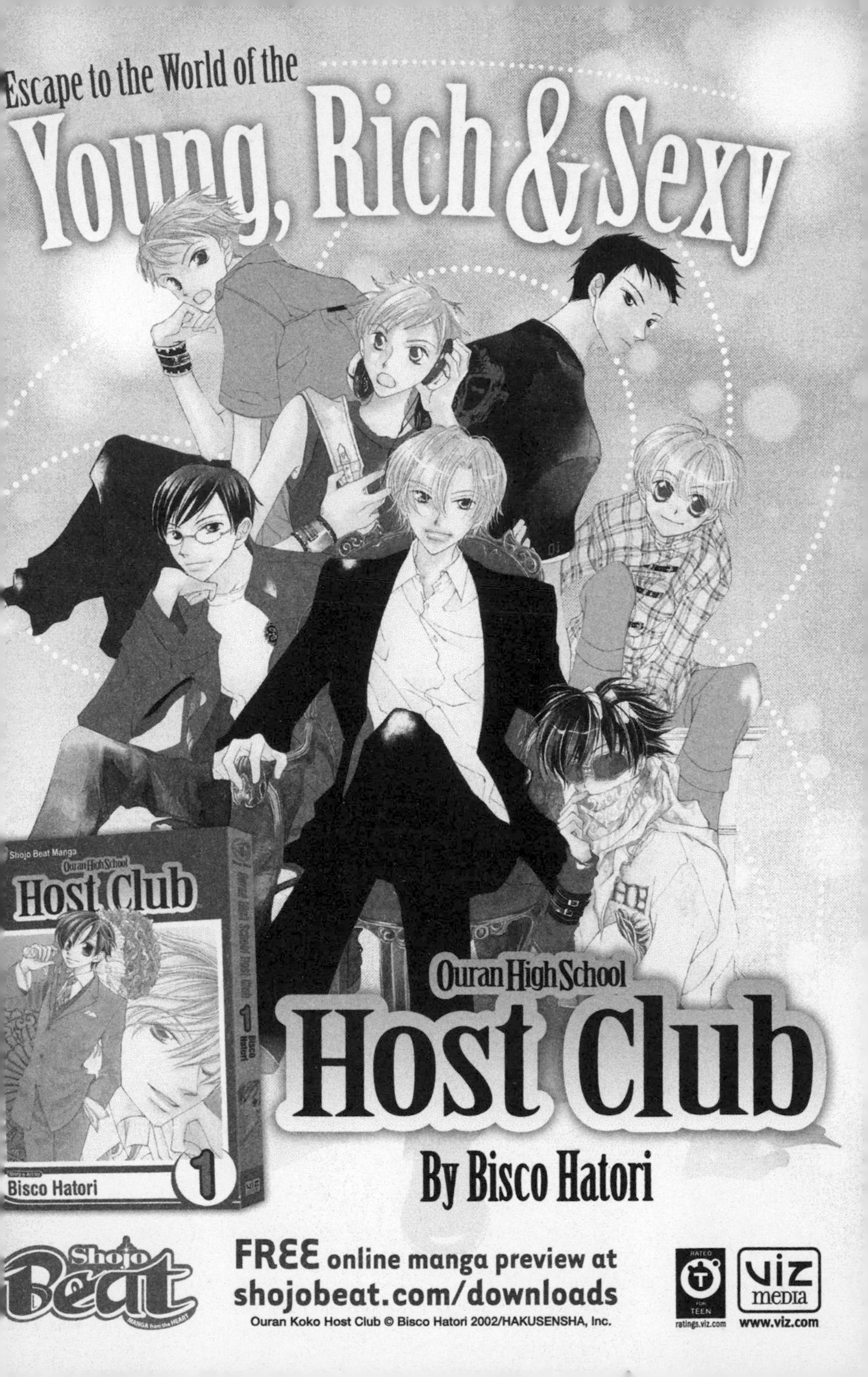
Escape to the World of the
Young, Rich & Sexy
Shojo Beat Manga
Ouran High School
Host Club
1
Bisco Hatori
Ouran High School
Host Club
By Bisco Hatori
Shojo Beat
MANGA from the HEART
FREE online manga preview at
shojobeat.com/downloads
Ouran Koko Host Club © Bisco Hatori 2002/HAKUSENSHA, Inc.
RATED
T
FOR TEEN
ratings.viz.com
viz media
www.viz.com

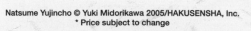

Cactus's Secret

Story and Art by **Nana Haruta**

Prickly Miku Yamada has a serious crush on her classmate Kyohei, but he's far too oblivious to pick up on her signals. How will Miku find her way out of such a thorny siuation?

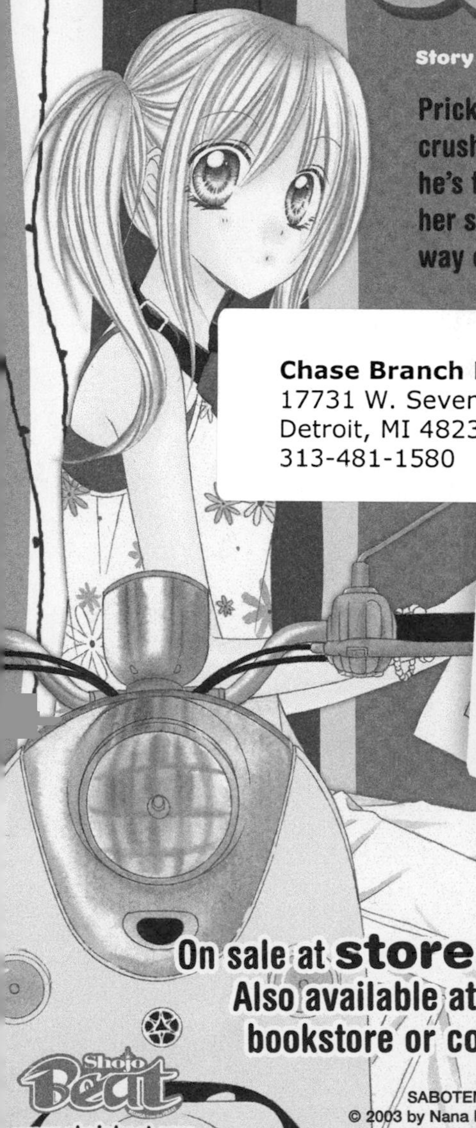

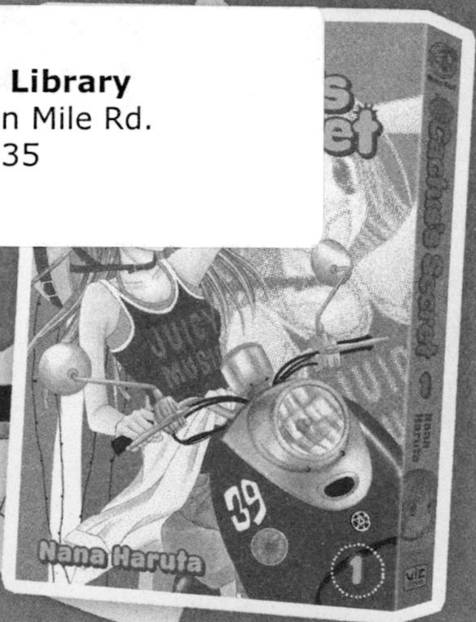
Cactus's Secret
Nana Haruta
1

$9.99 USA / $12.99 CAN / £6.99 UK *

ISBN: 978-1-4215-3189-2

Shojo Beat

www.shojobeat.com

SABOTEN NO HIMITSU

* Prices subject to change

RATED T TEEN ratings.viz.com

VIZ media www.viz.com